Introduction to
Politics *and* Society

Introduction to Politics *and* Society

Shaun Best

SAGE Publications
London • Thousand Oaks • New Delhi

SAGE Publications Ltd
6 Bonhill Street
London EC2A 4PU

SAGE Publications Inc
2455 Teller Road
Thousand Oaks, California 91320

SAGE Publications India Pvt Ltd
32, M-Block Market
Greater Kailash - I
New Delhi 110 048

British Library Cataloguing in Publication data

A catalogue record for this book is available
from the British Library

ISBN 0 7619 7130 0
ISBN 0 7619 7131 9

Library of Congress control number 2001 132937

Typeset by SIVA Math Setters, Chennai, India
Printed in Great Britain by The Cromwell Press Ltd,
Trowbridge, Wiltshire

Contents

Foreword   vi

1. Introduction: Reading the 'Social' and the 'Political'   1

2. Power, Authority and the State   6

3. Postmodern Politics   40

4. Marxist and Elite Theories of Power   78

5. Pluralism and Political Parties   105

6. New Social Movements   145

7. Globalisation and Power   166

8. War   209

9. Voting Behaviour   236

Index   271

Foreword

During the year 2000 I was involved in an interesting debate about the nature and purpose of sociology textbooks.* My argument was that textbooks in sociology look and feel the same; they have a similar content and layout, share similar prejudices and appear to be written largely by drawing upon earlier versions of textbooks. Sociology textbooks are written to a strict formula and have a fairly rigid conception of which authors and theories should be included, and, more importantly, which should not be included. Not surprisingly, a number of people asked me what I thought the contents of a textbook should be like. My answer was that there should be diverse texts for diverse folks.

This book represents my vision of what a textbook should be like. I have used the traditional textbook format to look at a number of theorists and theoretical issues that are not normally addressed in an introductory text. My one deviation from the traditional textbook format is that I have moved away from the customary chapter division and adopted a similar arrangement to that of Deleuze and Guattari in *A Thousand Plateaus* (London: Athlone Press, 1988). This approach involves having areas (plateaus) that readers can follow in any order that they wish.

The book was written during my time as Lecturer in Sociology and Social Policy at Burnley College. I would like to thank the staff and students for the many interesting times we had together. Many of the ideas in this book were also shared with friends and colleagues in the Association for the Teachers of Social Science.

I hope you enjoy the text.

Shaun Best

---

*Best, Shaun, 'The demise of the sociology teacher', *Social Science Teacher*, 29(1), Autumn 1999, 22–26. 'Replies' in 29(2), Spring 2000, 1–23.

1

Introduction: Reading the 'Social' and the 'Political'

Welcome to this introductory guide to politics in the contemporary world. The text is intended for a person who needs to get a quick grasp of a range of social and political issues, together with some understanding of the theoretical background to the arguments. I have attempted to do this in a way which is not patronising, but which is simple enough for a reader coming to contemporary social and political debates for the first time to be able to follow. However, fashionable writers are often very convoluted and inelegant in the way they express themselves. Zygmunt Bauman (1999), for example, has described the contemporary world by the term *Unsicherheit*. This German term incorporates uncertainty, insecurity and unsafety and involves 'the loss of livelihood, social entitlements, place in society and human dignity' (Bauman, 1999: 29). For Bauman, this state of *Unsicherheit* is linked to processes of globalisation and the inability of governments to have any real control over economic conditions within a nation-state.

In an effort to make such interesting and important ideas and arguments more accessible for a student readership I have included a great deal of information which is not specifically social scientific in nature, drawing on writers such as Angela Carter. The purpose of this material is simply to give you an opportunity to enhance your interpretative and evaluative skills, as well as to highlight key elements in the arguments I am discussing, with material that you may be more familiar with. From my own experience and that of the students whom I teach, many of us find reading original social theory texts daunting. How do you start to read the work of an author who often assumes that you are familiar with a range of debates, concepts and theories? How do you read authors who assume that you are familiar with every book and paper they have ever published? Moreover, how do you complete these difficult tasks in a short period of time, against deadlines for assignments and when you may have to write assignments and/or sit exams? I assume that the readers will at some point have to attempt an assignment or sit an examination in which they will be expected to discuss the ideas and arguments of the people in this book.

Before you attempt any assignment, in what many people might consider to be a very 'modernist' fashion, you need to be clear in your own mind what the nature of the assessment criteria is. In other words, what are you expected to do in the assignment and how will your work be judged? When I was an undergraduate, some years ago, I got an essay back from a professor, with a mark that was not particularly good. I asked the professor why he had given the mark that he did. His reply was that the essay did not give him a buzz! When I asked about the criteria I should look for in order to do this, he said that I should not be upset by the poor mark, because when he was my age he had never even heard of sociology, he was too busy killing Germans. The moral of this story is simply that it is important that the assessment criteria are transparent.

Using the web sites of a number of sociology departments, I carried out a simple content analysis of the advice given to undergraduate students on how to complete assignments. Essentially, you are expected to demonstrate three skills. First, you must be able to demonstrate that you can read the work of theorists or researchers and give an outline of their fundamental arguments. I hope this book will help you develop this skill.

Second, you must develop your skill of interpretation. Quite simply, you must give your own restatement of the theory or research. This exposition is *your* reading, *your* version of what the theory or research is about. A central element of this is your ability to demonstrate your understanding of the relevant material by making a connection with other sociological material and relevant non-sociological material; for example, news events, docudrama, film and your own personal experience. You must be able to demonstrate that the ideas you are discussing have relevance outside the world of academic books and papers. This is not simply taking lines from books and papers and rewriting them in your own words, but bringing the ideas to life by discussing the lives of the people who are being theorised about, including yourself, and showing how the sociological ideas affect people's everyday lives. Good sociology should inform you about your life; if a theory or type of research has no relevance to you or your life, then say so in your assignment. If you have a convincing justification as to why the theory or research is of little relevance to you and your life, then you are well on the way to demonstrating the third skill of evaluation. I hope this book will help you develop your interpretation and application skills.

Third and finally, you need to develop the skill of evaluation. In other words, you must make judgements or assessments of a theory or type of research. You will be expected to present a balanced argument, and to demonstrate the strengths and weaknesses of a theory or research. How do you do this? Outline the strengths and weaknesses of whatever the topic of your assignment is by looking at the published critiques and at those writers that endorse the theory or research you are looking at. But suppose you do not like a particular theory or cannot think of anything positive to say about it. In this case, outline the points made by the writers that endorse the theory and explain, with some justification, why you do not agree with them. As an undergraduate, you may feel more confident in doing this by drawing upon the published work of established sociologists. I hope this book will help you to develop this skill.

In other words, this textbook is about helping you to develop your skills to 'read' the key social and political debates.

In addition to this introduction, the content of this text is broken down into seven 'areas'. These areas can be read in any order. In Area 2, we consider the issues of power and authority. The difference between the legitimate use of power and coercion is considered by reference to the work of Max Weber. In this area we spend a great deal of time and space looking at what Weber had to say about bureaucracy. The reason for this extended discussion is that up until the emergence of New Social Movements (NSMs), all political organisations were essentially formal organisations, in the 'Prussian' style, with the rigid rules and formal hierarchies that Weber had so fully and clearly described in the latter part of the nineteenth century. Whenever you are assessing any organisation, it is always worth looking to see whether it has any of the features that Weber described. This is a good starting point for your evaluation.

Area 3 moves away from the 'modernist' concerns of Weber and looks specifically at what a range of writers have had to say about the nature of a postmodern politics. The area starts by looking at the characteristics of the postmodern condition; this is the idea that the world has become a very uncertain and highly fragmented place. Individuals may be experiencing 'epistemological insecurity' and 'ontological plurality'; do not be put off by the odd-sounding terms. Postmodernists are not averse to using strange and puzzling phraseology. Moreover, in this text, you will come across a great deal of it! Hopefully, such language will translate into a form that is easily understood. What these strange-sounding terms above mean is that we are unsure about what we know and how we know it ('epistemological insecurity'); similarly, we are unsure about what reality consists of ('ontological plurality'). Instead of one reality that we all accept without question as the truth, there may be a range of realities that we can move between. This is a situation not unlike an episode of *X Files*. In terms of practical politics, what were once stable political regimes may be giving way to a process of Balkanisation, within which Weberian formal bureaucratic organisations no longer have any significant influence. In contrast, the unstable tendencies that are evident in former Yugoslavia may be becoming common across the world. This raises questions such as 'Is postmodern politics based upon social class factors or upon more unstable forms of identity politics?'

Area 4 looks at the contribution of the distinctly 'modernist' Marxist and elite theories to our understanding of the nature and distribution of power within societies. We examine the contributions made by classical theorists, but also look at the relevance of these theories to the contemporary world. In particular, we look at the ways in which Marxist writers have attempted to come to terms with the views of postmodern writers.

In contrast, Area 5 looks at pluralism – the theory that power is widely shared within societies. We look at the nature and structure of political parties in Britain. In addition we outline the changes that they have gone through since the general election in 1997. The Blair Project, communitarianism, the 'third way' and the 'new deal' are all discussed. The membership of traditional political parties has declined over the past ten years; however, support for NSMs has significantly increased. This is further developed in Area 6, where we look at the rise of NSMs and evaluate their significance. Issues of power and politics are not confined to any one country, and in Area 7 we look at processes of globalisation and the possible decline of the nation-state. Area 8 looks at the contribution that sociologists have made to our understanding of war and how the nature of war-related activities may have changed with the emergence of the 'new world order' at the end of the twentieth century. Finally, in Area 9, we evaluate theories of voting behaviour with specific reference to the 1997 general election in Britain.

In all the areas, there is an attempt to look at the contributions of leading sociologists and other social theorists who are working today: Anthony Giddens, Jurgen Habermas, Richard Sennett and a range of postmodern writers – notably, Zygmunt Bauman, Richard Rorty and Jean Baudrillard.

During the time that this book was being written, Anthony Giddens became director of the London School of Economics and Political Science. Clearly, he has had a significant influence on the thinking and the approach of the Blair government. However, Giddens is notably 'cool' in his thinking about postmodernism. He is not directly hostile to the idea that modernity is coming to an end, but is unwilling to accept many of the assumptions that postmodern writers make about the nature of the world. Giddens prefers to describe the contemporary world as a place of 'reflexive modernisation' or 'late modernity'. In a number of the areas, readers are encouraged to contemplate Giddens's approach in relation to the range of postmodern approaches.

In the last analysis, this is a students' guide, and the idea is that by the time you reach the end of the text you should have a clearer idea of politics, the 'social' and debates about the postmodern condition. To aid this process, at numerous points in each area, you, the reader, are asked to do some of the work! You will be asked to reflect upon an issue, and to interpret or evaluate some text. The idea is that you should not function simply as a passive receiver of the information that the text is presenting. All texts are there to be challenged, and this text is no different. Postmodern writers have a tendency to say very provocative things, notably in relation to gender. Jean Baudrillard has a tendency to annoy feminists, simply as an end in itself. He and other postmodern writers have made highly contentious statements about gender. I have attempted to remain faithful to his provocation! Hence, many of the points that you will come across will, I hope, provoke you, especially in the area on a postmodern politics. The text itself is not written from a postmodern perspective. However, I have suspended both my belief and my disbelief about postmodernism and the postmodern condition while writing the text. Hopefully, this should allow you, the reader, to arrive at your own conclusion about the important issues raised in the text.

References

Bauman, Z. (1999) *In Search of Politics*. Cambridge: Polity.
Raskovic, J. (1990) *Luda Zemlja*. Novi Sad: Slavija.

2

Power, Authority and the State

Area Goals

By the end of this area you should:

○ Be aware of Anthony Giddens's conception of modernity
○ Have a critical understanding of the distinction that Max Weber made between authority and coercion
○ Have a critical understanding of the three types of legitimate rule outlined by Max Weber
○ Be familiar with the contribution of Michel Foucault to our understanding of power and authority
○ Be familiar with Jurgen Habermas's contribution to our understanding of the processes of legitimation within social systems
○ Be familiar with the contribution of Richard Sennett to our understanding of authority
○ Understand the postmodern conception of the state
○ Be familiar with the nature of state-centred theories

Understanding how some people effectively control the actions of others is one of the central questions in sociology. This is the question of power or domination. The central questions in the sociology of politics are 'How is power exercised?' and 'By what means is power made right, just or legitimate?' Authority, whereby people are seen to have a legitimate right to control the behaviour of others, is

Surveillance

(Control of information and
social supervision; for
example, the use of CCTV)

Capitalism

(Capital accumulation, the
accumulation of profits, in the
context of competitive
labour and productive markets)

Military power

(Control of the means of violence
in the context of the industrialisation
of war, the use of advanced
industry in the help to fight wars; for
example, in the Gulf War)

Industrialism

(Transformation of nature:
development of the 'created
environment'; in other words, all aspects
of natural places have been
refashioned in some way; there is no
true wilderness any more)

Figure 2.1   *The institutional dimensions of modernity (Giddens 1990: 59).*

also an important concept in political sociology. The meaning of power and authority has been summarised by Steven Lukes (1978). Lukes explains that, central to the idea of power is the notion of 'bringing about consequences', not unlike, for instance, the way in which your sociology teacher ensures that people in the class hand in their homework. This is about securing compliance, and compliance can be secured by the use of force or by people choosing to surrender to others. When people choose to accept the will of others as legitimate or right, we can describe the relationship as one of authority. You might want to reflect upon the different forms authority takes in our lives: religious authority, moral authority, academic authority, etc.

Power or domination is often thought to be right and legitimate; however, domination has also been described as a form of repression. In our everyday lives we have to deal with individuals and agencies that attempt to exercise power over us, making us do things which they want us to do. In this area we look at a number of contrasting writers who are all concerned with power and domination within the modern world; afterwards we shall look at the contribution made to these issues by postmodern writers.

Giddens on modernity

The clearest outline of 'modernity' is provided by Anthony Giddens in *The Consequences of Modernity* (1990). In this text he explains that the modern world has four characteristics, or 'institutional dimensions' (Figure 2.1).

For Anthony Giddens, 'power' is a fundamental concept in the social sciences. By 'power' Giddens means 'transformative capacity'; in other words, the ability to make a difference in the world. In Giddens's view, whenever an individual carries out a social action – by which we understand any action with an intention behind it – that individual makes a difference in the world. The consequences of a social action may go against many other individuals' vested interests. We all carry out social actions, so it follows that we all have power. However, the amount of power an individual has is related to 'resources'. Giddens outlines two distinct types of resources:

- Allocative resources – control over physical things such as owning a factory
- Authoritative resources – control over the activities of people; for example, by being high up in an organisation like the civil service

All social systems are viewed as 'power systems', and usually this means that they are involved in the 'institutional mediation of power' (Giddens 1985: 9). By this, Giddens means that institutions, such as schools, attempt to control the lives of individual people by the use of rules, which become deeply embedded in our everyday lives. The nation-state, such as France or Britain, a geographical area with recognised borders and a government, is described by Giddens as a 'power container' that has a high concentration of both allocative and authoritative resources. In other words, the state contains lots of institutions, with lots of resources and therefore lots of power. In particular, Giddens suggests that surveillance, both watching people and collecting information about them, is essential to maintaining the power of the modern nation-state and to maintaining any social system. As Giddens explains, 'All states involve the reflexive monitoring of aspects of the reproduction of the social systems subject to their rule' (1985: 17).

The modern state gathers all type of information about individual people, such as information about birth, death, income, notifiable diseases and travel overseas, to name but a few. You might want to ask yourself why the state should be interested in gathering such information about people:

- How much money people earn
- Notifiable diseases, such as tuberculosis
- How many people are in your house on the night of the census?
- If you travel overseas – why do we have passports?

The characteristics of the modern nation-state are outlined by Giddens as 'a political apparatus, recognised to have sovereign rights within the borders of a demarcated territorial area, able to back its claims to sovereignty by control of military power, many of whose citizens have positive feelings of commitment to its national identity' (1989: 303). This passage from Giddens is not the easiest to follow, but its key elements can be defined as follows:

- 'A political apparatus': a leader or government supported by institutions and other forms of organisation

- o 'Demarcated territorial area': a place or geographical area, usually a country
- o 'Sovereignty': control over a geographical area, including control over the people who live there
- o 'National identity': characteristics displayed by people which identify them with a particular place

All types of *rule* rest upon the mediation of power by the society institutions, and the modern state has become capable of influencing some of the most private and personal characteristics of our everyday lives. The Children's Act 1980, for example, allows the state to intervene in the relationship between parents and children. However, Giddens argues that modern nation-states are without fail 'polyarchic' in nature. This means that they have a set of legal rules which provide individual people with civil and political rights, such as free speech, which gives them a status as a 'citizen'. A key concept that Giddens develops here is his notion of the 'dialectic of control'. By this he means that all people have 'openings' that can be used to influence the activities of authorities that attempt to exercise domination over them. According to Giddens, even the prisoner alone in the cell still has opportunities to exercise power over the jailer; such techniques can involve: harming oneself physically, conducting a 'dirty protest', going on hunger strike, and refusing to wear prison clothes. The 'dialectic of control is fully explored in Area 5, 'Pluralism and Political Parties'.

However, can we accept the claim made by Giddens that all individual human agents have power? Researchers such as Joanne Finkelstein clearly believe that the answer is yes. In her book *The Fashioned Self* (1995), she gives an illustration that is worth quoting at length:

> Clearly, physical appearances are understood to do more than differentiate the sexes; they act as social passports and credentials, often speaking out more eloquently than the individual might desire. ... In the following example from Primo Levi, appearances are used as a credential of one's humanity. In his document of the Nazi concentration camps, *If This Be a Man* (1987), Levi described an episode where an inmate of Auschwitz, L, understood even in the torturous circumstances of the camps, that there was power to be gained through deliberately fashioning one's appearance. L went to extreme lengths to cultivate his appearance, so, in the barbaric conditions of the concentration camp where everyone was soiled and fouled, his hands and face were always perfectly clean, and his striped prison suit was also 'clean and new': 'L knew that the step was short from being judged powerful to effectively becoming so ... a respectable appearance is the best guarantee of being respected. ... He needed no more than his spruce suit and his emaciated and shaven face in the midst of the flock of his sordid and slovenly colleagues to stand out and thereby receive benefits from his captors. (Finkelstein, 1995: 136)

Here Finkelstein raises a number of interesting points; for example, that *appearances* can be seen as *social passports and credentials*; that L can have power; and that L has at least some control over the course of his own life. This is surprising given the circumstances in which L finds himself.

Max Weber – power, coercion and authority

Max Weber (1864–1920) was one of the founders of sociology, and he always described himself as a *bourgeois theorist*. According to Marianne Weber's biography (1926) of her husband, Weber could never have joined a socialist party, as he believed that private companies were the only source of power in society to challenge the state civil service and therefore guarantee freedom and liberty. As Weber himself explained, 'Superior to bureaucracy in the knowledge of techniques and facts is only the capitalist entrepreneur, with his own sphere of interest. He is the only type who has been able to maintain at least immunity from subjection to the control of rational bureaucratic knowledge' (Weber, 1978: 225).

Marianne Weber suggested that three assumptions underpin Max Weber's political analysis:

o *Economic individualism.* In other words, Weber believed in economic freedom, the freedom to buy and sell whatever one wanted in the market place.
o *Civil and political freedom.* In other words, Weber believed in civil rights such as the rights to free speech voting.
o *Personal autonomy and responsibility.* In other words, Weber believed in individual people taking responsibility for their own actions. The state should not control the life of the citizen.

The starting point for Weber's political analysis was the important distinction between power as *authority* and power as *coercion*. For Weber, authority is the legitimate use of power. Individuals accept and act upon orders that are given to them because they believe that to do so is right. In coercion, on the other hand, others force people into an action, often by the threat of violence, and this is always regarded as illegitimate. However, we might wish to question some of the assumptions that Weber made in this area.

But can we accept the distinction between coercion and authority, that Weber makes? Are Weber's conceptions of 'coercion' and 'authority' always based upon the point of view of the people with power? Richard Bessel's review of David Irving's book *Nuremberg* (1997) raises some of these issues:

> For more than three decades, David Irving has been engaged in a crusade to rescue the Nazi leadership from the enormous condescension of posterity, and to demonstrate that the Allies committed terrible crimes against the Germans. ...

> At various points, Irving attempts to pin responsibility for crimes during wartime on the Allies – not denying what the Nazis did, but insinuating that the Allies bear a substantial share of the blame. Characteristic of his approach is the following passage about 'the Nazi "extermination camps"':

'At many camps liberated by the British or Americans, including Buchenwald, Bergen Belsen and Dachau, they found and photographed for posterity disturbing scenes of death from starvation and pestilence – scenes which should not, in retrospect, have surprised the Allied commanders who had spent the last months bombing Germany's rail distribution networks and blasting the pharmaceutical factories in order to conjure up precisely these horsemen of the Apocalypse.'

Almost reasonable, after all, the bombing certainly was brutal, brought about the slaughter of hundreds of thousands of innocent people and caused untold suffering. But one does not have to be a militant supporter of 'Bomber' Harris or a moral relativist to point out that the bombing, horrible as it was, was part of a campaign to win a war which, after all, neither Britain nor the United States started, and that incarcerating and murdering Jews in Dachau was not. ...

Irving's text contains a number of photographs that have never been published before. Probably the most disturbing is a black and white photograph, from the United States National Archives, of the execution by American soldiers of 'regular German soldiers', shot against a wall, at Dachau shortly after the camp's liberation. Perhaps the most telling, however, is the colour photograph of the grave of Rudolf Hess – Hitler's deputy ('a dedicated, upright ex-aviator', according to Irving), which, as Irving makes a point of reminding us, 'is permanently heaped with flowers from all over Germany'. (Adapted from Bessel, (1997, 8: 14) 1997).

Richard Bessel clearly believes that the actions of the Allies had authority and the actions of the Nazis did not. However, the significance of the photograph of the execution of the German soldiers casts doubt on this view, as does Irving's reminder that Rudolf Hess's grave: 'is permanently heaped with flowers from all over Germany'.

Issues of coercion and authority affect us all in many aspects of our everyday life. Clive Harber outlines the Weberian distinction in relation to schools:

The teacher asks a pupil to do something for him which is rather out of the ordinary, like stand on one leg and write 'I am a Martian' on the board. The pupil, having complied, and they always do, the teacher asks why the pupil did what he did. Answer: 'because you told me to.' Teacher: 'Why do you do what I tell you to even when it's completely lunatic?' It's not far from here to the idea of authority as the right to influence others when they recognise your right to do so; i.e. the use of power is recognised as right and proper. Following this the teacher then describes how, due to the incessant droning of the teacher's voice, one of the pupils falls asleep at the back of the class and remains unnoticed until waking up in the dead of night long after the school has been locked up. It's a stormy night, the wind is howling and the school feels very spooky. All of a sudden, the sound of heavy footsteps in the corridor! They get closer and closer. The door creaks open and a hairy misshapen arm appears around the edge of it. ... It turns out to be the pupil used to illustrate authority and crazed by a thirst for revenge. He threatens to set about the second pupil with a huge, nasty club unless they write 'I am a Martian' on the board. The second pupil is then asked what they would do. Answer: 'comply'. 'Why?' 'If I didn't I'd be physically assaulted' – the use of power i.e. the ability to influence somebody, even against their will. (Clive Harber, 'The Best of the Social Science Teacher' ATSS 1995: 72)

In a similar fashion, Maya Angelou in *I Know Why the Caged Bird Sings* draws upon her own personal experience in Weberian fashion:

> Crossing the black area of Stamps, which in childhood's narrow measure seemed a whole world, we were obliged by custom to stop and speak to every person we met, and Bailey felt constrained to spend a few minutes playing with each friend. There was joy in going to town with money in our pockets (Bailey's pockets were as good as my own) and time on our hands. But the pleasure fled when we reached the white part of town. After we left Mr. Willie Williams' Do Drop Inn, the last stop before whitefolksville, we had to cross the pond and adventure the railroad tracks. We were explorers walking without weapons into man-eating animals' territory.
>
> In Stamps the segregation was so complete that most Black children didn't really, absolutely know what whites looked like. Other than that they were different, to be dreaded, and in that dread was included the hostility of the powerless against the powerful, the poor against the rich, the worker against the worked for and the ragged against the well dressed. (Angelou, 1984: 24–5)

Max Weber: the three types of legitimate rule

For Max Weber, there are three 'ideal types' of legitimate rule. Weber developed the ideal type as the starting point for a research project, and it is one of the most misunderstood methodological devices in the social sciences. The ideal type is a list of characteristics that the researcher considers the most significant. What is most significant is based upon the informed personal opinion of the researcher, a basis which Weber terms *'value relevance'*. From this starting point, the researcher constructs a model that is used to evaluate bureaucracies in the real world. Those who criticise Weber's ideal type of bureaucracy on the grounds that it differs from bureaucracies in the real world have clearly mis-understood the role and purpose of the ideal type as a methodological device. Weber's critics could be said to have different informed opinions about the nature of the bureaucracy.

Charismatic authority is the first of the three types of legitimate rule discussed by Weber, and it is concerned with how a political order can be maintained by the force of a leader's personality. Often such leaders will be seen as having supernatural powers or qualities. Weber explains that this form of authority is 'resting on devotion to the exceptional sanctity, heroism or exemplary character of an individual person and of the normative pattern or order revealed or ordained by him' (Weber, 1978: 215).

Traditional authority is the second type of legitimate rule discussed by Weber; it is concerned with how a political order can be maintained by the constant reference to customs, traditions and conventions. As Weber explains, this type of authority is: 'resting on an established belief in the sanctity of immemorial tradi-tions and the legitimacy of those exercising authority under rule' (1978: 215).

Rational legal authority is the third type of legitimate rule outlined by Weber; it is concerned with how a political order is regarded as *legal* in the eyes of the population. Weber explains that this form of authority is 'resting on a belief in the legality of enacted rules and the right of that elevated to authority under such rules to issue commands' (1978: 215). Rational legal authority is then a structure for making decisions, and the legitimacy of the structure is maintained by reference to a legal code. In addition, for Weber the legal code within rational legal authority is based upon 'natural law'. Weber's argument is that whenever people interact with each other they make expectations of each other's behaviour, and these expectations form a 'normative order'. In other words, Weberian natural law is a form of non-religious morality. This normative order puts pressure on people to behave in particular ways, and this becomes codified (written down) as a set of legal rules. The example of an ideal type of rational legal authority that is discussed by Weber is the bureaucracy.

Rational legal authority is legitimate because there is a set of legal rules, but you might want to reflect on the question, 'Why do people obey the law?'. Do people obey because they fear the consequences of getting caught, or do you accept that the Weberian concept of 'natural law' has some validity?

Weber argued that modern government inevitably means government by bureaucracy. This means that in any nation-state the politicians are seen to run the country; however, the implementation and interpretation of political decisions is carried out by the civil service. However, in Weber's view, the bureaucracy always lacks political leadership. There is a need, he claimed, for a strong parliament as a guarantor of individual rights and liberties. For this reason, Weber was always in favour of political democratisation, notably arguing in favour of votes for women. Weak parliaments produce extreme ideological divisions between the parties, a development which Weber termed 'negative politics', because it was little more than ideological posturing, while the state bureaucracy often took the important decisions.

Max Weber's ideal type of bureaucracy

An ideal type is a useful model by which to measure other forms of administration. This model contains the following characteristics:

o The organisation is in the form of a hierarchy
o Its operations are governed by a system of abstract rules
o The ideal officials conduct their tasks without friendship or favour to any clients
o All bureaucrats have a fixed number of recorded duties
o Employment in the bureaucracy is based upon qualifications
o From a purely technical point of view, this form of administration has the highest degree of efficiency

Bureaucracy

In Weber's analysis, there are two forms of bureaucracy which can be identified. The first one is built upon 'consent', whereby rules emerge through a process of agreement. This form is clearly regarded as 'legitimate', an example of it is liberal parliamentary democracy. The second form is 'punishment centred' and is clearly based upon the imposition of rules as an end in itself. It is concerned with the need to extract obedience from a population, as exemplified by the role of the 'secret police'. Clearly, the latter form of bureaucracy is not regarded as legitimate in the eyes of the people under its control. This form of bureaucracy was not fully investigated by Weber, but was looked at many years later by Richard Sennett (1980), (see below). The significance of Weber's ideal type spread far beyond the narrow study of political organisations. Weber made the very large claim that because of the process of rationalisation spreading into all areas of social life, all organisations in all areas of social life appear to be bureaucratic in nature.

According to Weber, the bureaucracy is both the most rational and the most efficient of all forms of administration. All forms of bureaucracy need rules. Modern organisations make use of quality assurance programmes or systems which are rational in exactly the way that Weber described them; examples include BS 5750, ISO 9000 (Quality Assurance Standards), and Investors in People, which all involve the establishment of systems to ensure that procedures are carried out. Quality is understood as making sure that the formal rules are followed.

The influence of Weber in this area of sociology is substantial. Since Weber's pioneering work, organisations have been defined as social units that aspire to achieve particular objectives or ends which they are structured to promote. In other words, organisations have been deliberately put together to carry out a specific task. They are usually bureaucratic in nature, and they usually carry out their function rationally.

All bureaucratic organisations were defined by Martin Albrow as 'Social units in which individuals are conscious of their membership and legitimise their cooperative activities primarily by reference to attainment of impersonal goals rather than moral standards' (Albrow, 1977: 1). To a large extent, Albrow's definition of bureaucracy is simply repeating Weber's earlier definition.

Organisations can be divided into a number of types depending upon what they do.

Total institutions

'Total institutions' is a term defined by Erving Goffman (1962) to describe five distinct types of institutions in which people live and work within a closed community, under fixed supervision, together with a rational plan which points towards a fixed number of goals. A mental hospital, for example, may have the goal of curing the patients. Examples of total institutions include such diverse organisations as armies, boarding schools, prisons, mental hospitals and leper colonies. People entering these institutions are subjected to 'rituals of degradation' in which both the staff and the inmates attempt to destroy the individual self of the newcomer. In other words, they must lose their individuality, and become like the inmates, who appear as a 'batch' to the outside observer as Goffman describes.

Voluntary associations

Voluntary associations provide a setting for people who share common interests. Again there are diverse examples to draw from: political parties, New Social Movements (non-class-based movements such as animal rights protesters), and local sports teams. As we shall see in our area on Marxism and elite theory, according to Robert Michels (1949) (1876–1936), all organisations are inevitably oligarchic; in other words, within any organisation we will find a few people who make the key decisions while the rest of the membership is powerless. Michels termed this the 'iron law of oligarchy', by which he meant that no organisation could ever be democratic or allow true participation in decision making by its members.

Postmodern organisations

The postmodern organisation should contain de-demarcated and multi-skilled jobs. Unlike the Prussian-style bureaucracy as outlined by Weber, the postmodern organisation should be 'de-Prussianised'; it should be free of formal rationality, loosely coupled and complexly interactive; it should be a 'collegial formation' with no vertical authority, but with forms of 'networking'. These networks should reflect the needs of the new 'cultural and social specialists' and cultural capital, and allow the specialists to resist control by traditional bureaucracy.

In a 'post-Fordist' world, which has an uncertain or postmodern feel to it, new forms of pluralistic or non-hierarchical organisation are possible. People can work within quality circles, in which workers are not constrained and powerless, as they would be under some form of Taylorist scientific management. They are not 'deskilled', as Braverman would suggest, but work within structures which empower individuals by allowing democratic participation in decision making. According to Frederick Taylor in his book *The Principles of Scientific Management* (1911), nineteenth-century management had little or no understanding of the techniques or skills needed, or the time it took, to produce a product. Managers were generally unpleasant to people who looked as if they were not busy. Taylor termed this form of management 'ordinary management'. Workers attempted to undermine ordinary management in the following two ways:

○ Natural soldiering – all individuals tending to do as little as possible
○ Systematic soldiering – work groups putting pressure on individual members to conform and work to an agreed speed

Scientific management empowered managers by giving them a full under-standing of all aspects of the production process. This allowed management to select the right people for the job. Production could be broken down into the simplest of tasks, which workers could learn in a very short period of time. Management would measure how much time was needed to perform each task, and individual workers would be given financial incentives to work as quickly as they could. This management style was most vigorously adopted by Henry Ford in his production of the model T car, and became known as 'Fordism'. This started the process that Harry Braverman (1974) was later to describe as deskilling, in which as the work tasks were broken down, workers lost both their skills and control of the planning of work tasks.

In contrast, postmodern organisations:

o Encourage initiative, autonomy (independence), flexibility (people have a range of different roles), multi-skilling (people have a range of different skills), decentralisation (people can make decisions within localised teams), and flat-ter hierarchies
o Yet retain a core of detailed rules and procedures, with a centralised overall structure of control, with careful monitoring of performance

If we take the postmodern college as an example of a postmodern organisation, its lecturers should be 'cultural and social specialists'. As new professionals, they should be the major carriers of the postmodern consciousness. We shall explore many of these themes in Area 6, 'New Social Movements'.

Formal and informal organisations

All organisations have both formal and informal aspects. The formal organi-sation contains the strictly laid-down patterns of authority, rules and procedures. It has a high degree of rationality and makes the most efficient use of the resources available to it. It aims to produce maximum predictability. The informal organisation includes friendships and personal relationships. Formal organi-sations have

o A well-defined, durable and inflexible structure
o A well-planned hierarchy
o Clear channels of communication
o A specified job for each member
o Well-defined objectives

Informal organisations have

o A loosely organised, flexible, ill-defined structure
o No defined goals or objectives
o No clearly defined relationships

The goals of organisations are difficult to measure; long-term goals may have to change while short-term goals may compete with each other. A long-term goal might be to maximise profits, but this may have to change if a company needs to recruit highly skilled workers in the short term. In this sense, it might be better to have an organisational structure which is less durable but which can change to meet the needs of its stakeholders better in new circumstances. This idea formed the basis of what came to be known as *contingency theory*.

In contrast to Weber, Henry Mintzberg (1979) argued for what he called 'adhocracy', which is a fluid and flexible administration based upon teams who form their own rules; like the informal organisation, this organisation does not attempt to standardise the activities of its members. Adhocracy gains the advantages of the informal organisation, that is, its flexible search for better ways of working in the face of new contingencies or circumstances and its innovative teamwork. These may take the form of quality circles that give individuals opportunities to develop their skills in a number of different areas.

The dangers of bureaucracy

As we suggested, for Weber, bureaucracy was precise, soulless and machine-like, a technical instrument for achieving preconceived goals. In addition, argued Weber, bureaucracy has an inherent tendency to exceed its function, and to become a separate force within society. Underpinning the growth of bureaucracy was the process of *rationalisation*, in which relationships between people were becoming more impersonal and dehumanised than in traditional societies. Life in the modern world was losing its meaning because of the process of rationalisation; for this reason, Weber was highly critical of the spread of bureaucracy into almost every area of modern life. In terms of political institutions, Weber believed that the spread of bureaucracy was a potential threat to democracy in the modern world, as the state bureaucracy became a more powerful and independent group in society.

It was for this reason that Weber could never be a socialist and always supported capitalism as an economic system. In capitalist societies, large companies are always bureaucratic in nature, and these private enterprise bureaucracies will compete with the state bureaucracy to hold power and influence in society. It follows, therefore, that in capitalist societies this competition ensures a degree of political competition and democracy.

The officials of the bureaucracy held a set of beliefs or a code of honour, which Weber termed its *Amtsehre*, including:

- A sense of duty to their office
- A belief in the superiority of their own qualifications and competence
- The view that parliament was a mere talking shop
- The view that they were above party politics

  ○ The view that they were the true interpreters of the national interest
  ○ Loyalty to interests of their own, which Weber terms their *Staatsraison*

The source of power for the bureaucracy is based upon knowledge, and by this Weber understood technical expertise protected by secrecy. Weber did not like the spread of bureaucracy; he saw it as a product of the wider process of rationalisation that was making all aspects of human life calculable and predictable but also lacking in meaning and feeling. In Weber's view, we know very little about how products in our society really work; for example, we know how to turn on the radio, but most of us have no idea how radio waves are generated or turned into sound. By contrast, do not so-called primitive people have a much greater understanding of their environment?

Nevertheless, as we saw in our exercises above, many sociologists could argue that Weber's conceptions of power, authority and legitimacy are too restricted in their focus. In contrast to Weber, Steven Lukes (1974) argues that power has three dimensions or appearances:

  ○ Decision-making, which is concerned with the activities of the decision makers, such as government departments
  ○ Non-decision making, which is concerned with the way in which power is used to limit the range of decisions that the decision makers can choose from, when people come into contact with an ideology
  ○ Shaping desires, which is concerned with the ways in which individuals can have their attitudes and beliefs manipulated so as to accept a decision which is not in their own true interests, as when people have their ideas manipulated by an advertising campaign

One of the most damning critiques of Weber's conception of bureaucracy is found in Zygmunt Bauman's book *Modernity and the Holocaust* (1989):

> In Weber's exposition of modern bureaucracy, rational spirit, principle of efficiency, scientific mentality, relegation of values to the realm of subjectivity etc., no mechanism was recorded that was capable of excluding the possibility of Nazi excesses ... moreover, there was nothing in Weber's ideal types that would necessitate the description of the activities of the Nazi state as *excesses*. For example, no horror perpetuated by the German medical technocrats was inconsistent with the view that values are inherently subjective and that science is intrinsically instrumental and value free. (Bauman, 1989: 10)

> *I propose to treat the Holocaust as a rare, yet significant and reliable, test of the hidden possibilities of modern society.* ... Modern civilization was not the Holocaust's *sufficient* condition: it was, however, most certainly its *necessary* condition. Without it the Holocaust would be unthinkable. It was the rational world of modern civilization that made the Holocaust thinkable. The Nazi mass murder of the European Jewry was not only the technological achievement of an industrial society, but also the organizational achievement of a bureaucratic society ... bureaucratic rationality is at its most dazzling once we realize the extent to which *the very idea of the* Endlosung *was an outcome of the bureaucratic culture.* ... At no point of its long and tortuous execution did the

Holocaust come into conflict with the principles of rationality. The 'Final Solution' did not clash at any stage with the rational pursuit of efficient, optima; goal implementation. On the contrary, *it arose out of a genuine rational concern, and it was generated by bureaucracy true to its form and purpose*. (Bauman, 1989: 12, 13, 15, and 17)

In contrast to this view, Guenther Roth, an eminent Weberian scholar, has said of these views that his disagreement is 'total' and that he could not agree with one sentence, because 'Weber was a liberal, loved the constitution and approved of the working class's voting rights (and thus, presumably, could not be in conjunction with a thing so abominable as the Holocaust)' (Bauman, 1989: 10).

In contrast to Weber, the work of Michel Foucault (1977) does explore fully the parameters of power that Lukes suggests. In addition, Foucault explores the issue of legitimacy that Weber first raised; Foucault's argument is, however, very different.

Michel Foucault – power, legitimacy and authority

Foucault developed what he called a 'capillary' model of power in which he attempted to understand the 'relations of power' by looking at struggle and resistance. In contrast to the Marxist conception of power, which is based upon the idea that the economic power of class is the only significant factor to be analysed and discussed. Foucault argued that there are a number of important struggles that are independent of class relations: those over gender, sexuality, madness, criminality and medicine, to name but a few. Foucault suggests that these struggles share a number of characteristics:

- They are *transversal*; in other words, these struggles are not limited to any one place or any one class – such as the struggle for gay rights
- They are concerned with resisting the effects of power on bodies or lives – as we find in the holistic medical movement
- They are concerned with resisting the role of government in individual self-formation
- They are concerned with opening up and making clear how power is used in a secret way to change people – as in the case of the militia movement in the USA
- They are concerned with the politics of self-definition and self-formation – as in the women's movement
- They are concerned with resisting the imposition of external standards of taste and decency – as in the case of the Internet
- These political struggles are local and personal in nature – as in the case of road protesters

There are a number of common themes running through Foucault's work. His central concern was with how human beings are made into subjects within the modern world. What Foucault means by this is he is concerned with how individual people become both citizens of a state and the effect that this has on them as people. In addition, Foucault is concerned with how people become subjects of investigation for 'new' sciences such as medicine, psychiatry, and psychology in the search for the causes of 'abnormality', the search for answers to the question of what makes some individuals sick or mischievous.

Let us start with 'the state'. For Foucault, the state is a political structure that emerged in the sixteenth century. The state attempted to look after the interests of everybody within the whole community. Towards this end the state started to gather information about all forms of human activity: birth rates, death rates, unemployment, public health, epidemic diseases and crime. All of these phenomena could be indicators of a serious threat to the community. Gathering statistics about the population became a major activity of the modern state. Data collection by the state forms an important part of what Foucault refers to as bio-power (the monitoring of a range of trends that may form a threat to the community). Bio-power, along with a number of new developments in disciplinary technology (new forms of control over the bodies of people), can be viewed as the dark side of the Enlightenment. The Enlightenment is usually thought of as a period in history which gave rise to new concepts in politics, philosophy and science that not only stressed 'reason', rationality and freedom but also questioned the ignorance of tradition.

In his introduction to *The Foucault Reader* (1986), the friend and colleague of Foucault, Paul Rabinow, explains that within Foucault's work it is possible to identify what he calls three 'modes of objectification'; in other words, three organising principles used by Foucault to explain how individual human beings become subjects: dividing practices, scientific classification, and subjectification.

Dividing practices

Dividing practices involves the exclusion of people who are viewed as a threat to the community. The most famous example of this was the forced withdrawal of lepers from the community into leper colonies during the Middle Ages. This exclusion did result in the eradication of leprosy from Europe; therefore, it was believed that other threats to the community could be solved by similar exclusions. The poor were forced into workhouses. Criminals were put in prison. The insane were excluded into mental hospitals, or 'ships of fools', which were said to be ships loaded with the insane who were sent out to sea to recover their sanity. Although the ship of fools may have been mythical, it is certainly true that the mad once played a recognised role within the local community, as in the village idiot, for example, a role that was taken away from the insane when they were locked up in secure institutions. Foucault turns on its head the idea of progress in relation to the treatment of the mentally ill; the common-sense assumption that the more we progress, the more we care is not true, in Foucault's eyes.

Scientific classification

The Enlightenment brought with it a number of new sciences which were concerned with understanding the 'nature' of individuals. In addition, these new sciences defined what is 'normal' so that the 'abnormal' could be treated. The key tool for these new sciences was the *examination* (such as the medical examination given by a doctor). This tool transformed visibility into power, classified people into *cases* and trapped them in a straitjacket of documentation, that clearly stated whether or not they were normal. Foucault refers to this as 'hierarchical observation': 'a mechanism that coerces by means of observation; an apparatus in which the techniques that make it possible to see induce effects of power and in which, conversely, the means of coercion make those on whom they are applied clearly visible' (Foucault, 1986: 189). For example, in psychiatry, the doctor has a notion of the 'normal' mind and classifies individuals as 'normal' or as exhibiting a range of various diseased states. In Foucault's work, power relationships are based upon surveillance and need not be based upon physical punishment.

Subjectification

Subjectification is concerned with the process of self-formation, self-understanding and the way in which conformity is achieved. Foucault is concerned with what it means to have a self and how we as individuals create ourselves. Individuals define themselves as 'normal' in relation to a number of factors: sex, health, race and many more. This is primarily concerned with what Foucault was to call the 'power of the norm', all individual actions are now within 'a field of comparison' which both pressurises and *normalises* people. Normal people could legitimately regard themselves as members of a homogeneous social body – society.

If we take the example of gender, there is great pressure placed upon individual people to behave in a 'normal' way. A female child is expected to behave in a 'feminine' fashion. She may be told by her parents that she is 'not a baby now', and must change her behaviour. When she goes to school, she may be told that she is 'not at home now', and must change her behaviour. When she goes to work, she may be told that she is 'not at school now' and must change her behaviour. In this way the behaviour of women is shaped to 'fit in' with expectations of normal female behaviour.

The philosopher Jeremy Bentham designed the panopticon that Foucault draws upon in his work, but it was never built. Bentham outlined a number of positive things which the panopticon could offer: moral reform, preservation of health, invigoration of industry, reduction of public burden, lightening of the economy and abolition of the poor laws. Was the panopticon unnecessarily harsh, cruel or dehumanising? However, Angela Carter (1984) does attempt to give her readers the feel and flavour of what life in a panopticon would be like:

With the aid of a French criminologist who dabbled in phrenology, she selected from the prisons of the great Russian cities women who had been found guilty of killing their husbands and whose bumps indicated the possibility of salvation. She established a community on the most scientific lines available and had female convicts build it for themselves out of the same kind of logic that persuaded the Mexican *federales* to have those they were about to shoot dig their own graves.

It was a *panopticon* she forced them to build, a hollow circle of cells shaped like a doughnut, the inward-facing wall of which was composed of grids of steel and, in the middle of the roofed, central courtyard, there was a round room surrounded by windows. In that room she'd sit all day and stare and stare and stare at her murderesses and they, in turn, sat all day and stared at her.

During the hours of darkness, the cells were lit up like so many small theatres in which each actor sat by herself in the trap of her visibility in those cell shaped like servings of *bab au rhum*. The Countess, in the observatory, sat in a swivelling chair whose speed she could regulate at will. Round and round she went, sometimes at a great rate, sometimes slowly, raking with her ice-blue eyes – she was of Prussian extraction – the tier of unfortunate women surrounding her. She varied her speeds so that the inmates were never able to guess beforehand at just what moment they would come under her surveillance.

By the standards of the time and place, the Countess conducted her regime along humanitarian, if autocratic lines. Her private prison with its unorthodox selectivity was not primarily intended as the domain of punishment but in the purest sense, a penitentiary – it was a machine designed to promote penitence.

For the Countess P. had conceived the idea of a therapy of meditation. The women in the bare cells, in which was neither privacy nor distraction, cells formulated on the principle of those in a nunnery where all was visible to the eye of God, would live alone with the memory of their crime until they acknowledged, not their guilt – most of them had done that, already – but their *responsibility*. And she was sure that with responsibility would come remorse.

(Carter, 1984: 210–11)

The significance of the panopticon was outlined by Zygmunt Bauman in his book *Freedom*: '*Panopticon* may be compared to Parsons' laboriously erected model of the social system. What both works seek is nothing less than a model of well-balanced, equilibrated, cohesive human cohabitation, adaptable to changing tasks, capable of reproducing the conditions of its own existence, producing maximum output (however measured) and minimum waste' (1988: 20).

Jurgen Habermas: legitimation crisis

No discussion of the legitimacy of any political regime would be complete without a discussion of Jurgen Habermas's influential book *Legitimation Crisis* (1976). In this text Habermas outlines the core structures of society and the crisis tendencies

Table 2.1 *The rank order of socio-cultural, political and economic systems*

Subsystems	Normative structures	Substratum categories
Socio-cultural	Status system; subcultural forms of life	Distribution of privately available rewards and rights of disposition
Political	Political institutions (state)	Distribution of legitimate power (and structural force), drawing upon available sources of organizational rationality
Economic	Economic institutions (relations of production, ownership) or non-ownership of means of production. With owners in one class and non-owners in another class	Distribution of economic power (and structural force); available forces of production – the forces of production are all the things from nature needed to produce commodities

Source: Adapted from Habermas 1976: 6

Table 2.2 *Possible crisis tendencies*

Point of origin	System crisis	Identity crisis
Economic system	Economic crisis	–
Political system	Rationality crisis	Legitimation crisis
Socio-cultural system	–	Motivational crisis

Source: Habermas 1976: 45

which can emerge within these structures. He is particularly interested in how liberal-capitalist societies are sensitive to problems of legitimation. He argues that most discussions of the legitimacy of regimes are written from a 'systems' perspective, and Habermas starts his analysis with a discussion of the notion of a 'social system'.

Social systems are 'life-worlds' that are 'symbolically structured'. The *life-world* is the 'world of lived experience' the taken-for-granted world of common-sense assumptions that people share within a given community. Inside the social system, Habermas identifies three subsystems: the socio-cultural system, the political system and the economic system. Within each of these subsystems, Habermas distinguishes between 'normative structures' and 'substratum categories', as shown in Table 2.1.

Habermas argues that crises within a social system can emanate from several different points, as shown in the Table 2.2:

An *economic crisis* emerges when the required number of consumable values is not produced – in other words, consumer demands are not fulfilled. A *rationality crisis* emerges when the required number of rational decisions is not produced – in other words, people question the nature of the decisions made by the state, and lose faith in the ability of institutions to make rational decisions. A *legitimation crisis* emerges when the required number of 'generalised motivations' is not produced – in other words, the encouragement for people to act and think in a supportive way about the system is absent. A *motivational crisis* emerges when the required number of 'action-motivating' meanings is not produced – in other words, the motivation for people to act becomes dysfunctional for the state.

Unlike Weber, Habermas did not believe that rationalisation was an unstoppable process.

The discussion of a 'crisis' within a social system must take into account the relationship between system integration and social integration. A crisis is brought about by a combination of the following two factors:

○ *Social integration.* This is concerned with how individual people relate to each other within the system of institutions.
○ *System integration.* This is concerned with the 'steering performance' of the social system, the ability of the social system to deliver to individual people protection from an uncertain and often hostile environment; system integration also includes the ability of the social system to maintain its boundaries.

If social integration and system integration break down, the social system will not only lose legitimacy but may also collapse. People within what was the social system will be unable to interact with each other in a civil fashion. It could be argued that such a situation did emerge in the 1990s.

Balkanisation

The conflicts in the former Yugoslavia have been analysed by Stjepan G. Mestrovic in *The Balkanization of the West: The Confluence of Postmodernism and Postcommunism* (1994). In contrast to modernist thinkers such as Jurgen Habermas, Mestrovic argues that the world is becoming less cosmopolitan, less global and less rational. It is moving towards smaller and smaller units with greater hostility towards each other. This is the process of Balkanisation, which is both a postmodern phenomenon and a rebellion against the grand narratives of the Enlightenment – it is a process of disintegration running counter to the optimism of the Enlightenment. A key element of Balkanization is 'narcissism' – whereby people feel that their religion, group, city, cultural identity, etc. is superior to all others – which unites with the collective feeling that 'others' have ambitions to exterminate their group. Such narcissism leads directly to hostility and the breakdown of society. The USA and Western Europe are not Balkanising along geographical lines, but along ethnic, gender and other lines. Among others, many Native Americans, Kurds, Haitians, Bosnians, Croats, and Palestinians feel that the Western notion of universal human rights has passed them by.

In both the West and the former Soviet Union, the popular belief was that the indigenous system was superior to the other. In the former Soviet Union, the culture which helped to maintain the belief in the superiority of communism has not gone away, but is now manifest in aggressive forms of nationalism and ethnic conflict, which in the West is referred to as 'tribalism'. To explain this attempt to 'demonise' the opposing culture, Mestrovic draws upon the work of a number of writers such as Lasch, Riesman and notably Jovan Raskovic's *Luda Zemlja* (*Crazy Land*) (1990), which discusses the narcissistic nature of communism. When communism came to an end, people in the former Soviet Union experienced a collapse of hope and self-esteem; their ontological security was shaken. Taking his starting point from Freud, Raskovic makes the following claims:

- The Croats have a castration anxiety; they are driven by fears that something will happen which will humiliate them and take away what they have worked for
- The Muslims have an anal frustration that makes them desire to be clean and good
- The Serbs have Oedipal conflicts that make them aggressive and authoritarian

The interaction between these forces is what underpins the Balkan conflict; hence violence is inevitable. However, Balkanisation, as we suggested above, is not confined to Eastern Europe. In the USA, for example, there was rioting on the streets of Dallas after the 1993 Super Bowl. Black Americans pulled white Americans out of their cars and beat them up – in revenge for slavery, they claimed. According to Mestrovic, Dallas is not Sarajevo, 'but disturbing similarities exist already' (Mestrovic, 1994: 109). In addition, the postmodern television camera induces the evils found within traditional cultures to come to the surface. Television does not induce racism, sexism or violence, but enhances a need for faith, and this is asserted as fundamentalism.

The social system exists within an environment. The environment has three distinct parts according to Habermas. The first part is the 'outer nature', which is concerned with the natural resources available to the social system. This control over nature gives the social system power. The second part is the 'inner nature', which is concerned with the development of norms and other acceptable ways of behaving as passed on via processes of socialisation. These include the ways in which parents bring up their children, and the ways in which the mass media influence people's ideas, opinions and beliefs about the nature of society and the way it works. The third part comprises other social systems that may benefit as well as threaten the present social system. The benefits may include such things as trade relationships, while the possible threats include military action. Either way, the relationships between social systems must be managed in some way.

Social systems, then, exist within an environment. Inside the environment the social system is involved in production, to satisfy the material needs of its members, and socialisation of its people into acceptable ways of behaving and believing. Inside the system, people relate to each other in rational ways that form 'reconstructable patterns'. In other words, individuals are made aware of appropriate ways of relating to each other, and whenever similar situations present themselves to an individual, that person can draw upon the appropriate pattern of behaviour to cope with the situation in a stress-free or mutually beneficial way.

Habermas's suggestion here is that the goals and values within a social system are limited by the development of 'world-views' – ways in which individuals within a social system make sense of their world by the meanings or moral systems that they share. These 'structures of intersubjectivity' (by which Habermas seems to mean 'sharing'!) also help people to secure an identity. A system's level of development in these areas is then dependent upon the openness of institutions in allowing individuals to learn. This seems to mean that social systems are limited by the amount of knowledge that the people within a social system possess.

With growing theoretical and practical insight, people within the social system have greater control over both the system's outer nature and its inner nature. Habermas refers to these developments as the system's 'steering capacity'. Steering can be problematic and produce crisis effects within the social system if issues or problems arise that are regarded as beyond what could possibly happen. Very high rates of inflation, investment strikes or large numbers of people dropping out of the labour force would all be examples of this. Ideas of 'what could possibly happen' are defined by 'organisational principles' which are highly abstract and which 'limit the capacity of a society to learn without losing its identity' (Habermas, 1976: 7). The 'organisational principles' are a framework of ideas that provide individuals with certainty about the system.

Habermas and liberal capitalism

Although Habermas outlines several types of social formation, he spends most of his time discussing the liberal-capitalist social system. Within this system, the 'principle of organisation' is the relationship between labour and capital. In other words, the type of society that we live in is dominated by the relationship between workers and employers. Within our social system these relationships have become 'depoliticised' and 'anonymous'. By this, Habermas means that the power of the state is used to make the conditions for capitalistic production. In other words, we have private individuals who own companies that make things for profit; this is usually referred to as 'private sector production'. What the state does is to provide the conditions under which unregulated markets become legitimate in the eyes of the people within the social system. The role of the state is to ensure that the capitalist social system is allowed to continue and to be reproduced again and again over time. As Habermas explains, 'Economic exchange becomes the dominant steering medium' (Habermas, 1976: 21).

Once the capitalist society has been established, the state's activity can be limited to four purposes:

- To protect commerce – one of the key purposes of the police and the justice system
- To protect the market mechanism from possible self-destructive side-effects; for example, the dangerous working conditions which damage the health of the workforce and reduce profit margins

- To provide an infrastructure, notably schools, and transport and communication systems, which allows capitalists to be more effective and efficient
- To provide a legal framework for business, banking and an efficient taxation system

In liberal capitalism, crises appear in the form of unresolved economic steering problems. It is commonly assumed that severe economic problems arise because government policies lack competence. Social change becomes unpredictable and this is seen as a direct threat to the living standards of working people and the profit margins of capitalists. There is a strong fear that economic depression will endanger social integration. Workers and capitalists repeatedly confront one another over the nature of their intentions, which, of course, are always incompatible; workers want maximum wages and capitalists want maximum profits. As Habermas explains, 'economic crisis is immediately transformed into social crisis' (Habermas, 1976: 29).

In summary, crises can be avoided by the use of 'steering imperatives'. In the case of economic crisis, the 'steering imperative' may involve increasing the level of state activity in the economy. The purpose of increased state activity in the economy is to enhance the level of mass loyalty to the social system. If this crisis management by the state were to fail, withdrawal of legitimacy would follow.

Case study. Northern Ireland and the absence of legitimate authority?

Northern Ireland was created in 1921 when the rest of Ireland was given self-rule. The majority of the population was and remains Protestant, unlike the rest of Ireland, which has a very large Catholic majority. From 1921 until 1968, Northern Ireland was given limited self-government, with the Stormont Parliament comprising a senate of twenty-four elected members and two ex officio members, and a House of Commons of fifty-two members elected for a five-year period. The province also sent twelve members to the House of Commons at Westminster. This was a period of majority rule and one-party government, and it is clear that during this period discrimination against Catholics was rife. On 24 March 1972, Stormont was suspended and the British government introduced direct rule from Westminster. Since that time, government policy for Northern Ireland has had three objectives:

- To contain and stabilise the problems of the province within the UK
- To create a form of cross-communal political consensus; in other words, to get the two sides of the community to tolerate each other
- To produce structures of devolved government, based upon cross-communal support – if necessary by intergovernmental negotiation, or, as it has been termed, the 'Irish dimension'

The positions of the major political forces in Northern Ireland are the following.

Non-negotiable issues

Constitutional Unionists – the main Unionist parties

1. British sovereignty – that the British government should have sole control over the running of Northern Ireland
2. No institutionalised political or administrative links with the Republic of Ireland
3. Protestant self-determination – the Protestant people in Northern Ireland, should be responsible for their own destiny.
4. Suppression of Sinn Fein and the IRA
5. No power-sharing, as of right, between the Catholic and Protestant communities in Northern Ireland.

British government

1. British Sovereignty
2. Self-determination for the Northern Ireland majority
3. Suppression of the IRA

Constitutional nationalists – including the Irish government and the Social Democratic and Labour Party (SDLP)

1. Recognition of the Irish dimension in Northern Ireland
2. Need for institutionalised links between Northern Ireland and the Republic of Ireland
3. Need for partnership/power-sharing, between the Catholic and Protestant communities in Northern Ireland

Republicans – including Sinn Fein (the political wing of the IRA) and the IRA

1. Irish sovereignty: a unitary Irish state for the whole island of Ireland
2. British withdrawal from Northern Ireland

Adapted from McCullagh and O'Dowd (1986: 4)

Steve Bruce (1986) views the struggle in Northern Ireland as a conflict between nationalists and an ethnic group, the Unionists, who share a common experience and a common historical tradition, of which Protestantism is the common thread. In particular, Bruce sees Ian Paisley as representing the core of traditional Orange-Loyalist culture. This culture stands at the very core of the traditional Loyalist world-view. The Free Presbyterian Church, formed by Paisley in 1946, represents a very conservative form of evangelicalism. Some Paisley supporters believe the Pope to be the AntiChrist and the Roman Catholic Church to be undemocratic and supportive of the IRA. Bruce maintains that it is this evangelicalism which gives Unionist politics its distinct identity. Without it, Unionists

Table 2.3 *Crisis in Northern Ireland*

	For Northern Ireland Catholics	For Northern Ireland Protestants
Motivational crisis	Yes/No	Yes/No
Legitimation crisis	Yes/No	Yes/No
Rationality crisis	Yes/No	Yes/No
Economic crisis	Yes/No	Yes/No

would not differ significantly from Catholics. Paisley, in his opening speech (a copy of which was kindly sent me) at the Brooke Talks, which was the start of the current peace process was very keen to point out that 'Ulstermen are not Englishmen living in Northern Ireland.' Moreover, he stated: 'I would never repudiate the fact that I am an Irishman, but that to me is a geographic term in relation to the island where I live. That does not call into question my Britishness.' In contrast, Bruce argues that among Northern Ireland Catholics, national identity has become so secure, and so taken for granted, that it can be separated from its religious base.

In summary, we could argue that before the introduction of direct rule, the political structures in Northern Ireland had legitimacy in the eyes of the Protestant community, but not the Catholic community.

However, can the work of Weber cast any light on why sections of the community in Northern Ireland regard the political structures as lacking in legitimacy? I would argue that Weber's arguments cannot be used to understand the conflict in Northern Ireland, because Weber's conceptions of authority lack a discussion of emotional attachment to a form of political regime.

Similarly, the work of Jurgen Habermas cannot shed much light on why sections of the community in Northern Ireland regard the political structures as lacking in legitimacy. I do not think the problems of Northern Ireland be diagnosed in the following tick-the-box way, which is where Habermas's argument leads us (Table 2.3). Like Weber, Habermas assumes that the state should have legitimacy in the eyes of the people under its authority; without this legitimacy, the state cannot survive.

In contrast to the work of both Weber and Habermas, stands the work of Richard Sennett (1993), to whom we shall now turn.

Richard Sennett: authority

One of the most thought-provoking accounts of power and authority is provided by Richard Sennett (1993). In sharp contrast to Weber, Sennett argues that authority need not be legitimate in the eyes of the population. For Sennett, authority is associated with a number of qualities: 'assurance, superior judgement, the ability to impose discipline, the capacity to inspire fear' (Sennett, 1993: 18). Above all, power has the image of strength, it 'is the will of one person prevailing over the will of the other' (Sennett, 1993: 170). For Sennett, 'authority' is both an 'emotional connection' between people and at the same time, a 'constraint' upon people. These bonds are seen as 'timeless' rather than 'personal'. Emotional bonds often mesh people together against their own personal or financial benefit. Even though the desire to be under some authority is regarded as indispensable, people fear the damage that authority can do to our liberties. Moreover, the emotional bonds of authority are seldom stable in nature.

In contrast to Weber, who believed that authority was built upon legitimacy in the eyes of the people who were subject to the control of the authority, Sennett argues that: 'We feel attracted to strong figures we do not believe to be legitimate' (Sennett, 1993: 26). How could this be? Taking his starting point from Freudian analysis, which argues that the mass of the population are always in danger of regressing to earlier phases of psycho-social development, Sennett maintains that we have a psychological need for the comfort and emotional satisfaction which a resolute authority can provide. Freud believed that we saw such a 're-infantilization of the masses' in Europe in the 1930s. These Freudian ideas were taken up and developed by the Frankfurt School, most notably in Theodore Adorno's *The Authoritarian Personality*. This influential psychological study is discussed in most psychology textbooks. In essence, it suggests that there is an F scale, passed on from parents to children, which can be measured. This scale includes hostility to outsiders, racism and sexism, hostility to people who are artistic or sensitive, a feeling of wanting to be conventional, belief in superstition and fear of authority. Those with a high score on the F scale are likely to become fascists. David Held (1980) suggests that the following nine personality variables make up the implicit pre-fascist tendencies:

- Conventionalism: rigid adherence to conventional, middle-class values
- Authoritarian submission: submissive, uncritical attitude towards idealised moral authorities of the in-group; in other words, the need to conform to authority
- Authoritarian aggression: tendency to be on the look out for and condemn, reject and punish people who violate conventional values
- 'Anti-interception': opposition to the subjective, the imaginative, the tender-hearted
- Superstition and stereotyping: the belief in mystical determinants of the individual's fate; the disposition to think in rigid categories
- Power and 'toughness': preoccupation with the dominance-submission, strong-weak, leader-follower oppositions, exaggerated assertion of strength and toughness
- Destructiveness and cynicism: generalised hostility; defamation of what it means to be human
- Projectivity: the disposition to believe that wild and dangerous things go on in the world
- Sex: exaggerated concern with sexual 'goings-on'

Although Sennett sees much of value in these Freudian-inspired analyses, he argues that there is a need for us to look at 'the actual give-and-take between the strong and the weak' (Sennett, 1993: 25–6). He outlines a number of 'bonds of rejection' which people use to counter authority, but which simultaneously allow us to depend upon the authority and be used by that authority. There are three such 'bonds of rejection'.

The first 'bond of rejection' is 'disobedient dependence'. This is a situation in which people rebel 'within' authority, rather than 'against' authority. By this, Sennett means that individuals become obsessed with what the authority thinks of them as individuals. Such rebellion often becomes a bid for recognition. Sennett explains that the key practice within disobedient dependence is 'transgression'. This practice involves not simply saying 'no' to the authority, but proposing an alternative which the authority cannot accept. However, the proposed alternative is rarely a real alternative; its purpose is to obliterate some aspect of the past which the individual did not like. To counter this transgression, the authority uses a range of strategies, which Sennett refers to as 'reverse responses'. The main reverse responses is 'indifference' to the subordinate's demands and requests. Reversed responses discredit points of view from the people who are subject to authority, suggesting that they have nothing 'intrinsically meaningful' to say. This puts pressure on the subordinate to bid for recognition, leading to emotional dependence. Individuals have a need to be given some recognition by the authority. Hence, according to Sennett, rebellion takes place within the terms and conditions laid down by the authority, and for this reason the emotional control of the authority tightens.

In other words, people rebel within authority usually in an attempt to gain recognition from the authority. The authority is in a position to enhance the self-esteem of the individual by giving recognition. If the authority refuses to give recognition, the emotional ties which constrain those under the authority become even tighter, as the need for recognition becomes greater, the longer it is denied.

The second bond of rejection is 'idealised substitution'. Here the authority serves as a negative model; whatever the authority does, the opposite is what we want. In this case, the authority also serves as a key point of reference, and we become dependent upon it. We have a fear of losing our link with authority, because without it we have no moorings. Individuals secure themselves with any anchor authority can provide.

Finally, the third bond of rejection is 'the fantasy of disappearance'. Sennett defines the fantasy of disappearance as a form of 'infantile scepticism', according to which 'everything would be all right if only the people in charge would disappear' (Sennett, 1993: 39). However, at the same time, there is a fear that if the authority did not make its presence felt, there would be nothing: 'The authority figure is feared, but even more the subject fears he will go away' (Sennett, 1993: 40).

In summary, people have a fear of freedom.

Table 2.4 *From social action to legitimate rule*

Type of social action		Type of legitimate rule
Zweckrational ⟶	social action motivated by a 'goal' ⟶	rational legal authority
Wertrational ⟶	social action motivated by a 'value' ⟶	charismatic authority
Tradition ⟶	social action motivated by customs ⟶	traditional authority
Affect ⟶	social action motivated by emotion ⟶	

Sennett has a number of interesting things to say about the effects of authority on 'the self'. He suggests that, in response to authority, there is a separation between an 'outer self' and an 'inner self'. The 'outer self' is the self that we present to others in our everyday life; it is our public self, made up of the various roles that we play, such as teacher or student. The 'inner self' is the self of our innermost thoughts and feelings. The 'outer self' obeys the rules of the authority without question, but the 'inner self' does not accept what the 'outer self' is doing. This leads to a permanent feeling of passivity and indifference, as if it were not really me that is obeying the authority; my actions do not really matter because I do not really believe in them.

As we suggested above, in contrast to Weber, Sennett believes that an authority does not necessarily have to have legitimacy in the eyes of those subject to it. However, this is not the only contrast with Weber. For Weber, any social action is an action that has an intention behind it, and there are four types of social action that suggest motives for or intentions behind people is behaviour. Three of these types of social action have corresponding types of legitimate rule, as shown in Table 2.4.

It would have been logical if Weber had developed a form of legitimate authority based upon emotion, but he did not. However, Sennett has done just this; he has developed a form of authority based upon emotion, as may be seen in his notions of disobedient dependence, idealised substitution and the fantasy of disappearance. In summary, in sharp contrast to Weber, Sennett holds that authority need not be legitimate in the eyes of the population.

The postmodern conception of the state

Area 3 will expand on the nature of the postmodern condition, and explore how the world is a very uncertain place because of the rejection of 'grand narratives', such as political ideologies like socialism. However, we need to remind ourselves that in the modern world, people are organised by the state in rational and logical ways. This state organisation is conducted via the education system, which provides people with the appropriate values and beliefs, and the health-care system, which defines the 'normal' body and how it should function 'normally'. This process reached its boundary or end point with the state socialism of the former Soviet Union, in which nature was controlled, rivers were redirected and people were moulded into a unified identity, in the interests of the collectivity. People are clearly defined as 'normal' or 'abnormal', and those who are not normal will be dealt with in the appropriate way, which may be imprisonment, hospitalisation or execution.

Postmodernists such as Crook et al. (1992) have argued that the postmodern state is a decentred, minimal and fragmented one. In other words, in the post-modern condition, the state does not have the power or influence over people's lives that it does in the modern world. By a 'decentred' state we mean a state which is disappearing. The term 'minimal' means that the state has little influence and is 'fragmented', or broken up into a range of units, some of which are in the public sector and some of which are run by the private sector. This was reflected in the policies of 'deregulation', allowing the private sector to bid for contracts to run public services, such as local bus services, and 'privatisation', the sale of assets from the state sector to the private sector, such as the sale of British Gas. These policies were followed by the Thatcher and Reagan governments in the 1980s and were not reversed by either the Clinton administration in the USA or the Blair government in the UK.

The fragmentation, diversification and disorientation of the state were reflected in what David Ashley (1997) refers to as the forms of postmodern 'civil and voca-tional privatism'. The postmodern condition has dissolved the need for state legitimacy, because we do not expect the state to be able to solve our problems. Moreover, legitimacy in the sense that Habermas discusses it is based upon acceptance of some form of 'grand narrative', or the manipulation of the masses into some common way of thinking again built upon a 'grand narrative'.

Area 3 will outline the nature of the postmodern condition and the concept of the 'grand narrative'. The term 'postmodernism' was popularised by Jean-François Lyotard (1984), who was chosen by the Council of Universities of Quebec in the 1970s to write a report on the condition of knowledge in the Western world. His conclusion was that all 'grand narratives' or 'meta-narratives' are exhausted. In other words, the enlightenment project is completed, and the big ideas such as Marxism and liberalism have nothing of value to say about the world and how it is now organised. In the postmodern condition, such 'grand narratives' as Marxism and liberalism break down, and with this break down we lose the dis-tinction between 'high' culture and 'low' culture; truth and fabrication; morality and immorality. In the postmodern condition, 'anything goes' – calves in formaldehyde become art, Harry Seecombe singing 1950s pop songs becomes religion, and even food and sex become life-threatening. The postmodern world is a very uncertain place. There are no universally accepted ways of behaving, no com-munally held beliefs, no agreed foundations for organisation of our personal, social or political lives. The world becomes impossible to predict, and our lives have an uncertain feel to every aspect of them.

On the one hand, this condition can be very liberating, individuals can con-struct any identity they wish, draw upon any lifestyle, any ideology, that they find

Table 2.5 *Modern/postmodern versions of privatism*

	Civil privatism	Vocational privatism
Modern	Based on familial or personal property ownership	Centred on professional occupational status, regulated by achievement within closed collegially organised groups
Postmodern	Increasingly includes sumptuary consumption, i.e., purchase of commodified semiotic privileges marking cultural distinctions	Includes attempt to promote hyperdiversity value commitment and ability to create new forms of expertise and cultural capital

Source: Ashley, 1997:180.

significant. Individuals are free. On the other hand, this freedom has a dark side. Individuals freed from morality are capable of great cruelty and may see no place in their world for justice, kindness and respect for others. The position of post-modernists also has implications for sociological conceptions of the state.

According to Ashley (1997), vocational privatism is the idea of professional service to the community based upon communal interests, such as district nursing services, while civil privatism is the loss of interest and involvement in careers, leisure pursuits and consumption (Table 2.5).

In the postmodern condition, 'the masses' cannot be manipulated. A postmodern culture is built upon a high degree of diversity and fragmentation. Postmodern politics is a form of politics without the need for legitimation. However, David Ashley takes a contrary view.

Ashley's critique of the postmodern view of the state

Crook et al.'s observations about the shrinking state are seriously out of kilter – first, because the capitalist state was never exactly motivated by the need to succour the needy and, second, because there is, in any case, little objective evidence that western states 'shrank' in power or size during the 1980s. The number of lobbyists in Washington, D.C., did not fall during the decade … nor did the number of civil servants in Britain. … Under Reagan, the U.S. federal budget nearly doubled from $591 billion in 1980 to $1,183 in 1988; during this period public spending as a proportion of national income actually rose. By 1996 the federal government was paying $240 billion a year in interest payments alone on the deficits created by the Reagan and Bush administrations. In Britain, government expenditure increased from £68.5 billion in 1979 to £190.7 billion in 1990. As a proportion of GDP, public-sector spending in the United Kingdom did not fall as much as a single percentage point from 1979 (the year that Thatcher assumed power) to 1993. (adapted from Ashley, 1997: 166)

The argument here is that 'state-centred' theories still have a high degree of validity. We shall turn our attention to these theories.

State-centred theories

According to Roger King (1986), people looked at 'the state' during the nineteenth century as something purposefully 'built' or 'made' that comprised a number of key elements:

- A centralised power within a defined territory – which made use of a number of agencies, including the use of force if necessary, to maintain its power
- A power founded upon consent that should be seen as legitimate authority.

As King explains,

The nineteenth century constitutional state is characterised by a unitary sovereignty which becomes manifest in a single currency, a unified legal system, and an expanding state educational system employing a single 'national' language. A literary tradition in this 'national' language erodes cultural particularism, and a system of national conscription, which replaced the local recruitment of ancient military units, also tends to overcome 'peripheral' or localist identities. Moreover, this increased monopoly of the means of violence by centralising states is sustained by the extension of the capitalist mode of production. (King, 1986: 51)

The state became bureaucratic, in the way that Weber described, a hierarchy of offices; a division of labour and depersonalised decision making based upon the application of abstract rules. Drawing upon the work of Poggi (1978), King explains that the state 'machinery' developed five distinct characteristics:

- *Civility*. This is most fully explained by Foucault, and it is concerned with the movement by states away from the use of violence and coercion towards forms of control and punishment such as community service, which are more effective and regarded as more legitimate.
- *Plurality of foci*. Politics and the political processes become very varied, with many governmental agencies acting in almost complete independence of each other. This gives the political process a many-sided or diverse feel.
- *Open-endedness*. Political processes have a constant unfinished feel to them.
- *Controversy*. People's views are freely expressed and act as a constraint upon the state.
- *Centrality of representative institutions*. The division between the state and society is clearly defined; the parliamentary assembly or parliament constitutes *the state,* and the electors constitute *the society*.

In state-centred theories, the state is assumed to be the most powerful institution in society, and it is said to have interests of its own, and to act independently to bring about social change. Therefore, the modern state is not the creation of capitalism, or of class relations within capitalism. There is no force in society pushing the state in any particular direction. Michael Mann (1986) suggests that there are four sources of social power: the economic, the political, the military and the ideological. Military threats from the outside world are one of the key factors in the process of state formation; and the state is the only body that can exercise power in a centralised, territorial fashion.

Eric Nordlinger (1981) defined the state as 'all those individuals who occupy offices that authorise them, and them alone, to make and apply decisions that are binding upon any and all segments of society' (Nordlinger, 1981: 11). His argument is that the state has become increasingly powerful and an independent body in society, as a consequence of the emergence of the welfare state, built upon Keynesian techniques for government intervention in the economy and society, in order to improve the living and working conditions of the population. He explains that the state is autonomous

> to the extent that it translates its preferences into authoritative actions, the degree to which public policy conforms to the parallelogram of the public officials' resource-weighted preferences. State autonomy may be operationally defined in terms of the overall frequency with which state preferences coincide with authoritative actions and inactions, the proportion of preferences that do so, the average substantive distance between state preferences and authoritative actions, or some combination of the three. (Nordlinger, 1981: 19–20)

Nordlinger suggests a number of ways in which the state can increase its independence of groups within society:

- By concealed methods of decision making
- By the honours system, providing employment or government deals with private companies to persuade people to accept its proposals
- By using the state's resources to weaken opponents; for example, the much-increased use of state advertising in Britain since 1979
- By changing policy

Perhaps the most convincing state-centred theorist is Theda Skocpol (1985), who outlines a number of examples of states behaving independently in pursuit of their own interests. Building upon the work of Weber and the historian Otto Hintze (1960), she argues that the state has a high degree of autonomy; in other words, the state can exercise power independently of social class or any other social force in the society. Skocpol conceives of state 'organizations claiming control over territories and people' (Skocpol, 1985: 20). The autonomy of the state has its origins in the following:

- The emergence of an inter-state system and the subsequent rise of geopolitical factors
- The development of economic and social relationships that are worldwide in nature
- The activity of political managers who build careers within the state machine
- Periods of crisis which need a collective response

Like Gramsci, she suggests that whether or not a state develops into a powerful independent body depends upon how well organised other groups in society are. However, states do not have to represent the interests of the bourgeoisie in the way that most Marxists would suggest. A strong state can shape the activity of classes, including the bourgeoisie.

However, state-centred theorists are often vague about their distinct theoretical assumptions. They are critical of the assumptions of Marxists, pluralists and elite theorists, but do not make clear their own assumptions about the links between the state and society. At times, they are neo-Weberian, at times neo-Marxist in nature. In addition, as we have seen in the discussion of Weber and the Marxist theorists, Weber considered state bureaucrats to be independent of party politics, and a number of Marxists have expounded the 'relative autonomy' of the state.

Area Summary

In this area we looked at a number of 'modernist' theories of power and the state. We started by looking at Anthony Giddens's conception of modernity and then moved on to outline the distinction that Max Weber made between authority and coercion. All of these theories and concepts are open to question. Did the Nazis have authority or did they rule by coercion? Reflecting on such questions should allow you to develop a critical understanding of the three types of legitimate rule outlined by Max Weber. From this, we moved on to look at the contribution of Michel Foucault to our understanding of power and authority and at Jurgen Habermas's contribution to our understanding of the processes of legitimation within social systems.

Giddens, Weber, Habermas, the state-centred theorists and, to some extent, Foucault all propose theories which fail to consider 'emotion' as a factor in the processes of power. In contrast, the contribution of Sennett to our understanding of authority does attempt to give 'emotion' a central role in our understanding of power. Finally, we looked at the postmodern conception of the state. Postmodernists reject all the modernist assumptions upon which all the theories in this area are based.

The world that postmodernists describe is one of fragmentation, diversification and disorientation, in which the need for state legitimacy has dissolved. Moreover, legitimacy, in the sense defined by the modernist writers we have looked at, is based upon acceptance of some form of 'grand narrative' or the manipulation of the masses into some common way of thinking, again on the basis of a 'grand narrative'. As we shall see in the following areas, postmodernists reject this above all else.

References

Adorno, Theodore, Frenkel-Brunswick, E., Levinson, D.J. and Sanford, N.R. (1950) *The Authoritarian Personality*. New York: Harper.

Albrow, M. (1977) *Bureaucracy*. London: Pall Mall Press.

Angelou, M. (1984) *I know Why the Caged Bird Sings*. London: Virago.

Ashley, D. (1997) *History Without a Subject: The Postmodern Condition*. Boulder, Co: Westview Press.

Bauman, Z. (1988) *Freedom*. Milton Keynes: Open University Press.

Bauman, Z. (1989) *Modernity and the Holocaust*. Cambridge: Polity.

Bessel, R. (1997) 'Just retribution', 8 August, *Times Literary Supplement*.

Best, S. (1997) 'Power and Politics', in Nik Jorgensen (eds), *Sociology: An Interactive Approach*. London: Collins Educational.

Best, S., Griffiths, J. and Hope, T. (2000) *Active Sociology*. Harlow: Longman.

Braverman, H. (1974) *Labor and Monopoly Capital*. New York: Monthly Review Press.

Bruce, S. (1986) *God Save Ulster. The Religion and Politics of Paisleyism*. Oxford: Clarendon Press.

Carter, A. (1984) *Nights at the Circus*. London: Picador.

Crook, S., Pakulski, J. and Waters, M. (1992) *Postmodernization: Change in Advanced Society*. London: Sage.

Finkelstein, J. (1995) *The Fashioned Self*. Cambridge: Polity.

Foucault, M. (1977) *Discipline and Punish: The Birth of the Prison*. New York: Pantheon.

Foucault, M. (1986) *The Foucault Reader*. P. Rabinow (ed.). Harmondsworth: Penguin.

Giddens, A. (1984) *The Constitution of Society*. Cambridge: Polity.

Giddens, A. (1985) *The Nation State and Violence: Volume Two of A Contemporary Critique of Historical Materialism*. Cambridge: Polity.

Giddens, A. (1989) *Sociology*. Cambridge: Polity.

Giddens, A. (1990) *The Consequences of Modernity*. Cambridge: Polity.

Goffman, E. (1962) *Asylums: Essays on the Social Situation of Mental Patients and Other Inmates*. Harmondsworth: Penguin.

Gramsci, Antonio (1957) *The Modern Prince and Other Writings*. New York: New World Paperbacks.

Haber, C. (1995) *The Best of the Social Science Teacher*. Watford: ATSS.

Habermas, J. (1976) *Legitimation Crisis*. London: Heineman.

Held, D. (1980) *Introduction to Critical Theory: Horkheimer to Habermas*. London: Hutchinson.

Hintze, O. (1960) *The Historical Essays of Otto Hintz*. F. Gilber (ed.). New York: Oxford University Press.

Irving, D. (1997) *Nuremberg*. Basingstoke: Macmillan.

King, R. (1986) *The State in Modern Society – New Directions in Political Sociology*. Basingstoke: Macmillan.

Levi, P. (1987) *If This Be a Man*. London: Abacus.

Lukes, S. (1974) *Power: A Radical View*. Basingstoke: Macmillan.

Lyotard, J.F. (1984) *The Postmodern Condition: A Report on Knowledge*. Minneapolis, MN: University of Minnesota Press.

Mann, M. (1986) *The Sources of Social Power*. Cambridge: Cambridge University Press.

McCullagh, M. and O'Dowd, L. (1986) 'Northern Ireland: the search for a solution', *Social Studies Review* (March).

Mestrovic, S. (1994) *The Balkanization of the West: The Confluence of Postmodernism and Postcommunism*. London: Routledge.

Michels, R. (1949) *Political Parties.* Glencoe: The Free Press.

Mintzberg, H. (1979) *The Structure of Organisations.* Englewood Cliffs, NJ: Prentice-Hall.

Nordlinger, E. (1981) *The Autonomy of the Democratic State.* Cambridge, MA: Harvard University Press.

Poggi, G. (1978) *The Development of the Modern State – A Sociological Introduction.* Stanford, CA: Stanford University Press.

Sennett, R. (1993) *Authority.* London: Faber and Faber.

Skocpol, T. (1985) *States and Social Revolution.* Cambridge: Cambridge University Press.

Taylor, F. (1911) *The Principles of Scientific Management.* New York: Harper and Row.

Weber, M. (1988; first published 1926) *Max Weber: Biography.* New Brunswick: Transaction Books.

Weber, M. (1978) *Economy and Society: An Outline of Interpretive Sociology.* 2 Vols. Berkeley, CA: University of California Press.

3

Postmodern Politics

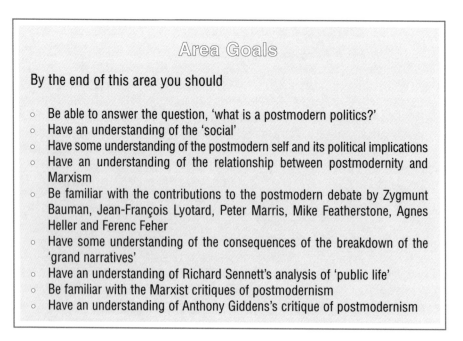

Whatever is understood by the term 'postmodernism', it suggests a radical break with the past, a fundamental split from theories of 'modernity'. In other words, post-modernism is historically and conceptually different from modernism or theories rooted in modernity. By modernity, sociologists mean 'the modern world', and theories rooted in modernity include Marxism, functionalism, feminism and any other 'grand narrative'. There is some debate about when the modern world came into existence, but most people assume that modernity is the industrial age from about 1760 to the late twentieth century. Grand narratives are 'big theories' which attempt to explain huge sweeps of history and everything that happens within those sweeps, as well as giving us advice on how to lead our lives and what to think. As Lyotard explains in his book *The Postmodern Explained to Children* (1992), 'These narratives aren't myths in the sense that fables would be (not even the Christian narrative). Of course, like myths, they have the goal of legitimating social and political institutions and practices, laws, ethics, ways of thinking' (1992: 29).

Modernity, postmodernity and postmodernism

Initially, some clarifications and definitions may be useful. As a set of theories or perspectives, 'postmodernism' is built upon the idea that 'modernism' or 'modernist' theories, such as Marxism, socialism, feminism and functionalism, can no longer explain the way in which the world works. Postmodernism suggests 'new times' and this means 'new theory' to explain the world. As a social system, postmodernity follows modernity.

The term 'modernity' means the modern world, and, according to Anthony Giddens (1992), modernity has the following institutional characteristics:

- Capitalism: the economy dominated by private companies
- Industrialism: the use of complicated technology to make products
- Centralised administrative power: a central government or state that employs surveillance
- Centralised control of military power

According to Zygmunt Bauman, there is a movement within modernity by the state to impose an approved identity upon all citizens. This can be seen most clearly in the activity of the education system, which, many people argue, attempts to impose accepted values, attitudes and beliefs upon all schoolchildren. Consider the debate in Britain about all children having a collective act of Christian worship each day at school. In contrast, postmodernism can be viewed as the culture of postmodernity. Within the postmodern culture, there are a range of lifestyles and social identities from which one can choose. You might ask yourself how would you react to someone who enjoyed eating dog? Why is eating dogs unacceptable in Western culture? Lifestyle choices include such diverse things as choices about the food we eat, the clothes we wear, the car we drive, our sexual preference and many more. Why did you choose to wear the clothes that you are now wearing.

Postmodernism is concerned with finding new techniques of describing and explaining the character of the world; these are needed because the theories of the 'modernist movement' can no longer explain how the world works in a satisfactory fashion. Postmodernism, then, is a direct response to modernist social theories such as Marxism, functionalism and feminism. All these theories assume that there is one true source, such as class, common values, or gender, of our behaviour as individuals which is external to us or beyond our control.

According to Rob Stones, 'Postmodernists argue, respectively, for: (1) respecting the existence of a plurality of perspectives, as against a notion that there is one single truth from a privileged perspective; (2) local, contextual studies in place of grand narratives; and (3) an emphasis on disorder, flux and openness, as opposed to order, continuity and constraint' (Stones, 1996: 22). In other words, postmodernists accept there are many different views of the world, not one that is better than all others; they question the notion of truth and the foundations of all knowledge. When they look at the world, they see confusion rather than ordered social systems, which functionalists see, or modes of production, which Marxists see.

Most sociologists place postmodernism or the postmodern condition in the context of the 'disorganised capitalism' of the consumer society and cultural mass production of the late twentieth century. The world does not have the clear and easily identifiable structure of owners of the means of production as opposed to non-owners of the means of production, as in Marxist analysis. The world now has a messy and highly uncertain feel to it.

Mike Featherstone (1988: 205–7) outlines three aspects of the sociology of postmodernism. First, there is the analysis of the change in the activities of artists and intellectuals in postmodern culture. Second, we have the analysis of the changing relationship between artists, intellectuals and the rest of society. The rise of `new cultural intermediaries' is central here. These are groups that create and distribute new cultural goods that we desire and make use of in our relationships with others. Finally, we have the most important area of sociological analysis, the significance of postmodernism in the everyday life of people, who may be developing new identities, new ways of relating to the world, and new forms of signification or meaning in their everyday experience. In other words, in the postmodern condition, people redefine what is important for them, redefine themselves and redefine the meaning of their place in the world.

In this area, I will look at the essence of the postmodern condition and the debates connected with what make up a postmodern politics.

The postmodern condition

But what is postmodernism?

Nigel Wheale (1995) outlines what he calls a lexicon of postmodern technique, in other words, a list of key terms that may be found in postmodern texts: 'An all-purpose postmodern item might be constructed like this: it uses eclecticism to generate parody and irony; its style may owe something to schlock, kitsch or camp taste. It may be partly allegorical, certainly self-reflexive and contain some kind of list. It will not be realistic' (Wheale, 1995: 42).

Glossary of key terms

- Eclecticism: a picking and mixing of styles and themes.
- Parody: a copy of an original, often in a satirical fashion.
- Irony: the quality of a postmodern item in not being based upon any moral code or other foundation that is separate from the item itself.
- Allegory: the idea that any item can have covert or secret meanings other than the obvious meaning.
- Lists: consumers' lists of paraphernalia or things from which a choice can be made.
- Schlock: nonsensical or frivolous things we give to others.
- Kitsch: 'bad taste' with bragging; ignorant gloating over the possession of items of bad taste.
- Camp: the culture of a minority clique or group, usually based on a closet or private language and often a key source of identity for the individuals involved.
- Simulacrum: a term first used by Baudrillard (1983) to refer to the fact that media products are constantly reproduced to the point that they take on a meaning mainly by reference to earlier versions of similar media products; hence, they have a pace and reason of their own. It is not possible to distinguish between the 'real' and the 'representation'; we live in a world of 'hyperreality', where media representations give an experience of the world which has a feel of being more real than real.
- Realism: the opposite of the postmodern way.

In essence, postmodernism is a way of looking at the world that assumes the following two factors:

1 *Epistemological uncertainty*. An epistemology is a theory of knowledge; it attempts to answer the question, 'How do we know what we know?' Within the postmodern condition, there is an argument that all knowledge, including what we, as individuals know, is undependable and ambiguous.
2 *Ontological plurality*. An ontology is a theory of what reality consists of; the argument here is that within the postmodern condition there are a number of different conceptions of reality that we experience, each having equal significance for the individuals involved.

These two points taken together suggest that in the postmodern condition there is no simple division between reality and unreality.

However, you may ask, 'Does postmodernism as a historical time period exist?' The simplest answer to this question is given in *Postmodernist Culture* (1997) by Steven Connor, who argues that postmodernism exists because people talk about it! Postmodernism is a construct. This means that it is a set of ideas and practices which people assemble in order to make sense of the world. Postmodernism is not a concrete object that exists in the world like a house or a school. Postmodernism exists in the way that the Renaissance is said to exist. Just as recognisably new styles of art, architecture and ideas spread from Italy in the fifteenth century throughout Europe, so, in the late twentieth century, there was a similar sea change, as new forms of art, new forms of architecture and new ideas, which people termed 'postmodern', spread across the world.

An alternative question may be, 'How do people experience postmodernism in their everyday lives?' In health care, there has been a questioning or rejection of many aspects of orthodox medicine. We no longer accept the views and opinions of the doctor without question. We also consider non-biological factors, such as dissatisfaction with lifestyle or body shape, to be significant in causing illness. We have seen the rise of alternative medical techniques and the emergence of what appear to be essentially postmodern health problems. Health problems such as AIDS are more prevalent because of specific lifestyle choices. Alternatively, postmodern health problems, such as CJD, are based upon human creations not found in nature. In addition, some contemporary health issues are directly related to self-dissatisfaction such as Koro syndrome and Capgras' syndrome. Capgras' syndrome, or Capgras' symptom as it is sometimes known, has been described as: 'the delusion that others, or the self, have been replaced by impostors. It typically follows the development of negative feelings towards the other person that the subject cannot accept and attributes, instead, to the impostor' (http://www.ncf.carleton.ca/~ah 787/Home Page.Capgras.html). If you wish to find out more about the Koro syndrome, see http://members.gnn.com/lono/psychosis/muyloco/koro htm.

This disbelief does not affect only medicine. In the postmodern world, people have also lost faith in science and scientific rationality. In the postmodern mentality, scientific rationality is just one perspective among many. It is the disappearance of our belief in the truth of science, politics and religion together with the corrosive impact of doubt that marks clearly the transition from a modern to a postmodern mentality: 'In practice, it means constant exposure to ambivalence: that is, to a situation with no decidable solution, with no foolproof choice, no unreflective knowledge of "how to go on"' (Bauman, 1991: 244–5).

The key word in this statement by Bauman is *ambivalence*. In the postmodern condition, irreconcilable desires characterise our psychological state. 'Ambivalence' is the name that Bauman gives to our postmodern psychological state, in which we are driven by an indecisiveness brought about not simply by being in two minds about issues, but by desires for things which are not compatible.

To the postmodernist, teachers do not now simply give out information and mark homework with ticks and crosses. Teachers are facilitators who assist students to construct their own knowledge. Individual subjects such as history reflect the experiences of different groups within the population, as in women's history, and the history of the black working class in Britain. In addition, postmodernism is essentially populist in nature; it breaks down the division between popular or commercial culture. The argument is that no cultural form is better or worse than any other; Shakespeare is no better or worse a contributor to culture than the Spice Girls.

Cinema has also gone through a number of changes. Films such as *Twister* contain little storyline or character but overemphasise special effects, style and spectacle. Moreover, even though the film *Twister* is about a naturally occurring event, the film seems to lack realism. Steven Spielberg's films also have a post-modern feel to them. They often rely upon previous knowledge of popular cultural forms such as Saturday morning television cartoons and adventure series, and have plots that involve the manipulation of time and space. We could make similar comments about food, television, literature, advertising, popular music or sexuality.

In the postmodern condition, we feel as if the social is dissolving. In other words, the universal bonds that bind people together into communities are no longer accepted without question. A new social formation emerges that is gener-ated by the random activities of individual people attempting to make sense of the world and their place within it.

What is the 'social'?

The 'social' is the bonds between people that come together into an integrated moral community. Our notion of the 'social' emerges with modernity. The 'social' is based upon a number of governmental interventions into the ordering of the population and incorporates all aspects of modern life, including the language of politics and morality. This is what Bauman (1989) refers to as a state-administered universal identity; in other words, individuals have themselves manipulated in order to erase any differences between them, according to a planned, managed and rational set of state actions. As you may recall from the previous chapter, the self is a person and in the modern world, for example, the state-administered education system might promote one language as the official language of society, which the self should speak. In a similar fashion, the health services define the 'normal body', and how to treat the abnormal body.

The notion of the 'social' suggests ideas of character, culture, race and nation. It is used to make distinctions between the personal and the public and to make distinctions between 'insiders' and 'outsiders'. Therefore, the 'social' has eco-nomic, biological, geographical and political boundaries that need to be policed. The notion of the 'social' makes governmental interventions into the area of the personal appear both natural and rational. At the same time, the power re-lations within modernity appear to be transparent, and the discipline within the power structures of modernity is given a high degree of legitimacy because the disciplinary practices, such as CCTV and prison, are viewed as normal by the population.

The state-administered universal identity within modernity is the starting point for Bauman's critiques of modernity.

Bauman's book *Postmodernity and Its Discontents* (1997) opens with a discussion of the notions of 'purity' and 'order' within modernity. Something is regarded as 'clean' if it is in the right place; the idea of 'dirt' reflects the breakdown of order in the world. A pair of shoes may be spotlessly clean on the shoe rack, but be regarded as dirty on the dining table. An omelette may be a thing of beauty on the plate but dirt if it falls on a pillow. In the modern world, order suggests purity and a thing in the wrong place suggests dirt. The argument also applies to human beings; if people are treated like dirt – they will be either assimilated, excluded or destroyed physically. This can take the form of assimilation; that is, change as a means of restoring order, as by imposing language or belief systems upon people, in an effort to make them 'normal'. It could also take the form of exclusion – expelling groups of people from society ('cleansing') or herding them into ghettos. Bauman (1989) talks at length about the creation of Jewish ghettos by the Nazis as a means of destroying people physically, and also discusses the creation of death camps by the Nazis.

For the benefit of beginners at sociology, Bauman, in his book *Thinking Sociologically* (1990) takes up these themes in Chapter 3, 'Strangers'. However, the fullest explanation of their significance is to be found in Bauman's work of 1989 *Modernity and the Holocaust*. This book states very clearly the dangers inherent within modernity. For Bauman, the Holocaust – the mass murder of Jews, homosexuals and others by the Nazis – was not some pre-modern accident of history. On the contrary, the Holocaust was a coming together, in a particular way, of factors that are not uncommon in all modern societies.

All postmodernists, including Bauman, perceive in the postmodern condition significant changes at the level of the self. What makes being a self such a complex activity in the postmodern condition is that the context of everyday life is open to a number of valid interpretations. This is a key factor in the ambivalence that postmodern people are said to feel. Within the postmodern condition, there is no agreed moral code to guide the self in the choice of right and good, and the absence of a moral code can generate feelings of insecurity. The self constantly has to cope with unforeseen consequences. This is a skill that the self must continually exercise. Therefore, in the postmodern condition, living has become a highly skilled activity, and our key human skill is to direct the course of the fragments which constitute human existence in an effort to feel comfortable and secure. Individuals as dynamic agents attempt to formulate all forms of solidarity including those of class, community, race and gender. This is because, for a number of postmodern writers, individual class, race and gender have lost all influence in terms of determining life events and life chances. In the postmodern condition, individuals have no independent identity other than that which they create for themselves. This is a world in which class, race and gender are immaterial. In the postmodern world you are what you appear.

This is particularly the case in the work of Deleuze and Guattari, who suggest that modernist thought takes the form of a hierarchy, in which some ways of thinking are seen to be superior to other ways of thinking. In contrast, Deleuze and Guattari draw upon the Nietzschean concept of 'the will to power'; people who have their ways of thinking accepted as superior are simply making use of their ability to dominate others. Deleuze and Guattari criticise those discourses and institutions that repress desire and proliferate what they call fascist subjectivities. The discourses and institutions of modernity impose a definition of normality from the perspective of the powerful. In contrast, Deleuze and Guattari suggest that ways of thinking should take the form of a rhizome. These are ways of thinking which are not horizontal and spread like a strawberry plant, sending out both roots and shoots upon runners. In addition, Deleuze and Guattari attempt to decode libidinal flows caused by the institutions within capitalism. They do this by attempting a 'schizoanalytic' destruction of the ego and the superego and putting forward the notion of a dynamic unconscious. They refer to this as a process of becoming. This 'becoming' leads to the emergence of two new types of decentred subjects, the 'schizoid' and the 'nomad', who are free from fixed and unified identities, modernist/Freudian subjectivities and their bodies. However, the only people who lead lives in this fashion are nomads and schizoids.

The postmodern condition is a world without certainty. However, we all need both meaning and predictability in our lives and relationships. As Peter Marris (1996) makes clear, 'Meanings are intentional structures which perceive, create and reiterate relationships for a purpose' (1996: 33). Marris argues that meaning has the following forms, all of which are associated with the creation of certainty in everyday life:

○ *Personal meanings*. These arise from attachment and allow us to make sense of the world around us; they underlie both our search for relationships and our personality.
○ *Mutual meanings*. These are concerned with the mutual expectations within a relationship and the expectations of what we should feel.
○ *Public meanings*. These are built upon an abstract structure of interpretations such as those of the law, and are independent of specific relationships.
○ *Metameanings*. These are concerned with appropriate modes of understanding for given circumstances and the ability to relate different forms of meaning to each other.

Meanings generate a basis or foundation for predictability in our social relationships; however, in the postmodern condition there is no legitimate order to provide such a foundation.

But when did postmodernity begin? It is very difficult for social scientists to explain when the transition from feudalism to capitalism occurred, and similarly it is difficult to mark the transition from modernity to postmodernity. However, it is clear that the term 'post-war' is becoming increasingly meaningless, as the late 1940s are not the same as the early 2000s.

> Our Time is the epithet David Wells attaches to modernity and its postmodern succes-sor. Princeton philosopher Diogenes Allen declared, 'A massive intellectual revolution is taking place that is perhaps as great as that which marked off the modern world from the Middle Ages.' It is a shift that shapes every intellectual discipline as well as the prac-tice of law, medicine, politics, and religion in our culture. ...
>
> Theologian Thomas Oden argues that 'modernity' began with the storming of the Bastille on July 14, 1789 and ended with the fall of the Berlin Wall in 1989, while art philosopher Charles Jencks decided to be even more specific: It ended at 3:32 p.m. on July 15, 1972, 'when the Pruitt-Ingoe housing development in St. Louis (a prize-winning version of Le Corbusier's "machine for modern living") was dynamited as an uninhabit-able environment for the low-income people it housed.' Obviously a lot of people have their own opinions about when the shoe dropped, but most agree that it was fairly recently.

(Michael Horton 'The Tower of Babel: modernity built the tower – now post-modernity must face the challenge of condemning the "unsafe structure."' In the September/October 1995 issue of *Modern Reformation*, a periodical available from CURE, 2221 East Winston Road Suite K, Anaheim, CA 92806)

As indicated earlier, in the postmodern condition identity has changed. For the postmodernist there is no self. As Michel Foucault made clear, before the end of the eighteenth century the self as we know it did not exist, and with the coming of the end of modernity, the self will be 'erased, like a face drawn in sand at the edge of the sea' (quoted in Ashley, 1997: 20). Many postmodern writers have recoiled from this startling conclusion of the death of the self. However, there have been very definite shifts in their conceptions of both self and identity.

Traditionally, identity, had the following two key elements:

o People sharing many group characteristics
o Common categorising of outward phenomena, such as ethnicity or the clothes people wear

According to Bauman (1996), identity in the postmodern world is becoming reconstructed, or rebuilt and redefined, beyond these two key elements. Bauman agrees with Foucault that identity was a modern innovation. In the modern world, the problem of identity was a problem of how to construct and maintain our iden-tity in an effort to secure one's place in the world and avoid losing the sense of meaning. This was because in the modern world the avoidance of uncertainty was seen as an individual problem, although support was always available from various professionals such as teachers and counsellors. The creation of modern identity was seen as a pilgrimage. Modern people viewed the city as a desert. The city was a place in which a person's name and identity were not fixed or given. The modern city was a place of nothingness through which people must find their way. Therefore, modern people would construct an identity not out of choice but out of necessity. Without their pilgrimage to a secure identity, they might become lost in the desert. In the first instance, on their journey to a fixed identity they needed a place to walk to. This was their life project, which ideally should have been established early in life and used to make sense of the various uncertainties, fragments and divisions of experience which make up the post-traditional world. In other words, by creating a fixed and secure identity, they attempted to make the world more ordered and more predictable for themselves.

In contrast, in the postmodern world, the problem of identity is one of avoiding a fixed identity and keeping our options open, avoiding long-term commitments, consistency and devotion. In place of a life project established as early as possible, which we loyally keep to, postmodern people choose to have a series of short projects that are not fixed. The world has a feel to it of being in a continuous present. The world is no longer agreeable to pilgrims. In place of the pilgrim, there are a number of other lifestyles that emerge: the stroller, the vagabond, the tourist and the player. These lifestyles are not new to the postmodern world, but whereas in previous times marginal people in marginal situations practised these life-styles, they are now common to the majority of people in many situations.

According to Bauman (1996), the pilgrim has been replaced by four successors, illustrating postmodern life strategies. The first is the stroller, or *flâneur*. According to Bauman, this became 'the central symbolic figure of the modern city' (1996: 26). This figure looks at the surface meaning of things in the metropolitan environment, where all meaning is found in appearance; there is no deeper meaning underneath the surface of anything. The shopping mall is the place where we are most likely to see the *flâneur* in the postmodern world. This is because the shopping mall is the place where we are most likely to see a rich collage of surface meanings, in a range of shops and architectural features.

The second successor is the vagabond. This identity type is continually 'the stranger'; like the pilgrim, this person is perpetually on the move, but the movement has no preceding itinerary. In the modern and pre-modern world, the vagabond was unable to settle down in any one place because the vagabond was always unsettled: 'The settled were many, the vagabonds few. Postmodernity reversed the ratio. ... Now the vagabond is a vagabond not because of the reluctance or difficulty of settling down, but because of the scarcity of settled places' (Bauman, 1996: 29). The world is becoming increasingly uncertain and unsettled. Vagabonds are often on the move, but usually because they are not welcome; for example, 'boat people' or 'New Age travellers'.

The third successor is the tourist. The tourist moves purposefully, from home to a place in search of a new experience; this was once a marginal activity rather than a marginal person. We are losing the need for a home in the postmodern world, but we have a greater taste for new experience. Home may offer security, but it also has the numbing boredom of a prison. An example of such a person would be an executive in a multinational company.

Finally, the fourth successor is the player. For the player life is a game; nothing is serious, nothing is controllable and nothing is predictable. Life is a series of 'moves' in a game that can be skilled, perceptive and deceptive. The point of the game is to 'stay ahead' and to embrace the game itself.

Life, then, is developing a rather shallow feel to it; it is fragmented and discontinuous in nature. Life has no great purpose or meaning in the postmodern condition. Life is made up of a series of 'mini-projects' that can be changed or rejected at any moment. By contrast, in the modern world, people were expected to choose a vocation or life project early in life and stay with it for the rest of their lives.

Wagner (1994) also outlines the notion of self in the postmodern condition. He argues that modernity gave individuals scope to construct their own identities; in the postmodern condition, there has been a superabundance of material products, cultural orientations and consumer practices, leading to a momentous increase in the range of identity constructions available. People can change any aspect of physical appearance, including such radical changes as 'gender migration'. People can adopt a range of therapies and change their attitudes and perceptions of the world, just as they can change their taste in music or politics. In addition, the 'enterprise culture' has led directly to the 'enterprise self' – and a significant increase in individual autonomy: 'Rather than resting on a secured place in a stable social order, individuals are asked to engage themselves actively in shaping their lives and social positions in a constantly moving social context. Such a shift must increase uncertainties and even anxieties' (Wagner, 1994: 165).

Modernism was a form of social organisation that attempted to refashion and control the irrational forces of nature in the interests of satisfying human need or human desire. The relationships between people in the modern world were almost always rational and logical in nature, with legal codes put together on the basis of 'due process' of law and policed by rational organisations using bureaucratic methods. Within modernity, life had a secure and logical feel to it. In contrast, postmodernity is the form of society we are left with when the process of modernisation is complete and human behaviour has little or no direct dealing with nature; we now live in a fashioned or manufactured environment. In the postmodern condition, the world has an abandoned, relative and unprotected feel about it for the individual human agent. Even sex and food, which for thousands of years were the pleasurable building blocks of life, are now among the numerous sources of danger. Lacking the protection of class and communal togetherness, lacking any given racial and gender identities, individuals are left to experience feelings of isolation and detachment, having to create their own bonds of solidarity, selfhood and rectitude. This is the postmodern predicament; for individuals, *anything goes*: morally, spiritually, communally. For many of us, life is in fragments and we experience everyday life as an open space of moral, political and personal dilemmas.

What is the nature of self and self-identity in the postmodern condition? Above all, what are the life strategies that individuals employ to make their passage in the world? How do individual selves navigate a life in fragments?

What makes being a self such a complex activity in the postmodern condition is that the context is open to a number of valid interpretations. In the absence of an agreed moral code to guide the self, the choice of what constitutes 'right' and 'good' can generate feelings of insecurity. This makes the construction of an imaginary world for the self a much more difficult activity, and having to cope with unforeseen consequences is a skill that the self must continually exercise. Further-more, living is now a highly skilled activity, and our key human skill is to direct the course of the fragments that constitute human existence in an effort to feel com-fortable and secure. Individuals as dynamic agents attempt to secure or form-ulate all forms of solidarity including those of class, community, race and gender. In an effort to create forms of solidarity that they feel comfortable with, people join New Social Movements (NSMs), which we discuss in area 6. These NSMs have a key role to play in both the creation of a person's identity and the emergence of 'identity politics'. This is because, for individuals, class, race and gender have lost all influence in terms of determining life events and life chances. In the post-modern condition, individuals have no independent identity, other than that which they create for themselves; this is a world in which class and race and gender are immaterial. In the postmodern world you are what you appear.

The suggestion here is that even subjective experience has changed within the postmodern condition. The personality of people has changed within the postmodernity, from an identity imposed upon people within modernity, by the education system, family and organised religion, to a situation of almost total and complete choice within the postmodern condition.

What is a postmodern politics?

Postmodern ideas have had a significant impact upon the practice of politics; they have affected political theories about the influence of social class upon politi-cal ideologies and voting intentions, including the ways in which political parties now market themselves. Postmodern ideas have had an effect upon institutions, with the decline of Old Social Movements such as the trade union movement and the rise of NSMs, such as that of the 'eco-warriors'. In addition, postmodern ideas have had an effect upon the significance of, even the continued existence of 'the modern nation-state'. All of these themes are taken up in the following areas.

We are living in an era of significant social change, which many people have described as postmodern in nature. This means that politics has lost its certainty. Anything can happen, and we do not have the skills, the knowledge or the experience to deal with or to understand the changes taking place in the world. We have seen the collapse of the Soviet Union, the rise of nationalism and ethnic cleansing in Europe (what we called in Area 2 the process of Balkanisation), the declining significance of the nation-state in the face of processes of globalisation, and the idea that the world is becoming a single place: culturally, politically and economically. We have also seen politics become more tribal in nature, as people carry out acts of great cruelty against neighbours. Postmodern politics may be *neomedieval* in nature. What do we mean by neomedieval? We are observing a return to the politics of the Middle Ages. Politics appears to be developing a number of characteristics that are similar to the characteristics of the political system within medieval Europe:

- No strong, centralised nation-state
- No strong participatory democracy – in other words, individual people not actively involved in political processes; in the postmodern world, involvement in politics for many people a 'televisual experience'
- Violent challenge to the power of the central authority (the king in medieval times) from various sources; for example, the collapse of communist regimes in Eastern Europe
- Conflict between very different belief systems: church ideology in conflict with secular ideology
- Tension between the major institutions of the day: king against church
- Individuals unclear about their identity
- A politics without established rules
- Frequent resort to violence to resolve issues

As Bauman asks, 'Are we not back in the medieval world of beggars, plagues, conflagrations and superstitions' (Bauman, 1997: 22).

This is a very difficult point to grasp. On the one hand, postmodernist writers suggest that we are on the verge of a new era which is beyond modernity. Yet, at the same time, these writers often suggest we are experiencing a return to the Middle Ages. One writer who has attempted to explain this is some detail is Jean Baudrillard (1994). He argues that history is made up of a revival of earlier or even repressed values, as is particularly true of the situation in Eastern Europe since the collapse of the Soviet Union. The purpose of such a revival is to recreate a pure or positive history. However, the values do not reappear in their original form. This recycling of values recreates old conflicts and effectively means that history is going backwards. As Baudrillard explains, 'At some point in the 1980s, history took a turn in the opposite direction. ... In this perspective, the future no longer exists. But there is no longer a future, there is no longer an end either. *So this is not even the end of history*. We are faced with a paradoxical process of reversal, a reversive effect of modernity which, having reached its speculative limit and extrapolated all its virtual developments, is disintegrating into its simple elements in a catastrophic process of recurrence and turbulence' (Baudrillard 1994: 10–11). This recycling of past forms is referred to by Baudrillard as 'rehabilitation by *bricolage*' (1994: 35) and 'eclectic sentimentality' (35).

In this area we have attempted to sketch the broad cultural and social contexts within which these changes have unfolded. We have been doing this by looking at two central themes: politics and the decline of social class, and politics and the decline of 'meta-narrative' – big ideas and ideologies which not only guide people but also give meaning to their lives. Finally, in area 7, we will look at politics and globalisation, a theme which is also significant in a postmodern politics.

According to Anthony Giddens (1995), Zygmunt Bauman is *the* theorist of postmodernity. From Bauman's point of view, postmodernity does not start when modernity comes to an end, but is a condition which brings about the deconstruction of modernity by outlining its essential fragility. The notion of deconstruction is a key concept for postmodern thinkers; it involves closely looking at any text – for postmodern purposes, anything can be a text, a television programme, a book, food, a political ideology or a political regime – and breaking it down into its component parts to see what assumptions the text is built upon. As Bauman explains,

> Postmodernity is modernity coming of age: modernity looking at itself at a distance rather than from inside, making a full inventory of its gains and losses, psychoanalysing itself, discovering the intentions it never before spelled out, finding them mutually cancelling and incongruous. Postmodernity is modernity coming to terms with its own impossibility; a self-monitoring modernity is one that consciously discards what it was once unconsciously doing. (Bauman, 1991: 272)

In other words, postmodernity is reflexive; individuals and institutions are engaged in a constant process of looking at themselves, attempting to understand and change themselves.

For Bauman, modernity is a 'movement with a direction' (1992: 188), a direction driven by 'universalisation', 'systemisation' and 'rationalisation'. By universalisation, Bauman means the process by which people are manipulated so as to become the same in important respects; an example of this is the media manipulation of desire. By systemisation, social life exists within systems in which people are powerless to make changes. Finally, we have rationalisation, the process by which, according to Bauman, life is becoming more rational, calculable and predictable.

In other words, modernity is a way of organising society that is geared towards resolving the Hobbesian problem of order, which suggests that our life will be nasty, brutish and short if we do not have order imposed upon us by the state. The state 'works on' people in an effort to bring about a homogenisation of individuals – as a result, individuals are expected to share similar values, attitudes and beliefs. You may have come across the term 'homogenised' on cartons of milk! This means that the milk has been forced at pressure through a needle, a process which prevents the milk and cream from separating, and hence the milk has the same qualities throughout. In a similar fashion, Bauman suggests that people share fashions and passions in accepted ways. As Bauman explains, modernity is a form of society which has 'disqualified any "uncertified" agency; unpatterned and unregulated spontaneity of the autonomous agent was pre-defined as a destabilising, and indeed, anti-social factor marked for taming and extinction in the continuous struggle for societal survival' (Bauman, 1992: 190).

In other words, any human agent (individual person) who behaves in an unpre-dictable or unacceptable way will have to be changed in order to fit in.

Within the modern society, the education system, social policy and regulation of the mass media involve the state in a remaking and remodelling of its citizens, in an effort to make all people similar. Underpinning this institutional remaking and remodelling of the individual is a firm belief that progress can only be sus-tained when the state ignores the judgement of individuals, and acts in their own true interests, of which they are unaware.

From Bauman's perspective, modernity, in terms of structure, is a social totality similar in important respects to the modern social system described by the func-tionalist Talcott Parsons (1951). The Parsonian social system is a self-regulating and self-balancing system with its own shared values, attitudes, beliefs and mechanisms of self-reproduction. All human agents and institutions have a role and function to perform under the clear direction of a single authority; as we saw in Area 2 in Bauman's discussion of the Holocaust, modern authority often set targets that could not be reached, and that were often undesirable. Such pro-gress, in the eyes of the central authority was essential to maintain solidarity. The individual human agents within this form of modernity are cultural dopes charac-terised by 'universality' (behaving in ways that are common and approved of within the society) and 'homogeneity' (people are the same in terms of taste, style/fashion and ideas), and pushed about by forces outside their control.

In contrast, for Bauman, postmodernity is 'modernity conscious of its true nature' (1992: 187), by which he means that there is a great deal of difference between people in the postmodern world, and that individuals are not pushed by forces outside their control. An example you might want to consider is gay cabi-net ministers who 'come out' and continue in office. Postmodernity is, then, a form of modernity that is self-critical, and self-denigrating; in other words, it is highly critical of itself, and self-dismantling, by which it is suggested that there are tendencies within modernity that lead to its own deconstruction. An example of such a tendency towards deconstruction within modernity is hyperrationalisation. As we saw in the discussion of Weber in Area 2, modernity is bureaucratic in nature, but bureaucratic systems are often so time-consuming that they lead to inefficiency, the very thing that they were intended to avoid.

The most visible characteristics of this 'modernity for itself' are 'institution-alised pluralism, variety, contingency and ambivalence' (Bauman, 1992: 187).

Bauman is particularly concerned with the issue of 'ambivalence', by which he means that individual people hold both positive and negative feelings and ideas about people and things at the same time. Bauman has devoted a book to this condition of ambivalence. Ambivalence is characterised by action that takes place within a situation where individual human agents have to choose between many rival and contradictory meanings, as on an issue such as global warming; is it taking place or not? This is a situation where action is not determined by factors outside human control. In other words, people are responsible for their own actions, rather than being pushed about by forces outside their control. In postmodern politics, this ambivalence becomes the main dimension of inequality, as access to knowledge is the key to freedom and enhanced social standing. Postmodernity has its own distinctive features that are self-contained and self-reproducing, constructed within a cognitive space that is very different from that of modernity.

Jean-François Lyotard: the postmodern condition

In his book *The Postmodern Condition* (1984), Lyotard was highly critical of what he called the 'grand narratives', or meta-narratives, the myths, or popular stories, within the modern world which provide legitimacy to both institutions and activities. What are the role and purpose of the narrative for Lyotard? The narrative has the following three purposes:

- It bestows legitimacy upon institutions, a purpose which Lyotard refers to as the function of myth (1984: 20)
- It represents positive or negative models, a function which Lyotard refers to as creation of the successful or unsuccessful hero (1984: 20)
- It integrates individuals into established institutions, the process which Lyotard refers to as the creation of legends and tales (1984: 20)

As Lyotard makes clear, 'What is transmitted through these narratives is the set of pragmatic rules that constitutes the social bond' (1984: 21).

The narrative defines a community's relationship to itself and its environment. Moreover, the narration 'betokens a theoretical identity between each of the narrative's occurrences' (Lyotard, 1984: 22). I believe this means that the narrative contains within itself the pragmatic rules of when and why it should appear or the telling of the narrative should occur. Each time the narrative is drawn upon, something is suggested about the appropriateness of the narrative's use, role and purpose in holding together the social bond. Narrative has to be put into 'play' (1984: 23) within institutions by people. In this way, the narrative defines what is right and what is appropriate within a culture. At the same time, the narrator has a need for collective approval; the narrator must be seen to be competent.

In other words, narratives permit a society in which they are told to fix the limits of its basis for competence and to determine according to those limits what actions are carried out or what actions can be carried out. However, in an effort to distance himself from modernist ways of thinking, Lyotard outlines what he calls a non-universalised pragmatics for the transmission of narratives. He is keen to point out that this does not mean a set of pre-existing categories. Instead the pragmatics of the narrative is 'intrinsic to them' (1984: 20); for example, a narrative may follow a fixed formula. In addition, the narrator has no other claim to capability to tell the story than having heard it before. For Lyotard, then, postmodernity is about mourning the destruction of meaning because 'knowledge is no longer principally narrative' (1984: 26).

Socialism, communism and feminism can all be regarded as grand narratives. In other words, grand narratives outline the criteria of what to do, in what situation and for what reason. Socialism, communism and feminism attempt in their own ways to tell people what to think and how to think it. In other words, we can describe the grand narratives as universal, because they attempt to make statements about the nature of the whole of the social world and our place within it. Moreover, within the modern world, these narratives need no proof or justification because they are regarded by their supporters as true, and to argue against them is often regarded as 'politically incorrect'. In the postmodern condition, these grand narratives are dissolved; they become deconstructed.

Politics and the decline of social class

As suggested above, bonds of social class decline in significance within the postmodern condition. In other words, social class relations do not determine how people organise their lives. Most sociological theories of social class assume that there is some form of common values, or sharing of ideas and ways of living, within a social class. Marxists, for example, assume that working-class people are victims of false consciousness; that is, they have ideas placed in their heads by the ruling class. This set of ideas, which we term ideology, does not support the economic interests of working-class people. The notion that people have their ideas determined is undermined by the postmodern condition, in which individuals have to create their own thoughts and their own bonds of community.

Class theory has always been central to sociology. Many sociologists considered class to have an 'objective' economic existence. Class had an existence independent of the individual people within the class structure; hence class was something which could not be 'wished away'. Class was said to shape opportunities and life chances such as access to well-paid jobs or educational success. At the same time, 'class' provided sociologists with clear indicators of people's attitudes; awareness; collective consciousness or a shared culture; voting intentions; child-rearing practices; and much more. Postmodernists, in contrast especially to Marxists, believe that class is dead and that we live in post-class society.

In the twentieth century, ownership of the means of production, such as factories, became split from the control of the means of production. In other words, those who do the hiring and firing of employees are almost certainly going to be employees themselves, rather than the owners of the enterprises. We have seen the emergence of a 'new' middle class or 'service' class made up of 'professionals', often social and cultural specialists, people who provide services or work with ideas and images rather than making products. These 'new' middle-class or 'service' class 'professionals' may be culturally, but not necessarily financially, privileged. In addition to the emergence of the 'new' middle class, the working class 'fragments'. Some members of the working class have their skills upgraded, while others become part of a growing underclass, defined not in economic but in moral terms. These issues have been taken up by Bauman in his *Work, Consumerism and the New Poor* (1998).

As we shall see in more detail later in this area, since the mid-1990s, Bauman has been developing a theory of postmodern ethics which is in harmony with the way in which people lead their lives in the contemporary world. What Bauman does in this book is to apply his moral theory to the way that we view the 'underclass' in the present political climate. He questions the common assumption of the moral defectiveness and criminal intent of the poor, who are now viewed as the outright enemies of society. The poor take and give back nothing except trouble. People on welfare are seen as 'the natural catchment area for criminal gangs, and keeping people on welfare means enlarging the pool from which the criminals are recruited' (Bauman, 1998: 77). Bauman traces the history of the work ethic from the early years of the Industrial Revolution. Enterprising people were needed to create opportunities for themselves and others by providing the newly emerging working class with a meaning for their lives as factory employees, a sense of purpose in work. Throughout the post-war reconstruction, the poor were seen as a 'reserve pool of labour' that needed to be given skills and abilities through state-financed education and training, and adequate health and social security systems to keep the potential workforce fit, able and ready to work. However, as we approach the end of the century, the 'reserve pool of labour' is no longer needed. Companies have found ways of generating profits from low-cost products that do not require large numbers of workers to produce them. Hence, we have a growing section of the population that is classed as 'poor'. Nevertheless, the work ethic is still with us but is now used to class the poor as people who 'simply lack the competence to appreciate the advantages of working; they make wrong choices, putting "no work" above work' (Bauman, 1998: 71). In other words, the work ethic is used by us to define the poor as people who lack intelligence, will and effort.

What is Bauman's theory of morality? In a nutshell, we as individuals should be both with the other and for the other. And in the case of this most recent book, it is the poor who are cast as the other. The difference between *being with* and *being for* the other is about the level of commitment that we have for the other, about having an emotional engagement with the other. This involves regarding the other not as a type or a category but as a unique person. This involves the following points:

- Rejecting indifference towards the poor
- Rejecting stereotyped certainty about the poor, the view that 'they always behave that way'
- Viewing the poor in a manner that is free from sentiment

This moral stance means that we should assume some responsibility for the poor and to act on the assumption that the well-being of poor people is a precious thing calling for our effort both to preserve and enhance it.

What is Bauman's solution to the interesting question that he has posed? He argues that we should see the work ethic for what it is, as something that generates a 'moral economy' filled with 'concentrated and unchallenged discrimination'. In its place, we should have an 'ethics of workmanship' which recognises the value of unpaid work, which currently is classed as non-work. In addition, we should consider 'decoupling income entitlement from income-earning capacity' (Bauman, 1998: 97). This is an interesting choice of words, but it cannot hide the stale, old message, let's bring back socialism. What Bauman is saying is the same as Marx in the last century, 'from each according to his abilities, to each according to his needs.' Socialism has been rejected fully and comprehensively by almost everybody, and this approach highlights a flaw in both Bauman's analysis and socialism. When we take responsibility for the other, we run the risk of imposing our will on the other, and this can lead to cruelty. Bauman fails to take into account the ability of people to take responsibility for their own lives and their own actions. Forces outside their control do not push people about; some lone parents spend a lifetime on welfare, and others make successful lives for themselves. The contemporary world is a world of choice and we are all choosers.

According to Malcolm Waters (1997), the social stratification system is moving from a *class-based economic system* to a *culturalist or status-conventional phase*. He views this as part of a wider social transformation – the movement from modernity to postmodernity. This transformation is linked to several key ideas which are fully investigated in this textbook: detraditionalisation and reflexive modernisation (Area 6), postmodernisation (Area 3) and globalisation (Area 7).

The status-conventional form of stratification is built upon four concepts, which Waters identifies as follows. The first is culturalism, which is concerned with lifestyle choices such as whether or not to live in the country, aesthetic preferences such as the type of house or decor you choose and value commitments. Some lifestyle choices, aesthetic preferences and value commitments, such as having political values built upon either individualism or collectivism, are clearly thought to be better than others, and choice affects your position in any stratification system, because class is no longer solely economic in nature.

The second concept is fragmentation, in which fixed classes and statuses of the modern world give way to shifting and unstable associations and choices. Friendship groups, groups who choose to associate together because they enjoy common styles of music and/or dress, are all significant in people's lives, and the choices that individuals make within their lives give them a status within fragmented section of the population. As Waters explains, 'fragmentation ensures that individuals apprehend the stratification system as a status bazaar' (1997: 36).

The third concept is autonomisation, according to which within modernity subjective beliefs, preferences and ideas, such as which party to support and why, are clear, stable and predictable; in other words, automatic. In the postmodern condition, such automatic ways of thinking are disappearing; life is a consistent process of choosing. The concept of autonomisation suggests that the ordered nature of such preferences has gone; the logical nature for our preferences is always unstable. What we value at one moment we reject the next.

The fourth and last concept is resignification, that is, the constant change of subject interest, choice and emotion that constantly regenerates people's feelings and fears of distress, abuse and desire. We constantly have a fear that we have made the wrong choice, and what we believe to be 'cool' and status enhancing among our chosen groups will make us a laughing stock and damage our standing in the 'status bazaar'.

What is significant about these changes which Waters outlines is that 'occupation' is now only significant as a 'badge' of status that says something about a person's ability to make use of the nice things in the world. Occupation is no more important than our 'consumption status', our ability to demonstrate to others that we can fully appreciate nice things.

In the areas on 'New Social Movements' (Area 6) and 'Voting Behaviour' (Area 9) we shall look more closely at the effect of postmodern changes on political institutions.

Postmodernity and Marxism

The postmodern condition casts doubt upon all grand narratives, and, as such, all the key assumptions of Marxism are brought into question. In particular, we have seen that postmodernists reject class analysis, suggesting that the economic ruling class that Marxists outline has been replaced by a 'service class' that exploits its own knowledge/cultural resources. People who work in the new service class exploit their own skills, notions of good taste and abilities rather than employees in an effort to generate a profit.

Postmodernists reject the following key assumptions of Marxism:

- Class is the most important element in the construction of an individual's identity, political affiliation and relationships
- Economic factors are the most important variables in any explanation of social life
- Non-economic variables, such as race or gender, are of limited significance in any explanation of social life
- Political ideas are determined by economic factors
- The working class has impersonal economic interests such as class interests
- The working class has an exclusive historical role in bringing about revolutionary social change
- Socialism is the only genuine form of political action to liberate people from exploitation
- Marxism provides the only valid explanatory framework for understanding societies

Communism pushed the project of modernity to its very limits. It involved grand social engineering projects that attempted to control nature in the perceived interests of the working class. However, for Bauman (1992), individuals within communist societies wanted to share in the 'lavish consumption enjoyed under capitalist auspices': 'It was the postmodern, narcissistic culture of self-enhancement, self-enjoyment, instant gratification and life defined in terms of consumer styles that finally exposed the obsoleteness of the "steel per head" philosophy stubbornly preached and practised under communism' (Bauman, 1992: 179). In other words, communism collapsed because individuals behind the Iron Curtain wanted to participate in the processes of making unhindered and highly personal lifestyle choices that people in the West enjoyed. Consumer culture brings with it pleasure. State socialism in the former Soviet Union may have pushed modern rationality to its very limits, in an effort to control nature for the benefit of people. However, Soviet communists could never understand the pleasure of shopping!

The significance of this demise of socialism is that class-based political parties and conflict about the distribution of wealth and income do not play a significant role within postmodern politics. Because postmodern societies have solved their basic economic problems, they are post-scarcity societies where everyone's basic needs are catered for. In place of class politics, we have single-issue politics, which is often very emotional and very personal. A good example from the 1997 general election was the campaign of the late Sir James Goldsmith and his Referendum Party.

Sir James Goldsmith

What was Goldsmith up to? Before we can answer this question, we need to look closer at some of the theories of postmodernity. As we stated above, the key theorist in this area in the eyes of many commentators is Jean-François Lyotard (1984). For Lyotard, the postmodern condition is that in which individuals have lost faith in universal belief systems, or, as Lyotard calls them, 'grand narratives', which once provided assurance, or a secure feel for the world and the way that it works. Examples of such belief systems are religious ideas, moral codes and any other widely accepted ideas that constrain people's ideas and behaviour. In the postmodern world, social bonds exist as flexible networks of 'language games' in which individuals create their own rules.

The idea of language games in Lyotard's analysis is what sociologists would call the social. There are a number of different ways of defining the social or social relationships. The idea of the language game is concerned with the manner of grouping different types of descriptions of how society or social relationships are organised in terms of the rules of everyday life, as devised and legitimised by the participants in that social relationship. The rules specify the properties of the social relationships that the people who made up the rules choose to live by and the uses to which the rules are put. In other words, the language game is a set of principles, devised by the participants as a group, on how to organise their every-day lives:

> The social bond is linguistic, but is not woven with a single thread. It is a fabric formed by the intersection of at least two (and in reality an indeterminate number) of language games, obeying different rules. ... We may form a pessimistic impression of this splintering: nobody speaks all of these languages, they have no universal meta-language, and the project of the system-subject is a failure. ... That is what the post-modern world is all about. Most people have lost the nostalgia for the lost narrative. (Lyotard, 1986: 40–1)

The postmodern world encourages 'little narratives', or local social bonds, rather than 'grand narratives'. In terms of a postmodern politics, this means that macropolitics has been replaced by micropolitics. In other words, politics is dominated by a large number of single-issue movements, such as the peace movement or OutRage.

Sir James Goldsmith's actions can be viewed as both rational and irrational, democratic and autocratic or despotic, philanthropic or altruistic and selfish. The absence of any one true interpretation of Goldsmith's actions gives them a post-modern feel. A postmodern politics is one of single-issue movements in which traditional party politics has been replaced by the politics of imagined communities; in which communities are held together by similarities that individuals feel or believe that they have in common. For the Euro-sceptics, there is a fear that the Britishness of our community is under threat. Goldsmith's actions are about the politics of identity, which will always have an irrational and highly emotive feel. If individuals feel that their identity is under threat, part of the certainty of everyday life is lost. When Goldsmith threatens to place candidates in marginal con-stituencies, he is saying to the government, if you attempt to take away my cer-tainty, I will attempt to take away yours. Goldsmith appeared to be involved, together with the government, in what Lyotard would refer to as a language game.

However, unlike the structure of the social system within a modern analysis, the rules of the language game are constantly under revision and in dispute. Every utterance is seen as a move in the language game, making the activity like a joust. This involves clear minds and cold wills. Resolution is possible only via some form of 'dialogic democracy' in which participants must re-establish trust with others in the language game. All political issues are to be resolved via the joust within the language game. How can the government establish trust in the face of unreason? The rules of the game implied by this question have to be negotiated and established by the participants in the game itself, and, in many respects, such rule creation is the key skill. For example, in the 1997 election campaign the Conservative government attempted to undermine Goldsmith's position by attempting to establish a 'rule' that you cannot hold views about the relationship between Britain and the European Union if, like Goldsmith, you are based outside Britain.

What are the implications for democracy? The ability or inability of the government to inspire trust is what Goldsmith brought to the surface in British politics. This is beyond simple partisan dealignment, whereby people switch their allegiance from one political party to another. This issue raises serious ques-tions about the party structure, our expectations of what a government can do and the state's ability to generate legitimacy, as we know it.

As Mike Featherstone suggests, postmodernism is a situation that emerges with consumer culture. In this form of society, politically, socially and morally 'any-thing goes', and this situation

> has to be understood against the background of a long-term process involving the growth of a consumer culture and expansion in the number of specialists and inter-mediaries engaged in the production and circulation of symbolic goals. It draws on ten-dencies in consumer culture which favour the aestheticization of life, the assumption that the aesthetic life is the ethically good life and that there is no human nature or true self, with the goal of life an endless pursuit of new experiences, values and vocabular-ies. (Featherstone, 1991: 126)

This process adds to the feeling that the 'social' is dissolving.

This situation has developed within the consumer culture of contemporary cities. Moreover, because of the influence of the city, wherever we live our lives become 'urban'. Within this condition there is an aesthetisation of life; by this, we understand that things which look beautiful are believed to be morally good. Individuals are unable to evaluate the moral worth of something from the way it looks. In addition, there is an undermining of the difference between high culture, such as opera, ballet and fine art, and mass culture, such as popular music, television and film. As we said above, in the postmodern condition, no cultural forms are better or worse than any others; for example, classical music is no better or worse as a contribution to culture than popular music.

In the postmodern analysis, the focus is upon the self-constituting human agent, who operates within a habitat. In other words, this analysis concerns individuals creating and recreating what they like about themselves. The concept of habitat is explained by Bauman (1992) as a 'complex system', a term derived from mathematics, which suggests, firstly, that the system is unpredictable; secondly, that it is not controlled by forces outside the control of the human agents that live with it. There are no goal-setting, managing or coordinating institutions within the complex system; this makes constraint by the state over people's lives fall to an absolute minimum. Therefore, the human agents cannot be discussed by reference to their functionality or dysfunctionality for the social system. Moreover, Bauman assumes that no one agency can determine the activity of any other agent, although he explains that 'the postmodern eye (that is, the modern eye liberated from modern fears and inhibitions) views difference with zest and glee: difference is beautiful and no less good for that' (Bauman, 1991: 255). However, for Bauman, postmodernism is not a situation in which 'anything goes'. In his books on postmodern ethics, Bauman attempts to outline a postmodern ethics that has its origin within the human agent: 'Contrary to both the popular opinion and hot-headed "everything goes" triumphalism of certain postmodernist writers, the postmodern perspective on moral phenomena does not reveal the relativism of morality' (Bauman, 1993: 14).

In a similar fashion, Bauman rejects the postmodern slogan of replacing the moral with the aesthetic. However, there is still an ethical crisis, because within postmodernity we need help and advice on how to conduct ourselves morally, but we are more unwilling than ever to accept such advice. As we shall see more clearly in Area 5, the significance for political theories of this moral debate is that theories such as liberalism, conservatism and socialism all claim to have a moral basis. If morality disappears, so does the foundation for the politics we have taken for granted in Europe and North America.

The postmodern approach to ethics does not reject the moral concerns of individuals in the modern world. However, it rejects the coercive response within modernity to ethical issues by any central authority. The simple division between the 'right way' and the 'wrong way' becomes subject to forms of evaluation that allow actions to be viewed as 'right' in one way or 'wrong' in another. Bauman (1997) divides actions into the 'economically pleasing', 'aesthetically pleasing' or 'morally proper'. The modern world became secular as individuals lost belief in religious dogma. Their lives became increasingly fragmented, to the degree that any unitary vision provided by a religion could never be satisfactory in explaining aspects of an individual's life. At this point, the state intervened to attempt to create a comprehensive moral code and impose it upon individuals. One way in which this was done in Britain was by introducing religious classes into the

Education Reform Act 1988, requiring children in state schools to have a collective act of Christian worship each day. The motive behind the state's action was to free minds from contradictions and unresolvable situations. Human behaviour, when free from such regulation, was not only unpredictable, but also a major source of instability for the social system. From the point of view of the modern state, instinct must be subject to rationally designed enforcement – the principle of universality – and without the exceptionless rule of one obligatory moral code, supported by a foundation of coercive practices, modernity would end in chaos.

Bauman (1995) believes that humans are morally ambivalent, and no rationally coherent moral code can be imposed upon people to resolve this condition of uncertainty. We have to live with ambivalence, and every choice that we make can be defined as objectively good or bad. Even the moral impulse to care for another person can lead to the immoral consequence of destroying their independence. Bauman thus defines morality as non-universalisable; there is no clear and widely accepted notion of what is right across society. Moreover, for Bauman, morality is irrational: 'Moral responsibility is a mystery contrary to reason' (Bauman, 1993: 13). What, then, is the moral self? Individuals have moral impulses and moral capacities. To act in a moral fashion is to assume moral responsibility: 'being for the Other before one can be with the Other' (Bauman, 1993: 13). This is the first reality of the moral self. To be a moral self is to act in an unselfish way, to do something for another person, without taking into account self-interest. This morality has no other foundation, no other origin, yet it is deeply felt as real. Moreover, to act in this moral way is a key element in the postmodern construction of self-identity.

A postmodern politics, then, is about the redefinition of the nature of social solidarity. What Bauman is arguing here is similar to the point of view of Richard Rorty. In his essay 'Solidarity' (1989), Rorty argues that bonds of solidarity are strongest within collectivities that are small and local, in contrast to critics such as Ernest Gellner (1992), who argues that postmodernism cannot provide any foundation for political action or belief. Moreover, in contrast to the critics described by Best and Kellner (1997) who present postmodernism as the terrifying vision of a 'non-society devoid of cohesive relations, social meaning and collective political struggle', Rorty (1993: 18–19) attempts to provide a distinctly postmodern notion of rights that is not built upon 'grand narratives' or similar universal criteria. In Rorty's view, all human beings need emotional attachment and to feel sympathy for others. In addition, by education, we can reinforce individual identification with others, so that we view all individuals as fully and truly human. His foundation for human rights assumes that the human body is delicate, and that some bodies are much weaker than others are. All of us have a feeling to protect bodies that are weaker than ours. This makes Rorty's theory of human rights one of a collective, shared compassion for other human beings that still exists within the postmodern condition.

However, this view of morality as self-discipline could be seen as another universal foundation for a value system which is an internally coherent, impersonal attempt to suppress ambivalence. In other words, Bauman is attempting to show us how to return to a modern type of morality and with it a modern type of politics; to show us how to distinguish 'right' from 'wrong',' just' from 'unjust', and 'legitimate' from 'illegitimate'. Self-interest is defined and discussed by Bauman as a universal, and within his work there is a constant search for the universal, as in the following passage: 'The right of the Other to his stranger hood is the only way in which my own right may express, establish and defend itself. It is the right of the Other that my right is put together. The "I am responsible for the Other", and "I am responsible for myself", come to mean the same thing.' (Best 1998)

In other words, you should help others in trouble, and they should help you when you are in trouble – a universal ethical code of human conduct. Although Bauman may be right, he would do well to remember Bernard Shaw's comment: 'Don't do unto others as you would have them do to you – their tastes might be different.' Moreover, it is not so easy to define self-interest. Individuals can be honest and helpful in their dealings with others out of self-interest, if only to aid continued rewarding dealings with other individuals. It is also possible to live a totally abstemious life (a life that involves doing without things) out of self-interest; for example, not forming close relationships because you might be deserted, not indulging in expensive food to reduce the risk of indigestion. All moral codes involve imposition, and Bauman's universal view of morality has no place within any formulation of postmodernity. For a full outline and explanation of these issues, see Best (1998).

Bauman's view of a postmodern politics

Bauman (1997) argues that a political community should be built upon the principles of liberty, difference and solidarity, and that individuals should be free to achieve and continue to live in freedom. In the postmodern politics, 'individual freedom' is the yardstick by which all ideas, beliefs and practices are to be measured.

In the postmodern condition, macropolitics has been replaced by micropolitics. There is said to be a deeply embedded democratic impulse towards a pluralistic order. This impulse includes a rejection of the politics of 'totality', 'unity', and 'universalism'. Moreover, unlike the politics of modernity, there is no need for 'a gardening state' to weed out uninvited guests and any others who are seen as a potential threat to the system. Such potential threats would include the poor, immigrants and political extremists. Postmodern politics is the politics of single-issue movements in which party politics has been replaced by the politics of 'imagined communities'; groups of people who feel that they have something in common. This pluralistic order, in which power is not centrally controlled by a strong state, has no foundation in principles that are outside the control of individual people, externally imposed, or readily accepted by the members of the community. In other words, this is a social and political system in which everything is open to negotiation and everything is subject to change. In Bauman's view, communism collapsed because it could not cope with the postmodern condition. The optimistic view of a postmodern politics is outlined by Bauman as follows: 'Whatever value or means championed by postmodernity we consider, they all point (if only tacitly or by elimination) to politics, democracy, full-blown citizenship as the sole vehicles of their implementation' (1991: 276).

Postmodernism: a pessimistic view

Therefore this politics has a tendency towards the irrational and unstable, particularly when the imagined communities become tribal in nature, as we shall see below. Because the postmodern condition, as we have seen, leaves people to cope with ambivalence, the tendency to share is very strong. In these conditions, the politics of identity is crucial for many individuals, and we have seen that the ethnic component of such a politics in Europe has given rise to forms of nationalism in which individuals attempt to cope with ambivalence by adopting a fanatical ethnic identity. Brutalising the other can then become an essential condition in avoiding exclusion from the community. This is the very condition that modernity's totalising impulses were designed to control. Postmodern politics reflects a dark side of postmodernity.

There is a political dimension to the postmodern habitat, and that has to be 'the politics of agents'; that is, a form of politics created by individual people, and not a politics imposed upon individual people. This has come about because the state's monopoly of control has eroded within the postmodern habitat. Responsibility for policy has been taken over by localised or partial agencies; these are often single-issue movements and short-term social movements, such as protesters against road-building. The old conflicts of modernity over redistribution; notably the redistribution of wealth and income by the state, as a solution to the problems of poverty, has become a non-issue. As in New Right politics, individuals are to blame for their own poverty; as individuals they made the wrong choices.

Within the postmodern community, then, the monopoly of control by the state has been eroded, and is being replaced by local social movements. Unfortunately, this can develop into a fanatical ethnic identity. According to Bauman, these conditions bring about the following forms of politics.

Tribal politics. The tribes are the imagined communities formed by individuals coming together because they feel that they share values, attitudes and beliefs. This can be seen most clearly in the response of Muslims to Salman Rushdie's *The Satanic Verses* (1988) or of Christians to Madonna's 'Like a prayer'. There is a return to fundamentalism in the postmodern condition. Individuals draw upon shared symbols and rituals in an effort to construct a common self-identity. Nationalism can help individuals cope with the uncertainty that they experience in the postmodern world.

Politics of desire.   Individuals have a need to acquire tribal tokens. To show that they are full members of a community, people need to make use of these tokens. In the postmodern condition then, the citizen and the consumer are one and the same. What people wear, what they eat, and where they are seen have all become highly politicised. These tokens are signs of wanting to belong to the community, of sharing its beliefs and aspirations. We can say, then, that in the postmodern condition the political becomes the personal. The politics of identity is crucial, and the ethnic component is central to this.

Politics of fear.   This is concerned with the avoidance of potentially harmful effects. In particular, there is a fear that the products supplied to enable individuals to fulfil their desires may have harmful effects upon the body. The possible link between BSE and CJD, the link between diet and heart disease, and the link between oral contraceptives and a number of possibly life-threatening conditions are all examples of this. The uncertainty that this generates leads to a growing dependency upon experts, but at the same time individuals question the advice of experts as they had never done previously.

Politics of certainty.   This is primarily concerned with trust. Experts attempt to produce and distribute certainty; however, most individuals are unable either to challenge or endorse the arguments of such experts. Individuals exercise their choices on the basis of trust, and the manipulation of this trust forms the basis of the politics of certainty. Loss of trust is viewed as a major threat to the self-identity of individuals in the postmodern condition.

Liberty, diversity, and tolerance inspire the postmodern political mentality. However, liberty becomes nothing more than consumer choice, diversity nothing more than marketable lifestyle choices, and tolerance nothing more than spectator curiosity in front of the TV screen. Postmodern politics represents the dark side of postmodernity.

The dark side of postmodernity

Why does Bauman want to reject the 'anything goes' view of postmodernity and discover a need for an ethical code? The answer to this is that postmodernism has a dark side that is tribal, unequal and violent. As we have seen, the postmodern condition provides us with no real opportunity to escape from uncertainty. However, the condition generates within us a need to share: 'A shared idea ... promises a shelter: a community, an ideological brotherhood, fraternity of fate or mission. The temptation to share is overwhelming. In the long run it is difficult to resist' (Bauman, 1991: 245).

The need to share is the basis of any community in the postmodern world. These communities are described as aesthetic communities or imagined communities, with their own tribal conceptions of right, truth, and beauty. They invent tradition, and exist because individuals follow the 'symbolic traits of tribal allegiance' (Bauman, 1991: 249). The problem with this is that the obsessive search for community becomes the key element in the self-definition of the individual. Without the protection of rationality, the door is open to all forms of barbarism against others that are not seen to be part of one's community. Here you might consider again the points we made in Area 2 about the process of Balkanisation. Satisfying the need for security in the face of ambivalence can produce a foundation for self-definition which involves irrational cruelty and the need to humiliate others who are outside the community. When we see such acts of cruelty on our TV screens, our postmodern response is a privatised one; we see such acts as none of our concern and as the work of evil individuals. The political has again becomes the personal within the postmodern condition.

Other forms of selfishness can also be generated; on the one hand, there are the rich and resourceful consumers who exercise their choice from the available diversity. The choices that consumers make to acquire happiness are screened by a 'protective wall of playful unconcern': 'The playgrounds of happy shoppers are surrounded by thick walls, electronic spies and sharp-toothed guard dogs. Polite tolerance applies only to those allowed inside. And thus drawing the line between the inside and the outside seems to have lost nothing of its violence and genocidal potency' (Bauman, 1991: 260).

In the postmodern condition, then, the citizen and the consumer are one and the same, and the response of the consumer to individuals on the outside is, again, a privatised one. Without guilt or shame, the poor are told that they them-selves are to blame for their own poverty. Poverty is their own choice. This is not a mere by-product of the postmodern condition, but an essential element of it.

A postmodern politics: Heller and Feher

The Postmodern Political Condition (1988) by Agnes Heller and Ferenc Feher defines postmodernity as: 'the private-collective time and space, within the wider time space of modernity, by those who want to take it to task. ... The very foundation of postmodernity consists of viewing the world as a plurality of heterogeneous spaces and temporalities' (1988: 8). In other words, from this point of view, modernity and postmodernity coexist, and postmoderns are people who have superseded the grand narrative. That is, postmoderns are people who choose not to make use of 'grand narratives' to make sense of the world. Moreover, the postmodern world-view can be described as 'the end of history', the idea that from this moment in time onwards there will be no more historical epochs such as feudalism, or great historical experiments such as communism or fascism. We shall explain this in more detail before we summarise and again in Area 7.

In addition, Heller and Feher argue that post-structuralism has a specific meaning within postmodernity: 'It indicates the social and political prevalence of the functional over the structural, the gradual weakening if not total disappearance of a politics based solely on class interests and class perceptions' New Social Movements (NSMs) appear 'which are the epitomes of functionalist-postmodern politics'. What Heller and Feher are arguing here is the obsolescence of class-based politics, and the institutions and organisations that go with that politics: Old Social Movements such as pressure groups, notably trade unions; class-based political parties, notably the Labour Party before the leadership of Tony Blair. This type of politics has broken down, and the institutions that we now consider Old Social Movements do not appear to be significant in the lives of individual people. It is now single-issue NSMs, such as the Green movement, the anti-poll tax movement, and anti-roads protesters, all of whom make use of 'direct action', that have significance for our lives. It is now these groups which we see as 'functional' within the postmodern condition. For a more detailed discussion of NSMs, see Area 6.

The breakdown of 'grand narratives' has the following consequences:

- The postmodern political condition becomes pluralistic in nature, with many (what postmodernists would term '*a plurality of*') 'cultures and discourses', each with its own 'small narrative', which may be local, cultural, ethnic, religious or ideological in nature, living alongside each other
- A foundation for what Habermas (1979) termed 'domination-free' discourse becomes possible; people can talk to each other free from ideology. This is what Habermas terms 'communicative competence'. The idea of 'communicative competence' is used by Habermas to suggest a way of communicating with others that is not distorted by ideology or prejudice.
- The replacement of the state as a 'class agency'. Class politics was always rational and calculable because it was based upon economic interests. However, without the economic interests of classes, politics becomes irrational and unpredictable.
- Politics loses its sense of 'taboo'. Racism becomes politicised within a form of 'moral relativism' in which even the assessment of a mass deportation and genocide becomes a matter of taste.

In contrast to many postmodernists, Heller and Feher argue that certain moral principles of democratic politics can be extracted from the arguments and debates about the postmodern condition. This is possible because, without direct financial economic reward as the sole measure of success and well-being, the postmodern condition promotes various non-economic forms of satisfaction, such as being seen to be Green, which can be incorporated within an individual or collective lifestyle. The postmodern political ethos is therefore said to be democratic in nature. With the decline in the grand narratives, there is a greater emphasis upon individuals actively making their own personal choices about such things as lifestyle, rather than being pushed about by forces outside their control, as they would be under modernity. It is this freedom of personal choice that upholds the postmodern democracy.

Postmodern politics is much more irrational and emotional than the politics that went before it.

Richard Sennett

In *The Fall of Public Man* (1977), Sennett argues that 'public life' has gone into decline since the end of the nineteenth century and has been replaced by the widespread belief that all problems in the world are caused by impersonality or coldness. Sennett presents a rather pessimistic view of both the self and of city life. Sennett argues that the public space in the city is viewed as 'dead', and that the inhabitants of the city are isolated. They are inhibited from fulfilling personal relationships, transported in cars which diminish their relationship with the surroundings and isolated at work in buildings under a high degree of constant surveillance.

The world of personal intimate feelings has lost its boundaries, so that, for example, political leaders are judged on what kind of person they are, rather than on policy or action. Sennett refers to this society as 'the Intimate Society', which is organised on the basis of the following two principles:

- ○ Narcissism, that is, 'the search for gratification of the self which at the same time prevents that gratification from occurring' (Sennett, 1977: 230). In this type of society, the more individuals strive for personal fulfilment, the less likely they are to achieve it, because fulfilment involves ignoring the feelings of others.
- ○ Destructive *Gemeinschaft*, or 'a market exchange of intimacies', in which individuals are encouraged to make revelations on the grounds that this activity is a moral good in itself. Destructive *Gemeinschaft* is characterised by repression, loss of participation, and violence, because true intimacy is not possible.

However, Sennett warns that 'When people today seek to have full and open emotional relations with each other, they succeed only in wounding each other. This is the logical consequence of the destructive gemeinschaft' (Sennett, 1977: 223).

Richard Sennett on 'the intimate society':
narcissism and destructive Gemeinschaft

The following quotations give the clearest idea of what Sennett understands by narcissism and destructive *Gemeinschaft*.

In such a society, the basic human energies of narcissism are so mobilized that they enter systematically and perversely into human relationships. ... Narcissism [is] a character disorder, it is self-absorption which prevents one from understanding what belongs within the domain of the self and self-gratification and what belongs outside it. ... This absorption in self, oddly enough, prevents gratification of self needs; it makes the person at the moment of attaining an end or connecting with another person feel that 'this isn't what I wanted.'...

The withdrawal of commitment, the continual search for definition from within of 'who I am', produces pain. ... Narcissism withdraws physical love from any kind of commitment, personal or social.

The most common form in which narcissism makes itself known to the person is by a process of inversion: If only I could feel more, or if only I could really feel, then I could relate to others or have 'real' relations with them.

[Destructive gemeinschaft or the market exchange of intimacies] reinforces this fruitless search for an identity. ...

Narcissism and the market exchange of self-revelations structure the conditions under which the expression of feeling in intimate circumstances becomes destructive.

(Sennett, 1977: 8–10)

Broadly stated, when people today seek to have full and open emotional relations with each other, they succeed only in wounding each other. This is the logical consequence of the destructive gemeinschaft.

(Sennett, 1977: 223)

In recent years similar points have been made about Bill Clinton (president of the USA) and Tony Blair (British prime minister). The suggestion is that both these people have few, if any, policies or principles, but present themselves as credible and trustworthy individuals. Readers might consider whether Iain Duncan-Smith (Conservative Party) is a credible leader or about former Party leaders Neil Kinnock and William Hague (Labour and Conservative respectively).

If we accept Richard Sennett's views, we cannot wonder that people want to move away from the cities. Outside the city, people can develop themselves in a reflexive fashion, changing their behaviour, making choices about how they want to live their lives; they can fashion themselves and create an identity of their own choosing. It is possible, then, to point to the suburbs as places of diversity. This is particularly the case if we accept the idea of the postmodern condition, according to which people are much more likely to be free from constraints over their lifestyle choices.

The culture of the modern world puts pressure upon people to act narcissistically; therefore, disclosure of our feelings to others becomes destructive. This is because narcissism makes a person attempting to form an intimate relationship feel that 'this isn't what I wanted'. The end result is a withdrawal of commitment.

The critique of postmodernity

Marxist critics of postmodernism advance the following arguments:

- Postmodernity attempts to restabilise bourgeois identity, maintaining capitalism and people's places within it
- Postmodernity is a catalyst for working-class fragmentation – it decentres working-class identity; in other words, it breaks down working-class people's sense of a shared identity
- Postmodernism is a diversionary tactic to obscure the class struggle
- Postmodernism discards both realism and socialist realism
- Postmodernism is relativist in nature; in postmodernism, everything is appearance and nothing is substance
- Postmodernism's association with Nietzschean thought, libertarian individualism, deep ecology, and mysticism, render it right-wing and reactionary

The essential point here is that the Marxist perceives postmodernism as a set of ideas that undermines the class struggle by directing our attention away from the conflict between labour and capital. Hence postmodernism is ideological in nature, concerned with filling people's heads with notions of culture, style and identity that, in the Marxist analysis, are merely products of economic determinism. Any evaluation of these points depends upon your acceptance or rejection of the assumptions upon which the Marxist analysis is built. However, you do not have to accept or reject either Marxism or postmodernism. In Area 4, which deals with Marxist theories of power, we shall look at two very different attempts to combine Marxism and postmodernism. First, we will discuss Fredric Jameson (1991), who argues that postmodernism is a stage in the development of capitalism, and then Ernesto Laclau and Chantal Mouffe (1987), who replace the economic basis of the Marxist analysis with more postmodernist presuppositions.

However, at this point, let us take up the point about the 'decentring', 'fragmentation' or dissolution of working-class identity. This breaking up of working-class identity began in the 1950s, with the rise of rock music, the increase in the spending power of teenagers, and the impact of commercial television with its US influences such as the game show, which equated happiness with material possessions. With 'pop' culture came a rejection of parental discipline by teenagers and a reduction of restraints on sexual freedom, both of which were significant at the level of individual people reflexively creating or forming their own identity. These new identities were often far removed from traditional working-class identities. The 1950s 'pop' culture also brought with it a redefinition of the relationship between the working class and the Labour Party. People no longer had an automatic party identification; in other words, there was a redefinition of the 'collective working-class identity'. One of the most influential analyses of the breakdown of the culture of working-class communities is Richard Hoggart's case study of the Hunslet area of Leeds in the 1950s in *The Uses of Literacy* (1956).

In addition, the New Right critics of postmodernism are also vocal, but they tend to be political activists rather than academics. For the New Right, postmodernism embraces multiculturalism, choice in sexual orientation, the 'direct action' of NSMs and a number of other causes they believe to be left wing in nature. New Right thinkers believe that Western civilisation is under threat from homosexuals, foreigners, single parents and others who adopt non-traditional lifestyle choices.

In contrast to both Marxists and the New Right, one of the most influential sociological critics of postmodernism is Jurgen Habermas (1989). Habermas believes that the Enlightenment project remains unfinished and that postmodernism is based upon irrational anti-Enlightenment theories that are also the roots of fascism. In Habermas's view, the rejection of reason and the embracing of irrationalism found in postmodern analyses will have dangerous political consequences. People who are free from reason have no constraint over their behaviour, and are capable of acts of great cruelty. Postmodernism is not only critical of modernity, but also rejects all of its positive aspects, which, Habermas argues, are worth saving, notably modernity's notions of individuality and citizenship rights.

Habermas is critical of many aspects of modernity; in particular, the spread of rational/bureaucratic ways of behaviour throughout society, causing great damage to the meaning that people give to their lives. As we shall see in Area 6, 'New Social Movements', Habermas has developed a theory of 'communicative action' that allows us to escape the oppressive aspects of modernity, and provides us with opportunities for true democratic participation in all aspects of political life.

Steven Best and Douglas Kellner (1991) spell out the critique of postmodernism, making the following points:

- Postmodernism does not supply a satisfactory examination of the economy, or of recent developments within capitalism. Postmodern analysis is mainly cultural in nature.
- It is too subjectivist; in other words, postmodernists do not attempt to provide an objective or value-free vision of the world.
- Postmodernists have no satisfactory theory of human agency – the self. As we suggested, some postmodernists, taking their lead from Foucault, believe that the individual self may disappear completely.
- It does not provide a satisfactory examination of the state. Although the state may have lost much of its influence because of the spread of global processes, it can still have a significant impact upon people's lives.
- There is no substantive explanation of the relationship between the state, the economy and other areas of everyday life.
- There is no analysis of institutions or organisations within the postmodern condition.
- There is little concrete social or political analysis; some postmodernists assert the end of history, politics and society.

In response to the argument that we now live in 'new times' and new social conditions which require very different forms of theorising about the nature of the world than the theories provided by modernist writers such as Durkheim, Weber and Marx, modernist thinkers make the following points:

○ The postmodernist claim that the world is a very different place from that described by modernist theorists is not validated by evidence
○ To validate the claim that the world is a very different place in the postmodern condition requires a 'meta-narrative' or 'grand theory', an approach which is rejected by postmodernists
○ There is no satisfactory political response to the postmodern condition as described

In other words, postmodernism does not have a satisfactory or convincing theory of a radical break with modernity.

Sociologically speaking, however, it is possible to reject postmodernity as a cultural model. The contents of arcades, department stores, etc., have to be manufactured. This manufacture has to take place within a social relationship, usually between employers and employees, that has not changed significantly since the nineteenth century. Alternatively, critics attempt to dismiss postmodernism as a mere 'cultural' theory; the contents of the arcade may have been produced by a multinational company operating within a global economy. If entrepreneurs do not produce the contents of the arcade, they will be produced by bureaucratic management. Therefore, the economy in its effects upon social relations is still an important factor in explaining political relationships within any society.

The construction and consumption of lifestyle choices by an urban middle class has always existed, often as a form of 'café society', such as existed in Paris of the nineteenth century. Today, because of the proliferation of media within the postmodern world, middle-class people can make use of a range of different resources to express their lifestyle choices, and more middle-class people can experience a feel of café society. However, these cultures, and the media for their transmission, are manufactured, mass produced for a mass audience, and are clearly modern in nature.

Giddens's critique of postmodernism

Most theorists of postmodernity view the postmodern condition as the absence of any foundation of reliable knowledge, a situation which makes it impossible to have any systemic understanding of social action, or to be engaged in any form of social engineering. However, as Giddens points out from this perspective, 'To speak of post-modernity, as superseding modernity appears to invoke that very thing which is declared (now) to be impossible: giving some coherence to history and pinpointing our place in it' (1990: 47).

According to Giddens (1990), instead of investigating postmodernity, we need to have a closer look at modernity itself, which, he argues, has been poorly grasped in sociology. Modernity is becoming more radicalised or unpredictable, and it is becoming universal or global. It is attempting to develop a greater under-standing of itself, and life has a much more uncertain feel because we have to live through a radicalisation of modernity, in which the traditions which gave us comfort are swept away. In this radicalised modernity, there is a self-reflexivity. The individuals and institutions within the modern world constantly question modernity, turning its rational powers of analysis upon itself in a critical way that never happened in the past. The postmodern condition, for Giddens, would involve a radical transformation of the present institutional dimensions of moder-nity, capitalism, industrialism, military power and surveillance, towards a new social order.

Whatever is beyond the far side of modernity, this postmodern condition would be institutionally complex, global, and a post-scarcity system in which the goods needed for life are readily available to everyone. The postmodern will also be capitalist, but the market will merely indicate choice, not be a source of depriva-tion. The politics will be life politics, and polyarchic in nature; this means that power will be widely shared, and individuals will be free to choose from a rich variety of lifestyles. However, it is also possible that the postmodern could be a dark, dangerous and unpleasant place, characterised by the growth of totalitar-ian power, collapse of economic growth mechanisms, ecological decay and nuclear conflict or other large-scale warfare. These are the high-consequence risks of the current dimensions of modernity, and, in Giddens's eyes, at the moment modernity is still with us.

What brings about the postmodern condition?

Many postmodernists do not explain what brings about the postmodern condi-tion. To return to Lyotard, why do grand narratives dissolve? In a world that is global in its media and communication links, we all observe how others live their lives and the reasons that they give for the choices that they make. In a democra-tic society, individuals constantly have to choose, and, as many theorists suggest, industrial societies have a tendency towards greater polyarchy. This means greater democratisation and greater opportunities for choice. Even if the view we hold is that all other people are wrong, we still have knowledge of other lifestyle choices and other views of the world. Globalisation breaks down grand narratives by giving people a view of the world from the perspective of a number of 'little narratives'. In a similar fashion, movement of people as tourists or migrants also provides opportunities for meeting individuals who share a narrative with which we are unfamiliar. Overall, globalisation has the effect of relativising – in other words, removing the foundation from – all narratives.

Area Summary

All postmodernists discuss the consequences of the breakdown of 'grand narratives'. In this Area we have attempted to answer the question 'What is a postmodern politics?' To do this, we have had to look very critically at what is understood by the 'social'. We have also attempted to look at the postmodern self and its political implications. This involved looking at the relationship between postmodernity and Marxism, and assessing the contributions to the postmodern debate by Zygmunt Bauman, Jean-François Lyotard, Peter Marris, Mike Featherstone, Agnes Heller and Ferenc Feher.

In response to postmodernist positions, we looked at Richard Sennett's analysis of 'public life', the Marxist critiques of postmodernism and Anthony Giddens's critique of postmodernism.

References

Ashley, D. (1997) *History Without a Subject: The Postmodern Condition*. Boulder; Westview Press.

Baudrillard, J. (1983) *Fatal Strategies*. (translated by Philip Beitchman and W.G.J. Niesluchowski). New York: Semiotext(e) and Pluto.

Baudrillard, J. (1994) *The Transparency of Evil: Essays on Extreme Phenomena*. (translated by James Benedict). London: Verso.

Bauman, Z. (1990) *Thinking Sociologically*. Oxford: Blackwell.

Bauman, Z. (1991) *Modernity and Ambivalence*. Cambridge: Polity.

Bauman, Z. (1992) *Intimations of Postmodernity*. London: Routledge.

Bauman, Z. (1993) *Postmodern Ethics*. Cambridge: Polity.

Bauman, Z. (1994) *Alone Again: Ethics After Certainty*. London: Demos.

Bauman, Z. (1995) *Life in Fragments: Essays in Postmodern Morality*. Oxford: Blackwell.

Bauman, Z. (1996) 'From pilgrim to tourist – or a short history of identity', in S. Hall and P. Du Gay (eds), *Questions of Cultural Identity*. London: Sage. pp. 18–36.

Bauman, Z. (1997) *Postmodernity and its Discontents*. Cambridge: Polity.

Bauman, Z. (1998) *Globalization: The Human Consequences*. Cambridge: Polity.

Bauman, Z. (1998) *Work, Consumerism and the New Poor*. Buckingham: Open University Press.

Best, S. (1997) 'Power and Politics', in Nik Jorgensen (eds), *Sociology: An Interactive approach*. London: Collins Educational.

Best, S. (1998) 'Zygmunt Bauman: personal reflections from the mainstream of modernity', *British Journal of Sociology,* 49(2)

Best, S., Griffiths, J. and Hope, T. (2000) *Active Sociology.* Harlow: Longman.

Best, S. and Kellner, D. (1997) 'The postmodern adventure', http://ccwf.cc.utexas.edu/~panicbuy/HaTeMail/marxopomo.htm.

Best, S. and Kellner, D. (1997) *Postmodern Theory.* Basingstoke: Macmillan.

Connor, S. (1997) *Postmodernist Culture.* Oxford: Blackwell.

Deleuze, S. and Guattari, F. (1988) *A Thousand Plateaus: Capitalism and Schizophrenia.* London: The Athlone Press.

Featherstone, M. (1988) *Postmodernism.* London: Sage.

Featherstone, M. (1991) *Consumer Culture and Postmodernism.* London: Sage.

Gellner, E. (1992) *Postmodernism, Reason and Religion.* London: Routledge.

Giddens, A. (1984) *The Constitution of Society.* Cambridge: Polity.

Giddens, A. (1990) *The Consequences of Modernity.* Cambridge: Polity.

Giddens, A. (1992) *Modernity and Self Identity.* Cambridge: Polity.

Giddens, A. (1993) *The Transformation of Intimacy.* Cambridge: Polity.

Giddens, A. (1994) *Beyond Left and Right.* Cambridge: Polity.

Giddens, A. (1995) *Politics, Sociology and Social Theory: Encounters with Classical and Contemporary Social Thought.* Cambridge: Polity.

Habermas, J. (1979) *Communication and the Evolution of Society* (translated by Thomas McCarthy). London: Heinemann.

Habermas, J. (1989) *The New Conservatism.* Cambridge: Polity.

Habermas, J. (1989) *The Philosophical Discourse of Modernity.* Cambridge: Polity.

Heller, A. and Feher, F. (1988) *The Postmodern Political Condition.* Cambridge: Polity.

Hoggart, R. (1956) *The Uses of Literacy.* London: Chatto and Windus.

Horton, M. (1995) 'The Tower of Babel: modernity built the tower–now post-modernity must face the challenge of condemning the "unsafe structure"', in *Modern Reformation.* Anaheim, CA: CURE.

Jameson, F. (1991) *Postmodernism: or the Cultural Logic of Late Capitalism.* London: Verso.

Laclau, Ernesto and Mouffe, Chantal (1987) 'Post-Marxism without apologies' *New Left Review,* No. 166, November/December. pp. 79–106.

Lyotard, J.F. (1984) *The Postmodern Condition: A Report on Knowledge.* Minneapolis, MN: University of Minnesota Press.

Lyotard, J.F. (1986) *The Differend: Phrases in Dispute* (translated by George van den Abbeele). Manchester: Manchester University Press.

Lyotard, J.F. (1992) *The Postmodern Explained to Children – Correspondence 1982–1985* London: Turnaround.

Marris, P. (1996) *The Politics of Uncertainty: Attachment in Private and Public Life.* London: Routledge.

Parsons, T. (1951) *The Social System.* London: Routledge.

Rorty, R. (1989) *Irony, Contingency and Solidarity.* Cambridge: Cambridge University Press.

Rorty, R. (1993) *Objectivity, Relativism, and Truth: Philosophical Papers. Vol.* 1. Cambridge: Cambridge University Press.

Rushdie, S. (1988) *The Satanic Verses.* Dover, DE: Delaware Consortium, Inc.

Sennett, R. (1977) *The Fall of Public Man.* London: Faber and Faber.

Stones, R. (1996) *Sociological Reasoning: Towards a Post-modern Sociology.* Basingstoke: Macmillan.

Wagner, P. (1994) *A Sociology of Modernity: Liberty and Discipline.* London: Routledge.

Waters, M. (1997) 'Inequality after class', in D. Owen (ed.), *Sociology after Postmodernism.* London: Sage.

Wheale, N. (ed.) (1995) *The Postmodern Arts: An Introductory Reader.* London: Routledge.

4

Marxist and Elite Theories of Power

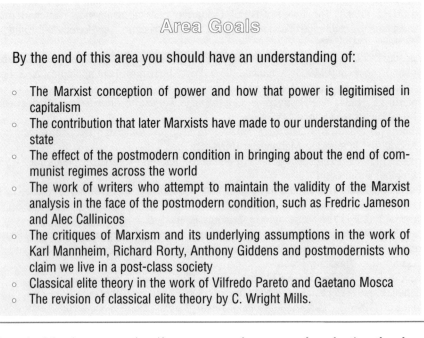

Area Goals

By the end of this area you should have an understanding of:

- The Marxist conception of power and how that power is legitimised in capitalism
- The contribution that later Marxists have made to our understanding of the state
- The effect of the postmodern condition in bringing about the end of communist regimes across the world
- The work of writers who attempt to maintain the validity of the Marxist analysis in the face of the postmodern condition, such as Fredric Jameson and Alec Callinicos
- The critiques of Marxism and its underlying assumptions in the work of Karl Mannheim, Richard Rorty, Anthony Giddens and postmodernists who claim we live in a post-class society
- Classical elite theory in the work of Vilfredo Pareto and Gaetano Mosca
- The revision of classical elite theory by C. Wright Mills.

From the Marxist perspective, if a group own the means of production, they have not only economic power but also political power. The state is viewed as an institution that helps to organise capitalist society in the best interests of the bourgeoisie. Working-class people are said to hold values, ideas and beliefs about the

Key assumptions of Marxism:

The mode of production

> **Superstructure:**
>
> this is the realm of culture, politics and ideas
> the **superstructure** is determined in the last
> analysis by the **economic base**

> **The economic base:**
>
> this is made up of two parts
>
> 1. the **relations of production** – this means
>   **Class Relations**
> 2. the **forces of production** – is made up of all the
>   things from nature that we need to produce
>   commodities

Figure 4.1 *The key assumptions of the Marxist analysis.*

nature of inequality, that are not in their own economic interest to hold. Working-class people have their ideas manipulated by the media, schools and religion, and regard economic inequality as fair and just.

In contrast, classical elite theories are the work of anti-democratic theorists who assume that in any political system a few will lead and the majority will be led. In other words, there is a small self-conscious elite with power and the masses, who have very little power.

All societies have broadly this type of social structure in which *oligarchy* (the rule of the few) is inevitable. In addition, most elite theorists view the masses as being psychologically incapable of holding power and also as having an instinctual need to be dominated. Only the elite can satisfy that need; Robert Michels (1911) has termed this 'the iron law of oligarchy'. For this reason, democracy is not a realistic alternative, according to the elite theorist.

Marxism

Classical Marxism is based upon the writings of Karl Marx and Friedrich Engels. In the nineteenth century Marx and Engels constructed a philosophy of history, commonly known as 'dialectical materialism', which singled out class divisions as the motor of history – the ingredient which pushed history forwards. For Marx, the type of society in which we live, including its politics, culture, art and literature is determined by the 'mode of production' (Figure 4.1). Within capitalism, the mode of production is divided into two parts: the economic base – which is made up of the 'relations of production'; in other words, class relations – and the 'forces of production'; in other words, all the things from nature that we need to produce commodities. The mode of production also shapes 'the superstructure' – this is the area of culture, politics and ideas. In the Marxist analysis, people's ideas and beliefs are determined in the last analysis by economic factors.

The opening chapter of Marx's most influential book *Capital* (1867) is about 'the commodity'. This concept plays a key role in Marxist analysis. Any human creation can be a 'commodity' and the commodity contains 'value', both 'use' value, which is the personal value that a person gains from consuming the commodity, and 'exchange' value, which is the value in monetary terms that another person will give to own the commodity. Workers are the people who put the value into any commodity. Moreover, Marx builds his theory of class exploitation upon these simple ideas.

What does Marx understand by the term 'class relations'? For Marx, capitalist society is a form of society in which factories, shops and offices are privately owned, rather than owned by the government. There are a number of economic classes within capitalism, and Marx investigates two: the bourgeoisie, who own the means of production, and the proletariat, who do not. These two groups have a structural conflict of interest; to make profits, the bourgeoisie must exploit the proletariat, while to improve their own living standards, the proletariat must reduce the profits of the bourgeoisie by transferring more profit to the workers as wages.

The labour theory of value

Marx characterises the relationship between the bourgeoisie and the proletariat as an exploitative one. The bourgeoisie exploit the proletariat. The theory that Marx develops to explain class exploitation is called 'the labour theory of value'. The stages of the theory follow a logical order:

1. The capitalist starts with an amount of
[]
2. money, which is put into the purchase of
[]
3. commodity inputs, these are
[]
4. materials of production and
[]
5. labour power, these come together in the
[]
6. production process, to form
[]
7. the commodities, which are sold in the market place for
[]
8. money

According to Marx, because the bourgeoisie buys the materials of production from other capitalists, who have a rational perception of their situation, these materials are bought at their true market value; hence the source of profit can come only from exploiting labour power. It is extracting *surplus value* from the labour force that provides the difference between the amount of money it takes to set up the production process and the amount of money made at the end of the production process. In addition, we should note that surplus value is not simply profit; it also includes the cost of setting up the production process again for the next production run.

In summary, the value of any commodity reflects the amount of labour power needed to make that commodity. In addition, workers are not paid the 'true' value of their labour power, and this is what Marx means by 'exploitation'; workers add value to a commodity, but are paid only a fraction of the value that they have added.

The perceptive reader will have noticed that, by Marx's theory, if the capitalist replaces workers with machines, profits should fall. For the individual capitalist, this is clearly not the case. However, if large numbers of capitalists replace workers with machines, a fall in profits will result, because individuals will not have sufficient spending power to buy the commodities produced; this is referred to by Marxists as a *realisation crisis*. In these circumstances, capitalists have to find new markets or sources of cheap raw materials from overseas.

Strengths of the Marxist approach

o   Marx provided a cogent description of capitalism and class
o   Marx had an informed theory of inequality, and its persistence
o   Marx predicted that there would be a long-term tendency for the rate of profit to fall
o   The labour theory of value has generated a great deal of research
o   Marx provided the motivation for working-class people to join together and improve their position in society
o   Marx provided a justification for socialism

Weaknesses of the Marxist approach

o   The Marxist conception of class cannot deal with automation; it suggests a fall in profits, but this does not happen
o   Marx's labour theory of value is both sex-blind and race-blind; he does not take into account the race or gender of the bourgeoisie or proletariat
o   In late capitalism, 'ownership' of the means of production has become divorced from 'control' of the means of production – the bourgeoisie and the proletariat no longer exist

The dominant ideology

For Marxists, the dominant ideas of any historical period are the ideas of the ruling class, the bourgeoisie. The notion of a 'dominant ideology' refers to a system of thought which is manipulated by the bourgeoisie and imposed upon the proletariat in support of capitalism. The Marxist conception of ideology is based upon the humanistic notion that consent should be based upon an authentic consciousness free from any distortion. For Marxists, the term 'ideology' suggests that the bourgeoisie control the way in which working-class people think about the world. The bourgeoisie create a 'world-view' for the proletariat, which is shaped by the mass media, the education system and organised religion, together with other institutions concerned with ideas. Class interests shape ideas, and the bourgeoisie distort the ideas of the proletariat by imposing 'false' consciousness upon them. Television's manipulation of the ideas of individual people is a commonly discussed example. Working-class people make use of their false consciousness to justify their own subordination within the capitalist system.

However, the Marxist analysis undervalues the role of the human agent. Marxists assume that people are moved by forces that are outside their control. This deterministic assumption, shared by all Marxists, may not be correct. In addition, Marxists have a very simplistic notion of the 'representation', things as they appear, contained within the notion of the ideology. As we have suggested, in the Marxist analysis, working-class people's ideas and world-view are manipulated. The bourgeoisie are said to be capable of taking any object or idea and giving it a new representation or meaning in the minds of the working class. This new representation is supportive of capitalism, justifies the position of the bourgeoisie and legitimises the exploitation of the working class in their own minds. The problem here is that Marxists do not explain how this happens. What goes on, at a cognitive level, inside the minds of working-class people to cause them to reject their own economic interests so fully and totally? How can the 'agency' – the ability to make decisions in our own interests for our own reasons – of working-class people be so completely destroyed without their revolutionary potential not also being destroyed?

The term 'dominant ideology' could mean at least two very different things. On the one hand, the term suggests that there is one ideology that all people accept because it is imposed upon everybody. On the other hand, the term could also mean that there is one dominant ideology and any number of non-dominant ideologies. The suggestion here is that any group of like-minded people could construct a set of ideas and beliefs in opposition to the dominant belief system. As we shall see in Area 6, the construction of new ideologies is one of the key activities of New Social Movements (NSMs).

In summary, the Marxist analysis of ideology contains a very simplistic view of 'representation'. Representation is concerned with how something we see or hear reminds us of something else; for example, a heart shape may remind a person of love and romance, while a smile is a representation of happiness. These are issues of 'cognition'; something happens inside our mind – the process of cognition – which suggests that we think about a person, place or thing when a representation of it presents itself to us. In the Marxist analysis of ideology, people's ideas are manipulated.

You might want to ask how the bourgeoisie can intervene in the processes of cognition, substituting representations and planting new meanings in our heads.

Strength of the Marxist concept of ideology

The concept explains why a revolutionary working class has not emerged within capitalist society.

Weaknesses of the Marxist concept of ideology

- The structure of the argument is 'functionalist' in nature
- The argument places too much emphasis on shared values and beliefs
- There is an overemphasis upon class interests
- It is not clear whether the bourgeoisie accept the dominant ideology or simply impose a set of known false beliefs upon the proletariat

Marxism and the state: modernist perspectives

For Ralph Miliband (1973), the UK has a coherent, well-organised capitalist class who hold top positions in both industry and the state, and most of whom were privately educated before going to Oxbridge. These privileged individuals use the state as an instrument for continued bourgeois domination.

In contrast, Nicos Poulantzas (1973) argues that the class background of individuals in top state positions in unimportant. The structure of society is capitalist, and the role of the state is to maintain that structure. The state must have a high degree of autonomy, or independence, of individual capitalists, in order to choose effectively between the competing demands for state action by different capitalists. In other words, the state is always functional to the needs of capital, even though individual members of top state institutions are not from an upper-class background.

Antonio Gramsci rejected the economic determinism contained in the type of argument that Poulantzas is putting forward. Writing from his prison cell in the 1930s, Gramsci made the following distinction between two parts of the state:

- First, political society, which contains all the repressive state institutions, such as the police and the army
- Second, civil society, which contains all the institutions, such as the mass media, which attempt to manipulate our ideas

The state rules by consent although it has the ability to use force if necessary. However, the state would always prefer to use negotiating skills to secure a compromise. The state attempts to form a *historic bloc*, which involves making compromises with different groups in an effort to maintain solidarity. Consent is maintained by *hegemony*, a body of ideas, which becomes part of our consciousness, and which we accept as right. Capitalism can be overthrown only by challenging and reformulating hegemony and establishing a new historic bloc.

Building upon this analysis by Gramsci, David Coates (1984) suggests that the state must make compromises with various bodies both at home and overseas. In addition, new forms of ideology have to be created in an effort to maintain legitimacy; Thatcherism may be such an example. The nature of Thatcherism was populist. It attempted to appeal to the people by identifying similarities between key elements of common sense and Thatcherite ideology.

Abercrombie et al. (1980) reject approaches that overemphasise the ideological aspects of state power. There are numerous studies, they claim, which show that working-class individuals reject a dominant ideology. For example, Paul Willis's study *Learning to Labour* (1977) shows how a group of working-class 'lads' attempt to import masculine shop-floor culture into the classroom in an effort to reject the dominant ideas that the teaching staff attempt to impose. Abercrombie and his colleagues argue that it is economic factors, such as fear of unemployment, that are the key in maintaining the structure of inequality within capitalism. Many workers do not rebel for fear of losing their jobs.

Marx on ideology

For Marx, the relationship between a person's economic interests and attitudes could be one of the following two types:

- People could have 'true' consciousness – that is, they are aware of their economic interests and their attitudes support those interests
- People could have a 'false' consciousness – that is, they are unaware of their economic interests and therefore may hold views in conflict with their true interests; an example of this would be working-class people hostile to the trade union movement

Baudrillard, postmodernity and Marxism

As we saw in Area 3, Jean Baudrillard is a postmodernist who is critical of all forms of 'Enlightenment' thinking – Marxism, structuralism, critical theory, and Foucault's work. He rejects all epistemenology (theories which attempt to answer the question, 'How do we know what we know?') and all truth claims and a priori concepts (concepts which are true for all time). All of the theories mentioned are based upon 'meta-narratives' or 'foundations' that are used by their authors and followers to distinguish between 'the truth' and various forms of non-truth, notably ideology.

The postmodern condition casts doubt upon all grand narratives, and, as such, all the key assumptions of Marxism are brought into question. The Enlightenment values – most notably claims to have found 'the truth' – are seen by Baudrillard as a source of error and evil. The special place that Marx gave to labour power, and that other thinkers, notably Weber, give to rationality as a foundation of truth, is itself without foundation.

For Baudrillard, 'reality' is a human creation of media products and our feedback on these products. Our values are brought about by consumer demand that is itself influenced by an endless rotation of interpretations, reflections and advertising codes. In all this, there is no clear division or objective criteria that can be used to distinguish between what is true and what is ideological. Baudrillard has argued that imagery has had the following evolution over the course of history:

- Initially, any sign once stood for a truth; for example, a pain in the chest as a sign of heart disease.
- In the nineteenth century with the development of Marxism, signs began to be seen as concealing or deliberately distorting the truth; this is the Marxist conception of ideology.
- As we move into the twentieth century, signs begin to be seen as masking the absence of the truth; this is the idea that style is used to make up for the lack of substance.
- Finally, in the contemporary world, we believe that there is no link between an image and truth. In other words, in the postmodern condition, there is no representation; what you see is what there is. The image is real.

In other words, it is no longer possible clearly to state the difference between what is seen on television and the world it is meant to represent. As we shall see below, there are similarities between Baudrillard's and Rorty's (1998) accounts of the nature of truth.

In his book *The Mirror of Production* (1973), Baudrillard casts doubt upon the Marxist distinction we outlined above between 'use value' and 'exchange value'. 'Use value' is seen by Marxists as based upon genuine need, whereas 'exchange value' is brought about by capitalists distorting the consciousness of the population by ideology and alienation. According to the Marxist theory of alienation, we are essentially creative in nature. However, in the capitalist system, work so is dull and boring that we are unable to express our creativity. In contrast, in a socialist society, people would work for the common good. Making use of the Marxist concepts we outlined above, we could say that socialist society is based upon the principle of 'from each according to his ability, to each according to his needs'. In other words, solely taking care of our 'use values' would satisfy all our needs. For the Marxist, the concepts of 'value' and 'labour' are non-negotiable concepts; they cannot be questioned, and they are essential for any analysis of the world.

In contrast, for Baudrillard, genuine need is impossible to identify without taking into account how our needs are manipulated, explained and even created by the mass media. It is at this point that Baudrillard introduces us to his concept of 'simulacra', which is explained by David Ashley (1997) as follows:

> In the same year [1992], the line between image and reality became so confused that TV viewers were able to watch a sitcom character ('Murphy Brown') pose as a real journalist criticising an allegedly real vice president (Dan Quayle) for condemning her fictional pregnancy. (The baby's TV shower was, of course, attended by 'real' reporters.) Viewers were subsequently treated to the spectacle of Quayle discussing with 'real' journalists Murphy Brown's criticism of him as if this attack had been launched by a real newswoman on a real news show. Needless to say, the vice president's increasingly bizarre behaviour – which included persistent attempts to send flowers to a character he seemed not to understand was fictional – was itself covered as a major news event about which the public needed to be kept fully informed. (Ashley, 1997: 27)

Thus, people make use of the media, both fictional and news programmes, not only to make sense of the world but also to give their own views, beliefs and feelings enhanced validity. Baudrillard uses the term 'hyperreality' when he discusses the simulacra, a concept introduced in Area 3.

In summary, Baudrillard's argument rests upon the following three points:

○ The truth is an 'unreal' creation, and the search for the truth by Marxists and others is doomed to fail
○ All arguments are ideological and distorted; there can be no rational argument, because all ways of thinking, including rationality, are ideological in nature; there is no truth
○ There is no distinction between the real and the unreal or ideological

By way of criticism however, we could start with Baudrillard's implicit claim to present a correct explanation of what goes on in the world. He appears to offer what his analysis suggests he cannot offer, that is, a true account! In other words, his argument is self-refuting.

Baudrillard's work has generated a very mixed response:

> Baudrillard is a first-rate diagnostician of the postmodern scene, but thoroughly inconsequent and muddled when it comes to philosophising on the basis of his own observations. For it just doesn't follow from the fact that we are living through an age of widespread illusion and disinformation that *therefore* all questions of truth drop out of the picture. (Norris, 1990: 140)

It is no longer possible for us to see through the appearance of, for instance, a 'free market' to the structuring 'real relations' beneath (e.g. class conflict and the expropriation by capital of surplus value). Instead, signs begin increasingly to take on a life of their own referring not to a real world outside themselves but to their own reality – the system that produces the signs. (Hebdige, 1990: 141)

Post-communism

A communist society is one that attempts to base itself upon the ideals outlined by Marx. However, contrary to the views of many Marxists, such regimes were seen as anti-democratic with rigid state control over areas of social life.

The anti-communist rebellion started in 1989 and was most apparent in Eastern Europe. In August 1991, Latvia, Lithuania, Estonia and Georgia became independent sovereign states. In addition, communist regimes had been overthrown in Poland, Bulgaria, Czechoslovakia, East Germany, Hungary and Romania, and four of the six republics that made up Yugoslavia had non-communist governments. Communists were also falling from power in the rest of the world: Benin, Mongolia, Ethiopia, Mozambique, Angola and Congo, to name a few. By December 1991, the Soviet Union itself had ceased to exist. Finally, the anticommunist movement was brought to an end in China in June 1989 by a massacre of protesters at Tiananmen Square in Beijing and the imposition of martial law.

Bauman (1992) argues that communism pushed the project of modernity to its very limits. It involved grand social engineering projects that attempted to control nature in the perceived interests of the working class. However, individuals within the communist societies wanted to share in the 'lavish consumption enjoyed under capitalist auspices': 'It was the postmodern, narcissistic culture of self-enhancement, self-enjoyment, instant gratification and life defined in terms of consumer styles that finally exposed the obsoleteness of the "steel per head" philosophy stubbornly preached and practised under communism' (Bauman, 1992: 179).

In other words, communism collapsed because people behind the Iron Curtain wanted to participate in the processes of making unhindered and highly personal lifestyle choices which people in the West enjoyed. Consumer culture brings with it pleasure. In the former Soviet Union, state socialism may have pushed modern rationality to its very limits, but it could never understand the pleasure of shopping!

John A. Hall (1994) argues that sociologists have 'largely failed to understand the collapse of state socialism' (1994: 525). In addition, he suggests that a 'variety of regimes will follow the immediate post-communist period' (1994: 538). The break was made early by some post-communist countries, such as Slovenia, which also has close links with Austria and is the former communist country most likely to gain European Union membership. The Baltic States could further develop their links with Scandinavia. These countries have managed to avoid the 'symbolic politics' of nationalism and have made a speedy transition to liberal democracy.

In contrast, most post-communist societies have so far had great difficulty in constructing a constitutional political system, with legitimacy in its legal and political rules. This lack of legitimacy creates a political vacuum. As Hall suggests, 'Civil society has not yet been born' (1994: 537).

Political vacuums tend to be highly unstable. Individuals in post-communist societies exhibit the following characteristics:

○ No fixed identity
○ A loss of trust in possible political arrangements
○ A loss of faith in elections as shown in low turnout in voting, as in Poland and Hungary
○ An inability to cooperate politically

These factors have created a democratic deficit in post-communist societies. In other words, the lack of trust and cooperation is so great that people are unable to generate the 'volitions', the feeling states – to be discussed in Area 5, 'Pluralism and Political Parties' – that are needed to formulate an agreed set of rules about how to organise a democratic society with competing political parties. As Hall makes clear, 'It is hard to take a venal and weak state and to turn it into a body capable of co-ordinating and co-operating with society' (1994: 537).

This situation is made worse, according to Hall, because – except for the case of the reunification of Germany – North America and Western Europe have chosen to have little or no active involvement in the reconstruction of post-communist societies. The end result is that the political vacuum is filled by nationalism, a violent and highly emotionally charged ideology that claims that one's country is always right.

Nationalism

Nationalism is a return to the 'local', by which we mean a respect for local roots. Nationalism is a counter-politics of the local in which people attempt to maintain or assert their local identity. Nationalism has become synonymous with intolerance, inhumanity and violence.

Giddens on nationalism

Giddens (1981) makes a distinction between the nation-state and nationalism – although both are European in origin. The nation-state is essentially an institution, what Giddens terms the dominant 'power container', whereas nationalism is a psychological phenomenon 'involving felt needs and dispositions' that 'feeds upon, or represents an attenuated form of ... primordial sentiments' (1981: 193). Therefore, 'nationalism is not merely a set of symbols and beliefs force fed to an unwilling or indifferent population' (1981: 192).

For Giddens, the foundations of everyday life in the modern world are built upon routines. If the security which these routines give is broken in some way, as by any form of 'radical social disruption', individuals can become attracted to the security that nationalistic symbols provide, most notably when this is associated with strong leadership. For Giddens, nationalism can provide reassurance for 'repressed anxieties' which are primitive in nature.

What is significant for social and political theory about the collapse of the Soviet Union and other communist societies? Most importantly, it is that the people who live in these countries appeared to have lost faith in both socialism as a form of society and in the ability of the Marxist analysis to describe and explain the world. However, a number of writers have attempted to maintain the credibility of the Marxist analysis in the face of the postmodern condition; for example, we shall look at the work of Ernesto Laclau and Chantal Mouffe (1984) and Fredric Jameson (1991).

Post-Marxist approaches

Laclau and Mouffe provide one of the most influential of the post-Marxist analyses. In their book *Hegemony and Socialist Strategy* (1984), they cast doubt upon the whole Marxist tradition, claiming that its 'totalising' logic – in other words, its attempt to theorise about the whole of society – is both flawed and anti-democratic. In contrast, they argue that society is highly pluralistic in nature, and that people have an identity that is independent of economic forces. New Social Movements provide the basis for bringing about social change and a source from which individuals can build an identity. Marxists took up many of these ideas in the 1990s.

Fredric Jameson

For Fredric Jameson (1991), postmodernity is at the end of the process of modernisation. What he finds striking about the postmodern condition is the way in which many diverse articles, objects and ideas come together into a new 'discursive genre', or distinct perspective or notion of what reality consists of. Postmodernism is a 'systemic modification of capitalism itself' (Jameson, 1991: xii). Capitalism has gone through a radical change and is now built upon assumptions that Marx was unaware of in the nineteenth century. This distinct stage in capitalism is described by Jameson as a 'schizophrenic present', by which he means that there is not one accepted theory of what reality consists of but many, and this represents a significant break with the modernity of late capitalism. Society appears to be very different, but in its essential features it is still the same; postmodernity is a capitalist society with more choice of commodities, ideas and lifestyles.

Unlike most postmodern writers who reject Marxism, Fredric Jameson has attempted to absorb postmodern insights into the Marxist analysis. Jameson sees postmodernity as the third great stage in the global expansion of capitalism. These stages were as follows:

- The first stage was the 'national market', in which we have capitalism in one country but limited international trade
- The second stage was the 'older imperialist system', in which countries were colonised for economic reasons
- The third stage is postmodernity, viewed as a historic socio-economic reality

Jameson sees postmodernity as a 'broad cultural logic', a new stage in the cultural development of capitalism that has new forms of consciousness, and, as we suggested in Area 3, is dominated by fragmentation, pastiche and simulacra. For Jameson, postmodern culture has a high level of class content. However, Jameson departs from the fundamental presuppositions of the Marxist analysis, in that he rejects the distinction between 'base' and 'superstructure' that we outlined above. In the postmodern condition, we need to think about cultural phenomena before we think about the economy; in this sense, contrary to the traditional Marxist analysis, 'superstructure' becomes more important than the 'economic base' as the factor bringing about social change. Moreover, the superstructure is a source of conflict and the basis for formulating radical political positions. In Jameson's eyes, the relationship between base and superstructure is no longer coherent in the way that Marx described, and this is partly because, in the postmodern condition, people feel that nature has been abolished. Everything is cultural and is understood by reference to earlier cultural products (you may notice how Stephen Spielberg's films often refer to Saturday morning cartoons).

Jameson's account of this new stage of capitalism has the following characteristics:

- A new depth, which is found in both current social theory and in the new culture of the simulacrum
- A weakening of historicity, or, in other words, of our idea of history, both in our relationship to public history and in the new forms of our personal lives
- A new 'schizophrenic' structure which inclines us towards new types of syntax or syntagmatic relationship, especially in the more short-lived arts, such as popular music
- A whole new type of emotional foundation for people
- The deep and creative relationship of the above points to new technology

- A completely new world economic system
- A confusing new deregulated space in the world for multinational capital to do as it pleases, outside the control of governments

In contrast to Lyotard (1984), whom we discussed in Area 3, Jameson argues that grand narratives have not evaporated or otherwise gone away. Moreover, for Jameson, it is still possible to view the world in terms of class struggle. All areas of personal and social life, he argues, have become dependent upon commodities, as advertising makes people feel that they can be happy only through consumption. Jameson goes on to argue that the fragmentation of the working class through the development of new occupations and the deskilling of others has not altered the organisation of class relations or politics.

However, there is a need for what Jameson calls 'cognitive mapping'. Individuals are unable to place themselves within the network of classes that make up capitalism; they are unable to define themselves within, or as part of, a collectivity that has a class identity. Radical politics is about cognitive mapping, through which people are able to define their place in the world. Novels could provide such cognitive maps, helping people to define their place in the world and formulating political demands. Within the postmodern condition, radical politics is built upon the activity of New Social Movements (which we shall discuss at some length in a later area). Radical politics is no longer about the proletariat but about finding commonality and building alliances between groups who have experienced oppression within capitalism, such as women, ethnic minorities, gays and lesbians, etc.

What is the cognitive map meant to do? Jameson's answer is far from clear: the map is meant 'to enable a situational representation on the part of the individual subject to that vaster and properly unrepresentable totality which is the ensemble of society's structures as a whole' (1991: 51). In other words, cognitive mapping gives us a heightened sense of our place in the global system. This involves the mapping of the social space in terms of our class position and where we stand in both a national and international context, and how we view our individual social relationships in terms of class. This process should raise in our minds practical political issues that prompt us to take political action.

An example of cognitive mapping?

The problem here is that the groups that Jameson has in mind, women, ethnic groups gays, etc., may have little if anything in common with each other, and could also be in conflict with each other. Women can be racist, ethnic minorities can be homophobic, etc. Moreover, the oppression that these groups may experience often predates capitalism, and, as such, may have little or nothing to do with the existence of capitalism. In addition, these groups may favour a form of capitalism which is deep into the postmodern condition, where individuals are free to define and redefine themselves in any way they wish: sexually, ethnically, morally, or whatever.

In addition, Jameson also redefines the relationships contained within the 'labour theory of value' as a 'linguistic account'. In the traditional Marxist analysis of the labour theory of value which we have outlined, the value of very different things (e.g. hammers, linen, television sets) will still be the same if they contain the same amount of labour power. In Jameson's view, 'value' emerges as something else, independent of the labour power that went into making it. This 'value' is an 'abstraction' or 'concept', and the market place becomes a place for the 'symbolic exchange' of value.

In other words, 'value' is said by Jameson to be independent of the labour power that produced it. 'Value' is a concept, an idea, and must be explained in cultural terms that are free of the traditional Marxist terminology such as 'economic exploitation'. The significance of this is that Jameson has collapsed the economic base into the superstructure, and suggested that we can make sense of the world only in cultural terms. The economic base, including the relations of production, is irrelevant in the postmodern condition. The economic base is no longer the force which moves history forward; that force is culture and the ideas which generate social change.

It can be noted, then, that, although Jameson does not reject the labour theory of value, he rejects its traditional form, and redefines it as a cultural or super-structural thing. We could argue that he places the labour theory of value outside the traditional Marxist analysis.

Can Jameson be described as a Marxist?

Jameson rejects the traditional Marxist view of the following:

- The nature of class
- The nature of class conflict
- The role of the economic base
- The role of the superstructure
- The source of ideas, culture and ideology

Alex Callinicos on postmodernism and socialism

In contrast to Jameson, Alex Callinicos (1991) argues that there has been no radical break with modernity, and that the notion of postmodernism is politically or ideologically motivated. It is a right-wing attempt to save capitalism by diverting attention away from the class struggle. In addition, he points to the many contradictions contained within the contributions of postmodern writers:

Postmodernism corresponds to a new historical stage of social development (Lyotard) or it doesn't (Lyotard again). Postmodern art is a continuation of (Lyotard) or a break from (Jencks) modernism. Joyce is a modernist (Jameson) or a postmodernist (Lyotard). Postmodernism turns its back on social revolution, but then practitioners and advocates of a revolutionary art like Breton and Benjamin are claimed as precursors. (Callinicos in *The Polity Reader in Social Theory*, 1994: 384)

He then goes on to quote approvingly the comment that postmodernism is: 'another of those period descriptions that help you to take a view of the past suitable to whatever it is you want' (Callinicos in *The Polity Reader in Social Theory*, 1994: 384).

In *The Revenge of History: Marxism and the East European Revolutions* (1991), Callinicos attempts to outline what he sees as the implications for socialism of the collapse of Stalinism, the doctrine named after the Soviet dictator Joseph Stalin, who maintained his own rule by 'liquidating' people who were seen as a threat to his domination. Callinicos's argument is that the collapse of Stalinism cannot be used to justify the argument that Marxism is irrelevant to the modern world. In addition, Callinicos points out that as long ago as 1947 socialists such as Tony Cliff had argued that Stalinist regimes such as that of the Soviet Union would be brought down by the working classes. Hence Callinicos argues: 'The East European revolutions and the turmoil in the USSR itself are thus the vindication, rather than the refutation, of the classical Marxist tradition' (1991: 20).

The following passages from Callinicos (1991) outline his position on why the Soviet Union collapsed:

The industrialization of the USSR could only proceed by pursuing economic autarky... that is 'by exploiting the peasants, by concentrating resources of the peasantry in the hands of the state'. (31)

Real wages in 1932 were at most 50 per cent of their 1928 level. If this analysis is correct, then 'socialist' industrialization in the USSR was made possible not simply by the destruction of the peasantry but by the intense exploitation of the very class which in theory ruled the country and was supposed to be the main beneficiary of the changes involved. (32)

Strikes were quite frequent in the period 1928–34 [despite] the very harsh methods used to crush them. (33)

The class structure of the Soviet society was crystallising around the intensive exploitation of the mass of workers and around intensive exploitation of the mass of workers and peasants. (35)

The historical record leaves little doubt of the qualitative difference between Bolshevism and Stalinism. (37)

In the late 1980s, the Soviet leader Mikhail Gorbachev attempted to introduce greater openness and both political and economic reforms of the Soviet system. The economic reforms involved attempting to implant a market mechanism into the state planning systems. In the view of Callinicos, this produced the worst of both systems with little or no benefits.

For Callinicos, a socialist society need not have a Stalinist-style planned economy and an absence of democracy. In a socialist economy, individual workers would direct production, and this would be in the interests of providing people with the consumption that they believed they needed. In addition, claims Callinicos, Soviet democracy could achieve much greater accountability than is possible in liberal democracy, because in a socialist society people are active politically rather than remaining passive. Moreover, people make their political decisions face to face in the workplace, rather than after being lulled into passivity by a mass media which distorts reality in the interests of capitalists. Soviets are groups of workers and may be viewed like multiparty organisations. In this view, socialism is liberating and stresses individual diversity.

Callinicos on Marxism

Marxism is the *only* tradition with the theoretical and political resources needed to confront the issues currently facing us.... It is radically at odds with its monstrous Stalinist distortion.... Marx and his successors developed a perfectly feasible strategy for overthrowing capitalism and constructing a better society in its place. (Callinicos, 1991: 135)

In response to Callinicos's view of postmodernism, we could argue that the lack of any agreement on the basic assumptions of postmodernity is in itself an aspect of postmodernism. However, we could also point out that individual writers within any perspective often disagree about the fundamental concepts of that perspective, and this, as we have seen here, is clearly the case with Marxism.

Karl Mannheim: the transition from the theory of ideology to the sociology of knowledge

Karl Mannheim provides one of the earliest and best-informed critiques of Marxism. Mannheim (1893–1947) is regarded by many as the founder of the sociology of knowledge. In his most influential work *Ideology and Utopia*, (1936), Mannheim argued that there were two distinct meanings of the term 'ideology'. The first is the 'particular conception' of ideology; in this, individuals are sceptical of the opinions and ideas of opponents and believe them to be lying. The second is the 'total conception' of ideology; this originated in the work of Marx and is concerned with the ideology of an age or the ideology of a class.

Mannheim rejects the distinction in Marx between the true consciousness, which is free of ideology, and the false consciousness, in which working-class people are unaware of their true class interests because their ideas and beliefs have been manipulated. In Mannheim's view, all ways of thinking are ideological in nature. In many respects, what Mannheim is describing is similar to thinking about politics; it is not possible to think about politics without taking up a position – in other words, without thinking ideologically. For Mannheim, there are only competing ideological ways of thinking. Therefore, Mannheim uses Marxist concepts against Marxism, and, in this sense, he moves beyond Marx. Once we all come to view ways of thinking as ideological, rather than as true or false, we experience a major shift in our thinking.

The relationship between the criteria of truth (the things that we use to justify to ourselves that we have discovered the truth, such as the scientific method) and the historical situation is mediated by the existential situation. In the modern world, knowledge is said to be *Seinverbundernheit* knowledge. What this means is that knowledge is produced cooperatively by people. This new knowledge also contains an *activistic* element; this means that people have basic interests, such as economic interests, and these interests help individuals play a role in the processes of defining the nature of the world.

Mannheim refers to the notion of cooperative knowledge as a 'synthesis'. The synthesis can be used to organise the economic and political system in the interests of the population. This involves drawing upon all the different political perspectives in order to generate a form of knowledge that is better than any one political perspective. The notion of synthesis is usually associated in Mannheim's work with the idea of a free-floating intelligentsia, a group of intellectuals who are above politics, and who create the synthesis. For a commentary on the intelligentsia in Mannheim's work, see Best (1990: 55–57).

Marxists respond to Mannheim's argument by claiming that it is 'relativist' in nature. In other words, Mannheim is claiming that there is no such thing as objective knowledge or truth, because he is arguing that all ways of thinking are ideological in nature. Mannheim responded to the claim that he was putting forward a relativist position by arguing that his position was 'relationist' in nature rather than 'relativist'; relationism involves producing a dynamic synthesis of partial truths, taken from competing ideologies, rather than denying the existence of truth. The reader may like to note that Richard Rorty has taken up the themes that Mannheim addressed in recent years.

Richard Rorty

Richard Rorty (1989) argues that it is possible to develop a theory which treats both our individual need for self-creation – in other words, the drive to make ourselves how we want to be, often referred to as a 'life narrative' – and our collective need for human solidarity – our need to live together in groups – as equally convincing and proportionate, and yet, at the same time, as distinct. He defines his key figures as 'liberal' – 'people who think that cruelty is the worst thing we do' (Rorty, 1989: xv) and 'ironist' – 'the sort of person who faces up to the contingency of his or her own central beliefs and desires'. In other words, 'ironists' are aware that their core convictions and aspirations are related to the circumstances that they choose to place themselves in. The 'liberal ironist' is, then, a person who wishes to end the suffering and humiliation of other human beings; a person who is moved by the sight of starving people, for example.

In Rorty's view, human solidarity is something which we, as people, have to accomplish; it is not simply 'given'. In other words, solidarity is created, not discovered; and a key element of this accomplishment is our ability to see 'others' not as strange people whom we can marginalise, but as fellow human beings who can feel pain. The task of bringing about a change in our perception of 'the other' is not one for theory, but a task for ethnographers, who observe and record information about people in their natural settings; docudrama makers; and especially novelists. Works of fiction can show us the kind of cruelty we are able to inflict upon other humans and at the same give us an opportunity to redefine ourselves.

At the end of the eighteenth century, intellectuals across Europe started to accept the notion that 'truth' was something to be created rather than discovered. This was highly significant for politics because, as a consequence, it meant that humans were capable of creating forms of society that were previously unknown. Rorty is not suggesting that there is no truth.

However, Rorty makes a distinction between the two statements 'the world is out there' and 'the truth is out there'. The first statement suggests that the world is a 'thing' which exists independently of human thought. The world was created without the use of the mental processes of human beings. In contrast, the statement that 'the truth is out there' is not acceptable, because individual people create the truth. The truth is built up of sentences constructed by people and used to describe and explain the world. The sentences that we devise to explain and describe the world can be either true or false, but they are only there in time and space because we place them there. Truth is a property of any sentence. As Rorty explains, 'only sentences can be true, and [it is clear] that human beings make truths by making languages in which to phrase sentences' (1989: 9).

We can outline Rorty's argument as follows:

○ Truth is a characteristic of sentences
○ Sentences can exist only if vocabularies exist first
○ Vocabularies are created by human beings
○ Hence it follows that, so too are truths created by human beings
○ There is no truth other than the truth that we create by the use of our language

In addition, the human self is also created by vocabulary. The traditional view of the self was that we had a 'core self' which held beliefs and desires. These beliefs and desires were expressed by the self if and when the self thought it was appropriate to do so. The views expressed by the self could be criticised on the grounds that they did not agree with reality. Rorty's argument is that the core of the self is a network of beliefs and desires; and just as a truth statement is a human creation dependent upon sentences and in the last analysis upon vocabulary, so, too, is the self. The self is made and it is a linguistic entity. In getting to know ourselves, we come to accept that we cannot discover a 'true' self, but we can create a self. Moreover, in dealing with the situations that individual selves find themselves in, we have to create a new language, upon which our own selves will be built.

However, Christopher Norris, in his book *Uncritical Theory: Post-Modernism, Intellectuals and the Gulf War* (1992), casts doubt upon Rorty's conception of truth. From a left-wing perspective, Norris argues that, for Rorty, there is no reality or truth except what counts as such within an 'interpretative community'. This makes it impossible to challenge the validity of any statement by looking at historical evidence, factual evidence or ethical principles; to challenge, for example, the 'just war' principles of the USA and its allies in the Gulf War. For Norris, Rorty's postmodernism is another version of the 'end of ideology' thesis of the 1950s. The end of ideology suggested that the USA was the nearest thing we have to the perfect society because the USA had moved beyond ideological conflicts. People in the USA were all agreed on how to organise their society; they disagree only about the details of specific policies. From this point of view, Rorty is simply an apologist for American aggression and expansion.

What is wrong with Marxism?: Giddens's critique of Marxism

- Marxists do not have a satisfactory account of power; in particular, they have no real analysis of military power or of the use of violence by individuals
- Within the Marxist analysis there is no real account of administrative power or what is distinctive about administrative power within the nation-state
- Marxists do not take into account non-economic sources
- Marxists do not take into account conflicts which are not related to class issues
- Marxists do not take into account non-class-based politics – such as the Green movement or gender politics

Classical elite theory

The anti-democratic classical elite theorists assume that in any political system a few will lead and the majority will be led. In other words, there is a small self-conscious elite with power and the masses who have very little power. The assumption is that all societies have broadly this type of social structure, where *oligarchy* (the rule of the few) is inevitable. In addition, most elite theorists view the masses as being psychologically incapable of holding power and having an instinctual need to be dominated. Only the elite can satisfy that need; Robert Michels (1911) has termed this 'the iron law of oligarchy'. For this reason, democracy is not a realistic alternative for the elite theorist.

Pareto

Vilfredo Pareto (1847–1939) starts his analysis with a theory of non-logical actions; there are six basic human drives or instincts, which he terms 'residues'. The residues are manipulated by the elite through the use of four political strategies that Pareto terms 'Derivations'. The six residues are as follows:

○ *Residues of combination*. All people have an instinct to live together in groups.
○ *Persistence of aggregates*. Once groups are established people have an instinctual need to maintain them.
○ *Sentiments of activity*. People attempt to reinforce the bonds that hold groups together by forming rituals, such as those we find in religions.
○ *Residues of sociality*. People have a drive for uniformity and an instinctual hostility to outsiders.
○ *Self-preservation*. Individuals have an instinct to maintain their own security, property and social position.
○ *Sexuality*. Sexuality has a role to play in maintaining the social bonds of society.

The four derivations are as follows:

○ *Simple assertion*. People in elite positions simply state that something is right, and this is accepted as a satisfactory justification.
○ *Authority*. The masses accept what they are told by the elite because they accept the latter's position as legitimate.
○ *Sentiments or principles*. The masses accept what they are told by the elite because they believe the latter are conforming to public opinion.
○ *Verbal proofs*. The masses are persuaded to behave in a particular way, or to accept a belief, by the convincing arguments of the elite.

For Pareto, the elite can behave as either foxes or lions; in other words, the elite can choose to rule by cunning or by force.

Mosca

Like Pareto, Gaetano Mosca (1858–1911) believed that society could be divided into a small, well-organised elite with its own common purpose and the masses, who have no organisation and no common purpose. There are several types of elite groups, such as military, priestly, the wealthy and landowners. Moreover, although the elite may have a monopoly on legitimate violence, they do not hold their position by the use of violence. The elite attempt to justify their rule by political theories based upon common sense or by ethical systems that provide the elite with their source of legitimacy.

For Mosca, elites are essential to the continuation of civilisation. Within any society, there are a number of conflicting and competing social forces, and the stability of a society can be measured by the ability of the elite to control these social forces. The elite attempt to do this by imposing a political formula. This is a principle that, if accepted by the population, should bring political stability. In Britain such a political formula would be the principle of 'government by due process of law'.

Pareto may be criticised for not clearly defining his key terms; for example, a residue can be a sentiment, an instinct or a principle. The theory of non-logical actions is diminished by this inability to be clear on these terms. In addition, he provides no analysis of the structure of institutions, and discusses very few practical political situations. Mosca is also vague about many of his key terms, such as the idea of a social force; in addition, he, too, does not give many examples from the everyday practice of politics. However, what many people find offensive about elite theory is that it has been used to justify fascism.

Before we move on, it might be useful to outline the similarities and differences between Marxism and elite theory, as many students wrongly assume that they are one and the same. The similarities are as follows:

- Both Marxism and elite theory expound the existence of a small ruling class that holds power, and a large mass of powerless people.
- Both Marxism and elite theory are zero-sum conceptions of power; in other words, they assume that there is a fixed amount of power in society.
- Both Marxism and elite theory assume that the ruling class maintains its power by manipulating the ideas of the powerless.

The differences are as follows:

- In the Marxist analysis, the ruling class is always an economic class; in elite theory this is not the case.
- Marxism is a very optimistic theory – the powerless will one day rise up and take power. In elite theory, oligarchy (the rule of the few) is inevitable.
- In the Marxist analysis, the relationship between the bourgeoisie and the proletariat is one of economic exploitation. In contrast, in elite theory, the masses have a psychological need to be dominated.
- Marxism, is used as a political justification for socialism. In contrast, elite theory is used as a political justification for fascism.

C. Wright Mills – 'the power elite'

One of the most influential elite theorists of the twentieth century is C. Wright Mills, whose book *The Power Elite* (1956) introduced a number of new elements into the classical elite theory of Pareto and Mosca. With the USA as his focus, Mills argues that national power resides in three domains: the economic, the political, and the military. Top decision making is becoming more centralised and coordinated between these three domains. However, the elite are not dependent upon the structures in themselves for their power; if the elite so decide, they can break up and restructure the institutions. It is also important to point out that, in contrast to Marx, Mills holds that political and military power cannot be reduced to economic power; all three are distinct. The elite is said to have 'more of what there is to have ... money, power and prestige' (Mills, 1956: 9). Moreover, these factors are cumulative; the more that you have of them, the more you get. In terms of power, Mills takes his lead from Max Weber and argues that the powerful are those 'who are able to realise their will, even if others resist it' (Mills, 1956: 9).

The power elite is something compact in both a social and psychological sense. The members of the elite know that they share a range of characteristics. One of the novel and most interesting features of Mills's analysis is his discussion of prestige. Although Mills suggests that the power elite are never fully visible, prestige is linked to the notion of celebrity. Celebrities are people who need no introduction; they are recognised because they are well known and well publicised. Celebrities are 'stars'. Television personalities are seen at gatherings with top politicians, members of royal families and leading industrialists. What is significant for Mills is the fact that politicians compete for the same attention; in effect, they aspire to become celebrities. It was for this reason that Tony Blair was seen heading a football with the then Newcastle United manager, Kevin Keegan, during the 1997 general election campaign, or that Bill Clinton was seen playing sax with a jazz/rock band in the 1996 presidential campaign. It is not simply 'psychological gratification' that elite figures are searching for. Prestige brings with it a unifying function; it supports power by transforming elite power into authority.

The media has a significant role to play in transforming the population from a 'public' into a 'mass'; this is another key factor in Mills's analysis. What do we understand by 'the public'? This is probably the key element in any theory of pluralistic democracy. Mills's definition of the 'public' includes the following attributes:

- Expressing opinions and receiving opinions
- Immediate and effective response to any opinion expressed
- Opinions formed by discussion
- Outlets for effective action
- Communities with a high degree of independence of authoritative institutions

In contrast, the 'mass' is characterized by:

- Little expression or sharing of opinions
- People receiving opinions and impressions from the media
- Few effective channels for people's response
- No independence of authoritative institutions

In contrast to Charles Cooley's (1909) optimistic view that the media enhances democracy and individualism by breaking down local prejudices, Mills argues that the media creates a form of 'psychological illiteracy'. Individual people do not trust even their own experiences, unless the media confirms them. Mills goes on to argue that the media is crucial for the creation of each person's self-image, making the following points:

o   The media gives people an identity
o   The media gives people aspirations
o   The media informs people how to fulfil those aspirations
o   The media gives people an escape from their feelings

In the modern metropolitan society, people no longer encounter real disagreements or contrasting viewpoints, or discuss genuine issues. People are a mass; they do no formulate their own ideas or desires. These things are placed into people by the media. In the last analysis, this process of massification makes people anxious and isolated, and deprives them of goals. As Mills explains:

> The top of modern American society is increasingly unified, and often seems wilfully co-ordinated: at the top there has emerged an elite of power. The middle levels are a drifting set of stalemated, balancing forces: the middle does not link the bottom with the top. The bottom of this society is politically fragmented and even as a passive fact, increasingly powerless: at the bottom there is emerging a mass society (Mills, 1956: 324).

Elite theory: developments in the 1990s

Since the publication of Mills's *The Power Elite*, most academics in Europe and North America, apart from a number of 'modernisation' theorists, have turned away from the use of elite theory as an explanation for how political systems work. The reason for this shift in academic choice of explanation is that elite theory has an association with fascism and justifications of fascism or other forms of unpleasant political practice. For example, consider the following passage:

> Kemalism [the Westernising/modernising ideology of the first Turkish leader Mustafa Kemal (Atatürk) in the 1920s] was an ideology imposed on people from above. Its self-declared mission was to revolutionize the society for the good of the people. For the good of a backward and uncivilised people, however, a people whose commitment to progress and civilisation could not be relied on – could not be trusted to take part in its own revolution. (adapted from Kevin Robins, 'Interrupting identities: Turkey/Europe', in Hall and du Gay, 1996: 70)

For this reason, most academics do not wish to be associated with elite theory. However, one researcher who has attempted to make use of the key concept of elite theory in an effort to understand political situations is Beng-Huat Chua.

Beng-Huat Chua

Beng-Huat Chua (1995) looks at the way in which the government of Singapore, initially under the control of the People's Action Party in the 1960s, successfully spread the 'non-ideological ideology of pragmatism', based upon Confucianism, to the wider population. This non-ideology of pragmatism/Confucianism (pragmatism is a political ideology which makes no assumptions about the world) became transformed into the common-sense notion of the pursuit of further financial reward. This process of spreading issues within Singapore is described by Chua as 'unavoidably elitist' (1995: 36). Chua discusses this process of elite dissemination in Weberian terms. Pragmatism/Confucianism becomes common sense for the people of Singapore in the form of Asian values such as thrift, industry and respectful devotion. These adopted 'Asian' values stand in sharp contrast to Western values. Chua describes this with reference to the Weberian notion of *Zweckrational*, a form of 'instrumental rationality' that is not restricted to public life, but which reaches into people's personal lives as well. The people of Singapore are concerned with improving their own personal living, standards as Chua makes clear:

> While specific terms may change, discourses of culture and morality were always cast in terms of the 'immoral West' against the 'moral East'. ... The language of Prime Minister Goh Chok Tong clearly reflects his invocation of the dichotomous discourse of Orientalism, in reverse. According to him, 'bad Western values are: 'Me first, society second; the trend towards promiscuity, fun-loving, free-loving kind of society' ... and, of course, the 'good Eastern values' are all the opposite terms, above all 'society first, me second'. (Chua, 1995: 158)

The notion of instrumental rationality in everyday life is discussed later in Area 6 'New Social Movements', when we look at Jurgen Habermas (1976).

Beng-Huat Chua and the 'non-ideological ideology of pragmatism': Confucianisation of Asia

Confucianism is said to be the cultural root of the people of Japan, Korea, Taiwan, Hong Kong and Singapore, the loci of ascendancy of Asian capitalism. The Confucian package is said to contain the following unchanging elements: hard work, emphasis on education, pragmatism, self-discipline, familial orientation and collectivism. ... Confucianism is a philosophical justification of government by benevolent bureaucracy under a virtuous ruler; a leader's benevolent rule is reciprocated by the loyalty and obedience of his subjects; in short, benevolence ensures harmony and obedience within stratified and unequal social relations. (Beng-Huat Chua, 1995: 151)

Area Summary

In this area we have compared and contrasted the Marxist theory of power with the elite theories of power. Classical elite theory, such as that of Vilfredo Pareto and Gaetano Mosca, was seen as a justification for fascism; and their analyses largely ignored economic factors. Later

continued

elite theory by C. Wright Mills is an attempt to redefine the earlier position by introducing an economic dimension and notions such as celebrity. The Marxist conception of power is economic in nature, and Marxists describe how that power is legitimised in capitalism through the use of ideology, which takes the form of a false consciousness. For Marxists, ideology is a process which actively involves the thinker, but the real motive forces behind those thoughts are unknown to the thinker – this is the nature of ideology for the Marxist.

We looked at the contribution that later Marxists have made to our understanding of the state. In addition, we assessed the effect of the postmodern condition in bringing about the end of communist regimes across the world. However, a number of Marxists, such as Fredric Jameson and Alec Callinicos, have attempted to maintain the validity of the Marxist analysis in the face of the postmodern condition. It is questionable whether we can still view Jameson as a Marxist, as he appears to redefine all the key Marxist concepts in a 'cultural' form. In contrast, Callinicos views the collapse of communist regimes in the world as a great opportunity for Marxism; with the world now largely free from Stalinism, true Marxism can develop.

We also looked at a number of 'modernist' critiques of Marxism and its underlying assumptions in the work of Karl Mannheim, Richard Rorty and Anthony Giddens. Finally, we looked at the claim that we now live in a post-class society, a theme that we shall return to in later areas.

References

Abercrombie, N., Turner, B. and Hill, S. (1980) *The Dominant Ideology Thesis*. London: Allen and Unwin.

Ashley, D. (1997) *History Without a Subject: The Postmodern Condition*. Boulder, CO: Westview Press.

Baudrillard, J. (1973) *The Mirror of Production*. Paris: Gallimard.

Bauman, Z. (1992) *Intimations of Postmodernity*. London: Routledge.

Ben-Huat, C. (1995) *Communitarian Ideology and Democracy in Singapore*. London: Routledge.

Best, S. (1990) 'Karl Mannheim: the myth of the free-floating intelligentsia', *Social Science Teacher* (Spring).

Best, S. (1998) 'Zygmunt Bauman: personal reflections within the mainstream of modernity' *British Journal of Sociology* 49(2): 311–320.

Best, S. (1997) 'Power and politics', in Nik Jorgensen (eds), *Sociology: An Interactive approach*. London: Collins Educational.

Best, S., Griffiths, J. and Hope, T. (2000) *Active Sociology*. Harlow: Longman.

Callinicos, A. (1991) *The Revenge of History: Marxism and the East European Revolutions*. Cambridge: Polity.

Coates, D. (1984) *The Context of British Politics*. London: Hutchinson.

Cooley, C.H. (1909) *Social Organisation*. New York: Scribner.

Giddens, A. (1981) *A Contemporary Critique of Historical Materialism*. Vol. 1. *Power, Property and the State*. Berkeley and Los Angeles, CA: University of California Press.

Gramsci, A. (1977) *The Modern Prince*. New York: International Publishers.

Hall, J. (1994) 'After the fall: an analysis of post-communism', *British Journal of Sociology*, 45(4): 525–543

Hebdige, D. (1990) in R. Boyne and A. Rattansi (eds), *Postmodernism and Society*. London: Sage.

Jameson, F. (1991) *Postmodernism: or the Cultural Logic of Late Capitalism*. London: Verso.

Laclau, E. and Mouffe, C. (1984) *Hegemony and Socialist Strategy*. London: Routledge.

Lyotard, J.F. (1984) *The Postmodern Condition: A Report on Knowledge*. Minneapolis, MN: University of Minnesota Press.

Mannheim, K. (1960; first published 1936) *Ideology and Utopia*. London: Routledge.

Marx, K. (1976; first published 1867) *Capital: A Critique of Political Economy*. London: Penguin in association with *New Left Review*.

Michels, R. (1949; first published 1911) *Political Parties*. Glencoe: The Free Press.

Miliband, R. (1973; first published 1969) *The State in Capitalist Society*. London: Quartet.

Mills, C.W. (1956) *The Power Elite*. Oxford: Oxford University Press.

Mosca, G. (1939) *The Ruling Class*. New York: McGraw-Hill.

Norris, C. (1990) in R. Boyne and A. Rattansi (eds), *Postmodernism and Society*. London: Sage.

Norris, C. (1992) *Uncritical Theory: Post-Modernism, Intellectuals and the Gulf War*. London: Lawrence and Wishart.

Pareto, V. (1935) *The Mind and Society: A Treatise on General Sociology*. London: Jonathan Cape.

Poulantzas, N. (1973) *Political Power and Social Classes*. London: Verso.

Robins, K. (1996) 'Interrupting Identities: Turkey/Europe', in S. Hall and P. Du Gay (eds), *Questions of Cultural Identity*. London: Sage.

Rorty, R. (1989) *Irony, Contingency and Solidarity*. Cambridge: Cambridge University Press.

Rorty, R. (1998) *Truth and Progress: Philosophical Papers*. Vol. III. Cambridge: Cambridge University Press.

The Polity Reader in Social Theory. (1994) Cambridge: Polity.

Willis, P. (1977) *Learning to Labour*. London: Saxon House.

5

Pluralism and Political Parties

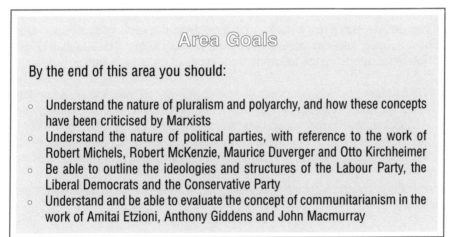

Area Goals

By the end of this area you should:

○ Understand the nature of pluralism and polyarchy, and how these concepts have been criticised by Marxists
○ Understand the nature of political parties, with reference to the work of Robert Michels, Robert McKenzie, Maurice Duverger and Otto Kirchheimer
○ Be able to outline the ideologies and structures of the Labour Party, the Liberal Democrats and the Conservative Party
○ Understand and be able to evaluate the concept of communitarianism in the work of Amitai Etzioni, Anthony Giddens and John Macmurray

Pluralism describes a condition within a community in which power is widely shared among a multiplicity of groups and organisations, all of whom have their own sectional interests, and their own views of the world and policies on how to achieve their objectives. In sharp contrast to both Marxist and elite theories of power, power for the pluralist is widely shared within a society. In addition, unlike Marxist and elite theories, pluralism is not a 'zero-sum' conception of power. For the pluralist, the amount of power in society is not fixed, but can expand. For the

Marxist, in contrast, if the bourgeoisie gain power, then the proletariat must have lost some power; similarly, if the proletariat gain some power, then the bourgeoisie must have lost some power. In other words, for the pluralist, the amount of power in society is not fixed. As shown very clearly in the work of Talcott Parsons (1951), every social action involves the use of power, because every social action makes a difference in the world. For example, whatever I do will affect other people in some way, albeit in only a minor fashion. Social actions are carried out within roles; for example, your reading this book may be within your role as student. Therefore, if the number of social roles within a social system were to increase, the amount of power within that social system would increase. Similarly, if the number of social roles were to decrease within a social system, the amount of power within that social system would decrease.

The sociology of citizenship

According to Bryan Turner (1999), societies face two contradictory principles. Firstly, there are issues in relation to scarcity, which result in social structures that exclude people, as in forms of stratification such as class; secondly, there is the need for solidarity.

The debate about the nature of citizenship in the civil, political and social spheres usually takes its starting point from the sociologist T.H. Marshall (1964). For Marshall, there are the following three types of citizenship rights:

- Civil rights or our legal citizenship – rights associated with individual freedom, such as the right to free speech, to own property and to equality before the law
- Political rights – rights associated with democracy, such as the right to vote
- Social rights – mainly our welfare rights, such as the right to education, health care and social security, the concepts that underpinned the welfare state

Marshall recognised that those citizenship rights were not based upon a universal standard:

> Citizenship is a status bestowed on those who are full members of a community. All who possess the status are equal with respect to the rights and duties with which the status is endowed. There is no universal principle that determines what those rights and duties shall be, but societies in which citizenship is a developing institution create an image of an ideal citizenship against which achievement can be measured and towards which aspiration can be directed. The urge forward along the path thus plotted is an urge towards a fuller measure of equality, an enrichment of the stuff of which the status is made and an increase in the number of those on whom the status is bestowed. Social class, on the other hand, is a system of inequality. And it too, like citizenship, can be based on a set of ideals, beliefs and values. It is therefore reasonable to expect that the impact of citizenship on social class should take the form of a conflict between opposing principles. (Marshall, 1964: 84)

Marshall attempted to create a form of citizenship that took into account the two contradictory principles of scarcity and the need for solidarity. He defined citizenship as a collection of rights that provided the individual with a formal legal identity. However, at the same time, 'citizenship' institutions control the access of individuals to scarce resources; they determine who gets social security, health care, housing, etc. Turner argues that an adequate understanding of the problems surrounding issues of citizenship in contemporary societies must go well beyond Marshall's framework.

Citizenship provides not only criteria for inclusion and exclusion of people from the wider society, but also the foundation for a cultural and political identity. We have moved from a discussion of inclusion and exclusion in relation to class advantages to disputes about sexual identity, gay rights, asylum seeking, residence and criteria for membership of a political community.

Turner's criticisms are, firstly, that Marshall's notion of citizenship is 'incomplete' in that he did not regard control over the workplace by the citizen as significant. In other words, Marshall had no conception of 'economic citizenship' based upon industrial democracy. Secondly, Marshall did not take 'cultural rights' into account. In the early part of the twentieth century, many governments attempted to suppress minority languages and force people to speak the majority language. In the latter part of the century, there was a rise in the notion of multiculturalism and a growing recognition that people should not be restricted in their choice of language, religion or other cultural practices. Thirdly, Marshall has been criticised by feminists on the grounds that his work is built upon Fordist assumptions that men go out to work and women stay at home doing domestic work. Marshall also naively assumed that the citizenship rights that we enjoy are both evolutionary and cumulative, as if, once an individual had won a civil or political right, it could not be taken away. Finally, Turner argues that Marshall had a one-dimensional view of citizenship; he did not distinguish between an active citizen and a passive citizen. Some forms of citizenship, such as those that emerged from the French Revolution, were based upon active involvement in social and political struggle; other forms of citizenship, such as those described by Weber, were based upon the idea that citizens select a leader but are otherwise generally passive.

Pluralism

For the pluralist, the state is seen as the rule maker or umpire; in other words, it is conceived as the 'honest broker' that attempts to balance opinions within the community in an effort to strike a balance between the various sectional interests. In addition, there is always political competition and a balance between competing interests.

For Robert Dahl (1961) there are the following four primary patterns of competition within pluralism:

- All active groups, such as political parties and pressure groups, exercising some influence over decision-makers
- Formal democracy, in which competition takes place between organised groups, again, the most often cited examples being political parties
- 'Inclusive hegemony', usually a one-party state, in which we find competition within the state bureaucracy and between party members and party officials
- 'Competitive oligarchy', in which elite groups, such as party leaders or the very wealthy, compete for power

The best-developed form of pluralism is known as '*polyarchy*'. According to Dahl (1961), polyarchy is the government of a state or city by many. The example that Dahl gives is the USA, where, he believes, there is government of the people, for the people and by the people. This contrasts with a monarchy, such as the UK, where people are subjects of the Crown rather that citizens with citizenship rights that the government cannot take away. Polyarchy includes a set of authoritative rules assigned in response to the citizen's wishes. This is necessary for the democratic process to work. The rules guarantee our civil and political rights, which according to Charles Lindblom (1977), include the following:

- Freedom to form and join organisations
- Freedom of expression
- Right to vote
- Eligibility for public office
- Right of political leaders to compete for support
- Right of political leaders to compete for votes
- Free and fair elections (open, honestly conducted, one person one vote) to decide who is to hold the top authority
- Alternative sources of information; free access to information
- Institutions for making government policies that depend upon votes and other expressions of preference; in other words, governments and government departments attempting to carry out whatever policies will help get them re-elected

The rules are based upon '*volitions*', that is, choices that are created by the citizens themselves in consultation with each other.

According to Lindblom, within polyarchy there is a common core of volitions. First, we have simple preference, in which a person holds a view without the need for calculated thought or reason; for example, when a person says, 'I like Blair better than Hague.' Second, we have complex judgement, in which an individual holds a view after some consideration and analysis. For example, a person claims to want closer ties with the European Union after an examination of the relevant policies, issues and consequences. Third, there are moral or ethical rules, as when an individual chooses a view on IVF or abortion on the basis of a moral code. Fourth, there is simple preference between complex judgements, as when an individual chooses between a range of complex judgements with little calculated thought. Lindblom give the example of a person saying, 'No, I don't believe in foreign aid, but don't ask me why' (1977: 135).

According to Anthony Giddens (1985), all nation-states tend towards polyarchy because all governments need to have the consent of the people in order to govern. In a similar fashion, Dahl argues that polyarchy is both a product of the democratising of nation-states and a type of regime. It is characterised by high tolerance of opposition and widespread opportunities to influence the conduct of government. The institutions within polyarchy have evolved in an effort to help democratise the political process.

However, there are a number of criticisms of pluralism and polyarchy. Within this perspective, researchers are concerned only with decision-making, and they ignore the idea of non-decision-making. Thus, those in power have the ability to manipulate which decisions will be made and which will not be made. In addition, pluralists are said to ignore the effects of ideology; in other words, they do not take into account that individuals' ideas, which Lindblom termed volitions, may be manipulated by others more powerful than themselves; notably, by capitalists or the mass media. Dahl has had to accept that the unequal distribution of wealth can sustain an unequal division of political power. In other words, we have the problem of under-represented interests within the system. In particular, Marxists make this criticism, and we shall evaluate it fully below.

Critiques of pluralism

Paul Hirst (1988) outlines the nature of pluralism and polyarchy and evaluates the critiques. Hirst argues that Marxists view pluralism as a 'misdescription of the realities of power'. This Marxist view disregards the inequality of income and wealth that is the key characteristic of Western societies, it focuses on the surface aspects of the political system – the actual process of decision-making and efforts to influence decision-making processes by individuals and groups – rather than on the 'deep' causes, such as class factors.

Misrepresenting pluralism

Three Marxist critics of pluralism, Miliband (1973: 4), Pateman (1970: 15) and Shin'Ya Ono (1965: 61), quote the following sentence from Dahl: 'A central guiding thread of American constitutional development has been the evolution of a political system in which all the active and legitimate groups in the population can make themselves heard at some crucial stage in the process of decision' (Dahl, 1956: 137). However, as Hirst (1988) makes clear, all three critics quote only part of the passage, starting with 'all ...'. Quoting only part of the sentence does significantly change the meaning. As Hirst comments, 'the whole sentence makes clear that this is not a description of a state of affairs, but an aspiration in a process of political development. … It is obvious that the sentence is not merely radically qualified, but that its whole meaning is changed' (Hirst, 1988: 156).

In the critic's eyes, pluralist theory is an apology for inequality and exploitation within capitalism. Marxists assume that if the working class were actually to enter politics, the illusion of the pluralistic democracy, as outlined by Dahl and others, would be broken. However, as Hirst (1988) has made clear, since the end of the nineteenth century in both Europe and North America the working class has played an active role in politics. At a practical level, we could point to the construction of welfare states in many Western societies as evidence of working-class involvement or influence in politics. The Marxist response to this view would be, firstly, that authentic socialist policy is not presented to the electorate, and, secondly, that control of the economy, the political agenda and the means of violence remain in the hands of capitalists.

In the Marxist analysis, a crucial role is given to ideology – the argument that working-class people's ideas and beliefs are manipulated by the bourgeoisie, by institutions such as the educational system, the media and religion. However, according to Hirst, 'The very idea that regularly socialist alternatives *are* presented to the electorate and turned down is impossible to accept as such' (1988: 160). Hirst cites the example of the Communist Party of Great Britain, which has regularly contested elections. In addition, the population is well aware that revolutionary socialism exists as an alternative to capitalism. In other words, as the quote makes clear, people always have the alternative of a socialist party to vote for, but they choose not to. Hirst continues: 'Moreover, authoritarian socialism does exist too and is so actively disliked by most ordinary people that, if they have a choice between it and a minimalist form of democracy, they overwhelmingly choose the latter' (1988: 161).

Even though capitalist society shows a high level of economic inequality and the economically powerful have disproportionate influence over political structure and decision-making, this does not mean that pluralism is an invalid perspective. The ruling class is divided into a number of factions, each with interests of its own; for example, capitalists who work in financial services or the media have interests very different from those of industrial capitalists. In addition, even if we accept the Marxian notion of ideology, this ideology can never be a closed system. The ideology of capitalism will reflect divisions with the capitalist class and therefore can never be all embracing. In other words, unlike a backward, rural and paternalistic society, in the modern capitalist society all adults have rights, and a significant number exercise those rights. This gives working-class people a degree of power and influence over capitalists, irrespective of their economic inequality. Similarly, there are other significant divisions within the modern capitalist society which are non-economic, and which both divide the population and integrate the population across economic divisions: race, gender and regional divisions are cases in point. As you may recall, this was a theme we took up in Areas 3 and 4 when we looked at the relationship between postmodernity and Marxism.

Political parties

Despite the many differences between the main political parties in Britain, they are all mass parties; in other words, the parties attempt to gain the support of the broad mass of the population. In addition, the parties also aim to have the following qualities or features:

- Strong leadership
- A central administration which supervises the party
- A grass roots organisation which mobilises people locally
- An organisation of MPs in Parliament
- An organisation which links the party in Parliament with the party members up and down the country
- An annual conference which gives members a chance to have their say

These points have had a significant impact upon pluralistic theories. According to Lindblom, 'In polyarchal politics, to move, to initiate, or to innovate requires the cooperation of a coalition. To stop or to block a change is a legal privilege to many.' Moreover, as Paul Hirst explains,

> Polyarchy is a system in which a plurality of organisations compete for influence and specifically where formally equal electors have a choice between a number of parties in elections. It leads not to 'majority rule', but to minorities rule: such a polity does not consist of an amorphous citizenry who cast their votes directly for policies, but a highly differentiated body of supporters of organisation who cast their votes for parties. (Hirst, 1988: 166)

Although the Labour and Conservative parties do not make information about their members readily available, Seyd and Whiteley (1992) found, among a number of other things, that the Conservative membership is predominantly at or near retirement age, and the Labour membership is predominantly middle class.

In terms of ideology, there have been significant differences between the two main parties. Under the leadership of Mrs Thatcher between 1975 to 1990, the Conservatives became closely associated with New Right ideas. These included the following:

- An emphasis on personal liberty and personal freedom
- Advocacy of the free market and opposition to state planning
- Popular capitalism – notably privatisation and home ownership
- The promotion of the conventional heterosexual family
- Reduction of public spending
- Giving people incentives to work by lowering both taxes and welfare benefits
- Making people less dependent upon the welfare state

For New Right thinkers, the welfare state removed freedom and responsibility, reduced incentives, produced waste, promoted social grievances and restricted individual freedom. In other words, the welfare state produced a dangerous underclass. John Major did not abandon the Thatcherite politics totally, but moved towards improving standards of service provision in the public sector with his citizens' charter.

Within the Labour Party there has been an uneasy relationship between the 'traditionalists' and the 'modernisers'. The traditionalists want the party to maintain its commitment to public ownership and bringing about greater equality by more government intervention in the free market. However, under Tony Blair's leadership of the party, the traditional socialists have lost influence. Blair's modernisers have moved Labour policy away from traditional socialism towards a more market-oriented position which they believe fits more closely the values and aspiration of the majority of the population. This policy change has been termed 'communitarianism' or 'new realism', and it may have come about because of the decline of the traditional working class or because of the weakening link between social class and political parties. As we shall see in Area 9, there was a growing recognition in the 1980s that 'Old Labour' was not electable. Some commentators have suggested that the society we live in has many 'postmodern' elements. One of the possible consequences of this postmodernisation is that people no longer define themselves in terms of social class. Many people are turning away from traditional class-based political parties and moving towards greater involvement in New Social Movements.

Commentators on the nature of political parties

Robert Michels

Robert Michels has provided major statements about the nature of political parties, influencing Robert McKenzie (1963), Maurice Duverger (1990) and Otto Kirchheimer (1990). As his book *Political Parties* (1911) reveals, Michels, like all other classical elite theorists, is an anti-democratic theorist who assumes that in any political system a few will lead and the majority will be led. In other words, there is a small self-conscious elite with power and a large mass that has very little power. All societies have broadly this type of social structure, rendering oligarchy (the rule of the few) inevitable. In addition, most elite theorists view the mass as psychologically incapable of holding power and having an instinctual need to be dominated. Only the elite can satisfy that need; Michels has termed this 'the iron law of oligarchy'. Therefore, democracy is not a realistic alternative:

> Organisation implies the tendency to oligarchy. In every organisation, whether it is a political party, a professional union, or any other association of the kind, the aristocratic tendency manifests itself very clearly. The mechanism of the organisation, while conferring a solidity of structure, induces serious changes in the organised mass, completely inverting the respective positions of the leaders and the led. As a result of organisation, every party or professional union becomes divided into a minority of directors and a majority of directed. (Michels, 1962: 32)

In other words, as organisations get bigger in size, their power increases, the power of the leader increases and the level of democracy diminishes. The mass holds its leaders in adoration and shows 'perfect docility'; indeed, without leadership, the mass is incapable of taking action. The 'principal means of domination', according to Michels, is found in the 'better instructed minds', of the leaders, especially their ability to make themselves indispensable. Leaders also develop a tendency to isolate themselves from other members of the organisation; leaders form a kind of 'brotherhood' and only allow individuals who accept the leadership point of view to enter. Michels refers to this 'closure' at the top of political parties as 'the transformation of the leaders into a closed caste' (1962: 156); consequently. 'The natural and normal development of the organization will impress upon the most revolutionary of parties an indelible stamp of conservatism' (1962: 162–163). In addition, Michels observes that 'The bureaucratic spirit corrupts character and engenders moral poverty. In every bureaucracy we may observe place hunting, a mania for promotion, and obsequiousness towards those upon whom promotion depends; there is arrogance towards inferiors and servility towards superiors' (1962: 189).

Robert McKenzie

McKenzie attempts to evaluate the work of Michels by looking at the history of the major political parties in Britain. He argues that the modern party system developed as a result of the growth of the electorate from 1832 onwards. According to McKenzie, Michels does not clearly define what he means by 'the iron law of oligarchy'. However, the issue of 'democracy' within political parties is an issue. McKenzie argues that there is 'ample evidence' of the 'technical' and 'psychological' factors that support the 'iron law', such as the power of party leaders to impose their will on the decision-making bodies within their parties. However, he also found that party leaders have been overthrown; for example, Mrs Thatcher was removed from office because the party feared that she would lose the next election. Therefore, any party leadership must hold its supporters.

Michels assumes that a democratic party is a party under the control of its members. In the British political system, MPs must hold themselves accountable to the electorate, not to the members of the party. In addition, there are practical problems in allowing the mass membership to make policy, as issues often emerge quickly and demand a swift response from the party leadership.

McKenzie outlines the functions of the Labour and Conservative Parties in Britain as follows:

- Providing a two-way channel of communication between the leaders of the party leadership and the supporters in the country
- Explaining the position of the party or the government to the supporters in the country
- Informing the party and the government of currents of opinion in the country

- ○ Providing politically active people with opportunities to contribute to policy formation
- ○ Exposing the electorate to political debate and stimulating public interest
- ○ Integrating bodies of opinion, including interest groups, into the political process

However, in the last analysis, according to McKenzie, 'The mass membership is capable of no more than "yes" or "no" responses to initiatives that come from their leaders' (1963: 16).

Maurice Duverger

Duverger identified a number of the organs of the political party. For example, we have the caucus, which is a closed group that runs the party in a fashion similar to the parties described by Michels. Membership of this ruling group is usually by invitation from the caucus itself. Then we have the branch, which is a centralised, hierarchical organisation built upon active local groups. Socialist parties most often adopted this form of organisation, as Duverger explains, 'the choice of the branch by Socialist parties was perfectly natural. They were the first to try and organize the masses, to give them a political education, and to recruit from them the working class elites. ... In contrast to the caucus, the middle class organ of political expression, it seemed the normal organ of political expression for the masses' (Duverger, 1990: 40).

Duverger also distinguished between 'cadre parties' and 'mass parties'. This distinction is based upon structure; the mass party appeals to the public, most notably in terms of the financing of the organisation, whereas the cadre party appeals to 'influential persons'. 'If we define a member as one who signs an undertaking to the party and thereafter regularly pays his subscription, then cadre parties have no members' (Duverger, 1990: 42).

Otto Kirchheimer

Kirchheimer suggests that successful political parties in the modern world move towards 'the catch-all' party. This is a party that attempts to appeal to the majority of people in the population by focusing upon issues that meet the least resistance within the community. An example that Kirchheimer discusses is the French UNR (National Republican Union) under General de Gaulle, who adopted the line of French national purpose and unity. This was 'vague and flexible enough to allow the most variegated interpretation and yet attractive enough to serve as a convenient rallying point for many groups and isolated individuals' (Kirchheimer, 1990: 55).

The 'catch-all' parties have contributed to the de-ideologisation of politics in Europe. For Kirchheimer, ideology has shifted from a class-based set of ideas and beliefs for motivating collective action by working-class or middle-class people, to a 'general background atmosphere, both all-embracing and conveniently vague enough to allow recruitment' from a number of different sections of the community (Kirchheimer, 1990: 55).

The motive for parties to change to the 'catch-all' form is to become more competitive, even if this involves adopting an opponent's style and content. From the end of the nineteenth century to the end of the twentieth century, parties have shifted from being:

○ Channels for integrating individuals and groups into the existing political order
○ Instruments for modifying or replacing the political order
○ Means to determine individuals' political preferences
○ Means to influence the political process into accepting the party's view of the world – the expressive function
○ Means for nominating political office-holders and presenting them to the public

As parties shift to the 'catch-all' position, they attempt to:

○ Drop their ideological baggage, in favour of short-term tactical advantage
○ Strengthen their leadership
○ Downgrade and disempower the individual party member
○ Recruit voters from many sections of the population rather than a single class
○ Approach special interest groups for advice and support

Kirchheimer thinks that catch-all parties should flourish because they can appeal to a wide range of voters, not simply a particular class or religious denomination. However, parties cannot stretch their appeal indefinitely, as any new appeal will open up new divisions or lead to a loss of old supporters. Kirchheimer's view is clearly spelt out in the following passage.

> If the process of programme convergence approaches the point where all distinctions are cancelled, the electors become unable to choose for want of separate identities, and participation in political life approaches meaninglessness, except when professionally motivated. The old parties will then be either exposed to schisms or threatened by new entries. A more or less durable revamping of the ideological stance, hence of the identity, of a party may be the most convenient response. The Thatcher case in the United Kingdom, followed by the organizational reform in the Labour Party, which has increased the power of the 'ideological core' of its supporters, can be restated when policy constraints have blurred all distinctions. There is another suggestion here that the convergence/divergence path of parties' programmes may follow a cyclical pattern. (Pizzorno, 1990: 64)

Let us turn our attention to the structure and ideology of the political parties in Britain.

The Labour Party

In 1900, Keir Hardie defined the purpose of the Labour Party as the promotion of legislation in the interests of working people. In other words, the party was created to defend a sectional interest in society. However, up until 1918, the party could be viewed as a pressure group within the Liberal Party. In 1918, Labour adopted a new constitution and attempted to focus its ideology on public ownership. This was set out most clearly in Clause 4 of the 1918 constitution.

The 1918 conference also created a constitutional structure for the party that included individual membership. All party members belong to a ward or 'branch' Party that covers the geographical area represented by a local councillor. The number of members within a branch varies depending upon the ability of the local party to attract members. The local ward or branch of the party has its own chairman, secretary and treasurer, and possibly a press officer, as well as people delegated to produce newsletters and so on. All of these people are volunteers. The main function of the branch or ward party is to select the candidate to stand in local elections, to either the district or city council, depending on the type of area.

The branch or ward party also sends delegates to the General Management Committee (GMC), the constituency level of the Party. Usually one in ten branch members are delegates to the GMC. Local trade unions also send delegates to the GMC, as do other affiliated bodies, such as socialist societies, Labour Clubs and the Cooperative Party. Members of the GMC are the activists of the constituency party. Before 1987, the GMC selected the parliamentary candidate for the Labour Party, but since the 1992 general election candidates have been selected by an 'electoral college' based upon the principle of 'one member – one vote' (OMOV).

All GMCs send one delegate to the Labour Party conference. Among its many functions, the party conference:

○ Makes Labour Party policy
○ Elects the National Executive Committee – which administers the party

However, up until the late 1990s, the decisions of the party conference were dominated by the block votes of the trade unions. In addition, for many years, the policy of the Parliamentary Labour Party and the policy of the conference were in total opposition to each other.

Tensions between the right and the left in the party have a long history, but a key moment was in 1973 when the annual conference voted to nationalise the top twenty-five companies in Britain. This was a key element in what became known as the 'alternative economic strategy'. However, the party leader, Harold Wilson, rejected both the nationalisation decision of the conference and the 1974 manifesto commitment to: 'bring about a fundamental and irreversible shift in the balance of power and wealth in favour of working people and their families'. In its place the 1974–9 Labour government introduced the so-called Social Contract, which called for pay restraint and cuts in public expenditure.

As a consequence, many party activists demanded a more democratic policy-making structure within the party, and towards this end the Campaign for Labour

Party Democracy was formed, and became closely identified with the left-wing figure Tony Benn. The campaign put forward the following recommendations for constitutional reform:

○ MPs must be reselected before each general election
○ An electoral college should elect the leader of the party from the party as a whole – not just the Parliamentary Labour Party (PLP)
○ The leader must lose the right of veto over the contents of the manifesto
○ The National Executive Committee (NEC) should write the manifesto
○ Every Labour candidate should sign a pledge to be bound by party policy
○ The rules of the PLP should be vetted by the annual Labour conference
○ The conference should hear a verdict by the NEC on the performance of MPs
○ The conference should deliver its own verdict on this with a full debate and vote

In 1979, the party conference accepted mandatory reselection of MPs, so that all Labour MPs have, in effect, to reapply for their jobs with their constituency parties before a general election. In 1980, the conference accepted that an electoral college should elect the leader. The votes within this electoral college are weighted so that the unions had 40 per cent of the votes, constituency parties 30 per cent and the PLP 30 per cent. Neil Kinnock was the first leader to be elected under this system. John Smith and later Tony Blair were elected under the OMOV system.

The party conference also elects the NEC, which is the 'administrative' arm of the party. It enforces the rules of the party, taking action where necessary, and resolving disputes within the party.

Under the leadership of Kinnock, Smith and Blair, policy making has shifted to specific policy forums and subcommittees, which were first used during the policy review (1988–90), with the conference voting to accept or reject a policy package that emerged from this process. The major constitutional change under Blair's leadership was to rewrite Clause 4 of the constitution. The 'old' Clause 4 stated the objective 'to secure for the workers by hand or by brain the full fruits of their industry and the most equitable distribution thereof that may be possible upon the basis of the common ownership of the means of production, distribution and exchange, and the best obtainable system of popular administration and control of each industry or service.' However, Clause 4 of the Labour Party Constitution now reads as follows:

By the strength of our common endeavour we achieve more than we achieve alone, so as to create for each of us the means to realise our true potential and for all of us a community in which power, wealth and opportunity are in the hands of the many, not the few, where the rights we enjoy reflect the duties we owe, and where we live together, freely, in a spirit of solidarity, tolerance and respect.

At his first party conference as prime minister, Blair pushed forward a radical reform of the party's policy-making structures (Figure 5.1).

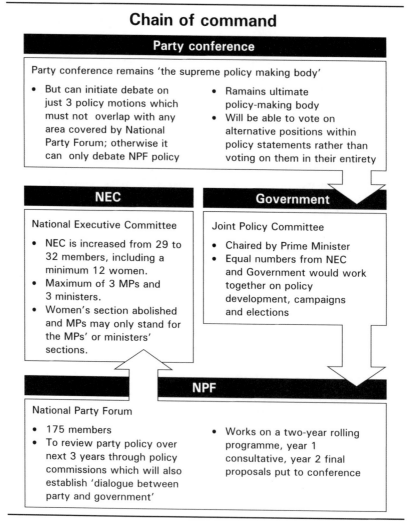

Figure 5.1 *Labour Party Policy Making Structure*

A joint policy committee was established which is concerned with the development of policy, campaigns and election strategy. A national policy forum will review party policy; this forum allows constituency parties, unions and other affiliated bodies have a voice in policy making. However, the party conference remains the supreme policy-making body; it decides what is to be adopted as party policy and what is not.

Within the Labour Party, there is no one accepted definition or view of socialism. Although all socialists believe in democracy, liberty and community, there is still a great deal of disagreement on the nature of socialism. Below is an outline of some of the ideologies within the party.

Social democracy

Social democracy is based upon the belief that capitalism is not self-regulating. Supporters of this ideology still believe in private enterprise and self-help or individualism, but think that the state should provide a safety net for people who are sick or old, or who for any other reason cannot benefit from capitalism. Hence the need for a welfare state. Government should intervene to make capitalism run efficiently, abolish injustice and poverty, and provide regulation where it is needed. Social democrats still accept inequality, but it must be inequality with a sense of fairness. In other words, there should be no barriers preventing people from making the best use of their abilities. Equality means 'equality of opportunity'. If inequality is to exist, it must benefit society as a whole.

Fabian socialism

The Fabian socialists have a very different view of equality from that of social democrats. Not equality of opportunity, but equality of outcome is their principle. In other words, everybody should be educated, everybody should be healthy and the government should do more than simply provide ladders and exits from poverty. Government action should bring about both a greater sense of community and a greater sense of social justice, because there would be no class conflict. Unlike Marxists, however, Fabians believe in the 'inevitability of gradualness'; they aim to bring about socialism over a long period of time rather than by revolution, and to reform the institutions within capitalism rather than destroy them through revolution.

Marxism

Marxism is probably the least influential of the ideologies presented here. As we have seen in Area 5, Marxists hold that if a group owns the means of production, it not only has economic power but also political power. They view the state as an institution that helps to organise capitalist society in the best interests of the bourgeoisie. The legitimacy of the system is maintained by making working-class people the victims of a false consciousness. In other words, working-class people are said to hold values, ideas and beliefs about the nature of inequality that are not in their own economic interests to hold. Working-class people's ideas are manipulated by agents such as the media, schools and religion; consequently, they regard economic inequality as fair and just.

In the UK, according to Ralph Miliband, a coherent well-organised capitalist class, who hold top positions in both industry and the state, and most of whom were privately educated before going to Oxbridge, control the state and use it as an instrument for continued bourgeois domination.

In contrast, Nicos Poulantzas argues that the class background of individuals in high state positions in unimportant. The structure of society is capitalist, and the role of the state is to maintain that structure. The state must have a high degree of autonomy, or independence of individual capitalists, in order to choose effectively between the competing demands for state action by different capitalists. In other words, the state is always functional to the needs of capital, even though individual members of elite state institutions are not from an upper-class background.

Antonio Gramsci rejected the economic determinism contained in the type of argument that Poulantzas puts forward. Writing from his prison cell in the 1930s, Gramsci made a distinction between two parts of the state, 'political society', which contains all the repressive state institutions such as the police and the army, and 'civil society', which contains all the institutions that attempt to manipulate our ideas. The state rules by consent although it has the ability to use force if necessary. However, in disputes, the state would always prefer to use negotiating skills to secure a compromise. The state attempts to form a 'historic bloc', which involves making compromises with different groups, in an effort to maintain solidarity. Consent is maintained by 'hegemony', a body of ideas that becomes part of our consciousness, and that we accept as right. Capitalism can be overthrown only by challenging and reformulating hegemony and establishing a new historic bloc.

Extending this analysis by Gramsci, David Coates suggests that the state must make compromises with various bodies both at home and overseas. In addition, new forms of ideology have to be created in an effort to maintain legitimacy; Thatcherism may be an example.

Abercrombie et al. reject approaches which overemphasise the ideological aspects of state power; numerous studies, they claim, show that working-class individuals reject a dominant ideology. Abercrombie and his colleagues argue that economic factors, such as fear of unemployment, are the key in maintaining the structure of inequality within capitalism.

Marxists hold that it is not possible to reform capitalism in the interests of working people. What is needed is to abolish capitalism and establish socialism. Marx (1863) himself, however, is not very specific about the nature of a socialist society; in his 'Critique of the Gother Programme', he describes the socialist society as one based upon the principle of 'from each according to his abilities to each according to his needs'. In view of Gorbachov's programme of perestroika, and the subsequent collapse of the Soviet Union, most people have lost confidence in the government's ability to plan the economy, and this has discredited these traditional approaches to socialism.

Communitarianism

What was strong then is fragile now. (Tony Blair, Labour Party conference, 1996)

Under the leadership of Tony Blair, the Labour Party has moved towards a much more 'communitarian' stance. Barry Barnes (2000) argues that communitarianism is a reaction against particular types of lifestyle choice; in particular, it reflects the idea that people have too many rights and too few responsibilities. The communitarian view also suggests that institutions that mediate between individuals and the government, most notably 'the family', have become undervalued. This view is said to be neither left-wing or right-wing; it is a combination of the free market/individualism of the Thatcher-Reagan years and the state planning of the 1945–51 Labour governments. It is concerned with the responsibility of the individual to the community. In contrast to current belief and practice, the community should become a 'stakeholder' in all its children. At the moment, the decision to have a child is a personal act that is of concern only to the prospective parents. In addition, divorce laws have become more 'open' in recent years, making divorce much easier to obtain. Moreover, during the 1990s, parents have had to spend much more time at work. As a consequence, many parents are said to be neglecting their duties as parents; this argument has been most fully developed by Amitai Etzioni in *The Parenting Deficit* (1992).

According to Etzioni, communitarianism is 'dedicated to the betterment of our moral, social, and political environment … and [is] dedicated to working with … fellow citizens to bring about the changes in values, habits, and public policies that will allow us to do for society what the environmental movement seeks to do for nature: to safeguard and enhance our future' (1993: 2–4).

COMMUNITARIANISM

By and large, citizens like the idea of the welfare state to be there if they fall on hard times. But, increasingly, governments everywhere are realising that the public purse cannot afford it at present levels.

Right-wingers say that health, education and social security should be cut because it induces a dependency culture and saps individual initiative. But social ills are not merely the product of moral turpitude. Left-wingers say that if unemployment were reduced then governments would have extra taxation income to pay for existing levels of payments. But nobody is simply a helpless victim – everybody has some contribution to make.

A midway position is quite possible, however. Some services now provided by the welfare state should and could be undertaken by people on their own. At the same time, society must continue to share the burdens.

Communitarians purpose a principle of subsidiary in which the primary responsibility belongs to the individuals nearest the problem; if a solution cannot be found, then the responsibility moves to the family; if there is still no solution, then to the community; then and only then, when no solution is possible at all, should the state be involved.

(Habitats-mini articles http://www.on-the-net.com/interskills/minis/habitat.htm#comm)

Sociologically, the notion of communitarianism can be seen as an attempt to rebuild the idea of 'the community' within the postmodern world. In the postmodern condition, cultures appear to be fragmented, In addition, this fragmented culture allows individuals to select their own identities.

A number of religious groups have taken up the communitarian message. The Rev. Samuel A. Trumbore is a keen supporter of the notion of communitarianism. In a sermon to the Unitarian Universalist Fellowship of Charlotte County, USA, he suggested principles in a new balance between rights and responsibilities:

- The right to vote should be conditional upon regular participation in elections
- Protection against illegal search and seizure should be lost after conviction of a serious crime
- The right to a jury trial should be conditional on being willing to serve or having served on a jury

According to Trumbore, Communitarianism is a 'non-coercive path towards building a stronger community' (Trumbore, 1996: 3). It could be argued that the emphasis on 'community' conceals a significant loss of liberty in Trumbore's view of communitarianism.

Anthony Giddens

Another advocate of communitarian ideas, who is said to have had an influence upon Tony Blair, is Anthony Giddens. On a practical level, Giddens's short book *The Third Way* (1998) advises Blair on the policies the Labour Government should adopt. Giddens's argument is that the Blair government should be involved in a 'renewal of social democracy' to create a 'social investment state'. In this state, the government would invest in education and welfare provision to enable citizens to become fully active in the life of the community.

For Giddens (1985), nation-states are polyarchic in nature, as individuals enjoy a number of citizenship rights which have been won by their participation in forms of 'emancipatory politics'. Within the nation-states, democracy is moving towards a 'dialogic democracy' similar in many respects to a 'pure relationship':

> There is a close tie between the pure relationship and dialogic democracy. Dialogue, between individuals who approach one another as equals, is a transational quality central to their mutuality. There are remarkable parallels between what a good relationship looks like, as developed in the literature of marital and sexual therapy, and formal mechanisms of political democracy. Both depend on the development of … a principle of autonomy. (Giddens, 1994: 118–19)

In Giddens's view, we need to have a theory of democratisation that takes into account both everyday life and globalising systems. To this end, Giddens developed his notion of 'dialogic democracy', which stands in opposition to all forms of fundamentalism and attempts to 'create active trust through an appreciation of the integrity of the other. Trust is a means of ordering social relations across time and space' (Giddens, 1994: 116). We attempt to live with others in a relation of 'mutual tolerance'. As Giddens suggests in the long passage just quoted, our political relationships take on many of the characteristics of the 'pure' relationship.

All individuals strive for a 'pure' relationship in Giddens's analysis; this is a relationship based solely upon trust, and it cannot be underpinned by any guarantee. In previous ages, it was possible to trust individuals in an intimate relationship, because of their family or professional background. This guarantee of trust can no longer be given in the 'new times' of 'high' modernity. The 'pure' relationship then expresses a prime difference between the traditional and present-day marriage. Today, marriage has become a signifier of commitment; commitment within a couple provides meaning, stability and large tracts of relative security in daily life. Within the 'pure' relationship, the marriage contract has taken the form of a Bill of Rights; it is an ethical framework for a personal democratic order, an intimacy based upon autonomy and democracy. Autonomy brings with it the successful realisation of the 'reflexive project of self' – the ability of individual people to create and re-create themselves in any way they choose. In other words, people can change any or all aspects of their lives that they become dissatisfied with. In addition, autonomy gives people opportunities to find ways of avoiding the meaninglessness and dread that are common in life today. Giddens suggests that all relationships can become democratic, including the relationship between a parent and young child. For Giddens, it is the right of a child to be treated as the equal of an adult. If it is not possible to negotiate with children because they are too young to understand the issues in question, the adult should provide counterfactual justifications. In other words, the adult should provide the child with hypothetical examples that draw upon the child's experience.

In terms of politics, the significance of these developments is that within modernity we have moved from 'emancipatory politics' – which is itself a product of modernity – to 'life politics', which is the key factor driving New Social Movements (NSMs). NSMs campaign for a new form of polity that is on the far side of modernity (Giddens dislikes the term 'postmodernity').

From emancipatory politics to life politics

'Life politics is a politics, not of life chances, but of lifestyle. It concerns disputes and struggles about how (as individuals and as collective humanity) we should live in a world where what used to be fixed either by nature or tradition is now subject to human secessions' (Giddens, 1994: 14–15). Life politics emerges from emancipatory politics and is a politics of self-actualisation, in other words, life politics 'concerns debates and contestations deriving from the reflexive project of the self' (Giddens, 1991: 215). This means that life politics is about the unhindered creation of a self that you are happy with. If you wish to be gay, straight, a New Age traveller, or an office worker, you should be free to do so without others making judgements about you.

Emancipatory politics has the following two main elements:

- An effort to break free from the shackles of the past
- An overcoming of illegitimate domination (coercion) that adversely affects the life chances of individuals

Moreover, as we have suggested, its central principle is that of enhancing autonomy, by moving away from all forms of exploitation, inequality and oppression, as well as promoting justice, equality and participation. In the last analysis, within a political system dominated by emancipatory politics, individuals have greater control over their circumstances. Life politics recognises that nation-states have very limited effectiveness in areas significant to individuals. Giddens gives the example of IVF research or nuclear power; if a nation-state were to ban research in these areas, it would have limited significance upon global scientific developments.

Giddens adopts a rather optimistic view of these issues that emerge with globalisation: 'Unpredictability, manufactured uncertainty, fragmentation: these are only one side of the coin of a globalizing order. On the reverse side are the shared values that come from a situation of global interdependence, organised via the cosmopolitan acceptance of difference' (1994: 253). By 'manufactured uncertainty', Giddens means uncertainties about problems created by people that have no real precedents; for example, global warming or nuclear power. It is possible to criticise both Etzioni and Giddens by arguing that they make impractical assumptions about the role and the authority of moral or ethical ideals within a society. In addition, both Etzioni and Giddens assume that 'the self' or the 'human agent' is a unified whole; in other words, that people have one firm identity and are clear about their role in the world, and their place within it. As we suggested in Area 2, political identity in the postmodern condition is often multiple, fragile and incomplete. This is because people do not have 'grand narratives' to give meaning to their lives. How such postmodern or reflexive selves could form a political community is difficult to say. This goes back to the age-old sociological question: how is society possible? We need to rephrase this age-old question and ask both Etzioni and Giddens: in your schemes how is community possible, what binds people together into such communities and how are they maintained?

John Macmurray

Tony Blair himself has stated that the philosopher John Macmurray, whom Blair met as a student at Oxford University, has influenced his views. At a practical level, Macmurray's ideas helped shape Blair's conception of the relationship between the individual and the community, the conception that individuals should be responsible for their own actions but should always take into account how these actions can affect the community.

A community is a group of persons, each one an 'agent' capable of making a difference in the world. For Macmurray, we, as individuals, should always think 'from the standpoint of action'; when we act we bring about a change in the world and all action involves choice. Before we make our choice, we have to consider the possible consequences of our actions, which will be either 'good' or 'bad'; this is important because action is irreversible. To behave in a moral fashion is to do good knowing that we have the freedom to act otherwise.

The agents who form a community are united in a common life; they act together and they create an association or a fellowship. In other words, there is more to a community than simply a common purpose; it assumes love and a consciousness of the common life. This consciousness is to be found in all personal associations within a community. Individuals carry out actions that can either help or hinder others; as Macmurray explained, 'The morality of an action is inherent in the action itself' (Macmurray, 1961: 117). Within the community the freedom of each person is dependent upon the intentions of every other individual within the community, as my freedom is dependent upon your acting in a way which does not constrain or harm me. This interdependence of persons, for Macmurray, is the foundation for morality: 'If we call the harmonious interrelation of agents their "community", we may say that a morally right action is an action which intends community.' (1961: 119). Accordingly, Macmurray suggests that there are the following three modes of morality:

- The 'communal mode' of morality rests upon a positive motivation to act in a way that benefits others without benefiting oneself. This communal way of behaving reinforces the bonds of community. Therefore, to act in a communal way is regarded as a 'positive' form of morality because it involves actively bringing about a change for the better.
- The 'contemplative mode' of morality is concerned with 'fitting in' with the ways of behaving which are regarded as normal or acceptable within the community. In many respects, this would appear to have more in common with manners than morality. This contemplative mode is regarded as a 'negative' mode of morality, because it involves not acting in a way that may be seen as to the disadvantage of the community.
- The 'pragmatic mode' of morality takes the form of obedience or a morality of self-control, as individuals limit their own independence for the benefit of the community.

Let us look again at Clause 4 of the Labour Party constitution:

By the strength of our common endeavour we achieve more than we achieve alone, so as to create for each of us the means to realise our true potential and for all of us a community in which power, wealth and opportunity are in the hands of the many, not the few, where the rights we enjoy reflect the duties we owe, and where we live together, freely, in a spirit of solidarity, tolerance and respect.

We can identify many communitarian assumptions within the new Clause 4, most notably in terms of the assumptions that the redrafted clause makes about the relationship between the individual and the community.

Table 5.1 *The Third Way*

Social democracy (old left)	Neoliberalism (New Right)	Third way (centre-left)
Class politics of left	Class politics of right	Modernising movement of centre
Old mixed economy	Market fundamentalism	New mixed economy
Corporatism: state dominates over civil society	Minimal state	New democratic state
Internationalism	Conservative nation	Cosmopolitan nation
Strong welfare state, protecting 'from cradle to grave'	Welfare safety net	Social investment state

Source: Giddens, 1998: 18

The 'third way'

The 'third way', an alternative approach to politics developed by Giddens, is said to be neither right-wing nor traditional social democracy. Influenced by communitarianism, the 'third way' entails radically changing our notions of citizenship away from something that is 'given' as of 'right' to something that must be 'achieved' by work and other contributions to the community. In addition, the 'third way' entails the creation of a 'social investment state' by eliminating social exclusion and segregation through training and reskilling the young unemployed in 'the new deal'.

According to Giddens (1998), people at the bottom of the class ladder have become increasingly excluded from social and political life. The children of the poor make limited use of the education system and have limited opportunities to become socially mobile. In a similar fashion, professional people increasingly exclude themselves from public institutions; they do not make use of the National Health Service and their children do not attend state schools.

The 'new deal'

The 'new deal' was one of Labour's election pledges; its intention is to reduce 'youth unemployment' through a programme of 'welfare-to-work'. The principal aim is to assist the transition from benefit to work for 18–24-year-olds who have been in receipt of benefit for over six months. After an initial interview, young unemployed persons will be invited into the 'gateway': a four-month period of personal assessment to determine what they are already capable of, and what type of option is suitable to their needs. It is also a stage where difficulties such as illiteracy can be dealt with, any personal problems such as drug or alcohol abuse can be identified, and rehabilitation, often with the aid of mentors, can be provided. After the 'gateway', there are the following four options:

- Work in the private or public sector
- Work in the voluntary sector

- Work with the Environmental Task Force – cleaning rubbish from rivers, cleaning graffiti etc.
- Full-time education or training

If the young person goes into full-time work, the employer will receive a subsidy of £60 per week plus £750 training expenses, to allow the young person to receive training one day a week over a six-month period. If they choose one of the other options, they will receive an extra £15 per week in addition to their benefits.

It is commonly assumed by right-wing critics that the benefits system created a dependency culture, and that reform of the system has not broken the cycle of dependency. The 'new deal' involves investing in individuals through training and increasing employment skills. As a consequence, the individual helps create economic prosperity and competitiveness in the global market, as well as gain employment experience. The communitarian edge to this policy is that persons who take from the community must give something back in return. From this perspective, citizenship rights are earned by work. As Raymond Plant explained, 'The ideas of reciprocity and contribution are at the heart of this concept of citizenship: individuals do not and cannot have a right to the resources of society unless they contribute to the development of that society through work or other socially valued activities, if they are in a position to do so' (1998: 30). As Tony Blair himself explained in a party political broadcast, 'Everybody who has a contribution to make can' (BBC1,1998, 9.00 pm).

The Labour government claims to be committed to the eradication of social exclusion. As David Muligan, the director of Demos, (an independent think tank) has explained, the unemployed 'are more properly defined as excluded because they live outside the worlds of work, of education, of sociability itself.'

Although we looked at the nature of communitarianism and some of the criticisms of it, it is worth looking at the evaluation of Etzioni's work by Richard Sennett. Sennett (1997) views communitarianism in the metaphor of a bicycle rider endeavouring to balance individual rights on one side against coercive conservatism on the other. In his critique of Etzioni's *The New Golden Rule* (1997), Sennett observes that:

> [Etzioni] thinks the 'moral infrastructure' of society resembles a 'Chinese nesting box' beginning with families, around which there are schools, then communities proper ('peer groups, voluntary associations, places of worship, community spaces') and, the biggest box of all, 'the community of communities' (society at large). Everything falls nicely into place: strong family values are necessary to behave well in schools, firm rules in school make for sociable adults, and sociable adults make for good citizens. Bicycling through the boxes (the mixed metaphor is inescapable), a human being helps soften the rigour of rules by communicating his or her needs for autonomy, while the selfish or egoistic propensities of the self are softened by group firmness. (Sennett, 1997: 3)

Sennett makes the following criticisms of Etzioni's work:

- There is no debate about the nature of either political or economic power
- Etzioni disregards Durkheim's (1897) argument that the stronger the social interaction between individuals, the more separated they become; sharing values is effortless for people who have a more detached relation to each other
- People who do not share the same values often construct constraints such as the fundamentalist norms and beliefs
- Etzioni 'wants more agreement on "core" values, such as "community spirit", without discouraging disagreement'
- Etzioni's work does not satisfactorily deal with 'commitment'; he cannot explain the motivation of people to act in a communitarian fashion

Richard Rorty: critique of communitarianism

Rorty (1991) argues that those who are labelled as 'communitarians' reject the 'individualistic rationalism of the Enlightenment', and reject the idea of 'rights'. In other words, according to communitarianism, liberal institutions and culture need the philosophical justification given by the Enlightenment. They cannot survive without this justification. But in a post-Enlightenment world, there is no guarantee that individuals will behave rationally and no automatic conception of rights. For these reasons, the institutions and culture of democratic states are now without foundation.

For Rorty, there are three strands within communitarianism. First, there is the argument that no society in which individuals do not share the same notion of 'moral truth' can endure. Such societies often turn to 'pragmatism', which is not a 'strong enough philosophy to make [a] moral community possible' (Rorty, 1991: 177). Rorty quotes Bellah and others who suggest that 'pragmatism' leads to ideological fanaticism and extreme political oppression.

The second strand is that the individuals produced by a liberal society are undesirable. The rich, managers and therapists, who are the only people who wish to defend such a society, dominate it. In rebuttal, Rorty argues that there is no reason to measure democratic institutions by the type of person they may produce: 'Even if the typical character types of liberal democracies are bland, calculating, petty and unheroic, the prevalence of such people may be a reasonable price to pay for political freedom' (1991: 190). What is important for Rorty is that personhood involves having the capacity to choose, and this ability is 'prior to the ends it chooses' (1991: 185).

The third strand described by Rorty is the idea that the liberal society presupposes a number of assumptions about the nature of human beings. In other words, the liberal society has an unstated theory of the self. Liberals generalise about the nature of the self from the philosophical foundations of liberal institutions, which they admire. In his philosophical papers, Rorty develops a notion of the self in which the community is constitutive of it. In other words, he holds that our notion of the self is generated from factors within the wider society. This notion of the 'community as constitutive of the self' is a widely accepted one in both philosophy and sociology; in particular, it is found in the work of G.H. Mead, Erving Goffman, Anthony Giddens and others.

Rorty goes on to develop a notion of the self as a 'web': 'Think of human minds as webs of beliefs and desires, of sentential attitudes – webs which continually reweave themselves so as to accommodate new sentential attitudes. ... All there is to the human self is just that web' (1991: 93). This means that for Rorty there is no thing called 'the self' that is different from 'the web of beliefs and desires that that self "has"' (Rorty, 1991: 185). This idea is further developed in his book *Irony, Contingency and Solidarity* (1989).

Rorty describes his argument as an attempt to 'dissolve the metaphysical self in order to preserve the political one' (1991: 185). Liberal social theory does not need a notion of the self. This notion does not provide a basis for liberal social theory. However, if we desire a notion of the self, then the 'self as web' model will fit with other assumptions that Rorty makes about the liberal society.

According to Rorty, Thomas Jefferson said, in defence of liberalism, that 'It does me no injury for my neighbour to say that there are twenty gods or no God.' (in Rorty, 1991: 195) This set the tone for American liberal politics; shared beliefs about issues such as religion were not necessary for the smooth and efficient running of liberal society. What was necessary was that individuals had a 'conscience'. As Rorty explains, the liberal society can get along without political philosophies. In a similar fashion, questions about human nature, the self, motives for moral behaviour and the meaning of life are also irrelevant to the politics of a liberal society. This neutralises many of the criticisms made about liberalism by communitarians and others.

Taking his lead from Rawls, Rorty holds that 'justice' is the first virtue of the liberal society, and the need for such legitimation decreases as the liberal society encourages the 'end of ideology'. 'Reflective equilibrium', or the balance of opinion, principles and argument, is the only method needed in discussing policy. In addition, Rorty argues that fanaticism threatens both freedom and justice, and it is for this reason that liberals will use force against fanatics. Fanatics threaten liberal democratic institutions, because they challenge the individual conscience. The absence of fanaticism is one of the conditions of citizenship in a liberal society. This is built upon the notion that 'anybody who is willing to listen to reason – to hear out all the arguments – can be brought around to the truth' (Rorty, 1991: 188).

A key political question here is how far governments should intervene in the lives of ordinary people – for example, in labour markets – by limiting the number of hours that employers can demand from their workers per week.

In summary, for Rorty, communitarianism has defined itself by rejecting individualistic theories. However, as Barnes (2000) points out, communitarians present the following alternative versions of human agency to the one that Rorty has in mind:

- ○ Michael Sandel: Being an individual is partly to do with the community that that individual identifies with
- ○ Charles Taylor: Human agency is seen as a self that is socially constructed: the individual has to cross a moral desert, and how this exercise is conducted determines how a person is judged morally by others
- ○ Alasdair MacIntyre: Morality is derived from the roles that we play in the social order

Feminist critique of communitarianism

Amitai Etzioni's book *The Spirit of Community* ... says that about 20 years ago mothers did what men did: they ran away from their children by going out to get paid work. Their children were abandoned, as Etzioni puts it, to 'the drinks cabinet and the television'. But is it true?

We need to test the hypothesis. Jonathan Gershung at the Centre has researched the most substantive work on what parents actually do in their everyday life in Britain for Micro-Social Research at Essex. Mapping, hour by hour, the activities of parenting and household responsibilities, he has come up with a very different picture from the one painted by Etzioni.

The work of parenting and housework has indeed changed. In 1961 women spent an average of 217 minutes a day and men 17 minutes a day on housework. In 1985 women spent 162 minutes a day and men something like double their previous figure – considerably more than they did, but considerably less than women.

The important thing here is the relationship between routine housework and routine parenting and *dedicated* parenting. How much time do parents spend eyeball to eyeball with their children? The average mother now with a full-time job spends more dedicated time with her children than the average homemaker of 30 years ago. ...

She may have been permanently present but she was also probably permanently 'absent'. Mothers were not people you played with or had conversations with. You played with and produced your culture with other children, your own generation. ... Parenting has indeed been refashioned ... the kind of mother who is lodged in the nostalgic crusade of the communitarians didn't exist. (adapted from Beatrix Campbell, 1996: 2)

The Liberal Democrats

After the 1979 general election, there was a period of conflict within the Labour Party, and on 26 March 1981 a number of MPs, including four former cabinet ministers, Roy Jenkins, Shirley Williams, David Owen and Bill Rodgers, left the Labour Party to form the Social Democratic Party (SDP). The SDP formed an alliance with the Liberal Party. After the 1987 general election, the Liberal leader David Steel proposed a merger of the SDP and the Liberal Party. After a great deal of discussion and some conflict within the parties, the Social and Liberal Democrats party was formed on 8 March 1988. The nature of liberalism in Britain was outlined in the preamble to the Liberal Party constitution:

> The Liberal Party exists to build a Liberal Society in which every citizen shall possess liberty, property and security, and none shall be enslaved by poverty, ignorance or conformity. Its chief care is for the rights and opportunities of the individual, and in all spheres it sets freedom first. (quoted in Meadowcroft, 1989: 1)

Is liberal democracy the same as liberalism? For many, the answer is clearly no. For example, the sociologist Peter Houghton (1990) asserts that

> Liberal Democracy is not and cannot be Liberalism. It is essentially a merger between those Liberals who saw enough common ground between Liberalism and social democracy to believe that a merger was the best way forward. Our view is that expediency cannot be confused with principle. ... We feel Liberalism needs its own home, its own Party, unimpeded by the need to acknowledge a different tradition. (*Liberal News*, 1 July 1990: 4–5)

Ralph Dahrendorf (1974) also defines liberalism as being in opposition to social democracy. He argues that social democracy has been in decline since 1945 and was finally 'killed off' by the oil crisis in 1973, because social democracy depended on having an economic surplus to distribute in the form of welfare payments. In 1973, the oil-rich states that formed the Organisation of Petroleum Exporting Countries (OPEC) increased the price of crude oil by 400%. Social democracy, or 'Labourism', as he calls it, is based upon the ideal that an economic surplus should be distributed or otherwise used to improve the position of the poorer members of the population; therefore, the disappearance of the surplus means the end of social democracy. This position was first developed in Dahrendorf's *The New Liberty* (1974), which identified two major factors bringing about the end of social democracy.

The first factor was the energy crisis; the Yom Kippur War in 1973, when its neighbours attacked Israel and 'disposed of the assumption that oil supplies can be regarded as a simple function of demand of the advanced countries' (Dahrendorf, 1974: 77). In other words, it produced 'the end of the post-war era', which had been characterised by a 'socio-economic syndrome consisting of growth expectations, a consumption orientation, the reliance on intellectual perquisites like free trade and convertibility as well as national ones like full employment and social welfare' (Dahrendorf, 1974: 7).

The second major factor of change which Dahrendorf points to was inflation: 'Inflation has become the medium of a more or less hidden redistribution struggle between those who are able to keep pace, because of their capacity, and those who are not; the potential of this conflict, like all concealed struggles, is nasty. It includes the danger of a return of variants of fascism' (Dahrendorf, 1974: 11). Those with little or no bargaining power in the market lose the most during periods of slow expansion and inflation. Dahrendorf's conception of liberalism is meritocratic in nature; in other words, he wants to create a society in which membership of the upperclass is based on intelligence and effort. Equality of opportunity is the basis of liberty. Equality of opportunity does not result in equality; some people will gain a much greater share of money, wealth and power. Equality of opportunity, then, does not mean equality of outcome, and an attempt to produce equal outcomes is illiberal in nature.

These themes are further developed in Dahrendorf's later books *Life Chances* (1979) and *The Modern Social Conflict* (1988). In *Life Chances*, he explains that social democracy is the synthesis of the following four attitudes:

○ The need for economic growth is never doubted
○ In terms of social policy, equality of opportunity is to be stressed
○ Institutions are the main instruments of change
○ Rationality is central

Dahrendorf argues that social democrats are 'historicists', a term coined by Karl Popper (1957), suggesting that social democrats ignore the individual to further the interests of the working class.

Social democracy as rationalisation

Rationalisation is a process in which modern life is becoming more rational, more calculable and more predictable. However, at the same time, we have less and less understanding of the world and the way it works. For example, I can read the train timetable, but I have no idea how the internal combustion engine works, or I know how to turn on the radio, but I have no idea how it transforms radio waves into sound. As was suggested above, Dahrendorf holds that social democrats are the main proponents of rationality in the Weberian sense. What does he mean by this? Weber discussed rationalisation in three contexts:

○ As the dominant ongoing cultural trend in the West; in other words, as part of Weber's philosophy of history
○ As the rationality of Weber's ideal type; that is, as part of Weber's scientific method/philosophy of science
○ As representing the disenchantment of life and its devaluation, in the sense of substituting purely technical instrumentalism for value-oriented conduct; that is, as part of Weber's philosophy of life, his moral critique

It is in this last sense that Dahrendorf uses the term. The social democrats have been responsible for the spread of such rationality in the modern world.

This line of reasoning has also been taken up by Jurgen Habermas; in *Towards a Rational Society* (1974), he argues:

Rationalization means, first of all, the extension of the areas of society to the criteria of rational decision. Secondly, social labour is industrialised, with the result that criteria of instrumental action also penetrate into other areas of life (urbanisation of the mode of life, technification of transport and communication). Both trends exemplify the type of purposive-rational action, which refers to either the organisation or the means of choice between alternatives. Planning can be regarded as purposive alternatives. Planning can be regarded as purposive-rational action of the second order. Moreover, the progressive rationalization of society is linked to the institutionalization of scientific and technical developments. (Habermas, 1974: 87)

The argument here is that social democracy is rational in the Weberian sense. However, as we saw in Area 2, many postmodernists, particularly Zygmunt Bauman, have been highly critical of Weberian rationality and its consequences. For Bauman, Weberian rationalisation leads to 'adiaphorization',that is, 'making certain actions, or certain objects of action, morally neutral or irrelevant' (Bauman, 1995: 149). There are two consequences of this: 'insensitivitization' to cruelty and the increasing of the distance between the victims and ourselves. In support of his view, Bauman quotes Michael Shapiro: '[The] objects of violence in the Gulf War were obscure and remote, both in that they were removed from sight and other human senses and that they emerged as appropriate targets through a tortuous signifying chain. More generally, they were remote in terms of the *meaning* they had for their attackers and the attackers' legitimating and logistical supporters' (quoted in Bauman, 1995: 151).

Policy-making structure of the Liberal Democrats

The Liberal Democrats are a highly centralised party, with power concentrated in two bodies, the federal executive and the federal policy committee (FPC); the non-federal elements within the party have the responsibility of overseeing local government, including coordination of local election campaigns. These bodies all report to an assembly which is called the federal conference.

Various bodies can send motions to be discussed by the federal conference, including constituency parties, the FPC, regions of the party and state parties. However, motions from constituency parties must first be submitted to a federal conference committee; this body is a subcommittee of the federal executive, and it has the power to veto motions before they are discussed by the conference.

The FPC is the most important body in terms of policy making within the party structure; it has responsibility for policy development and research, it writes the election manifesto and it provides the policy stance on issues of the day as they arise.

Critics of the party structure argue that in almost all circumstances the federal conference would be unable to create policy, as motions it agrees upon are passed to the FPC, who then produce a Green Paper on the subject that is debated at the next federal conference. If the Green Paper is passed, a White Paper is produced by the FPC, which is considered by the next federal conference. This procedure means that it would take at least two years for a motion to be debated that the party leadership did not agree with. Even in these circumstances, the leadership can do one of two things: call for a ballot of the membership or change the policy.

Former Liberal activists argue that the party structure is too centralised, too inward looking, too elitist and lacking in proper accountability.

The Conservative Party

Mrs Thatcher has dominated Conservative philosophy or ideology since the 1970s. It is commonly assumed that she broke the post-war consensus established by the Labour government of Attlee (1945–51). This consensus was based upon the redistribution of income via the tax and benefits systems, and the establishment of health care and education free at the point of issue as central elements in a comprehensive welfare state.

At the level of rhetoric, Thatcherism is seen as conviction politics, as enterprise culture pushing back the 'nanny state', and as giving unions back to their members. Many on the left, notably the sociologist Stuart Hall (1983), came to view Thatcherism as 'authoritarian populism' whereby Thatcher re-created common sense in the minds of the working class by the use of 'hegemonic messages'.

In his book *Thatcherism and British Politics: The End of Consensus?* (1990), Dennis Kavanagh provides perhaps the clearest statement on Thatcherism as a major break with the post-war consensus. Kavanagh sees Thatcherism as comprising both style and policy. At the level of style, Thatcherism was based upon the distinct personality of Mrs Thatcher herself. At the level of policy, Thatcherism stressed control of the money supply to control inflation, the reduction of the public sector or privatisation, freeing the labour market through reform and the restoration of the government's authority.

Similarly, Philip Norton (1987) suggested the following three propositions about Mrs Thatcher:

○ She changed the nature of the political debate in Britain
○ She imposed her will upon government policy and dominated the Cabinet
○ She abolished or reformed institutions that she saw as obstacles

S.E. Finer (1987) notes that all post-war governments accepted the triangle of public corporations, social services and full employment. However, the Thatcher governments favoured the following very different points of politics and the role of government:

- Keynesian deficit financing was out
- Physical controls over and subsidies to ailing industries were out
- Money-supply economics and financial management of the economy were in
- Unions were cold-shouldered
- Public expenditure was restrained
- Nationalised industries were told to make profits
- Privatisation increased
- Exchange controls were abolished
- The maximum possible scope was given to market forces

Finer explains that 'nothing – neither the rising unemployment that had stricken Macmillan and Heath with panic, nor waves of strikes such as had paralysed former governments – simply nothing was allowed to stand in the way of these policies' (Finer, 1987: 129). In many respects, this was because the Thatcherites blamed unemployment on the unemployed themselves; they had priced themselves out of jobs by demanding higher wages.

Like Kavanagh and Finer, other writers argue that Thatcher brought about a major change in values, attitudes and beliefs. For example, according to Stephen Haseler's *The Battle for Britain: Thatcher and the New Liberals* (1989), Thatcherism was a reaction to the dominant paternalist stance of the major political parties in Britain from 1945 onwards. We could add that Mrs Thatcher attempted to turn the political into the personal. 'Don't spend more than you earn' became economic policy; 'Don't trust foreigners' became foreign policy. Is this the hallmark of a postmodern politics? With the election of the first Thatcher government in 1979, the New Right philosophy of minimal state involvement and private market solutions to social problems had a significant influence on Britain's political system.

The New Right favour a return to 'Victorian values', a slogan that came to mean more privatisation of the welfare state. Instead of 'collective' or state provision, there was more private insurance for health and pensions; more contracting out of school and hospital cleaning services; the introduction of a voucher system for nursery education; and the replacing of student grants by student loans. The idea behind these moves was to make people less dependent upon the state and more independent. Like pluralists, the New Right believes that the state should be both 'rule maker' and 'umpire'. In other words, the state should police things such as the market; it should attend to market imperfections such as large companies fixing prices.

According to Julian Le Grand (1986), the welfare state includes the following features:

- A social security system that shifts cash from taxpayers to people on benefit
- A number of 'benefits in kind' provided 'free' because they are considered 'good' for society, including health care, education and a range of 'personal social services' such as the services of social workers, home helps, 'meals on wheels', etc.

- A range of price subsidies designed to reduce the cost to consumers of certain goods thought to be 'socially desirable', including rent subsidies, housing improvement grants and public transport subsidies

The state then, before the success of the New Right, was involved in social and economic activities in three ways, providing direct provision, subsidy and regulation.

Privatisation, which the New Right clearly supports (as reduction in state involvement), includes the following three types:

- Reduction of state provision: for example, the sale of council houses
- Reduction of state subsidy: for example, increases in charges for school trips and charges for NHS services, and the replacement of student grants with loans and the introduction of tuition fees for university students
- Reduction of state regulation: for example, deregulation of the bus services

According to the New Right thinkers, these changes are in the interests of efficiency.

Vic George and Paul Wilding (1982) give a very full and clear outline of the New Right philosophy. They argue that New Right thinkers such as Hayek, Friedman and Powell believe in what was known as liberalism in the nineteenth century. New Right thinkers are opposed to state intervention, which they term 'collectivism'; they support freedom or liberty, individualism and inequality. However, they see freedom or liberty in negative terms. You are free if you are not under coercion. In other words, if people are not forcing you to do something that you do not want to do, you are free.

In addition, these New Right thinkers believe that all people are irrational and unreliable. However, if individuals make mistakes, it affects only a small group of people. In contrast, if the head of a government, who is also a person and also irrational and unreliable, were to make an error in a big planning decision, millions of people would suffer.

The New Right philosophy also holds that inequality is good because it provides people with incentives to better themselves. In contrast, the state can bring about equality only by coercion or force; by taking money away from people in the form of unwelcome taxes. In addition, state intervention is socially disruptive, because, according to Enoch Powell (1966), the welfare state turns 'wants' into 'rights'. I might want health care, I might want my children to be educated, and I might want social security. However, if the state cannot afford to provide these things, I will feel that my 'rights' have been ignored, and I might turn to violence or crime to get what I believe is mine as of right.

In addition, from the New Right perspective, state services are wasteful of resources. Because state services are usually provided free of charge, people consume as much as they possibly can. Moreover, because state services have to be paid for out of taxes, there is always a lack of concern over individual freedom.

Under the leadership of John Major, the Thatcherite project was not abandoned. However, Major placed much greater emphasis on receiving value for money in the public services by imposing bureaucratic quality assurance systems (see Area 2, 'Power, Authority and the State'). In addition he introduced the notion of 'charter rights' (such as the Further Education Charter that explains all the rights that students can expect from their further education college) in all areas of public service.

The structure of the Conservative Party

The constitution of the Conservative Party is unwritten; it has been put together over several centuries, and is based upon custom and tradition. The nearest thing to a written constitution is the rules of the National Union of Conservative and Unionist Associations. These rules, however, cover only some of the structures that make up the modern party. Most importantly, the rules of the national union do not cover the role of the leader. This is significant because the leader appoints all the major officers of the party, including the chairman, vice-chairmen, deputy chairmen, party treasurers, major figures within the research department, the chief whip, all members of the Cabinet and all minor ministerial appointments.

The functions of the National Union are as follows:

o To promote the aims of the party
o To form and develop a Conservative association in every constituency
o To act as a link between leader and the party in the country
o To liase with the central office
o To liase with the party in Scotland and Wales

The work of the National Union is carried out through a central council, which was the governing body and rule maker of the National Union. In addition, an executive committee, a general purposes committee and provincial area councils all have roles to play within the National Union. The Conservative Party conference each year is the conference of the National Union. It is never clear whether the decisions of the conference of the National Union are binding on the party and its leadership, or whether the conference decisions are party policy or simply recommendations.

Until 1997, the structure of the Conservative Party was seen as very flexible to reflect the interests and views of the leader of the party, as well as the leader's priorities for the party. Under the leadership of William Hague, there were changes. However, before we outline the changes that Hague made to the party structure, let us look at his election to party leader and what he said about Conservative values.

Youngest Tory leader since Pitt

On 19 June 1997, a 36-year-old Yorkshireman, William Hague, became the youngest leader of the Conservative Party since the 24-year-old Pitt the Younger in 1783. His real task was considered to be to restore the morale of Conservative MPs and other activists, which had been severely damaged after the crushing 1997 election defeat. He first came to national attention at the age of 16 with a speech to the Conservative Party conference in 1977. At that time, he told the party they must cut taxes, restrict union power and roll back the frontiers of the state for the benefit of young people.

Diary of the leadership campaign

In the first ballot on 10 June, the favourite, Kenneth Clarke, came top of the poll with 49 votes, followed by Hague with 41, Redwood with 27, Lilley with 24, and Howard with 23. After the first ballot, both Lilley and Howard said they would back Hague for the leadership. On 15 June, Clarke said that he would not serve in the shadow Cabinet if he lost the leadership contest. In addition, Michael Heseltine declared that he would return to the backbenches. In the second ballot on 17 June, the result was Clarke, 64; Hague, 62; and Redwood, 38. Redwood had to stand down, but he declared that he would back Clarke's leadership bid, infuriating many of his supporters. Redwood was accused of being 'unprincipled' and told that his support for Clarke was an 'instability pact' that could damage the party. Lady Thatcher openly endorsed Hague's leadership bid. In the third ballot on 19 June, Hague won 92 votes, and became Conservative leader. Clarke won only 70 votes, and returned to the backbenches.

One of the major themes of Hague's leadership in the first year was the 'reform and renewal' of the Conservative Party. In his first speech to the Conservative conference, in October 1997, Hague attempted to give a clear picture of his position and his vision of the future of the party.

What did William Hague stand for?

Far from being dead we have embarked on a process of reform and renewal that will rebuild our party, rejuvenate our membership, restore our confidence and make us fit to return to govern at the next General Election....

I'd like to tell you about an open Conservatism that is tolerant, that believes freedom is about much more than economics, that believes freedom doesn't stop at the shop counter....

I'd like to tell you about a democratic, popular Conservatism that listens, that has compassion at its core....

I want to tell you about a Conservatism that is rooted in its traditions, but embraces the future....

I want to tell you about a clear Conservatism that is resolute in its support for freedom, for enterprise, for nation....

I want to tell you about a changing Conservatism that acknowledges its mistakes. But I also want to tell you about a proud Conservatism that has served this nation well and will do so again. ...

We won't just be a Party of power: we will be a Party of principle too. And you know, in the coming years, we'll be the only Party of principle. We might start with a lot of disadvantages – a heavy election defeat, a lot of ground to make up, a huge government majority. But, I can live with those disadvantages as long as I know that we have the one great advantage that dwarfs everything else: we believe in what we stand for. ...

So I believe in freedom. I believe in enterprise. I believe in education. I believe in self-reliance. I believe in obligation to others. I believe in the nation. ...

Some people think none of this matters any more. They think we've no more need for beliefs. We've reached the end of history. The battle's been won, the game is over the fat lady has sung!...

But I'm here to tell you they're wrong. Our beliefs and our values matter now more than ever. ...

We can protect our nation state or we can let them take it away and tell us Britain's gone out of fashion and have them tell us it matters no more...

The family that works hard, saves hard, tries to be independent of the state and that believes in their country, needs a Conservative Party. We shall speak for them. We will be on their side. (William Hague's speech to the Conservative Party conference, 1997 http://www.Tory.co.uk/)

'Members matter': reform of the Conservative Party

Hague made the former Asda chief executive and new Conservative MP, Archie Norman, a vice-chairman of the party, giving him the task of analysing and advising on party structure. In his speech to the Conservative Party conference, entitled 'Our party: blueprint for change', Archie Norman said:

Our ambition is not small:

o   We want to double the membership;
o   We want real involvement. I want to point to ideas in the next Manifesto that are members' ideas;
o   We want a new Conservative youth movement;
o   We want 25% of women candidates there on merit and selected by the constituency associations;
o   We want to double the number of Conservative councillors; and
o   Above all we want a United Party which is open to ideas and debate but intolerant of dishonesty in any form!

Norman claimed that the reform of the party should advance a new kind of political party that operates within the community, that urges active commitment from all members, whether they are MPs or local activists, and takes notice of all individuals' and groups' contributions to party policy. He summed this up with the phrase: 'members matter'.

Also delivered at the Conservative Party conference in Blackpool was a speech by Lord Parkinson, whom Hague had made chairman of the Conservative Party. Parkinson also took up the theme of 'reform and renewal':

> We must create a single united party which listens to and involves its members in a way that we have never seen before.
>
> Only if we achieve this;
>
> Only if we update our organisation;
>
> Only if we increase and broaden our membership;
>
> can the Conservative Party's future be assured.
>
> That is our aim.

The only real detail of what form the reform of the party should take was given in a speech by Archie Hamilton, MP, Chairman of the 1922 Committee. Hamilton said that Hague had made it a priority of his leadership that the Conservative Party learns the lessons of its heavy defeat in the 1997 general election. Hamilton argued that the Conservatives should have a single party that unites the three key institutions of the Conservative Party – the Central Office, the National Union and the Parliamentary Party – which have been autonomous. He also suggested that the rules for electing the leader of the Conservative Party should be changed:

> As you will know, the election of the leader of our party has been, until now, the sole responsibility of the Parliamentary Party. We always consulted with our constituencies; the National Union, the Conservative Peers and the MEPs but the decision remained with the Conservative Members of Parliament. However, the rules for the election of leader will be changed for the future.

'Fresh future'

The outcome of this process of consultation with the party was a document entitled *The Fresh Future*, which outlined the six principles – unity, dencentralisation, democracy, involvement, integrity, and openness – upon which the Conservative Party is to be based in the future, together with a clear picture of what the new structures are to look like.

Unity

○ A written constitution for the Conservative Party will outline the duties and responsibilities of all sections of the party: the elected members, the paid officials, and the voluntary organisations.

- A new governing body, known as 'the board', will be chaired by the party chairman, and will comprise twelve members, six elected and six appointed by the leader. The board will control all aspects of the party organisation.
- A 'constitutional college' will consider any future rule changes.

Decentralisation

- A national Conservative convention of key local activists will meet at least twice a year to provide a link between the party leadership and the grass roots.
- A national councillors convention will provide a link between the leadership and local government.
- Constituency associations will come together under 42 regional associations to coordinate local elections and oversee performance. These regional associations will also select the Conservative 'list' of candidates for the Euro Elections and elections to the Scottish and Welsh Assembly.
- There will be an annual party conference.

Democracy

- The party leader can be removed only by a 51% vote of 'no-confidence' by the Conservative MPs.
- A new system will elect the party leader. The first stage in the election of future Conservative leaders will be an 'MPs primary'. Conservative MPs will select two of the three candidates and the party members will select from this short list by a system of one member – one vote (OMOV).

Involvement

- A Conservative policy forum to survey members' views will suggest new policy and organise regional policy forums
- Recognised organisations will be established to attract women, ethnic minority and professional people to the party

Integrity

- An ethics and integrity committee will be established to investigate misconduct with the power to expel members

Openness

- Any donation of over £5000 to party funds will be published, and no foreign donation will be accepted

Devolution in Britain

In a pluralistic democracy, political parties should not only stand for Parliament; there should also be strong local and regional bodies. In September 1997, referendums were held in both Scotland and Wales on the issue of devolution. Although the Welsh voted for having their own Assembly by only the narrowest of margins, 74.3% of Scots voted for a Scottish Parliament, with 63.5% voting for the Scottish Parliament to have tax-raising powers.

Scottish Parliament

- 129 members elected for a four-year period by people living in Scotland: 73 members elected from the existing constituencies by 'first past the post' and 56 by proportional representation
- Has a 'first minister'
- Has taken over the work of the current government departments for Scotland and will be given a budget by the UK Parliament
- Has the power to increase or decrease income tax by 3 pence in the pound
- Can pass laws for Scotland on any issues except national security, foreign and defence policy and monetary policy

Welsh Assembly

- The Assembly will have 60 members: 40 elected by 'first past the post' and 20 by PR
- Although it has no tax-raising powers, the Assembly will take over the duties of the Secretary of State for Wales, with a budget of £7 billion from the UK Parliament
- The Assembly has control over local government in Wales

Area Summary

In this area, we have looked at the nature of pluralism. This theory assumes that power is widely shared in society among a number of groups and individuals. In addition, unlike Marxism and elite theory, pluralists have a non-zero sum conception of power. They assume that the amount of power in society can expand or contract. For example, Talcott Parsons holds that the amount of power in the social system reflects the number of roles that exist within the system. All people when performing their roles make a difference in the world and cause an inconvenience to other people, as they trample on their vested interests. In other words, all individuals need to have power to perform their

continued

roles effectively. Therefore, more roles means more power in the social system. However, there are problems with the pluralist position; notably, the relation of economic inequality to political power. Are people who are economically better positioned more likely to have greater political importance?

References

Abercrombie, N., Hill, N. and Turner, B.S. (1980) *The Dominant Ideology Thesis*. London: Allen and Unwin.

Barnes, B. (2000) *In Search of Agency*. Cambridge: Polity.

Bauman, Z. (1995) *Life in Fragments: Essays in Postmodern Morality*. Oxford: Blackwell.

Best, S. (1997) 'Power and Politics', in Nik Jorgensen (eds), *Sociology: An Interactive Approach*. London: Collins Educational.

Best, S., Griffiths, J. and Hope, T. (2000) *Active Sociology*. Harlow: Longman.

Campbell, B. (1996) 'The dangers of New Labour's communitarian ideas', *Sociological Research Online*.

Dahl, R.A. (1956) *A Preface to Democratic Theory*. Chicago: University of Chicago Press.

Dahl, R.A. (1961) *Who Governs? Democracy and Power in an American City*. New Haven, CT: Yale University Press.

Dahrendorf, R. (1974) *The New Liberty*. London: Routledge.

Dahrendorf, R. (1979) *Life Chances*. Chicago: University of Chicago Press.

Dahrendorf, R. (1988) *The Modern Social Conflict*. London: Weidenfeld and Nicolson.

Durkheim, Emile (1897) *Suicide: A Study in Sociology*. London: Routledge.

Duverger, M. (1951) (1964) *Political Parties*. London: Methuen.

Duverger, M. (1990) *Political Parties: Their Organisation and Activity in the Modern State*. London: Methuen.

Etzioni, A. (1992) *The Parenting Deficit*. London: Fontana.

Etzioni, A. (1993) *The Spirit of Community*. London: Fontana.

Etzioni, A. (1997) *The Golden Rule*. London: Fontana.

Finer, S. (1987) 'State and nation-building in Europe: the role of the military', in Charles Tilly (ed.), *The Formation of Nation States in Europe*. Princeton, NJ: Princeton University Press.

George, V. and Wilding, P. (1982) *Ideology and Social Welfare*. London: Routledge.

Giddens, A. (1985) *The Nation State and Violence: Volume Two of a Contemporary Critique of Historical Materialism*. Cambridge; Polity.

Giddens, A. (1992) *Modernity and Self Identity*. Cambridge: Polity.

Giddens, A. (1994) *Beyond Left and Right*. Cambridge: Polity.

Giddens, A. (1998) *The Third Way*. Cambridge: Polity.

Giddens, A. (1998a) 'After the Left's paralysis', *New Statesman and Society* (1 May: pp.18).

Gramsci, Antonio (1957) *The Modern Prince and Other Writings*. Lawrence and Wishart: London.

Habermas, J. (1974) *Towards a Rational Society*. London: Heinemann.

Habermas, J. (1976) *Towards a Rational Society: Student Protest, Science and Politics*. London: Heinemann.

Hall, S. (1983) *The Politics of Thatcherism*. London: Lawrence and Wishart.

Haseler, S. (1989) *The Battle for Britain: Thatcher and the New Liberals*, quoted in M. Horsman and A. Marshall (1994) *After the Nation State*. London: Harper Collins.

Hirst, P. (1988) *Politics After Thatcherism*. London: Macmillan.

Houghton, P. (1990) 'Liberal Democracy', *Liberal News* (July).

Kavanagh, Dennis (1990) *Thatcherism and British Politics: The End of Consensus*. Oxford: Oxford University Press.

Kirchheimer Otto (1941) *Changes in the Structure of Political Compromise*. Studies in Philosophy and Social Science. (New York: Institute of Social Research).

Kirchheimer, Otto (1990) Political Justice: *The use of Legal Procedure for Political Ends*. Princeton: Princeton University Press.

Le Grand, J. (1986) *Privatisation and the Welfare State*. Basingstoke: Macmillan.

Lindblom, C. (1977) *Politics and Markets*. New York: Basic Books.

Lloyd, J. (1997) 'New Deal' in *New Statesman and Society*, February 1997.

MacIntyre, Alasdair (1999) *Dependent Rational Animals: Why Human Beings Need Virtues*. London: Duckworth.

Macmurray, J. (1961) *Self as Agent*. London: Faber and Faber.

Marshall, T.H. (1964) 'Citizenship and social class', in T.H. Marshall (ed.), *Sociology at the Crossroads*. London: Heinemann.

Marx, K. (1863) *Capital: A Critical Analysis of Capitalist Production*. London: Allen and Unwin.

Marx, K. (1976; first published 1867) *Capital: A Critique of Political Economy*. London: Penguin, in association with *New Left Review*.

McKenzie, R. (1963) *Political Parties*. London: Heinemann.

Meadowcroft, M. (1989) *Liberalism Today and Tomorrow*. Coventry: The Liberal Association.

Michels, R. (1949, 1962; first published 1911) *Political Parties*. Glencoe: The Free Press.

Miliband, R. (1973; first published 1969) *The State in Capitalist Society*. London: Quartet.

Norton, P. (1987) quoted in M. Horsman and A. Marshall (1994) *After the Nation State*. London: Harper Collins.

Parsons, T. (1951) *The Social System*. London: Routledge.

Pateman, (1970) *Participation and Democratic Theory*. Cambridge: Cambridge University Press.

Pizzorno, A. (1990) *Political Sociology*. Harmondsworth: Penguin.

Plant, R. (1998) 'Citizenship', in *New Statesman and Society* (February).

Popper, Karl (1957) *The Poverty of Historicism*. London: Routledge.

Poulantzas, Nicos (1978) *Political Power and Social Classes*. London: Verso.

Powell, E. (1966) *Medicine and Politics*. London: Pitman.

Rawls, John (1973) *The Liberal Theory of Justice: A Critical Examination*. Clarendon Press.

Rorty, R. (1989) *Irony, Contingency and Solidarity*. Cambridge: Cambridge University Press.

Rorty, R. (1991) *Objectivity, Relativism and Truth*. Cambridge: Cambridge University Press.

Sandel, Michael (1998) *Liberalism and the Limits of Justice*. Cambridge: Cambridge University Press.

Sennett, R. (1997) 'Drowning in syrup', *Times Literary Supplement* (February).

Seyd, P. and Whiteley, P. (1992) *Labour's Grassroots: The Politics of Party Membership*. Oxford: Clarendon Press.

Shin'Ya Ono (1965) quoted in P. Hirst (1988) *Politics After Thatcherism*. London: Macmillan.

Taylor, Charles (1989) *Sources of Self: The Making of the Modern Entity*. Cambridge: Cambridge University Press.

Turner, B. (1999) *Current Sociology*. London: Sage.

Weber, M. (1922) *Economy and Society: An Outline of Interpretive Sociology*. Berkely: University of California Press.

6

New Social Movements

The study of social movements has a long history within sociology. Piotr Sztompka (1993) provides us with the following outline of definitions stretching back to the early 1950s:

Definitions of social movements:

'Collective enterprises to establish a new order of life' (Blumer, 1951).

'Collective efforts to effect changes in the social order' (Lang and Lang, 1961).

'Collective acting with some continuity to promote or resist change in society or group of which it is a part' (Turner and Killian, 1972).

'Collective efforts to control change, or to alter the direction of change' (Lauer, 1976).

'Collective attempts to express grievances and discontent and/or to promote or resist change' (Zald and Berger, 1978).

'Groups of individuals gathered with the common purpose of expressing subjectively felt discontent in a public way and changing the perceived social and political bases of that discontent' (Eyerman and Jamison, 1991).

(Sztompka, 1993: 276)

Finally, he provides his own definition of social movements: 'loosely organized collectivities acting together in an non-institutionalized manner in order to produce change in their society' (Sztompka, 1993: 276).

The discussion of New Social Movements (NSMs) takes place either against a background of the 'new times' of a postmodern politics or against the background of 'disorganised capitalism'. As we suggested in Area 3, postmodern politics is a very uncertain form of politics. For many researchers, NSMs have their roots in 'disorganised capitalism', a form of society in which economic relationships are global, and the distinct national economies and their governments decline in power. This is a form of society that relies heavily on computers, and power is maintained by a variety of forms of surveillance. According to Hall and Jacques, a 'feature of New Times is the proliferation of the sites of antagonism and resistance, and the appearance of new subjects, new social movements, new collective identities – an enlarged sphere for the operation of politics, new constituencies for change' (1989: 17). In other words, there has been a significant shift away from 'class-based' politics towards a new form of politics reflecting conflicts that were largely ignored for most of the period of modernity. NSMs have taken up this new form of politics. Although almost any form of collective action can be classed as a social movement, it is possible to outline the following four types of NSMs:

- *Alternative NSMs*. These movements aspire to bring about limited transformation in lifestyles.
- *Redemptive NSMs*. These movements aspire to bring about fundamental change in lifestyles.
- *Reformative NSMs*. These movements aspire to reform either a segment or the whole of society.
- *Fanatical NSMs*. These movements aspire to modify society completely, if necessary by violent forms of direct action or by the use of terror.

The distinction between Old Social Movements
and New Social Movements

Unlike Old Social Movements (OSMs), which tend to be largely class-based movements and to focus upon the state as the target for their collective activities, NSMs are said not to be class-based movements and not to direct their activities against the state alone.

The distinction between OSMs and NSMs has been broadly outlined by Paul Bagguley (1996), who explains that OSMs are influenced by economic factors that directly affect their members' future economic advancement, such as wages, job security and issues related to control at work. In contrast, NSMs are said to be 'post-materialist', and to be concerned with issues, such as peace, the environment and human rights, that do not directly affect the members' economic position. NSMs are primarily concerned with what might be termed 'identity politics', that is, issues about personal identity rather than ownership of the means of production. The support for OSMs mainly comes from working-class people. In contrast, support for NSMs is mainly drawn from the new middle classes, particularly white-collar public-sector employees. The organisational structures of the OSMs are built upon a central bureaucracy with a national committee structure. NSMs are built upon 'networks' that are largely informal, or what the textbooks on the subject refer to as 'polycephalus' in nature, meaning that they rely upon participation – often in the form of direct action – rather than representation. OSMs attempt to influence important people who have been elected to office or to influence some group that is powerful within a corporate structure. In contrast, NSMs are concerned with direct action, often involving symbolic protests such as obstructing the building of motorways.

Mark Kirby (1995) gives the following list of groups or loose collections of groups that are most often cited as examples of NSMs:

- The black civil rights movement
- The women's liberation movement
- The gay liberation movement
- The student movement
- The environmental movement
- The peace movement

These very diverse groups have the following facts in common:

- They favour protest that usually takes the form of direct action
- The basis of their protest is not solely concerned with who owns the means of production
- Their emergence is partly because of the failure of traditional political parties

The rise of NSMs

A number of reasons have been suggested for the rise of NSMs since the 1960s. As part of a wider discussion of the emergence of 'disorganised capitalism', Claus Offe (1985) suggests the following three possible reasons for their growth.

○ Capitalism has become much more bureaucratic in nature, and this generates a number of new discontents. For example, women workers can point to the similarity between male and female contracts of employment within an organisation and demand an end to discrimination against women.
○ There has been a significant change in the techniques of managerial control at work, and an increase in state intervention in the personal lives of citizens.
○ The class-based system of political representation has broken down. In other words, the concerns that people have over sexual and racial equality, the environment and peace-related issues could not be easily accommodated in the programmes of class-based movements, such as the labour movement or the Confederation of British Industry (CBI).

In Offe's analysis, two groups are important in the emergence of NSMs: the 'new' middle class – whom we will discuss below – and the 'new decommodified groups', such as students, the unemployed, and housewives. However, as Paul Bagguley (1996) points out, it is not clear how capitalism's becoming more bureaucratic can be directly related to the emergence of NSMs. In addition, the 'decommodified groups' would appear to lack both the financial and organisational resources to mobilise a NSM.

Disorganised capitalism

According to Scott Lash and John Urry (1987), the period in history since the end of the nineteenth century could be described as that of 'organised capitalism'. As Marx and Engels clearly outlined, capitalism brought order into people's lives by revolutionising production and making great changes in how labour time is organised. With the emergence of global processes (which we will look at in Area 7), capitalism becomes 'disorganised'. National markets are much less effectively regulated, and there is a decline in the size of the industrial working class with a consequent decline in class-based politics. Again, as we saw in Area 3, politics is now characterised by fragmentation, pluralism and the growth of NSMs.

Active participants often have little in common with people involved in other NSMs, giving politics a highly fragmented feel. For example, this fragmentation of politics within disorganised capitalism can be demonstrated by looking at a possible relationship between women's liberation movements and black liberation movements. Both movements integrate themselves around their own organised, cooperative and collective identity, which makes them distinct within the wider society. In part, the women's identity is built upon feelings of being sexually threatened, while black men can be viewed by women as sexually threatening. Hence, even though both NSMs seek liberation from oppression by collective action, and other forms of raising consciousness, the women can be said to reinforce racist assumptions within the wider society; both groups ignore each other's view of the world and their place within it. Under the Greater London Council, which was abolished by the Conservative government in the 1980s, the council's Women's Committee broke up amid accusations of racism.

NSMs: emotional recruitment

There is an emotional aspect of NSM recruitment that we do not find in the recruitment to class-based movements or traditional political parties. Julian McAllister-Groves (1995) outlines what he calls the 'emotions approach to social movement recruitment'. Traditionally, argues McAllister-Groves, it was asserted by functionalists such as Neil Smelser (1992) that people joined social movements because they had a grievance, brought about by some form of frustration, relative deprivation or other psychological condition caused by 'strains' within the social system. In contrast, McAllister-Groves explains that the most recent contributions to the understanding of NSM recruitment builds upon the work of Erving Goffman (1974), and is concerned with how NSMs attract people to their cause by 'framing'.

What is 'framing'?

Goffman's book *Frame Analysis: An Essay on the Organisation of Experience* (1974) is concerned with how people make sense of their personal experience, as Goffman explained:

> I assume that definitions of the situation are built up in accordance with principles of organisation which govern events – at least social ones – and our subjective involvement in them; frame is the word I use to refer to such of these basic elements as I am able to identify. That is the definition of frame. My phrase 'frame analysis' is a slogan to refer to the examination in these terms of the organisation of experience. (Goffman, 1974: 10–11)

Definitions of the situation can be viewed as informal rules or ways of behaving within a group; 'frameworks' are viewed as *'schemata of interpretation'*, organising principles that people use to give their lives and actions meaning. In some cases, such organising principles have no apparent shape, but all provide the individual and the group with a perspective. The frame not only organises meaning for the individual but also helps to organise involvement. NSMs therefore are involved in 'constructing sets of beliefs that encourage potential recruits to act because their beliefs appeal to them' (McAllister-Groves, 1995: 436).

McAllister-Groves goes on to explain that NSMs:

○ Are involved in providing a code that determines which emotions are common and acceptable for an ordinary person in any given situation

- Clarify and brand sentiments according to the NSM's own cultural categories
- Provide a place to avoid 'emotional deviance'

As McAllister-Groves explains,

> The animal rights activists that I studied experienced affection and empathy for the animals portrayed in animal rights literature as helpless victims of cruelty. Most of them, however, were attracted to the movement because of its ability to legitimate their affection and empathy for animals in a way that reduced difficult interactions with outsiders who viewed them as being too emotional and therefore irrational. (McAllister-Groves, 1995: 438)

In other words, the NSM provided men and women with an opportunity legitimately to share their emotions about an issue with other like-minded people. This was particularly true for men who join NSMs, and who are said to be embarrassed and unwilling to show emotion outside such a group. Such shows of emotion to non-activists would make a person feel great embarrassment or 'emotional deviance'.

In contrast to this emotional position, Day and Robbins (1987) suggest that middle-class people who joined CND and other parts of the peace movement in the 1980s did so not out of any emotional attachment to 'peace' but out of economic self-interest. As they explain,

> The mobilisation of welfare professionals must be seen in the context of the crises of social democracy and the sharpening of conflicts within the British state, between its repressive and productive arms. There has been a shift of resources from welfare services to the police and the military, and an accompanying tendency to legitimate the role of the state in terms of 'law and order' rather than social welfare. In the face of this material and ideological threat it is hardly surprising that the Peace Movement provides an avenue of mobilisation that is particularly attractive to members of the caring professions. (Day and Robbins, 1987: 232)

In other words, Day and Robbins see the rise of NSMs as directly linked to the economic interests of their members; the activity of the peace movement can be viewed as a form of institutionalised class action.

In comparison, postmodernists who take an interest in NSMs point to the variety of skirmishes and conflicts in the world which have little or no direct relationship to class divisions. Moreover, there is a rich diversity of groups that are attempting to impose their own view of how to organise society upon us. As Paul Bagguley suggests, 'New Social Movements have been characterised as postmodern because they reject modernist political discourses and class identities' (Bagguley, 1996: 606). Modernist political discourses are the ideologies, such as liberalism, conservatism, Fabian socialism, social democracy, etc., that are concerned with dividing up the economic cake between various groups.

Alain Touraine: NSMs, historicity and the end of the social

According to Alain Touraine (1985), collective action, via NSMs, is at the centre of social change. Moreover, people are involved with a NSM if they clearly identify the following:

○ An adversary, something or somebody they are in conflict with
○ The prize of the struggle, arguments not being just over different ways of solving the problem
○ The actors themselves, in whose name they are fighting

The views of the participants in these movements on issues such as the nature and distribution of power are central to how NSMs operate. As a result of his involvement in the events in Paris in spring 1968, Touraine initially argued that NSMs enhance participatory pluralistic democracy.

In the 1960s and 1970s, Touraine developed a sociology of action according to which the causes of social change were found not within social structures but within the activities and struggles of social movements. A central concept that he developed at this time was the concept of 'historicity', the ability of social action to bring about social change. Hence our capacity for reflexive social action is a key element in the transformation of social life. Historicity has the following three elements:

○ Knowledge – our understanding of nature and society
○ Accumulation – our economic activity
○ Cultural model – the interpretative process which underpins our social actions

These three factors constitute the self-transformative capacity within a society. Moreover, it is social movements that are at the forefront of this process of historicity. NSMs signify a change from the traditional modern industrial society, as outlined by Durkheim, Weber and Marx, to a post-industrial or 'programmed' society. NSMs are concerned with struggles over lifestyle, community, populism and anti-technological sentiments. NSMs have the capacity to transform the culture of a society, and historicity is about a shift in the cognitive basis of society.

However, in the 1990s, Touraine became increasingly pessimistic about the ability of NSMs to effect social transformation. One reason for this was Touraine's view that the 'social' was becoming assimilated within the 'cultural'. We were moving into a period of 'hypermodernity' or 'demodernization' in which class consciousness, rationality and community were becoming fragmented. We no longer had a unified modern society. He argues that there emerged at the end of the twentieth century a range of post-social movements that expressed nothing except their own individualism. The themes taken up by post-social movements are people's subjective experience of such diverse things as sexuality, consumption and the nation.

Boris Frankel (1987) has observed that the theory of NSMs has replaced class theory and class politics, as NSMs are concerned with issues that affect all social classes and draw members and supporters from all social classes. These movements are seen as the carriers of future social change.

Gerard Delanty (1999) outlines a number of criticisms of Touraine's work; essentially he makes the following two points:

○ Touraine has a tendency to overstate the end of the social; he takes away society but leaves only a void in its place
○ Touraine never spells out his conception of the subject

Beck – 'the risk society'

The environmental movement is a good example of a NSM which has emerged independently of class-based politics. In *The Risk Society* (1992), Beck argues that we are in the midst of a transition from an industrial society to a risk society. This means that we are moving from a social situation in which political conflicts and divisions are defined by a logic of the distribution of 'goods' to one in which conflicts are becoming defined by the distribution of 'bads' – in other words, the distribution of hazards and risks. This generates a new form of modernity, which Beck terms 'reflexive modernisation'. In this form of modernity, the state is concerned with providing a safety net in view of possible risks.

The risk society is not a class society, as both rich and poor are subject to eco- logical risks. Hence, in this form of modernity, anxiety replaces need. There is much confusion over how we are to define problems and possible solutions; we lose faith in experts and expert systems. There are seemingly no obvious answers to the problems that we face, and the enhanced reflexivity of individual people generates both new problems and new solutions. In place of the class- versus-class division of the industrial society, the risk society places sector in con- flict with sector, with some sectors becoming 'risk winners' (for example, chemicals, biotechnology and the nuclear industry), while others may become 'risk losers', (for example, the food industry, tourism and fisheries). The risk society knows no national boundaries, as shown by the effects of the Chernobyl nuclear disaster. Although, in practice, the poor, especially in the Third World, are more likely to be adversely affected.

In summary, for Beck, risks have the following characteristics:

○ Risks are made by society; they do not come from nature
○ Risks are the unseen and often unexpected side-effects of the attempts to control and refashion nature
○ Risks are abstract, often detached from people, and are experienced as beyond our immediate control
○ Risks are global

- Risks have a 'boomerang effect'; they have no respect for barriers of class, status or nation
- Risks are believed to have the potential to bring humanity to an end

The environmental movement

Is there a distinct Green political ideology? If so, what are the philosophical foundations of a Green ideology? The passages below should help you to form an opinion about Green ideology.

In his book *Green Political Thought* (1990), Andrew Dobson explains that

> Green politics explicitly seeks to decentre the human being, to question mechanistic science and its technological consequences, to refuse to believe that the world was made for human beings, and it does this because it has been led to wonder whether dominant post-industrialism's project of material affluence is either desirable or sustainable. (Dobson, 1990: 9)

Dobson sees Green politics with its source in the early Enlightenment, as a challenge to existing norms and practices; however, he warns us that Green politics 'should not' be seen as 'a form of reincarnated romanticism' (Dobson, 1990: 10).

There are however, the following two distinct forms of Green politics:

- *Shallow environmentalism*. It is good to care for the environment, as man will benefit.
- *Dark-green ecology*. Nature has an intrinsic value.

In *The Turning Point* (1985), Fritjof Capra defines the distinction as follows:

> Whereas shallow environmentalism is concerned with the efficient control and management of the natural environment for the benefit of 'man', the deep ecology movement recognises that ecological balance will require profound changes in our perception of the role of human beings in the planetary ecosystem. In short, it will require a new philosophical and religious basis. (quoted in Schwarz and Schwarz, 1987: 126)

Schwarz and Schwarz explain that Arne Naess (an ecological campaigner) coined the term 'deep ecology' in the early 1970s:

> The term deep is supposed to suggest explication of fundamental presuppositions of value as well as of facts and hypotheses. Deep ecology therefore transcends the limit of any particular science of today, including systems theory and scientific ecology. (Naess quoted in Schwarz and Schwarz, 1987: 130)

Naess draws upon Eastern philosophy, which is non-linear and unlike Western thought. The latter is said to have 'an excessive reliance on rational and scientific thought' (Schwarz and Schwarz, 1987: 131). This foundation of deep ecology places great emphasis upon theories and concepts such as the Gaia hypothesis,

Table 6.1   *Core value of shallow and deep ecology*

Shallow ecology	Deep ecology
Natural diversity is valuable as a resource for us.	Natural diversity has its own intrinsic value.
It is nonsense to talk about value except as value for humankind.	Equating 'value' with 'value for humans' reveals a social prejudice.
Plant species should be saved because of their value as genetic reserves for human agriculture and medicine.	Plant species should be saved because of their intrinsic value.
Pollution should be decreased if it threatens economic growth.	Decrease of pollution has priority over economic growth.
Third-World population growth threatens ecological equilibrium.	World population at any level threatens ecosystems, but the population and behaviour of industrial states does so more than any others. Human population today is excessive.
'Resources' means resources for humans.	'Resource' means resource for living beings.
People will not tolerate a broad decrease in their standard of living.	People should not tolerate decreases in their quality of life but in the standard of living in overdeveloped countries.
Nature is cruel and necessarily so.	Man is cruel but not necessarily so.

Source: Schwarz and Schwarz, 1987: 126–7.

the wilderness and bioregions. Schwarz and Schwarz list the major differences between the two Green approaches (Table 6.1):

This distinction between deep and shallow ecology makes it difficult to draw analogies with other parties and ideologies. Shallow ecology could be adopted by most of the political parties; however, adoption of deep ecology would involve a radical revision of ideology and practice. Moreover, as Dobson makes clear, there is a further problem: 'the tension between the radical nature of the social and political change that it seeks, and the reliance on traditional liberal-democratic means of bringing it about' (1990: 23). There are two contrasting views about the relationship between Green ideology and other ideologies, such as socialism. On the one hand, there is the view outlined by Dodds that 'we are all harmed by the ecological crisis and therefore we all have a common interest in uniting together with people of all classes and all political allegiances to counter this mutually shared threat' (1988: 45).

This view has a great deal in common with the 'end of ideology' thesis, which suggests that political differences and political conflict are coming to an end. In this case, it would be because of a common threat that makes class conflict redundant. Dobson supports this view: 'It makes no appreciable difference who owns the mode of production if the production process itself is based on the assumption that its development need not be hindered by thoughts of limits to growth' (1990: 32). In contrast, Schwarz and Schwarz see a much closer link with Marxism: 'New economics has taken from Marxism the restoration of the idea of needs and contributions – to each according to his need, from each according to his ability.' (1987: 25).

In an effort to produce a synthesis of Green thought, Dobson outlines what he considers to be the principal features of the natural world and the social implications of their adoption into political society:

○ Diversity – toleration, stability and democracy
○ Interdependence – equality
○ Longevity – tradition
○ Nature as 'female' – a particular conception of feminism

Classification of NSMs: Mario Diani

Mario Diani (1992) has attempted to pull together much of the relevant research and theories in the area and to produce a clear view of the nature of the NSM. Firstly, he explains that such diverse events and organisations as revolutions, religious and political groups, and single-issue campaigns have been defined as NSMs. Diani identifies four main trends within NSM analysis.

The first trend is collective behaviour approaches, as in the work of Turner and Killian (1972). As indicated earlier, they define a NSM as 'a collectivity acting with some continuity to promote or resist a change in the society or organisation of which it is part' (Diani, 1992: 4). These groups do not have a clearly defined membership or leadership, and their actions and views are determined by informal responses of the current supporters rather than by any formal management plan. In other words, this approach suggests that NSMs are networks of communication and action rather than formal organisations.

The second trend is resource mobilisation theory, as exemplified by the work of Zald and Berger (1978), who place much more attention on the role of the organisational factors within NSMs, which they define as 'a set of opinions and beliefs which represents preferences for changing some elements of the social structure and/or reward distribution of a society. A counter movement is a set of opinions and beliefs in a population opposed to a social movement' (McCarthy and Zald [1976], quoted in Diani, 1992: 4). In other words, this approach suggests that NSMs attempt to draw together resources in an effort to change some aspect of society.

The third trend is that of political process approaches, as in the work of Tilly (1985), who associates the development of NSMs with the exclusion of individual interests from the established political processes and political channels. NSMs are a product of social unrest among people with a shared identity who are ignored by traditional political parties. Tilly defined NSMs as a 'sustained series of interactions between power holders and persons successfully claiming to speak on behalf of a constituency lacking formal representation, in the course of which those persons make publicly visible demands for changes in the distribution or exercise of power, and back those demands with public demonstrations of support' (Tilly [1985], quoted in Diani, 1992: 5). In other words, this approach suggests that NSMs comprise individuals who are ignored by the major political parties.

The fourth and last trend is that of NSM approaches, as in the work of Touraine (1985). This approach attempts to link the rise of NSMs to wider structural and cultural changes within society. NSMs emerge as a consequence of the new contradictions which replace the class conflict between the bourgeoisie and the proletariat that we find in modern/organised capitalism as this form of society gives way to a post-industrial society. Touraine views the NSM as a 'combination of a principle of identity, a principle of opposition and a principle of totality' (Touraine [1985], quoted in Diani, 1992: 6). In other words, in the post-industrial society, individual people develop their own view of the world, their rivals and the rewards that can be gained from any conflict. NSMs are a product of the rise of a post-industrial society. In this post-industrial society, social classes disappear and the space they leave is filled by NSMs.

In summary, for Diani, the NSM is not an organisation, but is all of the following:

○ A network of informal interaction involving links between a number of individuals, groups and organisations
○ A form of solidarity built upon shared beliefs
○ A form of collective action outside the traditional political institutions, promoting or resisting social change
○ A basis for a collective identity

A 'queer' identity?

According to Diani, social movements are built upon a collective identity, and this collective identity is achieved through self-interpretation. If there is no collective identity, we might conclude that there is no social movement. Tim Jordan has suggested that 'It is not clear why a collective identity is constructed by actors in a movement' (1987: 677).

In the 1990s, there was a significant increase in the level of political activism among gay and lesbians who 'came out' since the beginning of the AIDS epidemic. In Britain, the activist group OutRage captured the headlines because of its tactic of 'outing' closet homosexuals (using a number of methods to force unwilling individuals to admit publicly that they were homosexual). OutRage has also been active in fighting anti-gay discrimination, prejudice and violence. In particular, building on the work of Michel Foucault (1977), OutRage has attempted to remake and remodel the identity of the homosexual man and lesbian woman, moving away from the notion of 'gay' and adopting the label 'queer'. In the eyes of OutRage, individuals who describe themselves as 'homosexual' are accepting a heterosexual and false-scientific view of sexuality in which the homosexuals are marginalised and can be accepted as a person only if they reject their 'queerness' or deny the legitimacy of their chosen sexuality. People who describe themselves as homosexuals are merely attempting to assimilate themselves into heterosexual life by accepting a role as a member of a distinct minority who ask for tolerance; but will always be regarded as sexually wrong. 'Queer' culture has the following features:

○ It is highly political, but above party politics
○ It rejects the rational sexual categories imposed upon us all, both homosexual and straight, male and female, in which we are asked to define ourselves as sexually 'normal'/heterosexual or otherwise
○ It aims to destabilise the power relations that maintain these categories that force homosexuals into a private world
○ It refuses to accept homosexuality as a minority group in the population

However, many lesbians and gays have questioned the notion of 'queer' and the identity that goes with it. Consider the following examples:

Assimilationism, as a term used to apply to minority groups in society, is the desire to merge – or the practice of merging – with the dominant majority.

(Toby Manning, *Gay Times*, April 1995: 19, 20)

Assimilationism is generally used in a slightly pejorative way to describe efforts amongst lesbian and gay men to become part of society. My own feeling is that (at Stonewall) we're not aiming towards a situation where everyone becomes the same – it's all about recognition and respect for difference. That's what makes life and society interesting. We're campaigning for social justice and equality. I don't see that as collaborating. (Angela Mason, executive director of the Stonewall Group, in *Gay Times*, April 1995: 19, 20)

Assimilationism has been the dominant lesbian and gay rights strategy for the last 30 years, emphasising law reform, and the idea that the best way to advance our interests is by quietly blending in with mainstream heterosexual society. However, since the legal system has been devised by and is dominated by heterosexuals, that inevitably means that we win equality on terms which are dictated by straights. The end result is the phenomenon of 'hetero homos' – queer versions of heterosexual lifestyle and morality. The opposite of assimilation is not separatism. It is the proud assertion of a distinctive queer identity and culture. Assimilation implies that there is nothing worthwhile or valuable in the lesbian and gay experience. Queer emancipation does not depend on us adapting to the heterosexual status quo, but on us radically transforming it. In questioning and rejecting the predominant social view that homosexuality is wrong and inferior, many of us also end up challenging other social assumptions. While equal rights are an important first step, they do not amount to full queer emancipation. There's a need for a complete overhaul for all the laws and values around sex – a post-equality agenda. This would benefit both heterosexuals and homosexuals and it creates the possibility of a new radical consensus for social change which transcends sexual orientation. (Peter Tatchell, OutRage activist in *Gay Times*, April 1995: 19, 20)

Most of us would agree that we should do whatever we can to protect members of our community. If 'outing' can help destroy the power and credibility of gay homophobes who harm other lesbians and gay men, then it is arguably the morally right thing to do. By not 'outing' gay public figures who are homophobic, we are effectively allowing them to continue to hurt other gay people. Our silence and inaction make us accomplices by default. (Peter Tatchell, 'The ethics of "outing"' *Gay Times*, February 1995: 37)

NSM: the anti-poll tax movement in Leeds?

In 1989, the Conservative government introduced a new local tax, the community charge, although this was commonly known as the poll tax. It was a regressive tax in that it hit the poorest the hardest. Everybody in a local area would pay the same amount of local taxation for local government services, irrespective of their ability to pay. The response to this tax was organised demonstrations, often violent, and a campaign of non-payment. Paul Bagguley (1995) conducted a case study of the anti-poll tax movement (APTM) in Leeds.

In Leeds, local APTM groups were highly informal organisations, coordinated by a city-wide federation, which was run by three elected officers: a secretary, a treasurer and a chairperson. Local organisations sent two representatives to the citywide federation although there was no control of the local groups from the centre. The Federation organised demonstrations – notably public poll tax bill burnings – transport, and leaflets and held advice sessions for people who were facing legal problems for non-payment.

Some of the local groups had formal membership schemes, issuing membership cards and collecting dues; other local groups were more informal, operating like a 'telephone tree'. Bagguley describes the structure as a 'series of concentric circles with a core of committed activists, surrounded by a ring of people who turn up for public meetings, demonstrations etc. and finally those who didn't pay but did not go to meetings etc.' (Bagguley, 1995: 713). Some local groups had the active support of left-wing groups such as Socialist Organizer and the Communist Party. In other areas of the city, radical Christians, the peace movement, CND and other single-issue groups were involved. Council estates often had the support of tenants' associations. Finally, the Leeds Trades Club provided the federation with office premises. However, the Labour Party and most trade unions, apart from NALGO, were unwilling to support the federation, because its activities – notably its most effective weapon of non-payment – often involved breaking the law.

Jurgen Habermas: NSMs and communicative competence

A key question about NSMs is whether they express *particularistic or universalistic* values. In other words, do NSMs advance the values and interests of small sections of the population and against the values and interests of the wider population? Or do they advance the cause of democracy and therefore improve the prospects for emancipation for all oppressed groups within the population?

Postmodernists clearly argue that NSMs further particularistic interests, as universalistic interests are built upon the *grand narratives* that postmodern writers, such as Lyotard (1984), have so forcefully rejected, as we discussed in an earlier area. In contrast, Jurgen Habermas (1976) takes his starting point from Weber's (1922) theory of rationalisation (which we discussed in Area 2). For Habermas, the *'lifeworld'*, or *the world of lived experience* – by which he means the taken-for-granted, common-sense, everyday world and the everyday assumptions we make and the beliefs we share that intertwine to form the relations and communications between members of a social community – is in danger of being destroyed by the rational economic and bureaucratic systems within modernity that destroy local cultures. This is the rationalisation process with its bureaucratic structures and formal, rule-based systems. The local process of social integration – how people bond together into communities – and local processes of socialisation – ways of informally teaching children and young people about the culture and informal rules about ways of living within a community – are changing from local systems based upon locally produced culture to a universal rational process. This is what Habermas terms the 'colonisation of the lifeworld', and it is a key part of the process of rationalisation.

Social movements attempt to defend the quality of life of people by becoming concerned with issues of personal and collective achievement that the process of rationalisation is taking away from them; these include issues such as equality, self-realisation, participation and human rights. They may take the form of *particularistic* concerns; however, social movements are also concerned with re-establishing a *communicative ethics*, which is entailed in the sharing of the same community norms. Although social movements may reflect differences of opinion and involve conflicts over a range of issues, such disputes can be resolved only if a movement is able and willing to listen to the other. This is what Habermas termed the ideal speech situation – a form of shared communication between people who want to resolve their differences.

Habermas defines an 'old politics', which is concerned with the economic issues that are a concern to OSMs, such as debates about the social security system and who gets what within it. In contrast, Habermas outlines a 'new politics' that is concerned with issues such as identity politics and human rights. This 'new politics' is the area of activity for the NSMs. Habermas draws parallels between the NSMs and what he terms the 'social-romantic' movements of the nineteenth century. These 'social-romantic' movements rejected modern rational capitalism. Examples of them include such diverse groups as craftsmen and 'escapist' movements such as the Ramblers Association or the Woodcraft Folk, which are often supported by middle-class people.

However, the following criticisms can be made of Habermas:

- Ralph Miliband (1985) asserts that the working class is not a spent force. Class-based politics can still provide the basis for mobilising the working population and bringing about change.
- Those who join the NSMs do not share the hostility that NSM theorists have for working-class politics; many would still label themselves as working-class. It

could be argued that the anti-poll-tax movement was an example of such a movement to mobilise the working class.

○ How 'new' are the NSMs? Those listed by Kirby – at the start of this area – for example, were all active and effective in the 1960s. It could be suggested that NSMs are not new; they are simply pressure groups that are not yet incorporated into the state decision-making structures. Alternatively, NSMs may be loosely-organised pressure groups or temporary pressure groups that exist only as long as an issue is newsworthy or until it is resolved. Motorway protests exist until the motorway is built or the decision is reversed.

More recently, Boris Frankel (1987) has developed these points. He notes that NSM theorists suggest that a 'new' politics has emerged to replace the class struggle. However, Frankel points out that their work provides much information on possible differences between OSMs and NSMs but very little on how NSMs are supposed to replace the structures and institutions of the state and private companies in political decision making. Very few NSMs support the idea of completely pulling down and rebuilding the state and its institutions, or support the idea of a stateless society. In other words, the important issue of state power is not well explained in the NSM analyses.

In addition, the members of NSMs have no clearly defined identity, and the movements themselves are rife with divisions. NSMs are treated as the substitutes for the working class; however, if we still live in a capitalistic society, where have the class conflict and the working class gone? Could it be that NSMs are simply the manifestation of working-class solidarity now that the Labour Party has shifted to the right and the trade unions have become much less effective because of the trade-union legislation since 1980?

Anthony Giddens: social movements and the far side of modernity

As we saw in Area 5, Anthony Giddens (1990) holds that within modernity all nation-states have a tendency towards polyarchy. You will recall that polyarchy is the most advanced form of pluralism – a condition within a community in which power is widely shared among a multiplicity of groups and organisations, all of which have their own sectional interests. The state is seen as the rule maker or umpire, or, in other words, as the 'honest broker' that attempts to balance opinions within the community in an effort to strike a balance between the various sectional interests. In addition, there is always political competition and a balance between competing interests. According to Robert Dahl (1961: 62), polyarchy is 'the government of a state or city by many: contrasted with monarchy'. Polyarchy includes a set of authoritative rules assigned in response to the citizen's wishes. This is necessary for the democratic process to work. These rules guarantee our civil and political rights.

Political/social movements operate with all of the following four dimensions of modernity that shape modern states in Giddens's analysis:

- Capitalism
- Industrialism
- Centralised administrative power – which makes use of surveillance
- Centralised control of military power

In Giddens's analysis, social movements have a key role to play in the transition from 'modernity' to 'postmodernity'. However, unlike most of the writers who consider the nature of postmodernity, Giddens views postmodernity as a form of 'utopian realism' at the far side of modernity which has institutional dimensions that have been changed by the activities of social movements. Not only do social movements have opportunities to exercise countervailing powers within society, but also their activities have moved the 'overall trajectory of development of modernity' (Giddens, 1992: 59) towards a 'radical democratisation' within which all people have greater opportunities to exercise power within society. Giddens provides us with a 'conceptual map' in which social movements are placed within the four dimensions of modernity, and are actively engaged in forms of struggle with the institutions that operate there. Social movements attempt to enhance the citizenship rights of individuals within each of the dimensions of modernity, and bring about significant change. Figure 6.2 shows the transition from modernity to postmodernity in Giddens's analysis and the key role that NSMs play in this process.

In the 1990s, Giddens argued that NSMs had important democratic qualities; they 'open up spaces for public dialogue in respect of the issues with which they are concerned' (1994: 17). NSMs give people opportunities to discuss issues that are not discussed by traditional political parties, including such issues as how people live their lives and the choices they make about any activity they choose to be involved in. Giddens refers to this as *dialogic democracy*, - the attempt by people to talk to each other in an effort to create active trust with others in order to further what Giddens calls *life politics*, the politics of self-actualisation or self-creation. However, as with many other writers we have looked at in this area, Giddens argues that NSMs cannot be viewed as 'socialist' in nature. In contrast to the class-based issues of socialism, NSMs 'have a deep involvement ... with the arenas of emotional democracy in personal life (1994: 121).

Giddens then looks at NSMs in terms of their use by individuals as a resource within late modernity or reflexive modernisation. Both Giddens and Beck view reflexivity in terms of changes in the institutional order. NSMs enhance the *knowledgeability* of the self but they cast doubt upon expert systems and therefore produce a loss of trust within the social order.

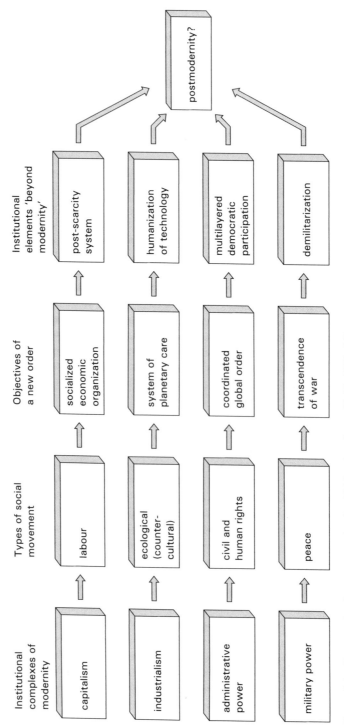

Figure 6.1 *From modernity to postmodernity: Giddens's scheme (Held, 1992: 34)*

Giddens's position on the role and purpose of NSMs is expressed in the following two passages:

> New forms of social movement mark an attempt at a collective reappropriation of institutionally repressed areas of life. Recent religious movements have to be numbered among these, although of course there is great variability in the sects and cults which have developed. But several other new social movements are particularly important and mark sustained reactions to basic institutional dimensions of modern social life. Although – and in some part because – it addresses questions which antedate the impact of modernity, the feminist movement is one major example. In its early phase, the movement was pre-eminently concerned with securing equal political and social rights between women and men. In its current stage, however, it addresses elemental features of existence and creates pressures towards social transformations of a radical nature. The ecological and peace movements are also part of this new sensibility to late modernity, as are some kinds of movements for human rights. Such movements, internally diverse as they are, effectively challenge some of the basic presuppositions and organising principles which fuel modernity's juggernaut. (Giddens, 1991: 208–209)

> New social movements cannot readily be claimed for socialism. While the aspirations of some such movements stand close to socialist ideals, their objectives are disparate and sometimes actively opposed to one another. With the possible exception of some sections of the Green movement, the new social movements are not 'totalizing' in the way socialism is (or was), promising a new 'stage' of social development beyond the existing order. Some versions of feminist thought, for example, are as radical as anything that went under the name of socialism. Yet they don't envisage seizing control of the future in the way the more ambitious versions of socialism have done. (Giddens, 1994: 3)

David Held (1992) makes a number of criticisms of Giddens's analysis of social movements. Although the quotation above suggests otherwise, Held argues that a number of social movements are excluded from Giddens's analysis, notably the feminist movement and religious groups. According to Held, these groups 'have no role in Giddens's scheme, suggesting ... that his conceptual framework may not make adequate allowance for some of the key pressure points in contemporary culture and politics' (Held, 1992: 37). In response to this, we note that in *The Nation State and Violence* (1985), Giddens does discuss both the women's movement and religious movements. Giddens explains that these movements can still be placed upon his 'conceptual map' or 'scheme' because these groups are concerned with the expansion of democratic rights, and therefore clearly concerned with issues of surveillance and governability.

Area Summary

In this area we outlined the distinction between OSMs and NSMs and the ways in which sociologists have classified NSMs. We suggested that OSMs are formal organisations in the Weberian sense and are more likely to be economic movements that have the financial well-being of their

continued

members as their focus. In contrast, NSMs are, on the whole, informal organisations that have little in common with the Weberian model.

Since the 1960s, NSMs have become very popular, as membership of political parties and OSMs has declined. We looked at the possible reasons, such as 'emotional' attachment, that people join NSMs. However, do people join the environmental movement, the gay liberation movement and the anti-poll-tax movement for 'emotional' or 'economic' reasons? Finally, we looked at Jurgen Habermas's and Anthony Giddens's contributions to the debate about NSMs.

References

Bagguley, P. (1996) 'Protest, poverty and power: a case study of the anti-poll tax movement', *Sociological Review,* 43(4): 693–719.

Beck, U. (1992) *The Risk Society.* London: Sage.

Best, S. (1997) 'Power and Politics', in Nik Jorgensen (eds), *Sociology: An Interactive approach.* London: Collins Educational.

Best, S., Griffiths, J. and Hope, T. (2000) *Active Sociology.* Harlow: Longman.

Blumer, H. (1951) 'Collective behavior', in J.B. Gittler (ed.), *Review of Sociology: Analysis of a Decade.* New York: Wiley.

Capra, F. (1985) *The Turning Point,* quoted in A. Dobson (1990) *Green Political Thought.* London: Routledge.

Dahl, R.A. (1961) *Who Governs? Democracy and Power in an American City.* New Haven, CT: Yale University Press.

Day, G. and Robbins, D. (1987) 'Activists for peace: the social basis of a local peace movement', in C. Creighton and M. Shaw (eds), *The Sociology of War and Peace.* Basingstoke: Macmillan.

Delanty, G. (1999) *Social Science: Beyond Constructivism and Realism.* Buckingham: Open University Press.

Diani, M. (1992) 'The concept of social movements', *Sociological Review,* 40(1): 1–25.

Dobson, A. (1990) *Green Political Thought.* London: Routledge.

Dodds, F. (1988) *Into the 21st Century.* Basingstoke: Green Print.

Eyerman, R. and Jamison, A. (1991) *Social Movements: A Cognitive Approach.* Cambridge: Polity.

Foucault, M. (1977) *Discipline and Punish: The Birth of the Prison.* New York: Pantheon.

Frankel, B. (1987) *The Post-Industrial Utopians.* Cambridge: Polity.

Giddens, A. (1985) *The Nation State and Violence: Volume Two of A Contemporary Critique of Historical Materialism.* Cambridge: Polity.

Giddens, A. (1990) *The Consequences of Modernity.* Cambridge: Polity.

Giddens, A. (1992) *Modernity and Self Identity.* Cambridge: Polity.

Giddens, A. (1994) *Beyond Left and Right.* Cambridge: Polity.

Goffman, E. (1974) *Frame Analysis: An Essay on the Organisation of Experience.* Harmondsworth: Pelican.

Habermas, J. (1976) *Legitimation Crisis*. London: Heinemann.

Hall, S. and Jacques, M. (eds) (1989) *New Times*. London: Lawrence and Wishart.

Held, D. (1992) in S. Hall, *Modernity and Its Futures*. Cambridge: Polity.

Hirst, P. (1988) *Politics After Thatcherism*. London: Macmillan.

Jordan, B. (1987) *Rethinking Welfare*. Oxford: Blackwell.

Kirby, M. (1995) *Investigating Political Sociology*. London: Collins Educational.

Lang, K. and Lang, G. (1961) *Collective Dynamics*. New York: Crowell.

Lash, S. and Urry, J. (1987) *The End of Organised Capitalism*. Cambridge: Polity.

Lauder, R. (1976) *Social Movements and Social Change*. Carbondale, IL: Southern Illinois Press.

Lyotard, J.F. (1984) *The Postmodern Condition: A Report on Knowledge*. Minneapolis, MN: University of Minnesota Press.

Manning, Toby, Angela Mason, and Peter Tatchell (1995) 'Assimilation' in *Gay Times*, April 1995. pp.19–20.

McAllister-Groves, J. (1995) 'Learning to feel: the neglected sociology of social movements', *Sociology Review*, 43(3): 435–461.

McCarthy, J.D. and Zald, M.N. (1976) 'Resource Mobilization and Social Movements: A Partial Theory', *American Journal of Sociology*, 82(6): 1212–41.

Miliband, R. (1985) *Capitalist Democracy in Britain*. Oxford: Oxford University Press.

Offe, C. (1985) 'New social movements: challenging the boundaries of institutional politics', *Social Research*, 52(4): 817–868.

Schwarz and Schwarz (1987) *Breaking Through: The Theory and Practice of Holistic Living*. Basingstoke: Green Print.

Smelser, N. (1992) 'External and internal factors in theories of social change', in H. Haferkamp and N. Smelser (eds), *Social Change and Modernity*. Berkeley, CA: University of California Press.

Sztompka, P. (1993) *The Sociology of Social Change*. Oxford: Blackwell.

Tatchell, Peter (1995) 'The ethics of outing' in *Gay Times*, February 1995. pp. 37.

Tilly, C. (1985) *Social Movements Old and New*. NSSR Working Paper No. 20. New York: Center for the Study of Social Change.

Touraine, A. (1985) 'Social movements and social change', in O.F. Orda, (ed.), *The Challenge of Social Change*. London: Sage.

Turner, R. and Killian, L.M. (1972) *Collective Behaviour*. Englewood Cliffs, NJ: Prentice-Hall.

Weber, Max (1922) *Economy and Society: An Outline of Interpretive Sociology*. Berkeley: University of California Press.

Zald, M.N. and Berger, M.A. (1978) 'Social movements in organizations: *coup d'état*, insurgency, and mass movements', *American Journal of Sociology*, 83 (4) 823–861.

7

Globalisation and Power

Area Goals

By the end of this area you should:

○ Be aware of the political, economic and cultural processes of globalisation
○ Be familiar with some of the major international organisations concerned with global governance
○ Have a critical understanding of the contributions to the debates about globalisation of David Held, Roland Robertson, Anthony Giddens, Francis Fukuyama, Immanuel Wallerstein, David Harvey and other Marxist writers
○ Appreciate how sociologists have attempted to make sense of the future
○ Be able to evaluate the contribution of postmodernist writers to the issues of international relations

What are the most recognised symbols around the world? The Christian cross, the International Red Cross or the logos for Coca-Cola and McDonalds? Who are the most famous names around the globe? The Secretary-General of the United Nations (UN) or Michael Jackson?

Globalisation takes the following forms:

1 *Economic.* Transnational corporations (TNCs) produce products in a number of countries and become involved in global markets looking for cheaper labour and raw materials. This involves capital shifts, as TNCs invest in a number of countries.

2 *Cultural.* Media images are transmitted around the world by multinational companies. This may lead to homogenisation of cultural forms (in other words, culture is becoming the same all over the world). In addition, some commentators, such as Ritzer (1996), have identified a process of McDonaldisation. Ways of working and tastes in such things as fast food become similar around the world.

3 *Political.* International organisations such as the UN, the International Monetary Fund and the G8 become involved in global governance. The collapse of communism in Eastern Europe has brought about a 'new world order' in which the Cold War has come to an end.

Underpinning the concept of *globalisation* is the notion that the world is becoming a single place. As a process, globalisation obviously has an effect on the life of everyone. Among many other things, drugs, sex tourism, the character of work, eating disorders and plastic surgery all have a global element. As Roland Robertson (1994) explains,

> The fact and the perception of ever increasing inter-dependence at the global level, the rising concern about the fate of the world as a whole and of the human species (particularly because of the threats of ecological degradation, nuclear disaster and AIDS), and the colonisation of the local by global life (not least via the mass media) facilitate massive processes of relativization of cultures, doctrines, ideologies and cognitive frames of reference. (Robertson, 1994: 87)

Robertson's argument is that the human race is becoming more interconnected, but, at the same time, we, as individuals, are becoming more anxious about the future of the human race. Moreover, at a cultural level, the global mass media wipes out local cultures to such an extent that people everywhere are even beginning to think in very similar ways.

Leslie Sklair (1993) has summarised the strengths and weaknesses of the main theories of globalisation. First, he considers Wallerstein's world systems model, which, as we have seen, takes its point of reference from Marx. In this approach, there is a worldwide division of labour within a global economy. The economy of a nation is linked in a number of ways to the global economy and can be either at its core, semi-periphery or periphery. Nations at the periphery of the global economy are much more likely to be in economic distress. However, because this model largely ignores cultural factors and overemphasises economic factors, it is said to be too deterministic in nature.

Second, we have Western 'cultural imperialism', in which the cultural products of multinational corporations based in the advanced countries destroy local or traditional cultures in the drive for higher profits. Ulf Hannerz (1989) has identified 'global homogenisation', the comprehensive supremacy of 'lowbrow' Western taste and lifestyles across the world. The large number of western products in the shops, Western cars in the streets, Western films, Western soap operas on television, etc. are all instances of this Western domination. This spread involves *Home and Away* rather than Shakespeare.

The third model is the global system based on transnational practices. This is Sklair's own model, in which TNCs pursue transnational practices, imposing their own ways of working upon the local population that they employ. Examples of this would include health and safety protocols imposed upon staff irrespective of the laws in the country, or customer-care policies that determine how staff are to treat customers irrespective of local customs and traditions. Such practices encourage economic, political and social or ideological practices, such as consumerism, to pass through state borders.

In addition, as we shall see below, in David Held's (1992) model, governments are becoming increasingly irrelevant in terms of their influence over a range of significant issues. For example, governments find it difficult to regulate their own economies, as global financial dealings can diminish the worth of a country's money. In addition, environmental issues cross national boundaries. These global processes are scarcely without problems. Although transnational governmental organisations, such as the UN, the European Union (EU), the North Atlantic Treaty Organisation (NATO) and the World Trade Organisation, have expanded their influence in the world, bringing people together from diverse cultures can still increase the chances of conflict between those of different ethnic identities. Globalisation can diminish what were commonly accepted political and economic structures without inevitably leading to the foundation of new systems.

Globalisation, then, can generate nationalist conflict in the world, because the governments of nation-states no longer make many of the political decisions. In addition, because globalisation as a process can destroy a person's cultural identity, people fight to protect their local ways of living. Although there is no one acceptable definition of nationalism from this perspective, we may consider it a counter-politics of the local. By 'a counter-politics of the local', I mean that local people come together with common ideas or shared beliefs, and stand in opposition to some outside power.

Nationalism

Nationalism is a counterpolitics of the local which contains its own distinct alternative view of modernity. It fosters a respect for local roots, in response to the impersonal and anonymous processes of globalisation, which can destroy any form of cultural identity. Alter (1985) explains the significance of this:

For the peoples of the southern Balkans, the struggle against Ottoman Turkey up until the first world war remained an important ingredient of their national consciousness; for the Irish it was conflict with England; while for the Poles, the catalyst of national fervour was resistance against the dividing powers of Russia, Prussia/Germany and Austria-Hungary. Likewise, in many of the African and Asian states that emerged after 1945, the fight against European colonialism and imperialism was the origin of a national consciousness which in most cases had yet to be created. (Alter, 1985: 20)

However, in constrast, Mark Kirby (1995: 208) has suggested that the following two critical points can be made against the globalisation thesis:

- The extent of the changes is overstated, particularly when it is implied that the whole world is involved
- Long-standing changes that result from larger historical trends are wrongly identified as being products of the 1980s and 1990s

Colonialism and racism

We must not lose sight of the fact that global issues have a long history within sociology. Ancient African kingdoms, such as Benin and Buganda, and ancient civilisations, such as the Aztecs of Mexico and the Incas of South America, were systematically pillaged, looted, and destroyed, and their people raped and enslaved. On the island of Tasmania (South of Australia), the white settlers hunted the Aborigines for sport until they had killed every single one – surely the worst holocaust, the worst case of genocide (the systematic extermination of a population), in history.

How could white Europeans have committed such terrible crimes against non-white populations around the world? The answer lies in the global/racist ideologies of colonialism.

The clue to comprehending racism is in the way in which one dominant group characterises the other in terms of a doctrine or set of beliefs that we term an ideology. Racist ideologies justify the cruelty of colonial exploitation and oppression outlined above. These ideologies share a number of assumptions, but the key one was a feeling of supremacy by the governing white Europeans based upon a belief in the laziness, immorality and stupidity of the oppressed non-white population.

Marxist writers, in particular, have discussed the economic consequences of colonialism and imperialism. Since Lenin in 1916, Marxists have argued that the development of capitalism has been dependent upon the economic exploitation of the labour and natural resources of the Third World. In addition, the Third World is used as a market place.

However, non-Marxist writers like Anthony Giddens (1985) have argued that European colonisers encouraged the development of plantations for the production of cash crops, such as tea, coffee and tobacco, which are for sale on world markets; and encouraged the setting up of farms and the sinking of mines. Concession companies that had a monopoly over the production of a particular commodity often directly controlled these enterprises, and these companies would take most of the profit gained from production. Many of these concession companies helped to form modern multinational companies.

Even in the post-colonial world, where First-World countries do not directly administer Third-World countries, a form of economic colonialism may still exist. This is called neocolonialism, and is defined by Andrew Webster (1990) as follows: 'Neo-colonialism literally means a new form of colonialism, a form of socioeconomic domination from the outside that does not rely on direct political control' (Webster, 1990: 79). In *The Global Society* (1995), William Cockerham discusses the neocolonial relationship between France and a number of her former colonies. As he explains, 'Cameroon, Chad, Central African Republic, Gabon, the Ivory Coast, Niger, and Senegal … are continually on the verge of bankruptcy. Yet … they share a currency based on the French Franc; maintain close political, economic, military and cultural ties with France; and have many French citizens in residence' (1995: 168).

Imperialism may have come to an end, but unequal relationships between countries still exist. Many researchers argue that neocolonialism describes how the First World continues to exploit, control and dominate the Third World. Multinational companies drain profits and resources from the Third World.

Theories of development

Has Europe helped to develop the rest of the world? Did colonisation by Europeans help Africa, Asia and America to modernise? Did European traders and Christian missionaries help to civilise 'primitive' peoples in 'backward' parts of the world? Walter Rodney's book *How Europe Underdeveloped Africa* (1981) argues that violent conquest and ruthless exploitation by European nations disrupted and smashed the highly developed cultures of the people of Africa.

The transformation or evolution of a traditional society into a modern society is referred to as the process of modernisation. Modernisation theory was developed in the 1950s by people who were influenced by the theories of Talcott Parsons (1951) and W.W. Rostow (1962). In Parsons's own theory of modernity, the modern world comes about by the following two overlapping types of social change:

- ○ Structural differentiation – in which institutions swap functions and become more specialised in those functions; for example, the family losing its economic functions but becoming more specialised in socialising young children
- ○ Long-term evolution – in which all social systems are on an evolutionary path that points in the direction of the perfect society

These forms of social change are explained by the following three concepts:

- ○ Adaptation – the idea that all social systems must adapt to their environment
- ○ Disintegration – the concept that in the process of change some institutions lose their functions, and for a time the social system loses its harmony
- ○ Reintegration – the concept that the social systems come back together in a reformed fashion that is better adapted to its environment

Rostow argues that, irrespective of their unique history or culture, all societies evolve through five stages of economic growth from the traditional society to the age of high mass consumption.

Both of these modernisation views are global theories. In addition, both assume that all societies want to be like the USA, because not only does this society provide the most for its citizens, it is also the society best adapted to its environment; it is the closest to the perfect society. They do not take into account that the pre-industrial social structure can act as a brake or affect the direction of future social change. The former Shah of Iran attempted to modernise his country along Western lines, but his people used the culture as a brake and changed the direction of Iran's development path away from a Western model and towards an Islamic society.

In addition, both Rostow's and Parsons's theories entail the following assumptions:

- ○ That lack of development is brought about by psychological factors, such as the laziness of people in the less-developed countries
- ○ That individuals are trapped within backward traditional cultures that prevent economic development
- ○ As with all theories that are evolutionary in nature, that individual human forces outside man's control determine behaviour

We may wish to challenge these three assumptions. Moreover, these two theories can hardly account for the variety of modern societies; for example, the Japanese in the 1870s under the Meiji government opted for a development path which gave them the material benefits of industrialisation, but allowed them to maintain many aspects of their traditional culture. Some commentators have suggested that this process should be termed Japanisation. In other words, modernisation theory needs to take account of each country's unique history and culture.

In contrast, dependency theory, which is Marxist in nature, but is still written from a global perspective, suggests that the First World was undeveloped but never underdeveloped. In other words, although countries such as Britain may have once been poor, they always had the possibility of future economic growth. Many Third World countries are unlikely to experience economic development because the First World keeps them poor and underdeveloped by exercising monopoly power over world markets. There is an unequal exchange between the two worlds. Capitalist countries continue to exploit the labour and resources of the Third World.

However, dependency theory also assumes that forces outside their control drive people. It also fails to explain the variety of development; why is it that some Third World countries have sizeable industrial sectors while others get poorer? Finally, dependency theory may have overstated its case. If the Third-World countries are constantly exploited, some development must be taking place there; if not, there would be no economic surplus for the First World to take. Dependency theory makes no attempt to account for this economic development within the Third World.

In summary, we can suggest that, as a process, globalisation threatens to dissolve the notion of territorial sovereignty, the idea that national governments, within recognised geopolitical boundaries, make their own policies and decide what is fair and equitable for their own citizens. This breakdown of sovereignty can be seen in the way politicians point to global factors as reasons or excuses for their own policy failures. Individuals, pressure groups and New Social Movements (NSMs) increasingly look to international bodies to resolve issues of concern to them rather than directing their protest at national governments. However, the momentum of globalisation is such that it may be surpassing the ability of any governments to supply the essential environment needed to create global rules and cooperative arrangements.

'Investing' or 'pooling' sovereignty

In an effort to resolve global problems, states 'invest' or 'pool' sovereignty in international organisations, as the following extract from Horsman and Marshall (1994) makes clear:

> The increases in the number of intergovernmental organizations has been phenomenal. In 1909, there were 37; by 1951, after the post-war reconstruction, there were 123; by 1984, the number had reached 365. The constituency of these organizations varied widely: the UN, with universal scope encompassing many agencies of its own; regional bodies, such as the European Community or the Organization of African States; and a host of sectoral bodies and others with limited agendas and mandates. ... With these organizations came another slow change, but one which its advocates thought could have a more profound effect: an attempt to introduce rules into international relations, in

the form of a profusion of treaties and agreements between states ... around six thousand bilateral treaties came into force in the period 1946–55; ten thousand between 1955 and 1965; and fourteen thousand in the decade that followed. In the first decade international organizations were party to some six hundred treaties; in the second over a thousand; and in the third, over two thousand. Most of these concerned economic subjects – cooperation, trade, aid and communications. Some, such as the United Nations Declaration on Human Rights, and the agreements of the Council of Europe, were devoted to incorporating an element of morality in international relations. The result was a gradual enmeshing of states in treaties, organizations and regular meetings. (Horsman and Marshall, 1994: 39–40)

Although we are some way from a world government, it is clear that any nation-state acting alone cannot solve many problems in the world. Human rights, development, AIDS, peace and order, and environmental issues such as global warming and biodiversity, are examples of issues that require international cooperation. In the area of environmental issues alone, there are important inter-national agreements such as the following:

- The UN Convention on the Law of the Sea (UNCLOS) 1982, revised 1995
- The Vienna Convention (1985) on CFCs expanded at Montreal (1987) and London (1990) to take into account other greenhouse effects
- The Framework Convention on Climate Change agreed in Rio de Janeiro (1992), reviewed in Berlin (1995) and reviewed again in Japan (1997)
- The Framework Convention on Biodiversity agreed in Rio de Janeiro (1992)
- The UN Conference on Environment and Development (1992), commonly known as 'Agenda 21' on 'sustainable development'

Global governance: an outline of some key institutions

The UN was formed after World War II, and held its first General Assembly meeting in London on 10 January 1946. The UN, like the League of Nations that preceded it, attempts to provide a forum for the following:

- The peaceful resolution of quarrels on the lines of trust, impartiality, universal justice and international law
- The open hearing of pleas from both participants in a dispute before the world forum of justice
- Examination of the meaningful facts of a dispute by fair scrutiny
- Collective security through the united support, including military support, of all its members to oppose armed assault
- Encouragement of international economic and social cooperation

The UN constitution gives power to the Security Council, which has five permanent members, the USA, Russia, China, France and Britain, together with six non-permanent members elected by the General Assembly for a two-year period, with half retiring each year. Each member of the Security Council has a veto over its decisions. What is significant about the Security Council is that its decisions are binding upon all members of the UN; hence, the non-Security Council members have surrendered their sovereignty to the UN, but the veto means that the members of the Security Council retain their sovereignty intact. Moreover, the UN does not confine its powers to its own members, but acts to prevent aggression by non-member states.

The other important body within the UN is the General Assembly, which gives all members of the UN an opportunity to discuss issues which are of concern. However, its decisions are not binding upon the Security Council but are treated as 'recommendations'. The UN also has a Secretariat, which is under the control of the Secretary-General, who can bring any issue to the attention of the Security Council that the Secretary-General believes can endanger the continuance of world peace.

Article 100 of the UN charter attempts to put beyond doubt the independence of the Secretary-General and the Secretariat: 'In the performance of their duties, the Secretary-General and the staff shall not seek or receive instructions from any government or from any authority external to the Organisation. They shall refrain from any action that might reflect on their position as international officials accountable only to the Organisation.'

In addition, the UN has a number of agencies such as the World Health Organisation (WHO) and the UN Educational, Scientific and Cultural Organisation (UNESCO). There is also the International Court of Justice, which is made up of fifteen judges. All member states agree to comply with the decisions of the UN. However, member states do not have to state in advance whether they will accept as binding any decision of the UN that might affect them. The significance of these agencies and the court is that they provide the population of the world with a clear idea of citizenship rights. In areas such as health, education and justice, all members of the human race can expect the UN minimum standard from their national governments. In this sense, the activities of the UN agencies and the court can be viewed as a form of cultural globalisation.

Although the UN was established to prevent international conflict, many nations in the post-war period still placed their trust in alliances that held a balance of power. Many nations felt unable to place their security needs in the hands of the UN. NATO is an example of an organisation which has for most of the post-war period attempted to hold the balance of power in the world. One possible consequence of balance-of-power alliances, a trivial dispute escalating into a major conflict, was clearly outlined by Crowley (1964):

> One of the reasons for the emergence of the League of Nations after 1918 was the fact that the First World War provided a notable instance of this. Germany was allied with Austria, Russia with France; Russia regarded herself as the protector of Serbia, and Britain had an understanding with France. A single act of murder, the victim being the

heir to the Austrian Imperial throne, resulted in Austria presenting an ultimatum to Serbia; Russia came to Serbia's assistance; Germany and France were drawn in almost immediately. So also, within a few days, was Britain, and eventually most of the world was involved. The result was the horror of 1914–18. (Crowley, 1964: 110)

In terms of issues of national sovereignty, what is significant about NATO is that its member states – the USA, Britain, Canada, the Netherlands, Belgium, Luxemburg, Denmark, Norway, Iceland, Italy, Greece, Germany, Turkey, Portugal and France (although France is part of NATO's political structure but not its military command structure) – have given control of their defence force to an international organisation. The purpose of NATO was to defend Europe and North America against the former Soviet Union and its allies, who themselves had a military alliance formed in 1955 by the Warsaw Treaty.

The European Union (EU) is another major institution involved in the dissolution of the nation-state and its loss of sovereignty. The EU has its origins in three institutions: the European Economic Community (EEC), a free trade area also known as the Common Market; Euratom, a body created to coordinate the joint development of nuclear power; and the European Coal and Steel Community, established to increase the efficiency of these industries by facilitating greater competition. With the Maastricht Treaty, the EU became a political union moving towards full economic and monetary union, with a central bank, a common currency and a common social policy, including a 'social chapter' that gives all EU citizens a minimum wage and common employment rights. Many people in Britain fear that they may be losing their national identity because of greater European integration.

World trade is another area in which there are international bodies that diminish the sovereignty of national governments. In 1947, 35 countries signed the General Agreement on Tariffs and Trade (GATT), in which all members agreed not to increase tax, duties or impose restrictions on each other's goods. In 1986, GATT held a meeting in Uruguay, with the intention of making significant changes to the GATT agreement. This 'Uruguay Round' dragged on into the 1990s. In the end, a new organisation was formed, the World Trade Organisation (WTO), which has two aims: firstly, to continue the GATT agreements on opening up world trade to competition; and secondly, to make world trade more responsible for the environment. On 24 March 1995, when Renato Ruggiero became head of the WTO, he was reported by *The Times* as saying: 'We cannot go back to the protectionism of the 1930s. Trade is the main tool of globalisation.' He was also reported as saying that the world had a vested interest in bringing both China and Russia fully into the world system.

One of the major global issues in the 1980s and 1990s was that of foreign aid. This issue shows more clearly than any other the argument between sociologists over global issues. As Best et al. (2000) make clear, aid is the giving of resources by one country to another, and it can take the following different forms:

- Development aid is given to help a country develop its economy or services in an effort to improve the quality of life for all people in the country
- Emergency aid is given after a disaster, such as famine or flood
- Military aid can include expertise as well as weapons
- Project aid is given for specific projects such as a dam, a school or a road; this is often referred to as 'tied' aid because the donor country usually has some control over the project, such as insisting that purchases made with the aid come from the donor country
- Programme aid is not linked to specific projects; it could be used to improve a country's trade imbalance

Aid can either be bilateral, as when one country gives help to another, or multi-lateral, in which countries give money to an international body such as the World Bank.

However, according to Teresa Hayter (1989), Western governments use the aid relationship to support pro-capitalist governments in the Third World:

> The World Bank and the IMF ... are dominated by the major Western powers; the United States and half a dozen other governments have an effective veto over their lending decisions through the weighted voting system, and other more subtle ways. In addition, the World Bank raises around 80 per cent of its money through Wall Street and other private financial markets; this means that they must defend the interests of those markets. (Hayter, 1989: 28)

Hayter's view is that the World Bank and the International Monetary Fund (IMF) will provide aid or loans only if the country is prepared to manage its economy in a way that the bank or the IMF approve of. The World Bank and the IMF insist upon 'structural adjustments' or 'stabilisation programmes'. Hayter explains the nature of such programmes:

> The stabilisation, or structural adjustment, programmes have been programmes to control government spending and the balance of payments by orthodox liberal means: by limiting credit, cutting public social expenditure and sometimes public investment, keeping down or cutting wages, eliminating subsidies, and devaluation. Cuts in military expenditure are not demanded; the issue is said to be 'too sensitive'. For example the government of Morocco, with the approval of the World Bank and the IMF, has been carrying out a programme of cuts in domestic public expenditure, especially on food subsidies which benefit the poor; at the same time it has been spending large sums on the war in the Sahara. (Hayter, 1989: 30–31)

However, possibly the most astonishing truth about the aid relationship is that most aid goes to states which are economically well off. For example, in 1992, the British government gave more aid to the oil-rich state of Oman than it did to poverty-stricken Ethiopia. Moreover, many aid-funded development schemes have 'strings attached'. A notorious British example was the Pergau Dam in Malaysia, built by Balfour Beatty and Cementation. The dam cost £397 million to construct, of which Britain gave £234 million in aid. However, it was suggested that the aid was directly linked to arms deals worth £1.3 billion to British companies.

In summary, modernisation theorists argue that aid can be used to facilitate the process of economic development. In contrast, dependency theorists argue that aid hampers economic development, and makes Third-World countries more reliant upon the First World.

David Held: globalisation and international governance

As suggested by the preceding passages, as political, social and economic action becomes global in nature and there are much higher levels of intergovernmental attachment, 'governance' may now be beyond the grasp of the nation-state. International organisations reduce the capacity of a nation-state to govern its citizens. However, nation-states still wish to become members of international bodies rather than to be isolated in the world.

Canada is an interesting case in point. At the beginning of 1995, the Canadians had a referendum on the future of the French-speaking province of Quebec, to decide whether Quebec should become an independent French-speaking nation. Jacques Chirac, then President of France, said that France would accept the new country if there was a 'yes' vote.

According to Held (1995), effective sovereignty is dependent upon the economic resources of the nation-state. However, economic globalisation has not been a uniform process throughout the world. Some nation-states have become much more economically influential than others, and, as such, they have a greater influence on the administration of international bodies. The international organisations we examined above are not wholly democratic in character; in addition, they abide by decisions taken in the interests of the most economically powerful states. Consequently, globalisation can bring about fragmentation as well as integration. Held finds important the following three factors in the process of globalisation:

- Economic, political and legal and military attachments are changing the sovereign states from 'above'
- New social movements and nationalist groups are questioning the trustworthiness and the ability of the sovereign state from 'below'
- Global organisations engender new relations between sovereign states and their citizens, as states have to take into account the possible reaction from international organisations when dealing with their citizens

Held argues that we have here a new 'cosmopolitan order', and this involves the obsolescence of the idea that the sovereign state has exclusive jurisdiction over its territory and the people who live within it. However, international organisations, as they are currently constituted, contain a serious 'democratic deficit'; in other words, they need to be made more accountable to the people of the world. The democratisation of the new world order requires the following changes:

○ More elected restraint over international bodies with responsibility for environmental, economic and security concerns
○ Regional parliaments for Africa and Latin America, and a renewed European Parliament
○ A renewed UN, with an 'authoritative assembly' to give deep-rooted political, social and economic rights to all people and bring a high degree of account-ability and regulation to national and international concerns

Roland Robertson: the world as a single place

Robertson (1994), one of the most influential theorists on globalisation, maintains that the processes of globalisation have a lengthy history, and that history can be seen as a succession of 'miniglobalisations' since early imperialism, the foun-dation of the great empires and the integration of conquered territories. Robertson traces the path of the globalisation process through the following stages:

1 The germinal phase
2 The incipient phase
3 The take-off phase
4 The struggle-for-hegemony phase
5 The uncertainty phase

The first stage lasted from about 1400 to the mid-eighteenth century, and is European in origin. This stage is related to a number of diverse global develop-ments such as the growth of the Catholic Church and the adoption of the Gregorian calendar. The final stage began in the 1960s and is associated with the expansion in demands for civil rights across the world, global environmental con-cerns, the moon landing, the Earth Summit, the conclusion of the Cold War and the dissolution of the Soviet Union, and the uncertainty and doubt that followed the creation of the new world order.

For Robertson, globalisation is associated with both modernisation and post-modernisation; as a concept, globalisation describes the processes that brought the modern world into being and at the same time account for the 'globally insti-tutionalised uncertainty' that people have experienced since the beginning of the 1990s. As Robertson explains, 'there is an eerie relationship between postmodern theories and the idea of postmodernity, on the one hand, and the geopolitical "earthquakes" that we (the virtually *global we*) have recently experienced, on the other' (1994: 50). In his opinion, the concept of globalisation is about 'the concrete structuration of the world as a whole' (1994: 53). This notion of 'structuration' was developed by Anthony Giddens (1984) to describe how individual people (human agents) have the skills and ability to generate structures which restrain their future behaviour. However, Robertson argues that Giddens's notion of structura-tion is lost in a 'quasi-philosophical context', from which it has to be removed: 'It has to be made directly relevant to *the world* in which we live. It has to contribute to the understanding of how the global "system" continues to be *made*. It has to be focused on the production and reproduction of "the world" as the most salient plausibility structure of our time' (Robertson, 1994: 53).

As Best *et al.* (2000) explain, Robertson provides concrete examples of how Giddens's theory works in everyday life, that is, to explain how the global system was made through a process of structuration. Robertson identifies the following factors which have helped to bring about the structuration of the world global system:

- The spread of capitalism
- Western imperialism
- The development of a global media
- Conflict within the contemporary world order

Robertson: taking Giddens out of the quasi-philosophical framework?

More precisely, I argue that systematic comprehension of the structuration of world order is essential to the viability of any form of contemporary theory and that such comprehension must involve analytical separation of the factors that have facilitated the shift towards a single world – for example the spread of capitalism, Western imperialism and the development of a global media system – from the *general and global* agency-structure (and/or culture) theme. While the empirical relationship between the two sets of issues is of great importance (and, of course, complex), conflation of them leads us into all sorts of difficulties and inhibits our ability to come to terms with the basic but shifting terms of the contemporary world order, including the 'structure' of 'disorderliness'. (Robertson, 1994: 55)

As Best *et al.* (2000) explain, any valid social theory has to identify those factors which have made the world into a single place. These factors include the spread of capitalism or Western imperialism, global media systems, individual human agents and the structures that we humans create, including the 'disorderliness' that we find difficult to come to terms with. In Robertson's view, our conception of 'world politics' needs to take into account the 'meaning' of the 'global-human condition as a whole', which he terms 'the new world order'. His belief is that global issues may form the basis of significant political, economic and military divisions in the twenty-first century. The boundary between the local and the global, once taken for granted, is now not so easy to distinguish, because, in Robertson's view, we have experienced the 'global institutionalisation of the life-world and the localisation of globally'. In other words, the world of everyday life (life-world) has a global feel to it, individuals have similar experiences in their local communities wherever they live in the world, and at the same time issues and problems on the other side of the world feel no more distant than events in our local community. You might want to reflect upon whether people make sense of Hollywood films in the same way everywhere in the world.

Waters (1995) argues that Robertson's conception of globalisation is built upon the 'establishment of cultural, social and phenomenological linkages between the following four elements' (1995: 42):

- The individual human agent (self) – no. 1 in the following quotation
- The national society – no. 2 in the following quotation
- The international system of societies – no. 3 in the following quotation
- Humanity in general – no. 4 in the following quotation

It is these four factors which come together to create the global system. Waters explains the relationship between these four elements in the following way:

- The individual self (1) is defined as a citizen of a national society (2), by comparison with developments in other societies (3), and as an instance of humanity (4).
- A national society (2) stands in a problematical relationship to its citizens (1) in terms of freedom and control, views itself to be a member of a community of nations (3), and must provide citizenship rights that are referenced against general human rights (4).
- The international system (3) depends on the surrender of sovereignty by national societies (2), sets standards for individual behaviour (1), and provides 'reality checks' on human aspirations (4).
- Humanity (4) is defined in terms of individual rights (1) that are expressed in the citizenship provisions of the national societies (2) which are legitimated and enforced through the international system of societies (3). (Waters, 1995: 43).

The major alternative theory of globalisation to Robertson's, is provided by Anthony Giddens (1985).

Theoretical detour: agency and structure
in the writings of Anthony Giddens

To understand fully what Robertson means by the structuration of the world, we need to have a clear idea of the relationship between agency and structure in the writings of Anthony Giddens. Giddens discusses the notion of agency as being made up of the following three elements:

1 *The unconscious*. This is a concept derived from Freud (1932) to denote those elements of ourselves that we are not fully in control of, that are beyond our immediate intentions.
2 *The practical consciousness*. This is a concept derived from Harold Garfinkel (1967) to explain that human action is not driven or determined by forces outside us. Giddens also accepts, as suggested by Garfinkel, that we have the ability to establish rules and routines for ourselves.

3   *The discursive consciousness*. This is a term borrowed from Alfred Schutz (1937) to suggest that individuals reflect upon their social actions to make sense of these actions.

Many sociologists look upon structure as a durable framework, rather like the metal girders within a concrete building. It constrains our behaviour, it is beyond our control and it is out of sight. In contrast, for Giddens, structure is always both enabling and constraining; defined as rules and resources, it is the property of social systems and gives shape to social systems. Structures themselves are reproduced 'through the regularized conduct of knowledgeable agents' (Giddens, 1984: 199). In other words, individual people do things on a regular basis, and the habit or expectations of what people do become structures which guide behaviour.

In *'The Constitution of Society'* (1984), Giddens's argument is rather complex, but contains the following points:

1   Human agents make rules
2   Rules form structures
3   Rules are used by agents to deploy resources
4   Resources help to form structures of domination
5   Structures are outside time and space in *virtual* existence

The concept of the 'duality of structure' brings all these points together. What does Giddens mean by 'rule'? Giddens (1984), views rules as 'generalizable procedures' that apply in a range of contexts and allow for the 'methodical continuation of an established sequence' as 'applied in the enactment/reproduction of social practices'. Rules tend to come in sets, and agents tend to reproduce social life with such consistency that the rules take on an objective property. Hence, for the human agent, social life is experienced as a fact. However, structures are outside time and space; they have what Giddens calls a 'virtual existence'. What does this mean? It means that they have no significance for individual human agents until they are made use of by those agents. Social systems, which depend upon 'situated activities of human agents', do not have 'structures', but rather exhibit the 'structural properties' found, for example, in the memory traces of social actors. These structural properties are key factors in orienting the conduct of knowledgeable human agents, most notably in terms of the deployment of both allocative and authoritative resources. Structures are not external to individuals in Giddens's argument, as, for example, they are in functionalism or structuralism.

The problem for Giddens is bringing together rules and resources with the regular social practices created by the human agents. His solution is the 'duality of structure': 'The constitution of agents and structures are not two independently given phenomena, a dualism, but represent a duality. According to the notion of the duality of structure, the structural properties of social systems are both medium and outcome of the practices they recursively organise' (Giddens, 1984: 25). Therefore, structure is defined as *rules* and *resources*. For Giddens, it is not possible to think of rules without also thinking of resources. Rules suggest 'methodical procedures' and relate to the 'constitution of meaning and to the sanctioning of modes of social conduct' (1984: 18). As such, rules allow us, as agents, to apply the right 'formula' or 'generalised procedure' in the right context and the right occasion. This rule-making and rule-following ability is at the 'very core' of our knowledgeability, according to Giddens, and is what constitutes our practical consciousness, a key element of the self. This means, that, for Giddens, our ability to make rules and to recognise and follow rules is what makes us people. (For an informed account of what Giddens has to say about the process of structuration, see http://www.clas.ufl.edu/users/gthursby/mod/gidcns.htm.)

What is Giddens's vision of the world order?

According to Giddens, there are two opposing views of globalisation. First, we have the view that there is nothing new about the notion of globalisation. Throughout the twentieth century there were a range of global institutions and processes, notably the international trading system and migration. The second view is held by a group of people, whom Giddens terms 'gee-whiz' types (Giddens himself claims to be one), who see globalisation bringing about a radical break with the past. Global changes are reflected in changes in technology, communication, the role of knowledge in production, and discoveries in the life sciences.

Globalisation refers to a complex of overlapping trends or changes that have taken place after 1989, since the fall of Soviet communism. Giddens (2000) identifies the following three trends:

○ The worldwide communications revolution; notably, the Internet
○ The 'weightless economy'; that is, the new knowledge economy, which includes such activities as the financial markets
○ Transformations at the level of everyday life that affect our family and emotional life; notably, the growing equality between men and women

According to Giddens, there are two broad theories about the nature of the world order. The first, Marxist in nature, views nations as instruments of economic domination. Capitalist society was created by the use of force. The second broad theory is described by Giddens as 'international relations', a perspective that views nation-states as social actors with meanings and intentions. Struggles inside nation-states are not regarded as significant. In contrast, in the Marxist analysis, the territorial character of states, their geopolitical involvement, is given a high priority. However, Giddens rejects both of these theories; he holds that the world system has come about because of several important processes 'associated with the nation state system, co-ordinated through global networks of information exchange, the world capitalist economy and the world military order' (Giddens, 1985: 290).

Nation-states do look as if they are 'social actors' because in the modern world they have became 'bounded administrative units'. All states have to negotiate reflexively with each other, and this involves continuously changing their opinions to fit better their own advantages, always taking into account the position and the goals of other nation-states. However, as Giddens explains, the 'actor'-like qualities of the nation-state have to be explained by looking at the internal conflicts and power relationships of states. The actor-like characteristics of nation-states cannot be regarded as a 'given'. The assumption that people who study international relations have to regard nation-states as person-like, with feelings, motives and intentions, is wrong. Nation-states do not exercise 'agency' independently of the people who live within the state; it is they who determine the state's course of action through their internal politicking.

In *The Nation State and Violence* (1985), Giddens argues that traditional imperialist states – such as the Ottoman Empire – and tribal societies became assimilated into more global units or have vanished altogether, because of the following two processes:

○ Global assimilation by industrial capitalism
○ Global dominance of the nation-state

Nation-states have the following four institutional clusterings of modernity:

○ Industrialised economy
○ Capitalistic production
○ Political integration
○ Military rule

Moreover, according to Giddens, the modern world system is characterised by an approximate transfer of these four institutional clusterings of modernity to the global setting, in the following way:

Symbolic orders/modes of discourse	Global information system
Political institutions	Nation-state system
Economic institutions	World capitalist economy
Law/modes of sanction	World military order

Giddens explains that modernity is fundamentally 'globalising' in nature, and the 'dimensions of globalisation' are, as suggested above, drawn from his four institutional clusterings of modernity: capitalism, the interstate system, militarism and industrialism. In nature, 'Globalization is not a single process but a complex mixture of processes, which often act in contradictory ways, producing conflicts, disjunctions and new forms of stratification. Thus, for instance, the revival of local nationalisms, and an accentuating of local identities, are directly bound up with globalizing influences, to which they stand in opposition' (Giddens, 1994: 5).

In contrast to the Marxist contention that globalisation is a single process with a single cause, Giddens holds that globalisation is a multiplicity of linkages and interconnections that surpass or exceed those of the nation-states. In other words, for Giddens, there are several global processes at work at the same time with a variety of causes. Globalisation, as a concept, describes a process by which incidents, opinions and actions in one part of the world can have both meaning-ful and important consequences for individuals and communities in quite distant parts of the world. In *Reflexive Modernisation* (1994), Giddens expands this point with the following example:

> The day to day activities of an individual today are globally consequential. My deci-sion to purchase a particular item of clothing, for example, or a specific type of food-stuff, has manifold global implications. It not only affects the livelihood of someone living on the other side of the world but may contribute to a process of ecological decay which itself has potential consequences for the whole of humanity. This extra-ordinary, and still accelerating, connectedness between everyday decisions and global outcomes, together with its reverse, the influence of global orders over indi-vidual life, forms the key subject matter of the new agenda. The connections involved are often very close. Intermediate collectivities and groupings of all sorts, including the state, do not disappear as a result; but they do tend to become reorganised or reshaped.' (Giddens, 1994: 57–58)

In summary, for Giddens, globalisation involves more 'than a diffusion of Western institutions across the world, in which other cultures are crushed' (1990: 175); it also involves 'a process of uneven development that fragments as it co-ordinates' (1990: 175). For Giddens, the major feature of globalisation is the compression of the world; this is the profound reordering of time and space in social life, what Giddens terms 'time-space distanciation'.

The central concern of Giddens's theory of structuration is with how social sys-tems *bind* time and space; for Giddens, the 'problem of order' is the problem of time. His key concept is that of time-space distanciation, which is the process through which society is 'stretched' over durations of time and space. In band societies or simple societies, there is a low level of time-space distanciation, almost all interaction is face to face, and little if any interaction takes place with people who are physically removed. Any time consciousness that does exist is maintained by tradition, kin relationships maintaining a link between the living and the dead. In modern societies, individuals interact with each other often over great distances of both time and space. Moreover, in modern societies, time becomes 'commodified'; that is, time exhibits a measured duration with distinct differ-ences between work time and non-work time. The emergence of a distinct linear time consciousness, with time moving in a progressive fashion from one point away to another, probably has its origins in the development of writing giving people the opportunity to organise their activities and have them organised. This is how we experience the day, individuals making their way through 'time space paths' of work time and non-work time: 'Authoritative resources are the prime carriers of time-space distanciation' (Giddens, 1981: 92). What does Giddens mean by this? He identifies the following three major forms of authoritative resources:

(a) Organisation of social time-space (the temporal-spatial constitution of society).
(b) Production/reproduction of the human body (organisation and relations of human beings in society).

(c) Organisation of human life-chances (constitution of chances of self development and self expression). (1981: 51–52)

Although these points may at first be difficult to follow for the reader coming to Giddens for the first time, the underlying message is a simple one; the control of time is a resource in the structures of power and domination.

Cultural globalisation

The division of the world into distinct, standardised time zones is perhaps one of the clearest examples of cultural globalisation. Political globalisation has advanced because there it attracts collective or shared global values and global problems. The clearest statement of this cultural/political globalisation, as discussed in Area 1, is Francis Fukuyama's 'end of history' thesis (1992). As you will recall, he argues that technology makes likely the unlimited amassing of affluence and an ever-expanding assortment of human wants and desires in the post-scarcity liberal democratic society. This process ensures an escalating homogenisation of all civilisations upon one liberal democratic model, irrespective of the historical origins or cultural inheritance of any one society. This makes liberal democracy the terminus of history; from now on, there will be no more great historical epochs (such as socialism, communism and fascism), just events.

Arjun Appadurai (1989) explains that the notion of political/cultural globalisation is brought about by the following flows:

- Ethnoscapes – the flow of people, tourists, immigrants, refugees, exiles and guest workers
- Technoscapes – the movement of technology
- Finanscapes – the rapid movement of money via money markets and stock exchanges
- Mediascapes – information and images generated and distributed by film, television, newspapers and magazines
- Ideoscapes – the movement of political ideas and ideologies

The significance of processes of globalisation is that, in contrast to the analyses of state-centred theorists (see Area 2), the nation-state is losing its significance in the world today and may cease to exist in its present form. We should keep in mind that nation-states are not simply splurges of colour upon a map; they are also important in terms of giving people a sense of identity.

In state-centred theories, the state is assumed to be the most powerful institution in society, and it is said to have interests of its own, and to act independently to bring about social change. The modern state is not therefore the creation of capitalism, or of class relations within capitalism. There is no force in society pushing the state in any particular direction. Michael Mann (1986) suggests that there are four sources of social power: the economic, the political, the military and the ideological. However, in particular, military threats from the outside world are one of the key factors in the process of state formation; and the state is the only body that can exercise power in a centralised territorial fashion. Eric Nordlinger (1975) lists the following ways in which the state can increase its independence of groups within society:

- By concealed methods of decision making
- By the honours system, providing employment or deals with private companies to persuade people to accept its proposals
- By using its resources to weaken opponents; for example, the much-increased use of state advertising in Britain since 1979
- By changing its policy

Perhaps the most convincing state-centred theorist is Theda Skocpol (1985), who outlines a number of examples of states independently pursuing their own interests. Like Gramsci (1957), she suggests that whether a state develops into a powerful independent body or not rests upon how well organised other groups in society are. However, states do not have to represent the interests of the bourgeoisie in the way that most Marxists suggest. A strong state can shape the activity of classes, including the bourgeoisie.

Creative destruction: the Marxist contribution to globalisation

Marxists have a history of criticising processes of globalisation; for example, Arthur MacEwan (1994) has described the process of capitalist global development as a process of 'creative destruction'. Perhaps the first contribution to our understanding of the characteristics of the relationship between nation-states, ownership of economic capital and the processes of globalisation was made by Robin Murray (1971). From his distinctly Marxist perspective, Murray attempted to outline a 'functional' view of global relationships, and identify the indispensable function that states can provide for capital. As capital expands overseas, it has the problem of ensuring that important state functions continue to operate. These state functions include guaranteeing property; guaranteeing contract by providing a system of legal sanctions; standardising currency and weights and measures; and making available land, labour, finance, infrastructure and the right macroeconomic conditions for capital to develop. If the nation-state is unable to provide these functions, the transnational company may have to provide them itself. In earlier times, this framework would have been provided by either colonial or neocolonial arrangements.

Colonialism and neocolonialism

Marxist writers particularly, Murray, have discussed the economic consequences of colonialism and imperialism. Since Lenin in 1916, Marxists have argued that the development of capitalism has been dependent upon the economic exploitation of the labour and natural resources of the Third World. In addition, the Third World is used as a market place.

Murray's argument should not be used to suggest that the age of independent nation-states has come to an end. Nation-states are still performing their economic role and still service foreign capital on the same basis as domestic capital. However, nation-states have lost many of their powers over economic activity because of the high level of activity by foreign capital, which is politically highly opportunist.

Robert Cox (1987) has built upon Murray's argument that the state provides 'indispensable functions' for capitalists. For Cox, the new world order – which we now have a clearer view of since the collapse of communism in Eastern Europe – has led directly to a transformation, but not a diminution, of the activities of the state. Cox argues that there has been an 'internationalisation' of the state, based upon an international consensus, and shown in international agreements. There is a common ideological framework, common goals, common criteria for judging economic events and a common assumption that an open world market needs common solutions by states. This internationalisation of the state is supported by various international agencies such as the World Trade Organisation, the World Bank, the IMF, the Trilateral Commission, the Club of Rome, the Bilderberg conferences and the Organisation for Economic Cooperation and Development (OECD). Together, these international organisations and agreements have produced a global centralisation of influence over policy. The end result has been the creation of what Cox terms the Thatcher-Reagan hyperliberal state form; in other words, all states are forced to support the liberal capitalist policies that maintain capital:

> There is a transnational process of consensus formation among the official caretakers of the global economy. This process generates consensual guidelines, underpinned by the ideology of globalisation, that are transmitted into the policy-making channels of national governments and big corporation. … The structural impact on national governments of this centralisation of influence over policy can be called the internationalisation of the state. Its common feature is to convert the state into an agency for adjusting national economic practices and policies to the national economy, where before it had acted as the bulwark defending domestic welfare from external disturbances. Power within the state becomes concentrated in those agencies in closest touch with the global economy – the offices of presidents and prime ministers, treasurers, central banks. The agencies that are more closely tied with domestic clients – ministries of industries, labour ministries, etc., – become subordinated. This phenomenon, which has become so salient since the crisis of the post-war order, needs much more study. (Robert Cox cited in Panitch, 1994: 71)

Manfred Bienefeld (1994) has also developed a Marxist critique of the processes of globalisation, which he defines as neoliberal in nature, and which he understands as the worldwide spread of systems and processes without regulation from the state. He takes his starting point from an analysis of Robert Reich's *The Work of Nations* (1992). Bienefeld describes Reich as a 'political liberal' who believes that globalisation will bring with it a 'peaceful, prosperous and dynamic future for the world economy as a whole' (Bienefeld, 1994: 98). Reich's analysis is based upon the following four assumptions:

- Globalisation is irreversible and inevitable
- Globalisation will provide the rich minority with an improved quality of life
- Globalisation can make people more active and competent
- Education and training can save people from impoverishment

The argument is that more economic liberalisation and greater deregulation of markets will always increase the efficiency of companies and the total output of the world economy. Moreover, any attempt to reverse global processes would be almost impossible and highly unfavourable. Reich gives us the example of the enactment of financial deregulation when the development of computer technology and communication systems makes it very difficult to regulate global markets. In contrast to this view, Bienefeld suggests that regulation is technically possible. In the case of laundered drug money, regulation has had a high degree of success. The problem is that governments do not have the political will to regulate global processes, as they are often blackmailed or coerced into neoliberal global agreements. He argues that 'globalisation has substantially undermined the material base of the nation state and has erected serious institutional obstacles to reverse this process' (Bienefeld, 1994: 124). In addition, Bienefeld casts doubt on the demand for more training, which Reich supports; not only do we not know what training is appropriate for the future, but also the training argument blames the individual for any future lack of success. In the last analysis, Bienefeld argues that globalisation leads directly to people demanding ethnically defined states:

> The current proliferation of such demands reflects the growing instability and economic insecurity spawned by globalisation and the growing inability of existing, territorial states to manage the regional or ethnic issues within their borders. But the creation of ethnic splinter states will not solve these problems and will generally create new and bigger ones. After all these little states will have the global market to contend with. In short, the resurgence of the ethnic state must be regarded as a major step in the direction of barbarism. Once the rights of citizenship depend on our ethnic genealogy, we will all end up living in apartheid South Africa. (Bienefeld, 1994: 123)

One of the clearest Marxist world system approaches, which discards the idea of the unified nation-state as an important factor in a global system, is that of Immanuel Wallerstein. Wallerstein (1979) argues that capitalism was always global in nature and was never confined by national boundaries. Wallerstein makes a distinction between the following two types of world systems:

○ *World empires*. These empires colonised areas of the world by military means and imposed a rigid bureaucracy on the population to extract taxes. These empires were displaced by world economies that are much more flexible.
○ *World economies*. These are market based and capitalistic as they are based upon capital accumulation. The world economy is neocolonial in nature, and is largely free from any influence of nation-states.

In Wallerstein's view, the modern world system is 'a single division of labour comprising multiple cultural systems, multiple political entities and even different modes of surplus appropriation' (Wallerstein, 1980: 5). The world system is divided into the following three components:

○ *The core*. In the beginning, this was Western Europe and North America, the places of origin of the first transnational corporations (TNCs) that come to dominate the global market and exploit the world's population for profit.
○ *The semi-periphery*. In the first instance, this was the Mediterranean countries and Eastern Europe; these counties did face exploitation from the TNCs but had some capital which was not directly under the control of the TNCs.
○ *The periphery*. This was the colonised and formerly colonised countries that are now visibly within neocolonial economic relationships.

The relationship between the core and the periphery is an exploitative one in the Marxist sense. The core – periphery relationship should be based upon the transfer of surplus value from the periphery to the core – the value can be extracted from workers either politically or economically. Ankie Hoogvelt (1982) describes the political/economic arrangements within the world system in the following way:

> The global distribution of wealth and poverty is seen as a result of market forces reinforcing an accident of history which gave a head start to the European nations. But there is also political interference in the market. While the single world market rewards some activities and penalises others, the actors can and do interfere with the operation of the world market by appealing to their nation-states to interfere on their behalf. And once we get a difference in strength of the state machineries, we get the operation of unequal exchange imposed by strong states on weak ones in peripheral areas – by core areas on peripheral areas. In this way capitalism involves not only appropriation of the surplus value by an owner from a labourer but an appropriation of the whole world economy by core areas. (Hoogvelt, 1982: 192)

In other words, the capitalist economy has built a division of labour that is neo-colonial and global in nature. Power and wealth shift to the core, while the periphery and semi-periphery are left comparatively poor and powerless.

Wallerstein's world system theory has been criticised by Giddens (1985) who argues that Wallerstein's view of capitalism is closer to Weber's than that of Marx, in that Wallerstein's conception of capitalism is one of unequal exchange within a market rather than one stressing exploitation based upon the labour theory of value. However, the appeal of Wallerstein's work is that he does not look upon nation-states as isolated or solitary individual entities, but as elements of a global structure brought about by the spread of global capitalism.

In addition, as Best et al. (2000) explain, for Wallerstein, the existence of semi-peripheral regions is explained by the 'needs' of the world system. He assumes that the world system has 'agency' in the same fashion as individuals do – but they do not. Wallerstein's account is both functional and economically reduction-ist in nature. In other words, the existence of the semi-periphery is explained by its functional necessity for the whole system, while the existence of the whole system explains the need for the semi-periphery.

Wallerstein also assumes that states have no other forms of power to draw upon other than economic power. Therefore, he had difficulty in dealing with the former Soviet Union; the Soviet Union had to operate with a global economy domi-nated by capitalistic institutions, yet it was militarily a superpower, so that it was clearly in a position to manipulate the world system. In general, it would be wrong to assume that nations outside the core are powerless simply because they lack economic development; as was seen in the events leading up to the Gulf War, economically less developed nations can have significance in the world.

Malcolm Waters (1995) also provides an informed evaluation of Wallerstein's analysis. According to Waters, business can unite geographically scattered pro-ducers and consumers. Capitalism is therefore economically globalising in nature. However, the declining contribution of world trade from Europe and the USA has moved the dependency relationship in the direction of greater harmony or balance during the post-war period. In addition, the following three recent globalising trends have challenged the validity of Wallerstein's division of the world into core, semi-peripheral and peripheral societies:

o A number of less developed countries, such as Singapore, South Korea, Taiwan, Malaysia and Thailand, have become newly industrialised countries; Wallerstein would find it difficult to account for such development
o Some multinational corporations have located production within less developed countries, which has brought about economic development there
o Taking their lead from the Organisation of Petroleum Exporting Countries, a number of less developed countries have managed to form cartels that have given them the power to push up the price of their products on world markets

Alternative futures

'Some people believe the future is the end of history; not so' 'Capt. James T. Kirk' (*Star Trek: The Undiscovered Country*, 1992)

Earlier in the area, we mentioned Francis Fukuyama's 'end of history' thesis. He suggested that cultural globalisation ensures an escalating homogenisation of all civilisation upon one liberal democratic model, and that liberal democracy is the terminus of history; from now on there will be no more great historical epochs (such as socialism, communism and fascism), just events. What gives Fukuyama's argument such force is that since the collapse of communism we find it difficult to conceive of alternative futures. Once people could argue that socialism was on the far side of modernity, but most people now assume that this is no longer the case. With the completion of the Uruguay Round and the formation of the World Trade Organisation, the future looks both Western and market dominated.

As Philip Sarre (1996) argues, any discussion of the future involves the following two aspects:

○   A prediction about which features of the present will survive
○   An evaluation of whether or not we will like what we find in the future

Will the future be a dystopia, as described in Orwell's *Nineteen Eighty-Four* and Huxley's *Brave New World*? Or will the future be a utopia, as described in *Star Trek*?

With the processes of globalisation, not only does the capitalist West rule economically, but also Western taste, fashions, and ideologies have spread across the world, destroying local cultures in the process. However, in his survey of civilisation from the first city-state to the birth of the modern industrial society, Michael Mann (1986) has shown that peripheral areas of the world have overtaken the advanced areas on a number of occasions. Mann cites the following examples: the Greeks overtaking the Persians, the Germans overtaking the Romans and the Americans overtaking the British. Many people believe that modernity is coming to an end, and the future is likely to be unpredictable and postmodern in nature.

In contrast to Fukuyama, Wagar (1992) suggests that there are three possible futures: 'the techno-liberal', 'the radical' and 'the countercultural'. The idea of the techno-liberal future is very much what Fukuyama is suggesting, more of the same liberal capitalism with similar powerful institutions dominating the world. The radical future is conceived as two opposed outcomes. It might be authoritarian in nature, reflecting the thesis of the political philosopher Thomas Hobbes that without strong government life would be nasty, brutish and short. Alternatively, the radical future may be libertarian in nature, with minimal government and people free to experience whatever they wish largely without constraint. The countercultural future is often said to be 'New Age' in nature, rejecting current values, attitudes and beliefs and suggesting very different lifestyles. This approach is often associated with New Social Movements, which we looked at in Area 6.

Some key global issues

In a survey of the research into problems affecting the lives of people in the Third World, Best et al. (2000) found that Third-World cities directly affect the health of the population because of their pollution of air, water and other things. However, many of the long-established risks to health are reduced in cities. A number of modernisation theorists would argue that economic development has brought with it a significant net increase in health when measured by indicators such as lower infant mortality rates and higher life expectancy.

However, because of environmental factors such as poor water, air and food quality, many communicable diseases are still major killers in the Third World. Tuberculosis, meningitis, whooping cough and other airborne diseases are often fatal in the Third World. Diseases transmitted via human faeces, such as polio, hookworm and hepatitis, and diseases communicable by human contact, such as AIDS, leprosy and VD, are much more widespread than in the First World, and are more likely to end in death.

Lack of a clean and safe water supply is often the major cause of many Third World diseases. Dumping solid wastes into disposal sites can pollute sources of groundwater used for drinking water. Even if a Third-World city does have a sewage disposal system, there is usually very little treatment before discharge into waterways. The World Health Organisation (WHO) estimates that patients with waterborne diseases take over 70 percent of the hospital beds in the Third World. In addition, according to the WHO survey of 151 countries in 1988, only two-thirds of people in urban areas in the Third World had any form of sanitation service; the other third had to dispose of waste by their own means. The Huangpu river in Shanghai, the Han river in Seoul and the Bogota river in Colombia all have mostly untreated sewage deposited in them.

Moreover, drinking water is often costly in Third-World cities. For example, water from tankers in Port-au-Prince, Haiti, can cost fifteen percent of poor families' monthly income. If there is a street tap nearby, all water has to be collected and carried home, almost always by women. If a family has no piped water, it is much more likely to make use of polluted supplies. In addition, urbanisation often results in overpumping of groundwater in the Third World, which in itself can lower water-tables and increase the chance of encroachment and contamination.

Critics of modernisation theory argue that Western curative medicine provides little for the poor within the urban environment, as increases in the number of hospital beds would do nothing to prevent these diseases. Moreover, Western-style hospitals in the Third World cities often serve only the affluent.

Education and employment

Many of the problems in Third-World cities are caused by the lack of well-paid work. Third-World economies do not have large industrial sectors. As a consequence, many people in the Third World work in what is referred to as the informal sector; such jobs include domestic service, selling newspapers, drug dealing, cleaning shoes, prostitution and collecting rubbish for recycling. As Aidan Foster-Carter (1985) explains, 'The informal sector is characterised by ease of entry, indigenous resources, family ownership, small scale, labour-intensive or adapted technology, skills acquired outside the formal school system, and unregulated and often highly competitive markets.' (1985: 68)

In complete contrast, the formal sector is difficult to enter, owned by large companies, capital intensive, etc. However, it is important to note that not all jobs in the informal sector are low paid. In both the formal and the informal sectors, people have to work long hours, and working conditions are often dangerous. In addition, there are close links between the two sectors, as work is often subcontracted from the formal to the informal sector.

Although the existence of the informal sector makes it difficult to measure the level of unemployment in the Third World, most commentators agree that underemployment is 'an even more serious problem' (Randinelli and Kasanda, 1993). They estimate that up to 40 percent of the urban workforce in Third World cities are underemployed. Gilbert and Guyler (1987) suggest that underemployment has the following three forms:

- Work linked to fluctuations in economic activity; i.e. seasonal work
- Work in which there are so many workers that a reduction in the number would not have an effect on output, i.e. street vending
- 'Hidden unemployment', often found in family firms where people are kept in employment, but have little work to do

Bienefield (1994) argues that the economy of many Third-World cities is like the medieval European city with large numbers of pedlars, beggars, jugglers and thieves.

Just as in First-World economies, where rates of unemployment are highest among people who have little education and few skills, a number of studies suggest that this is also true in the Third World; for example, Smith and Cheung (1986) in their study of the Philippines and Wolpert's (1991) study of India. In both the First World and the Third World, entry into the formal sector is usually via the education system and examination success. Therefore, the demand for education is high in most Third-World countries. Modernisation theory suggests that efficient education systems in the Third World are one of the most important factors in the process of development, as education improves a country's 'human capital'.

In contrast, dependency theory argues that Western-style education systems in the Third World may cause both economic and cultural damage. Western-style education systems are expensive to run and provide an academic education for only a minority of the population, producing, according to Frantz Fanon (1967), a 'colonised personality'. Those so educated are culturally dependent upon the West.

The environment

The physical environment is a central factor in the quality of life of all people in the world. Our quality of life is dependent upon such factors as the houses we live in, the air we breathe, the public services we use and the dangers we face in our everyday lives.

Air pollution is a major problem for Third-World cities. In Mexico City, levels of air pollution are said to be six times above agreeable levels while air pollution in Manila is between three and four times above. Even in cities without large industrial sectors, such as Caracas or São Paulo, air quality is poor because of vehicle emissions. In many Chinese cities, air quality is poor because coal is used to heat homes; in Shanghai, the smog is known to local people as the 'Yellow Dragon'.

Housing is often expensive in Third World cities. For those who choose to live on the fringe of cities in shantytowns, or spontaneous settlements, building materials are costly, and these people often have their homes pulled down by landowners. The inhabitants of such settlements have limited access to public services, and have higher rates of disease and industrial injury, as shown in the explosion and gas escape from the Union Carbide pesticide plant at Bhopal, India.

Desertification – the expansion of the desert because of salinisation, soil erosion and soil alkalinity – is also recognised as a major environmental problem in the rural areas of many Third World countries. As Smith (1991) explains, these problems are due not solely to changes in climate but also to changes in agricultural techniques and overgrazing. As long ago as the 1930s, the vegetation in West Africa was seen to be deteriorating; this became known as the 'advance of the Sahara'. As Smith stresses, 'Problems of desertification are widespread, and principally result from farmers pushing into lands where rainfall is too low for crop cultivation without irrigation. Environmental refugees, the result of deterioration of agricultural land caused by unsustainable methods, now form the largest class of refugees in the world, estimated at over 10 million' (1991: 77). Smith estimates, for example, that:

- Sixty-one percent of India's cultivated land is subject to land degradation including the build-up of salts in the soil water (salinisation)
- Eighty percent of the grass and crop areas of Madagascar shows falling yields because old soil is lost more quickly than new soil can be formed (soil erosion)
- As a result of the build-up of magnesium, potassium and sodium in the soil, fifty percent of the agricultural land in Australia is said to be experiencing land degradation (soil alkalinity)

Even in the affluent First World, with the support of subsidies from bodies such as the European Union, most farmers cannot afford to solve these problems.

Many researchers argue that traditional farming techniques give better protection to the soil.

Urbanisation

Urbanisation refers to the movement of people from rural areas into cities. More than one in three people in the Third World now live in cities. According to the UN assessment of urbanisation trends (UNDIESA, 1991), between 1970 and 1990, the number of city dwellers in the Third World more than doubled from an estimated 675 million to 1.5 billion. Modernisation theory suggests that urbanisation is part of an evolutionary global process of modernisation which was the same for all countries experiencing the 'take off' of modernisation. However, contrary to what modernisation theorists argue, rates of urbanisation in the Third World in the 1990s were higher than they ever were in the First World. Moreover, unlike in the affluent West, Third-World urbanisation often takes place without any meaningful industrialisation.

But why do people move from 'rural' to 'urban' areas? There is a combination of 'push' and 'pull' factors. Some central 'push' factors include the following:

- Rural population expansion
- Unemployment
- Low income

Some of the central 'pull' factors include the following:

- Higher wages
- Improved employment prospects
- Better amenities

A.S. Oberai (1993) argues that rural population increase is not a significant factor in the growth of Third-World cities:

> Rapid population growth was once considered a major cause of rural-urban migration, with rural poverty caused by excess labour supply providing a 'push' to the cities (e.g., Lewis, 1954). But rural out-migration now seems less strongly associated with rural population increase than with overall economic growth, changes in agricultural productivity, and land tenure systems that promote marked inequalities in landholdings and land-lessness. (Oberai, 1993: 63)

The nature and processes of the rural-urban migration differ between countries. In Central America, for example, most migrants make a permanent move to the city and never return to their former rural homes. This was also the case in the rural-urban migration in what were to become First-World countries. In contrast, African and Southeast Asian rural-urban migration is usually temporary in nature.

However, research suggests that poor rural conditions are a central factor in migration. Third-World cities offer people a better quality of life than is usually available in the rural areas. In India, for example, in the 1980s, infant mortality rates were fifty percent higher in rural areas. In Indonesia, almost fifty percent of rural families were in poverty, whereas in urban areas the figure was twenty percent. In Brazil, over forty percent of rural families were in poverty, whereas for urban families the figure was less than twenty-five percent. Moreover, urban populations are more likely to own a refrigerator, a television set and a car.

Demographic change

Population change is a product of three factors: births, deaths and migration. According to Frank Notestein's (1990) demographic transition theory, population growth has taken place across the world in the following three stages:

- *Pre-modern stage*. Population increase is limited because high birth rates are counterbalanced by high death rates.
- *Early industrial stage*. Industrialisation is associated with high rates of population in its early phase, when birth rates are still high, but death rates decline because of improved living conditions and improved public health.
- *Mature industrial stage*. Growth in the population declines as birth rates fall to a similar level to death rates.

However, according to Scott Fosler (1990), many Third-World countries have a demographic profile that does not fit this model. Accelerated population increase exceeds the capacity of the economy to support such increases, and the general economic well-being, suggested by the theory, is never reached because resources are never enough to maintain the population increase in comfort.

Edward Mburugu (1986) found that the fertility rate – the average number of children that women are anticipated to give birth to during their lifetimes – has continued to increase as economic development expands. However, many Third-World societies never develop to the point of mature industrialisation, and the population increase never stabilises. In other words, demographic transition theory cannot explain the situation of rapid population growth without economic development that we find in many Third-World countries. The consequences of this situation were outlined in the 1991 Human Development Report of the UN Development Programme, which reported the following conditions in the Third World:

- Income per head in sub-Saharan Africa declined in the 1980s
- More than one billion people live in poverty
- Two million people live without an adequate or safe sanitation system
- One and a half billion people do not have access to a clean and safe water supply
- One hundred and eighty million children experience continuous and extreme malnutrition

Postmodernism – *disetatisation* the end of sovereignty

For Crook (1992), the modernisation of politics comprises the following four interrelated processes:

o The detachment of political action from other forms of activity
o The incorporation of almost all power within the executive mechanisms of the state
o The expansion of political participation
o The rise of largely class-based 'power politics'

All four of these processes are now in decline, as societies in the contemporary world undergo an important transformation, which Crook refers to as 'postmodern' in nature. This transformation is taking place because the processes which brought about the modern world, according to both functionalists and Marxists – rationalisation, commodification and differentiation – are becoming 'hyperdifferentiated'. In other words, the processes of modernisation have become so exaggerated as to become free of all constraint. This has given the world an unpredictable, contradictory and fragmented feel. We are moving from a situation within modernity characterised by the following:

o *Commodification*. This is the process whereby business overrules notions of aesthetic value, a view held by both Marxists and theorists of mass culture. In other words, any physical item or service can be bought or sold.
o *Rationalisation*. This is the process whereby life in the modern world becomes highly consistent, calculable and predictable. We looked at this process in Area 2 in Weber's analysis of bureaucracy.
o *Differentiation*. This is the process whereby subsystems within the social system become functionally interdependent.

We are moving into a situation within the postmodern condition characterised by the following:

o *Hypercommodification*. This is the spread of the commodity form into all areas of social and personal life.
o *Hyperrationalisation*. This creates a series of tensions that become self-limiting to the point of irrationality.
o *Hyperdifferentiation*. Here an inexhaustible number of divisions emerge that effectively wear down the meaningfulness of distinctions between independent areas of social life.

Modern culture was built upon the idea of aesthetic 'progress' or the development of a cultural tradition. However, within the postmodern condition, such traditions and ideas of cultural development are fragmented. In the postmodern condition, individuals are faced with an 'archive of styles', 'pastiche' and 'parody'. In addition, these cultural transactions are global in nature. Culture is a product of supranational bodies, outside the control of a nation-state. A most important part of this movement is the decreasing relevance of the state. As Crook explains, we may see the following four elements in the decreasing relevance of the state:

- A horizontal redistribution of power and responsibility to autonomous corporate bodies, as private companies control people's lives in ways which only nation-states did in the past
- A vertical redistribution of power and responsibility to local councils, civic initiatives, and extra-state self-governing bodies, as the nation-state loses power to other non-state bodies, such as 'agencies' like the Child Support Agency
- The marketisation and privatisation of previously state-run enterprises
- An externalisation of responsibility by shifting it to suprastate bodies such as the European Union and the UN

The nation-state is dissolving, and both its economic significance and political and military power are becoming assimilated into global networks.

As Crook explains,

> The 'Gulf War' of 1990–1 might be seen as the first postmodernized war. It could not be fought in terms of the interests of a particular state but was legitimated in terms of the interests of the entire global community of states, with openly a few minor ones standing against it, that is, by claims to be a 'new world order'. The majority commitment of the US forces could only be accomplished under UN sponsorship and if bankrolled by the Arab oil-states and Japan – that is, only if detached from their own nation-state.

> Moreover, the war was a live-to-air mass mediated event in which much of the entire global community participated vicariously. It was therefore immediate, brief and available in every home with a TV set, a prime example of the reduction of time-space distances. (Crook, 1992: 45–6)

The state, then, has started to diminish because of the globalisation of politics.

The work of Cynthia Weber ('Something's missing: a feminist reading of the United States invasion of Panama', Annual Meeting of the International Studies Association in Atlanta [1995]), Jens Bartelson (*A Genealogy of Sovereignty* [1995]) and David Harvey (1989) also suggest that in the postmodern condition there has been 'an end of sovereignty'. In other words, the nation-state no longer has sole control upon what goes on within its borders.

David Harvey (1989) maintains that organised space and time are signposts for familiar social practices or common ways of behaving. These signposts provide a framework for our experience of society. The development of cartography (map making) allowed the accurate measurement of land, which assisted the emergence of capitalism. As Ankie Hoogvelt explained, 'The organisation of space holds the key to power. Today the freedom of capital to move wherever it wants to go world-wide gives the capital-owning international bourgeoisie a decisive advantage over the mass of workers who are restricted in their movements and migrations by the passports they carry' (Hoogvelt, 1997).

Global change in work practices

Richard Sennett (2000) argues that the nature of the work we do and the organisation of work has significantly changed:

> Corporations are shifting from being dense, often rigid, pyramidal bureaucracies to be more flexible networks in a constant state of inner revision. In flexible capitalism people labour at short-term tasks, and change employers frequently, lifetime employment in one firm is a thing of the past. As a result, people can't identify themselves with a particular labour or with a single employer. (Sennett, 2000: 176)

Moreover, within these flexible organisations, there has been a split between 'command' and 'response'. Sennett gives the example of Microsoft, whose bosses told the middle management in 1995 to 'think Internet'. This 'intention' had to be interpreted and put into action. The role of the chief executive within many corporations is now to state intentions while people lower down the organisation put the intention into practice. For Sennett, the changing nature of capitalism is global. Moreover, the nature of work is changing, and there has been a transition from ways of working that were said to be 'Fordist' in nature to ways of working considered to be 'Post-Fordist' in nature. For many writers, such as Crook (1992), this transition is part of a greater process of postmodernisation, in which the world is becoming a much more uncertain place.

Henry Ford (1863–1947) was one of the first capitalists to use the assembly line to mass-produce a standardised product. Ford made extensive use of the principles of scientific management developed by Frederick Taylor (1856–1915) to maximise the efficient use of resources in order to maximise profits. Fordism was said to have described a form of society and ways of working within advanced industrial societies for most of the twentieth century. According to Robin Murry (1989), Fordism was based upon the following four principles:

○ *Standardization*. Each task was performed in the same fashion and at the same pace as specified by management.
○ *Mechanization*. Machines were used where possible to do the work of people.
○ *Scientific management*. Forms of management were based upon the work of Taylor (1911).
○ *Flow-line production*. Products moved on a line that flowed past the worker.

Moreover, under the influence of the economist John Maynard Keynes, the effect of Fordist ideals spread beyond workplaces to other areas of social life. Increases in wages were used to buy the expanding production of 'massified' products such as cars, televisions, and other consumer durables. This strengthened the power of capital in society, as workers were dependent upon employers to provide employment and the wages needed to afford the consumer lifestyle.

However, Fordism had its limits. Work on the production line was often monotonous. In addition, workers attempted to assert some control over their work environment by taking industrial action or by forms of industrial vandalism or cutting corners. Moreover, the inflexible bureaucratic work organisations and their work practices were slow to respond to changes in consumer taste and fashion. By the early 1980s, the Fordist cycle of increasing wages, consumer demand and production broke down. As Michael Piore and Charles Sabel (1984: 189–91) explain, capitalist societies expressed a 'second industrial divide'. In imitation of the 'just in time' systems first used in Japan, new forms of flexible work practices were introduced by the early 1980s. New work practices needed fewer full-time, permanent workers and more part-time, temporary or subcontracted workers. These workers were thought to be more profitable, as they could be laid off at short notice, and employers could then be much more responsive to changes in consumer taste and consumer demand. In order to enhance profits, there was a need for workers to be multiskilled, versatile and able to work in teams. According to Lash and Urry (1987), post-Fordism signalled the end of 'organised capitalism', as employment became both less secure and more fragmented. Post-Fordism brought 'flexible firms' with 'flexible production' for 'niche' markets.

An Italian fashion wear company, for instance, does not even own its own stores. For example, the full cost of setting up a Benetton shop must be borne by the operator, although he or she must operate within the rules of Benetton's shop organisation; that is, no backroom stockholding, only one interior design and only Benetton products for sale. Benetton's production facilities employ only about 1500 workers, whose efforts are complemented by 200 subcontractors, each employing thirty to fifty workers. Commenting on such trends, Ashley (1997) remarked on the difficulty of trying to decide whether firms such as Benetton or Nike are 'big' or 'small'. 'Judged in terms of their core workers, both firms are small local operations; judged in terms of contract workers, however, they are sprawling multinationals. Indeed, organisations such as this are not so much single entities as fluid networks, adding value by coordinating activities across geographical and corporate boundaries. In other words, the best firms are both "big" and "small", depending on what they are doing.' (adapted from Ashley, 1997: 108–9)

The effects of these changes for young workers have been outlined by Gary Pollock (1997). Drawing upon longitudinal data from the BHPS study of 10,000 people every year since 1991, Pollock shows that for people aged between 20 and 24 the labour market trend is for lower levels of work for men, but for an increasing number to stay on in education. There has been an increase in labour market participation by women, but this trend had levelled off by 1997. However, the increase was associated with part-time work and short-term contract work. Many sectors of the labour market are becoming unavailable to young people, and young people find it difficult to predict what jobs they will have in the future, as the supply of labour is greater than the demand for it. Pollock describes the employment market for young people as 'a risk fraught system of flexible, pluralised, decentralised underemployment' (Pollock, 1997: 616).

David Ashley (1997: 95–6) gives the following summary of post-Fordism:

- A shift to new 'information technologies'
- An emergence of a more flexible, specialised and decentralised labour force, a decline of the old manufacturing base and the rise of computer-based, 'hi-tech' industries
- A contracting-out of functions and services hitherto provided 'in-house' on a corporate basis
- A leading role of consumption and a greater emphasis on choice and product differentiation; on marketing, packaging and design; and on the 'targeting' of consumers by lifestyle, taste and culture
- A decline in the proportion of the skilled, male manual working class, and a rise of the service and white collar class
- More flexi-time and part-time working, coupled with the feminisation and ethnicisation of the workforce
- A new international division of labour and an economy dominated by multinationals
- A globalisation of the new financial markets
- An emergence of new patterns of social division – especially those between 'public' and 'private' sectors, and between the 'new poor'

McDonaldisation

According to George Ritzer, the process of McDonaldisation characterises the production line approach that has been common in a number of industries for many years, especially the hospitality industries. Ritzer views this process as harmful because it reduces both diversity and choice. McDonaldisation has the following four key components:

- *Efficiency*. This involves 'choosing the optimum means to a given end' (Ritzer, 1996: 36). This efficiency is defined by the organisation rather than the individual and is, in effect, imposed upon the individual.
- *Calculability*. Here there is 'an emphasis on the quantitative aspect of products sold (portion size, cost) and service offered (the time it takes to get the product)' (Ritzer, 1996: 9).
- *Predictability*. Here there is an emphasis on 'discipline, order, systemization, formalization, routine, consistency and methodical operation. In such a society, people prefer to know what to expect in most settings and at most times' (Ritzer, 1996: 79). The experience is the same in every shop for the consumer, and work becomes routine for the workers.
- *Control*. Management must control both the workers and the customers in an effort to reduce the level of uncertainty within the organisation.

These processes have their own irrational outcomes, which Ritzer describes as follows: 'Rational systems inevitably spawn a series of irrationalities that limit,

Table 7.1 *Temporal and spatial changes in liberal, organized and disorganized capitalism*

Phase of capitalist development	Predominant temporal/spatial/ organizational structures	Spatial changes within each territory	Predominant means of transmitting knowledge and executing surveillance
Liberal	Large-scale collapsing empires that had been built up around dynastic rulers or world religions; emergence of weak nation-states	Growth of tiny pockets of industry. Importance of substantial commercial cities as well as the expansion of new urban centres in rural areas	Handwriting and word mouth
Organized	Nation-states within the ten or so major Western economies increasingly dominate large parts of the rest of the world through colonisation	Development of distinct regional economies organised around growing urban centres. Major inequalities between new industrial and non-industrial regions and nations	Printing developed through 'print-capitalism'
Disorganized	Development of world economy, an international division of labour, and the wide-spread growth of capitalism in most countries	Decline of distinct regional/national economies and of *industrial* cities. Growth of industry in smaller cities and rural areas, and the development of service industry. Separation of finance and industry	Electronically transmitted information dramatically reduces the time–space distances between people and increases the powers of surveillance

Source: Lash and Urry, 1989: 274

eventually compromise, and perhaps even undermine their rationality' (Ritzer, 1996: 121). The inefficiencies generated by these rational processes include the following:

○ Longer waiting times and more work for the customer – having to make your own salad in the salad bar, or fill your own glass in the fast-food restaurant
○ Dehumanisation of the worker and of the customer
○ The emergence of unforeseen anomalies

In some areas of industry in the 1970s, the ideas of Elton Mayo provided the basis for schemes of 'job enrichment' or 'job enlargement'. This often involved greater decision making within teams at work; for example, team working at Volvo was designed to enhance the workers' motivation and give them a greater sense of identity. Both of these approaches were concerned with the same end, to make modern capitalism better organised. During the economic slump in the 1920s and 1930s, Mayo (1935) and his team carried out a series of investigations at the Hawthorne plant of the Western Electric Company. Very much influenced by the ideas of solidarity and anomie of both Durkheim (1897) and Parsons (1935), Mayo and his team feared that during the slump workers were more likely to experience the sense of normlessness that Durkheim had termed 'anomie'. Mayo observed that this anomic uncertainty led workers to form informal organisations (compact social groups) at work to give their lives a degree of certainty.

In contrast to Taylor, people could not simply be motivated by money. Management had to take into account the deeper psychological motives of workers, and had to gain an understanding of these motives in order to manage both time and space more efficiently. The science of human relations makes the following assumptions:

o   A work organisation is a social system that has norms and defined roles
o   Feelings and sentiments influence workers' behaviour
o   The informal work group affects the individual performance of workers
o   Management should be democratic
o   Satisfied workers have higher productivity
o   Organisations should give opportunities for participation by workers and open channels of communication
o   The manager needs competent social skills

However, by the 1990s, many researchers, such as Lash and Urry (1987), were describing capitalism as having a 'disorganised' feel to it. Employers demanded greater flexibility from their workers, often employing only a small core group of permanent staff, with the rest on short, fixed-term, highly flexible contracts. This type of management practice can be described as Post-Fordist, and it has a post-modern feel to it.

This disorganisation that Lash and Urry outline has the following five components:

o   The breaking up of capitalist organisations
o   The decline of the working class and the emergence of a service class
o   The loss of state power, notably over the economy
o   Global markets
o   Cultural fragmentation

In contrast, Harvey (1989) views the postmodern condition as a new stage in advanced capitalism, as the system changed in order to cope with the problem of overaccumulation. Postmodern culture has an ephemeral or evanescent feel to it. We consume more and more products and services as we are bombarded with products to enhance our lifestyle choices. Postmodernity is also associated with a fundamental transformation of space and how we perceive space. In Harvey's view, we are experiencing a 'time-space compression'; in other words, space is becoming abolished because, unlike modernity, postmodernity has no need for physical movement (thanks to information technology and other media). These changes have a significant effect upon the nature of economic, cultural and political life. The world is being reconstituted into a single social space and life has become delocalised.

As Ankie Hoogvelt explains,

> Today people have social relations and even organised community relations regardless of space, that is: regardless of the territory that they share. This has enormous conse-quences not only for the role of the nation-state as territorially bounded community, but also, as we shall see below, for the organisation of economic production on a cross-border basis. It permits the emergence of virtual communities, cultures and even systems of authority and social control that cross borders. While we still have local lives as physi-cal persons, we also now experience phenomenal worlds that are truly global. It is this globalisation as shared phenomenal worlds, which, I argue, today drives the processes of economic globalisation. (Hoogvelt, 1997)

In capitalism, the costs of manufacturing are calculated in terms of the time it takes to complete the production process.

As we have suggested in both Area 3 and Area 4, postmodernism is in essence concerned with deconstructing, and casting doubt upon any 'grand narrative' or big theory which claims to hold the truth. For postmodernists, the truth is created, not discovered. In terms of international relations, each regime believes that its vision of international relations is the truth. President Clinton believes that his vision is correct; Sadam Hussein believes that his vision is cor-rect. Each vision forms a distinct discourse. However, in the international field, knowledge claims are conditional upon particular power relationships. In other words, there is no such thing as truth, but there are 'regimes of truth'. Some visions dominate others.

Area Summary

In this area, we have looked at the political, economic and cultural processes of globalisation, including an outline of the major international organisations concerned with global governance. As we saw, globalisa-tion has a number of dimensions: economic, cultural and political. With

continued

the collapse of communism in Eastern Europe, bringing about a 'new world order', processes of globalisation have come to the fore. Most of the area was an evaluation of various modernist positions, derived from either dependency theory (Marxist writers) or modernisation theory (functionalists such as Parsons or right of centre economists such as Rostow). We have also evaluated the contributions of David Held, Roland Robertson, Anthony Giddens, Francis Fukuyama, Immanuel Wallerstein and David Harvey to the debates about globalisation. In addition, we have looked at how sociologists have attempted to make sense of the future, with theories largely built upon the idea of 'progress' or the development of a cultural tradition that is positive about the future. Finally, we evaluated the contribution of postmodernist writers to the issues of international relations, most notably the notion of disetatization as the end of sovereignty. The processes of bring about this disetatization included hypercommodification, hyperrationalisation and hyperdifferentiation.

References

Alter, Peter (1985) *Nationalism*. London: Edward Arnold.

Appadurai, A. (1989) 'Disjunction and difference in the global cultural economy', in *Theory Culture and Society*, 7. pp. 295–310.

Aron, R. (1967) *Progress and Disillusion: The Dialectics of Modern Society*. New York: Mentor Books.

Ashley, D. (1997) *History Without a Subject*. Boulder: Westview Press.

Bartelson, J. (1995) *A Geneology of Sovereignty*. Cambridge: Cambridge University Press.

Bell, D. (1974) *The Coming of Post-Industrial Society*. London: Heineman.

Benedict, R. (1946) *The Chrysanthemum and the Sword*. Boston, MA: Houghton Mifflin.

Best, S. (1997) 'Power and politics' in Nik Jorgensen (eds), *Sociology: An Interactive Approach*. London: Collins Educational.

Best, S., Griffiths, J. and Hope, T. (2000) *Active Sociology*. Harlow: Longman.

Bienefield, M. (1994) 'Capitalism and the nation state in the dog days of the twentieth century', in *Between Globalism and Nationalism* Socialist Register (eds), R. Miliband and L. Panitch. London: Merlin Press.

Cockerham, W. (1995) *The Global Society*. New York: McGraw-Hill.

Cox, R. (1987) *Production, Power and World Order*. New York: Basic Books.

Crook, S. and Pakulski, J. (1992) *Postmodernization: Change in Advanced Society*. London: Sage.

Cuff, E. Sharrock, W. and Francis, D. (1998) *Perspectives in Sociology*. London: Routledge.

Crowley, D. (1964) *The Background to Current Affairs*. London: Macmillan.

Dahrendorf, R. (1990) *Reflections on the Revolutions in Europe*. London: Chatto and Windus.

Durkheim, Emile (1897) *Suicide: A Study in Sociology*. London: Routledge.

Eisenstadt (1992) 'The breakdown of communist regimes and the vicissitudes of modernity', *Daedalus* (Spring): 21–41.

Elger, T. and Smith, C. (1994) (eds) *Global Japanization: The Transnational Transformation of the Labour Process*. London: Routledge.

Etzioni, A. (1991) 'A socio-economic perspective on friction'. Washington: IAREP/SASE Conference (mimeo).

Fanon, F. (1967) *The Wretched of the Earth*. Harmondsworth: Penguin.

Feldman, A.S. and Moore, W.E. (1962) *Industrialisation and Industrialism: Convergence and Differentiation*. Transactions of the Fifth World Congress of Sociology. Washington, DC: ISA.

Fosler, S. (1990) quoted in Michael Carr, *New Patterns: Processes and Change in Human Geography*. Walton on Thames: Nelson.

Foster-Carter, A. (1985) *The Sociology of Development*. Ormskirk: Causeway Press.

Fukuyama, Francis (1992) *The End of History and the Last Man*. New York: New York Free Press.

Furtado, C. (1971) *Economic Development of Latin America: A Survey from Colonial Times to the Cuban Revolution*. Cambridge: Cambridge University Press.

Garfinkel, Harold (1967) *Studies in Ethnomethodology*. Cambridge: Polity.

Giddens, A. (1981) *Social Theory and Modern Sociology*. Cambridge: Polity.

Giddens, A. (1984) *The Constitution of Society*. Cambridge: Polity.

Giddens, A. (1985) *The Nation State and Violence*. Cambridge: Polity.

Giddens, A. (1990) *The Consequences of Modernity*. Cambridge: Polity.

Giddens, A. (1994) *Reflexive Modernisation*. Cambridge: Polity.

Giddens, A. (2000) 'Anthony Giddens and Will Hutton in Conversation', pp. 1–51 in.

Giddens, A. and Hutton, W. *On the Edge: Living with Global Capitalism*. London: Jonathan Cape.

Gilbert, A. and Guyler, J. (1987) *Cities, Poverty, and Development: Urbanisation in the Third World*. Oxford: Oxford University Press.

Gramsci, A. (1957) *The Modern Prince*. New York: New York International Publishers.

Grint, K. (1991) *The Sociology of Work: An Introduction*. Cambridge: Polity.

Gunder-Frank, A. (1969) *Latin America: Underdevelopment or Revolution*. Monthly New York Review Press.

Hannerz, U. (1989) 'Notes on the global ecummene', *Public Culture*, 1(2): 66–75.

Harvey, David (1989) *The Condition of Postmodernity*. Oxford: Blackwell.

Harvey, David (1989) *The Condition of Postmodernity: An Enquiry into the Origins of Cultural Change*. Oxford: Basil Blackwell.

Hayter, T. (1989) *Aid*. London: Earthscan Press.

Held, D. (1992) 'Democracy: from city states to a cosmopolitan order', *Political Studies*, 40: 32–4.

Held, D. (1995) *Democracy and the Global Order*. Cambridge: Polity.

Hoogvert, A.A. (1997) *Globalisation and the Postcolonial World: The New Political Economy of Development*. Basingstoke: Macmillan.

Hoogvelt, A. (1982) *The Third World in Global Development*. London: Macmillan.

Horseman, M. and Marshall, A. (1994) *After the Nation State: Citizens, Tribalism and the New World Disorder*. London: Harper Collins.

Hutton, W. and Giddens, A. (2000) *On the Edge: Living with Global Capitalism*. London: Jonathan Cape.

Inkeles, A. (1976) 'A model of the modern man: theoretical and methodological issues', in
C. Black, (ed.), *Comparative Modernizations*. New York: Free Press.

Kerr, C. Dunlop, J.T., Harbison, H. and Myers, C.A. (1960) *Industrialism and Industrial
Man*. Cambridge, MA: Harvard University Press.

Kirby, M. (1995) *Investigating Political Sociology*. London: Collins Educational.

Lash, S. and Urry, J. (1987) *The End of Organised Capitalism*. Cambridge: Polity.

Leggatt, T. (1985) *The Folking Paths*. London: Macmillan.

Lewis, O. (1970) 'The culture of poverty', in O. Lewis, *Anthropological Essays*. New York:
Random House.

Lewis, O. (1954) *Life in a Mexican Village: Tepoztian Restudied*. Urbana: University of
Illinois Press.

Lipset, S.M. (1967) *The First New Nation*. New York: Basic Books.

MacEwan, A. (1994) 'Globalisation and stagnation', in R. Miliband and L. Panitch *Between
Globalism and Nationalism*. London: The Merlin Press.

Mann, M. (1986) *The Sources of Social Power*. Cambridge: Cambridge University Press.

Mayo, E. (1935) *The Social Problems of an Industrial Civilization*. London: Routledge.

Murray, R. (1971) 'The internationalization of capital and the nation state' *New Left Review*,
67 May – June pp. 84–108.

Murray, R. (1989) 'Fordism and post-fordism', in S. Hall and M. Jacques, *New Times: The
Changing Face of Politics in the 1990's*. London: Lawrence and Wishart. pp. 83–103.

Mburugu, D. (1986) quoted in L. Inmberlake and J. Holmberg (1991) *One World for One
Earth: Overcoming Environmental Degradation*. London: Earthscan/Open University.

Nakane, Chie (1985) *Japanese Society*. Berkeley, CA: University of California Press.

Notestein, F. (1990) quoted in L. Inmberlake and J. Holmberg (1991) *One World for One
Earth: Overcoming Environmental Degradation*. London: Earthscan/Open University.

Nordlinger, E. (1975) *The Autonomy of the Democratic State*. Cambridge, Mass.: Harvard
University Press.

Oberai, A.S. (1993) 'Urbanisation, development, and economic efficiency', in J.D. Kasarda
and A.M. Parnell (eds), *Third World Cities: Problems, Policies and Prospects*. London:
Sage.

Panitch, L. (1994) 'Globalisation and the state' in R. Miliband and L. Panitch, *Between
Globalism and Nationalism*. London: The Merlin Press.

Parsons, T. (1935) *The Structure of Social Action*. New York: Free Press.

Parsons, T. (1951) *The Social system*. London: Routledge.

Parsons, T. (1970) *Societies: Evolutionary and Comparative Perspectives*. Englewood
Cliffs, NJ: Prentice-Hall.

Piore, M. and Sobel, C. (1984) *The Second Industrial Divide: Possibilities for Prosperity*.
New York: Basic Books.

Pollock, G. (1997) 'Uncertain futures: young people in and out of employment since 1940'
in *Work, Employment and Society*. Vol. II, No. 4: 616–38.

Randinelli, D.A. and Kasanda, J.D. (1993) 'Job creation needs in Third World cities', in
J.D. Kasards and A. Parnell (eds), *Third World Cities: Problems, Policies and Prospects*.
London: Sage.

Reich, R.B. (1992) *The Work of Nations*. New York: Vintage Books.

Ritzer, G. (1996) *The McDonaldization of Society*. Thousand Oaks, CA: Pine Forge Press.

Rodney, W. (1981) *How Europe Underdeveloped Africa*. Oxford: Harvard University Press.

Robertson, R. (1994) *Globalisation*. London: Sage.

Rostow, W.W. (1960) *The Five Stages of Economic Growth: A Non-Communist Manifesto*.
Cambridge: Cambridge University Press.

Rostow, W.W. (1962) *The Stages of Economic Growth: A non-Communist Manifesto*.
Cambridge: Cambridge University Press.

Sarre, Philip (1996) *An Overcrowded World? Population, Resources and the Environment*. Oxford: Oxford University Press.

Scott, J. (1997) *Corporate Business and Capitalist Class*. Oxford: Oxford University Press.

Sennett, R. (2000) 'Street and office: two sources of identity', in W. Hutton and A. Giddens (eds), *On the Edge: Living with Global Capitalism*. London: Jonathan Cape.

Shutz, Alfred (1937) *The Phenomenology of the Social World*. London: Heinemann.

Sklair, L. (1993) 'Going global: competing models of globalisation', *Sociological Review*, (Nov).

Skocpol, Theda (1985) *Bringing the State Back In*. Edited by Peter M. Evans and Dietrich Rueschemeyer. Cambridge: Cambridge University Press.

Smelser, N. (1959) *Social Change in the Industrial Revolution*. London: Routledge.

Smith, A.D. (1991) 'Towards a global culture?', in M. Featherstone (ed.), *Global Culture: Nationalism, Globalisation and Modernity*. London: Sage.

Smith, H.L. and Cheung, P.L. (1986) 'Trends in the effects of family background on educational attainment in the Philippines', *American journal of sociology*, 91: 1387–1408.

Sztompka, P. (1991) 'The intangibles and imponderables of the transition to democracy', *Studies in Comparative Communism*, 24(3): 295–311.

Sztompka, P. (1992) *Dilemmas of the Great Transition*. Cambridge, MA: Harvard Center for European Studies (Working Paper Series No. 19).

Sztompka, P. (1993) *The Sociology of Social Change*. Oxford: Blackwell.

Tiryakian, E. (1985) 'The changing centers of modernity', in E. Cohen, M. Lissak and U. Almagor (eds), *Comparative Social Dynamics*. Boulder, CO: Westview Press.

United Nations Development Program (1991) *Human Development Report*. New York: United Nations.

United Nations Department of International Economic and Social Affairs (UNDIESA) (1991) *World Urbanisation Prospects 1990: Estimates and Projections of Urban and Rural Populations of Urban Agglomerations*. New York: Population Studies No. 121 ST/ESA/SER.A/121.

Wagar, W. Warren (1992) *The Next Three Futures: Paradigms of Things to Come*. London: Adamantine.

Wallerstein, I. (1979) *The Modern World System II*. New York: Academic Press.

Wallerstein, I. (1979) *The Capitalist World Economy*. Cambridge: Cambridge University Press.

Wallerstein, I. (1980) *The Modern World System II*. New York: Academic Press.

Waters, M (1995) *Globalisation*. London: Routledge.

Weber, Cynthia (1995) 'Something's missing: a feminist reading of the United States invasion of Panama' *Annual Meeting of the International Studies Association in Atlanta* (1995) International Studies Association, Tucson: University of Arizona.

Webster, Andrew (1990) *Introduction to the Sociology of Development*. Basingstoke: Macmillan.

Wolpert, S (1991) *'India'* Berkeley, CA: University of California Press.

8

War

Area Goals

By the end of this area you should have:

- An understanding of the nature of war: limited war, total war, and post-modern war
- Knowledge of the contribution of Clausewitz on war
- Some awareness of the causes of war
- A critical understanding of the contribution that social scientists have made to our understanding of war: Chomsky, Giddens, Wallerstein, Deleuze, Baudrillard, Gunder-Frank
- Some understandings of 'the new world order'
- Some understanding of recent conflicts, particularly the Gulf War

Wars are deadly conflicts in which one society strives to attempt to impose its will on others through the use of armed force. However, as Ian Roxborough (1994) has pointed out, sociology has had very little success in generating a 'integrated corpus of theory about the nature of warfare'. This is because sociology has tended to look at internal working of societies rather than intersocietal processes: 'The sociology of war currently appears as an incoherent mass of widely divergent intellectual agendas' (Roxborough, 1994: 620). However, there is an ever-present threat of warfare across the globe. In this area, we attempt to answer the question: Why do wars happen? Do human beings have an inherent tendency for aggression that presents itself in warlike activities? Or is the notion of war inherently related to the idea of the nation-state and processes of state formation?

Clausewitz on war

Clausewitz argued that warfare was a complicated mixture of passion, chance and reason. In addition, he made a distinction between 'Absolute war', in which a state attempts to force an enemy to do its will by the use of 'untrammelled violence', and 'Real war', which is a more limited form of armed conflict. However, he describes both forms of war as the extension of politics by other means:

> War is nothing but the continuation of policy with other means. War is not merely an act of policy but a true political instrument, a continuation of political intercourse, carried on with other means.... The political objective is the goal, war is the means of reaching it, and means can never be considered in isolation from their purpose. (Clausewitz quoted in Roxborough, 1994: 623–4)

However, what did Clausewitz mean by 'politics'? Roxborough argues that when Clausewitz was writing, at the beginning of the nineteenth century in Germany, the word *Politick* meant both 'policy' and 'politics' in English. In this sense, the phrase, *'war as the extension of politics by other means'*, should be understood as the pursuit of foreign policy by an elite that dominates a state. With the arrival of mass democratic political systems, the phrase has shifted significantly in meaning.

Eqbal Ahmad (1996) argues that the history of the twentieth century was one of Western domination, achieved by means of force that was widespread, institutionalised and legitimised by religion and morality. However, the Vietnam War was a turning point in this process of Western domination, and its significance has yet to be fully understood. Moreover, this war reinforced the superiority of people over machines. The confidence that the US government had about its ability for global intervention was broken. US confidence in its ability to dominate the world did not return fully until the emergence of the new world order in 1989. The new world order is commonly assumed to include the following ideas:

- The acquisition of territory by force is unacceptable
- Violations of the UN charter are unacceptable
- UN Security Council resolutions shall be enforced strictly

Why war?

Below is a list of possible reasons why countries go to war with each other. You might want to reflect on which of the following motives you agree with and why:

- Seizure of territory
- Seizure of resources
- Need for domination
- Revenge
- To make profit for capitalists
- Instinctual aggression
- Misunderstanding of other countries' intentions
- Misunderstanding of other countries' strengths
- To maintain the balance of power in the world

In his account of the relationship between territorial ideology and international conflict, Alexander B. Murphy (1991) notes that in the early 1990s more than 175 sovereign states had borders that were in dispute. Moreover, claims Murphy, in the latter half of the twentieth century more than half of the world's states had some form of border dispute. In addition, as we saw over the last decade of the twentieth century, there are significant numbers of substate minorities seeking independence for a range of ethnic, historical or economic reasons. In other words, the idea that a nation-state should have exclusive sovereignty over a territory is a major factor in the often violent conflicts that take place within and between nation-states.

Murphy (1991) traces the concept of 'territorial sovereignty' back to the ancient Greeks, but argues that it was the Treaties of Westphalia (1648) that clearly established the concept in international law. Moreover, since the Treaties of Westphalia, threats to territorial sovereignty have become accepted as a legitimate reason for one nation-state to attack another. Writers such as Locke, J.S. Mill and Rousseau successfully fused the idea of 'the state' with 'the people'. In other words, the state should provide security for its people. This link creates a deep psychological attachment between 'the state' and 'the people' which manifests itself as nationalism and the belief that distinct ethnic patterns, such as language, shared perception and shared culture, are key elements in defining the state and its people.

The arguments about the economic causes of war have been most forcefully made by Marxist writers.

The new world order

With the collapse of the USSR in 1989, a new world order emerged. One major problem for this new world order was the conflict in the former Yugoslavia. At the end of World War II in 1945, the six federal republics of Yugoslavia – Bosnia-Herzegovina, Croatia, Macedonia, Montenegro, Serbia and Slovenia – were united in a federation under communist rule. For most of this period (1945–80), the federation was held together by Tito, but after he died in 1980 and the USSR collapsed in 1989, the various republics started to demand their independence from Yugoslavia. In the summer of 1991, two of the republics, Slovenia and Croatia, established themselves as independent states. President Milosevic denounced the declarations of independence, and the Yugoslav Parliament, now under the control of Serbia, ordered the Yugoslav army 'to undertake measures to prevent the division of Yugoslavia and changes to its borders'. Almost at once, wars started between Serbia and Slovenia and between Croatia and Serbia. In addition, serious civil disorder broke out in Bosnia-Herzegovina among Bosnian Serbs, Bosnian Croats and Bosnian Muslims.

Causes of war: the Marxist approach

All wars are a product of capitalism. This is because all wars are rooted in eco-nomic factors, and these factors reveal themselves in the processes of imperial-ism, first outlined by Lenin. Capitalists need to expand overseas in the search for new markets and sources of cheap raw materials. As the managing commit-tee of the bourgeoisie, the state involves itself in international conflicts to secure the economic advantages needed by capitalists to offset the long-term tendency for the rate of profit to fall. As all nation-states operate in this way, major inter-national conflict is inevitable. As Harold Laski wrote in his paper 'The economic foundations of peace', 'Men have sought an especially profitable source of invest-ment. They have been able to utilize their government to protect their interest; and, in the last analysis, the government becomes so identified with the investor, that an attack on his profit is equated with a threat to the national honour. In those circumstances the armed forces of the state are, in fact, the weapon he employs to guarantee his privilege' (quoted in Brodie, 1973: 285).

Economic motives can be seen in such diverse US wars as the following:

- The 'wars' against the Native Americans in the nineteenth century, which involved taking land by force
- The Mexican War of 1846–1848, which also involved taking land by force
- The American Civil War, fought over the issue of slavery

Psychological factors such as nationalism and chauvinistic ideologies are seen as 'false consciousness'; the *real* motive forces behind international conflict remain unknown to people.

In his book *Road to War 1914–1917* (1935), Walter Millis argued that US involvement in World War I took place because munitions companies in the USA had invested heavily on a credit basis in the Allied forces. These companies demanded that the US government support the Allies to protect their investment. Moreover, Millis claims that the US Ambassador to Britain, Walter Hines Page had played a key role in this process. However, Bernard Brodie (1973) has argued that there is no evidence that Hines Page was associated with munitions manufacturers. He was simply pro-British.

Similarly, World War II was more about stopping Hitler than any economic issues.

Brodie (1973) also points out that during most of the period of US involvement in the Vietnam War, stock prices had risen with hopes of peace and fallen when hopes of peace faded. The biggest drop in prices was when the US forces invaded Cambodia in April 1970, and defence industries fell more than most.

War and economic advantage

Many wars do not appear to have any economic advantage to be gained by either side. Consider the following examples of wars in the twentieth century and suggest some possible reasons for the involvement of the nation-state involved.

Example A

Our first example is the civil war in Cambodia (1970–5), the rule by the Khmer Rouge (1975–8) and the Vietnamese invasion (1979–89). The Khmer Rouge government of Pol Pot was involved in a programme of extermination of intellectuals, entrepreneurs, administrators and landowners. The Khmer Rouge blew up the central bank, abolished all property, and abolished all religion. Groups who resisted, such as The Chans, a group of about 60,000 who had followed Islam since the Middle Ages, were massacred.

Example B

The next example is the war in Afghanistan (1978–89). The borders of Afghanistan are arbitrary and were not drawn up by the Afghans themselves. The largest group of people in the region are the Pushtun, comprising some 6.5 million people resident in a region that is within Afghanistan and Pakistan. When India became independent in 1947 and the state of Pakistan was formed, the Afghan government asked for the Pakistani Pashtun region to become part of Afghanistan. The Pakistani government refused this request. The USA became an ally of Pakistan and the USSR an ally of the Afghan government. In 1965, the People's Democratic Party of Afghanistan (PDPA) was formed, but, by 1970, it had split into two factions; the Khalq, who were Leninist and wanted a communist revolution, and the Babrak, who believed in a gradual adoption of communism. In April 1978, PDPA supporters in the armed forces staged a coup and set about rebuilding Afghanistan as a Soviet-style communist society. However, by

March 1979, many people had become disillusioned with the new government. For this reason, Jabhai-yi-Nijat Melli (the National Liberation Front), led by Sigbratullah Mojadidi, a Sunni Muslim, declared a jihad against the secular Kabul government. From this date, the USSR became more and more involved in the conflict under the 'Brezhnev doctrine', which stated that the USSR would give support to any communist government that requested it. The USSR imposed its own favoured leaders in Afghanistan, first Babrak Karmal and later Mohammed Najib. However, these governments were very unpopular and, even with extensive military support and sustained direct military involvement by the USSR, were unable to avoid a military defeat at the hands of the Islami-Itehad-Afghanistan Mujaheddin. This group was a loose coalition of seven Sunni Muslim groups and a separate loose coalition of Afghan Shiites based in Iran.

Why did the USSR get involved in this long and costly war? Was it for 'economic' reasons? US commentators suggested that the occupation of Afghanistan would lead to the occupation of Iran, so that the USSR would have a presence in the Persian Gulf. It is also possible that the USSR wanted to prevent the spread of Islamic fundamentalism. Both of these objectives would have involved the occupation of Iran, but this was unlikely, as there were shorter routes to obtaining a presence in the Persian Gulf. As for preventing the spread of Islamic fundamentalism, it should be noted that the war in Afghanistan had started before the fall of the Shah of Iran. The most probable cause of this war was the application of the Brezhnev doctrine; Brezhnev did not want to be the first leader of the USSR to lose a communist country.

Example C

Our next example is the 'war' between the Tutsi and the Hutu in Burundi and Rwanda. This is one of the bloodiest and longest running conflicts in the history of the world. The Tutsi have ruled what is now known as Burundi for over 400 years and that control has been maintained by force. In October 1965, after the hereditary monarch Mwami Mwambutsa refused to accept that Hutu had made gains in the general election, a major Hutu revolt took place in which almost 5000 Hutu were killed. Again, in September 1972, there was a Hutu revolt in Bujumbura, in which the government claimed that 50,000 Tutsi were killed. Whether we accept this figure or not, what is not in doubt is that reprisals against the Hutu followed. Close to 150,000 Hutu fled the country, but about 100,000 lost their lives. There were similar events after the military coup in 1987 in which there was widespread killing of Tutsi by Hutu, and subsequent revenge massacres. Again, whatever were the causes of these awful events, there does not seem to be an 'economic' cause behind them.

Example D

The next example is the Kosovo conflict. In his short history of Kosovo, Noel Malcolm (1998) explains that in late 1997 and early 1998 occasional violent conduct by Kosovan Albanians was dealt with by the Serb security forces in brutal and often random fashion. One such incident was in the village of Vojnik near the town of Prishtina. On 25 November 1997, when the Serb police attempted to serve a court order on an Albanian man, there was a skirmish in which rifle shots were fired. The Serb police retreated, but returned with armoured cars. It was shortly after this event that the Kosovo Liberation Army (KLA) was formed, and there was a significant escalation in the conflict. By April 1999, Malcolm estimates that some 600,000 refugees had left Kosovo, in the face of a systematic 'ethnic cleansing' operation: random killings of civilians, and houses set on fire.

Since the formation of Yugoslavia, Kosovo had always been regarded as an autonomous region; even the 1974 Yugoslav constitution granted Kosovo its own direct representation in the main federal Yugoslav institutions, its own constitution, its own powers of economic management and some independence in foreign policy. In other words, Kosovo had almost the same autonomy as the six republics that made up the Federal Republic of Yugoslavia. It is important to note that the 1974 constitution stayed in force until the break-up of Yugoslavia. However, Slobodan Milosevic took this independence away from Kosovo and declared it a province of a greater Serbia. In addition, the European Union did not recognise the autonomy of Kosovo and instead regarded Kosovo as a subsidiary of Serbia.

On 9 March 1998, the 'Contact Group' – USA, Britain, France, Russia, Germany and Italy – introduced a limited set of sanctions, which were largely ignored by the Serbs. On 16 June 1998, after NATO jets had flown along the Kosovo-Serbia border, the Contact Group 'issued a 'strong final warning', which was also ignored. The 'ethnic cleansing' continued and many mass graves and stories of atrocities were reported in the West. On 24 March 1999, NATO started its air-strike campaign with cruise missiles and high altitude bombing.

The causes of war: psychological theories

Are people by their very nature warlike? The modern nation-states of Denmark and Sweden appear not to regard war as an option in their foreign policy, although made up of the descendents of warlike cultures. However, some strong emotions, such as nationalism, and the hostility that such feelings generate against 'others' are commonly believed to be a possible cause of war. However, defining 'the enemy' is never a simple matter. During The Gulf War, was 'the enemy' Iraq, Sadam Hussein or the Ba'ath Party? During World War II was Stalin a friend or a foe? The Cold War began before the end of hostilities, when it was clear that Eastern Europe, liberated by the Red Army, was going to be annexed by the USSR. Psychologically, we also have the problem of how to deal with all the 'goodies' on the side of the 'baddies'.

Sigmund Freud published two short pieces on war, 'Thoughts for the times on war and death' (1915) and an open letter to Albert Einstein, 'Why war?' (1932). Freud argued that war broke the illusion of morality that we had in modern society. War is a key factor in bringing about regression. For Freud, war demonstrates the universal instinctual aggressive drive of mankind. This approach was later taken up by Edward Glover in *War, Sadism and Pacifism* (1947) and Roger E. Money-Kyrle in the series of in-depth interviews with Nazis after World War II, published in his *Psychoanalysis and Politics* (1951). An interesting Freudian theory was developed by Arnaldo Rascovsky in a paper he gave to the UN Institute in 1970, entitled 'Towards the understanding of the unconscious motivations of war', in which he outlined the notion of *'filicide'*. The concept of filicide is a reversal of the Oedipus complex in which the son desires to kill his father and have sex with his mother. In *filicide*, the father unconsciously hatres his son and displaces his feelings of jealousy of others onto his son. This wish-fulfilment is achieved by the older generation sending the younger generation off to war. The problem with this approach is that terms like 'instinctual aggression' are a little vague. However, why are we aggressive towards Sadam Hussein, but not to a range of other world leaders that we have disagreements with?

Despite the psychological accounts, war is fought for a purpose. Wars are not an eruption of unreasoning passion.

Feminist peace research

During the Gulf War, women were presented by the media in very traditional roles, such as 'keeping the home fires burning' or waiting at military bases for their men to return from the war. As Gunder-Frank (1991) pointed out, Western television notably featured only two women in this distinctly male environment, an American soldier made prisoner by the Iraqis and the BBC correspondent Kate Adie.

According to Colleen Roach (1991), there are two sorts of feminist researchers that are of significance for war, peace and culture. The first are feminist peace researchers involved in the investigation of war and peace, such as Elise Boulding (Boulding, 1998), Betty Reardon (Reardon, 1995), Riane Eisler (Eisler, 1987) and Birgit Brock-Utne (Brock-Utne, 1985). Elise Boulding and Betty Reardon, for example, are developing a political economy of coercion and the consequences of militarism in the Third World. However, these feminist writers also see the need for a new and distinct moral development for women that makes them more prone to peace than men.

The second sort are the feminist researchers who have investigated the use of language (Thorne, Kramarae, and Henley, 1983), an approach which has provided a foundation for feminist critiques of the prevailing male discourse of the military. Roach cited the following statement made by Colin Powell, Chairman of the US Joint Chiefs of Staff, shortly before the launching of the ground phase of the Gulf War: 'First we're going to cut it off and then we're going to kill it.'

In this statement, 'it' refers to the Iraqi army, and feminist researchers have interpreted this as an attempt to view 'the enemy' not only as an 'other' but also a non-human 'other'. The following military euphemisms were used to prevent the public from thinking in terms of the loss of human life and the killing of other human beings:

- Collateral damage
- Saturation strikes
- Carpet bombing
- Flying sorties
- Engaging the Iraqi army
- Taking out Iraqi assets
- Softening up the Republican Guard

There is no word in this military idiom for 'peace'. As Carol Cohn argues, 'at the same time as the language gave me access to things I had been unable to speak about before, it radically excluded others. ... This language does not allow certain questions to be asked or certain values to be expressed. To pick a bald example: the word "peace" is not part of this discourse' (Cohn, 1987: 708).

In addition to language, feminist peace researchers have also at the centre of their analysis of militarism a critique of Western scientific rationality and technology. This critique can be found in the work of feminist scientists and science philosophers such as Sandra Harding and Evelyn Fox-Keller (Harding, 1986; Fox-Keller, 1985).

Freud put forward the idea that there is an instinctive aggressive drive within men. The same biological determinists are found at the roots of war and other forms of collective violence such as terrorism. Both men and animals share the same aggressive biological mechanisms. In contrast, feminist researchers argue that war is above all a cultural experience. Carol Greenhouse asks, 'Is human aggression innate? Are the causes of war in nature or in culture?... The orientation of the literature strongly suggests that war is a cultural phenomenon, that is, that its roots are in the human mind, and not in the genes' (1987:32). Robert Holt, a peace researcher and psychologist, agrees: 'The overwhelming consensus of behavioral scientists rejects the notion that something in human nature makes war inevitable' (1987: 9). His most important argument is that war is built upon a 'cultural complex' made up of 'value systems, ideology and mythology', all of which are disseminated by the media, mass culture, and formal education.

Moreover, the more militarised a culture becomes, the more probable it is that the degree of violence against women will also be higher (Eisler, 1987: 9–10). According to Roach, 'Women are not just victims of physical violence but are also much more oppressed than any other social group by the structural violence exacerbated in highly militarized societies' (1991: p. 28).

Donald M. Snow and Dennis M. Drew (1994) have examined the reasons why the USA enters wars: 'Rather than seeing peace as an interlude between wars (an attitude held by many Europeans whose history reflects such a view), we tend to look at war as a transgression of our normal circumstance.... The record, of course, does not fully support such a view' (1994: 327). They point out that the USA had been involved in six major wars in its history, three minor wars and a significant number of minor deployments. Some US wars have had strong support from the US people while others have not. Why? Snow and Drew argue that if the reason for involvement is seen as *absolute* and *moral* in nature, the war will be popular. They give the following examples:

○ The War of American Independence was seen as a 'just' resistance to British tyranny.
○ In the American Civil War, the Confederate side had popular support in the South, unlike the Federal side, which Snow and Drew claim did not have popular support, as many people in the North did not mind that some Southern States had seceded from the Union; this was certainly not seen as an issue worth fighting about
○ US involvement in World War I was seen to be making the world safe for democracy
○ World War II was also seen as necessary to destroy the evil of Hitler's fascism
○ In contrast, the wars in Korea and Vietnam had limited popularity because the issue of containing communism did not have the same moral edge to it

Popular wars must have clear political objectives, claim Snow and Drew, who out-line four criteria:

○ The objective must be clear and reducible to a catchphrase or slogan
○ The war should appeal to the moral sense
○ Losing the war would 'endanger the integrity of American soil' (Snow and Drew, 1994: 332)
○ The majority should see the objective as important

This would explain why 'limited' wars (for instance, for some geopolitical advantage) are much less popular than 'total' wars that are seen to exorcise some evil from the world.

What is 'limited' war?

According to Lawrence Freedman, we can identify a 'limited war' by the follow-ing three distinct criteria :

- ○ '*Limited*' wars are limited in their geographical scope – they are not global in nature
- ○ The ends and objectives are clearly defined
- ○ The means are limited and there is a restricted use of military capability

In other words, claims Freedman, a limited war must stay within political and military boundaries. Limited war is not based upon the notion of massive retaliation. The objectives of any limited war do not include the complete subordination of one state to another. Such wars would include the Korean War, the Vietnam War and the Gulf War. In both Vietnam and Korea, the USA and its allies were limited by their fear of provoking a great power to enter the war, notably China and the Soviet Union. In the Gulf War, the objectives were the expulsion of Iraqi forces from Kuwait. The war aims never officially included the overthrow of Saddam Hussein and the imposition of a political leadership on Iraq that was more to the taste of the West. The UN laid down the limited objective and it provided a clear criterion for success. Moreover, it was the UN that imposed limits on the means to fight the war. Attempts were made to avoid killing civilians, but this was not always successful. President Bush made the position clear: 'Our objectives are clear. Saddam Hussein's forces will leave Kuwait, the legitimate government of Kuwait will be restored to its rightful place, and Kuwait will once again be free' ('Address to Congress', 11 September 1991).

Some commentators, such as Stephen R. Graubard in *'Mr Bush's War: Adventures in the Politics of Illusion* (1992) and Jean Edward Smith in *George Bush's War* (1992), argue that the Gulf War was fought to provide a gloss over the personal and political shortcomings of Bush as president. However, as Freedman point outs, the Gulf War was not a *limited* war from Saddam Hussein's perspective.

In addition, according to Freedman, the other key objective of the Gulf War was the establishment of the 'new world order', which, contrary to the view of Jean Baudrillard (below) was not – in Freeman's eyes at least – an attempt to impose US/Western values on the Islamic world. For Freeman, the 'new world order' is 'a belief that traditional rights of states could now be protected if the world's great powers could both show respect themselves and demand it from others.' (Freedman, 1993: 212).

What was the Gulf War?

In his paper 'The conflict in comparative perspective', Oliver Ramsbotham provides us with the following list of possible interpretations of the Gulf War:

The conflict was
A traditional regional power struggle
A readjustment of power relations after the collapse of a superpower
A war fought for principle

A resource war
A one-sided massacre
A heroic victory
A setback for militarism
A reprieve for militarism
A war engineered by Mossad and the CIA
An inadvertent war
A war fought to lay the Vietnam Syndrome
A war fought to eliminate the 'wimp factor'
A war to prevent aggression
An attempt by the West to destroy the strongest Arab state
A Western pre-emptive strike against a resurgent Islam
A bid for geopolitical hegemony
A critical defence of the New World Order
A betrayal of the promise of a New World Order
A demonstration of the influence of the United Nations
A demonstration of the impotence of the United Nations
The harbinger of North/South conflict
A war to end war
An irrelevant anachronism
A just war
An unjust war
And so on. (Ramsbotham, 1991: 295–6)

Bush presented the Gulf War as a conflict between 'good' and 'evil'. The view that Iraq under Saddam Hussein was one of the worst violators of human rights was accepted without question. Television, radio and newspapers 'certified Saddam Hussein as the new Hitler and made him the personification of evil' (Aruri, 1991: 322). But, as Naseer Aruri points out, very few Arab countries have constitutions, and few have regard for civil and political liberties or social justice: 'Most Arab regimes fall short of the minimum international requirements for human rights.' (Aruri, 1991: 310).

Bush accused the Iraqi government and Saddam Hussein of violations of human rights and international law after the invasion of Kuwait. On the basis of a press release from Amnesty International (2 October 1990), Bush cited civil rights abuses by Iraq including arbitrary arrest, extrajudicial executions, beatings, torture and summary sentences to death. It was the defence of human rights that the USA cited as the main reason for the confrontation with Saddam Hussein. Middle East Watch, Amnesty International and the Arab Organisation for Human Rights all confirmed that violations of human rights are common in the Arab world – and in Iraq in particular. The right of assembly, freedom of speech, women's rights and workers' rights are all limited. In addition, there are violent limitations on political activity including brutal treatment of political dissidents, detention without charge, torture and executions. The government of Iraq also expelled undesirable nationals and the repressed ethnic minorities, most notably the Kurdish population in Iraq from March to September 1988. However, as Aruri explains, intelligence reports of the use of gas against the Kurds by the Iraqi forces in September 1988 are ambiguous. Moreover, during the Iran-Iraq War, both sides had made use of chemical weapons to attack the city of Halabja. A report by the US Army War College in Pennsylvania found that the Kurds had been killed by cyanide gas, which only the Iranians possessed.

In Iraq, any criticism of the head of state or the political system is a crime. Since 1986, insulting the president, the Revolutionary Council, the Ba'ath Party, the National Assembly or the government, has carried a life sentence together with confiscation of property. In addition, if the insult is believed to have the intention to bring about incitement, the punishment is execution.

A critical response to the Gulf War appears in Phyllis Bennis's paper 'False consensus: George Bush's United Nations'. Bennis argues that the UN was one of the victims of the Gulf War: 'UN independence, UN integrity and UN peace-keeping identity all were undermined by Bush administration coercion' (Bennis, 1991: 112). Bennis also asks why was there a Gulf War? She argues that the urgency of the response from the Bush administration took people by surprise. Iraq had benefited from the USA's backing during the eight-year war with Iran. Moreover, Bennis claims that the US Ambassador to Iraq had told Saddam Hussein five days before the invasion of Kuwait that the USA did not have a defence treaty with Kuwait and had no regard for any inter-Arab border squabbles. Bennis argues that since 1990 the USA has felt that it had to create a new unipolar framework to support its continued need to dominate international relations.

Noam Chomsky takes up a similar theme in his paper 'After the Cold War: US Middle East policy' (1992). He argues that the 'new world order' replaced the old world order when the USSR collapsed in 1989. In the old world order, what the US Government wanted was a 'grand area' in which it was dominant politically, eco-nomically and militarily. The threat to the world system was said to come directly from the USSR. However, since its collapse, the following changes have come about:

- New pretexts are needed for intervention in the Third World
- New prospects emerge for the 'Latin-Americanisation' of much of the former USSR
- The USA is now much freer to use force because the Soviet deterrent has dis-appeared

The USA and the new world order

Zbigniew Brzezinski, the former US National Security Adviser, made a balance sheet of the 'principal benefits and debits of the U.S.- led triumph':

The benefits are undeniably impressive. First, a blatant act of aggression was rebuffed and punished. An important political and even legal point, central to international decency, was reaffirmed. ...Second, U.S. military power is henceforth likely to be taken more seriously ... [and] is bound to have a chilling effect even as far away as North Korea.... Third, the Middle East and the Gulf region are now clearly an American sphere of preponderance. Pro-American Arab regimes feel more secure; so does Israel. U.S. access to oil is now not in jeopardy. Fourth, the Soviet Union ... has been reduced largely to the status of a spectator. (*International Herald-Tribune*, 22 April 1991)

However, Brzezinski also found a number of negative repercussions. Iraq's defeat changes the balance of power in the region. The Iraqi defeat was of great bene-fit to Iran, and, as a result, the ethnic, religious and tribal hostilities may be inten-sified and create a process of 'Lebanonization'. Furthermore the relationship between the USA and the rest of the Arab world may be changed significantly. There is also the moral question of the *proportionality of the response* to Iraq's aggression. Was the response of the Western allies too powerful to be considered a 'just war?'

André Gunder-Frank: the Gulf War and the new world order

According to André Gunder-Frank, the Gulf War may be termed a 'Third-World war' in the sense that it was a world war fought by the rich North against the poor South. The Gulf War aligned the rich North, the oil-rich emirates or king-doms, and some bribed regional oligarchies against Iraq, a poor Third-World country. In a series of essays, Gunder-Frank has examined the Gulf War and the new world order in this global context. Now the military victory over Iraq has become the cornerstone of the USA 'New World order.' Gunder-Frank surveys the social, political, economic motives of the USA, its actions and the consequences of what he sees as the violation of international law.

Gunder-Frank admits that the invasion and occupation of Kuwait by Iraq was wrong. However, he says that the claim by Bush and other Western leaders that the Gulf War was to protect the 'principle' of world order, international law and the charter of the UN from lawless might-is-right violation was 'a lie'. As he rightly points out, the following similar aggressions and violations of both the UN charter and UN resolutions had taken place without any such US/Western response:

○ Apartheid in South Africa
○ The USSR's invasion of Afghanistan
○ Israel's invasion and occupation of the Golan Heights, the West Bank, and the Gaza Strip, as well as Southern Lebanon
○ Syria's invasion of and exercises of military control over part of northern Lebanon
○ Turkey's invasion of Cyprus in 1974 and continuing occupation of the north of the island
○ Morocco's occupation of the Western Sahara
○ The USA's war on Nicaragua for a decade through the 'Contras', and its inva-sions of Grenada and Panama

Bush's 'just cause' for his invasion of Panama with 27,000 troops to catch one drug trafficker was 'a cynical lie', argues Gunder-Frank. In fact, the US Justice Department was unable to unearth a shred of documentary evidence to use in court against General Noriega. In addition, no Security Council resolutions were approved, or even proposed, to protect Bush's new world order from his own assault on the authority of Panama. Gunder-Frank argues that it was the danger of economic recession and military budget cuts that really inspired Bush invade Panama.

Why the Gulf War?

According to Gunder-Frank, the most obvious economic cause of the Gulf War was oil. On the one hand, Saddam Hussein invaded Kuwait for economic reasons and to lend political support to his regime in the face of increasing debts from the Iraq-Iran War and declining oil earnings with which to repay these debts. On the other hand under Bush, the USA also had severe economic problems, and it was to counter domestic recession, or at least the political consequences of recession at home, that both Saddam Hussein and Bush started the Gulf War.

Before the war, it was a common view in the USA that its economic and geo-political influence worldwide was diminishing. As Gunder-Frank aptly put it, 'the cold war is over – and Japan and Germany have won!' In other words, the Gulf crisis presented Bush with a golden opportunity to use military strength to compensate for economic weakness in the face of declining US ability to compete against its main economic rivals, Japan and Germany.

Gulf War: new departures in international political and economic relations

For Gunder-Frank (1991: 341), the Gulf War marked three important new departures in international political economic relations:

1. The powerful US response in the Gulf obviously resulted from a political-economic issue. The issue was oil without any Cold War or other ideological overtones. The conflict about oil and the massive American response were barely masked by appeals to the 'defence' of small states in international 'law'.
2. This mobilisation was entirely against (a part of) the South, without any pretence of an East–West ideological cover.
3. The third major departure in the Gulf was the near unanimity in the alliance of the North against the South.

The Iraqi invasion of Kuwait was not unexpected. The British arbitrarily fixed the border between Iraq and Kuwait in Mesopotamia before they had to relinquish their colonial empire. This border has always been disputed. Gunder-Frank's argument is that the British deliberately drew the border so as to deny

Iraq both oil fields and access to the sea. The colonial powers divided the Middle East into six large, populous but poor countries and six artificially created smaller states with oil reserves, ruled mostly by emirs: 'These have scarcely shared their oil-derived riches with their poor Arab "brothers" and have preferred to use them to flaunt their luxury at home and invest their surplus funds abroad in the West' (Gunder-Frank, 1991: 343).

Iraq has never fully accepted this neocolonial settlement of its borders. In particular, Iraq laid claim to two small islands off its coast that would expand its access to the sea to export its oil. Moreover, Iraq accused Kuwait of surreptitiously syphoning off increasingly more than its fair share of oil from the Rumaila oilfield, a common field crossing the border between Iraq and Kuwait, while Iraq was occupied by its war with Iran. In addition, Iraq claimed that the overproduction of oil by Kuwait and Saudi Arabia was deliberately planned to drive the price of oil down and economically weaken Iraq.

Saddam Hussein and other Iraqis regularly protested about this economic hostility against them and requested equitable treatment by their Arab neighbours. Saddam Hussein convened an Arab summit in Baghdad in May 1990 to protest against the 'economic warfare', against Iraq. Moreover, in his Revolution Day speech, he called the oil pricing policy by Kuwait and the other emirates 'a poisoned dagger' thrust into the back of Iraq.

Political costs of the Gulf War: violation of democracy at home

The Gulf War was depicted on television and in newspapers as a war fought against a merciless tyrant by the great democracies of the West. However, Gunder-Frank claims that the USA disregarded or destroyed the most important democratic foundations and institutions in the West, including the US Congress and other parliaments. Moreover, the political will of the vast majority of the people in the West was disregarded. Freedom of the press was subverted, as the media intentionally deceived the public. Moreover, it encouraged both racism and chauvinism, to aid the war. As Gunder-Frank observes, 'European civil society rapidly became shot through with rabid racism and chauvinism directed against any and all Arabs' (1991: 345).

Fairness and Accuracy in Reporting (FAIR) summarised the following 'eight (self-) censored stories national media ignored' in the USA:

- Secret U.S. arms shipments to Iraq during the Reagan administration
- The diplomatic scandal of Ambassador Glaspie's signal that the U.S. would not oppose Iraqi invasion
- The Kuwait connection of its financial clout in the U.S. and the conflict of interest of National Security Advisor Brent Scowcroft

- Racism and bigotry in the U.S. military
- Slave labor in the Gulf
- The true cost of the war including interest and veterans' benefits could be more than 10 times the official estimate
- The army that wasn't there poised to invade Saudi Arabia
- Bush's family ties in the Gulf.
  (quoted and paraphrased from Extra, [publication of Fairness and Accuracy in Reporting] May 1991: 16)

The first and most major institutional sacrifice and cost to peace was the perversion of the UN. The Secretary-General of the UN, Javier Pérez de Cuéllar, declared outright that 'this is a US war, not a UN war' and that 'the Security Council is controlled by the United States, Britain and France'. The Security Council disregarded the UN charter on various occasions; instead of maintaining its responsibility to keep the peace, the Security Council acted to 'legitimate' war. Other 'institutional casualties' were the American Congress and European parliaments. Most notably, the constitutional mandate of Congress to declare war was subverted by Bush for his own purposes.

Gunder-Frank concludes that the USA rushed into the Gulf War in a useless attempt to shore up its fading power in the world by the use of military power. However, without a satisfactory economic base, military power is insufficient to keep a superpower afloat. On the contrary, the foolish use of its military power may instead sink that power.

Wallerstein on the Gulf War

Immanuel Wallerstein (1991) outlines the following four reasons that may have influenced Saddam Hussein's decision to start a Gulf conflict:

1   The world debt crisis was imminent; seizing Kuwaiti assets offered some debt relief.
2   Israel had recently brought the peace process to an end, and the Palestinian *interfarda* had begun. Saddam Hussein may have seen the invasion of Kuwait as an opportunity to enhance the Palestinian bargaining power.
3   The end of the Cold War and the events in the former USSR might have made Saddam Hussein believe that he could affect the new world order, particularly given the Bush administration statement that the USA had no interest in inter-Arab border disputes.
4   The failure of domestic efforts to bring about social change meant that more drastic and external resources were needed to bring about change. An occupied Kuwait could be seen as a bargaining chip.

Baudrillard: the Gulf War did not take place

Jean Baudrillard provides one of the most interesting interpretations of the Gulf War. His account is a very serious one. The Gulf War was fought by the West to subordinate Islam to the new world order, which is to be both consensual and televisual. It was for this reason that the allied air forces carefully avoided bombing the Iraqi television transmitters. There was a Gulf War, but it was not a war in any traditional sense of a dirty, bloody war. Moreover, the Western powers were so able to outgun Saddam Hussein's forces that the events were more like a massacre. Baudrillard attempts to probe the nature of the Gulf War as a media event. For him, the Gulf War was not a 'real' war but a media event, a simulacrum of a war. Moreover, the issues surrounding the presentation of the Gulf War are important for all aspects of postmodern public life. What took place in the desert was out of sight of the television cameras. What the media presented was a fictional account of what happened on the ground, an idealised, clean and sanitised, or Hollywood, version of the events.

> Since this war was won in advance, we will never know what it would have been like had it existed … any more than the direct transmission by CNN of real time information is sufficient to authenticate a war. One is reminded of *Capricorn One* in which the flight of a manned rocket to Mars, which only took place in a desert studio, was relayed live to all the television stations in the world. (Baudrillard, 1993: 61)

Baudrillard builds upon some of his earlier ideas, notably the idea that no event is free from interpretation. According to Baudrillard (1993), the mass media is opposed to mediation, and is concerned with one-way communication; there is no exchange. This simple emission/reception of information can be viewed as the enforced silence of the masses. This apparent 'stupor' of the masses is said by Baudrillard to make them radically uncertain of their own desires. Media images are no longer distinguished from 'reality' or 'human nature', but this is not because of some simple manipulation in a Marxist sense, but because the masses have an almost infinite abundance of entertainment and other forms of useless information. They have a greater and greater desire for spectacle, and it is because of this demand that films become more and more expensive to produce, have better and better special effects, and have ever more intense promotion and hype; the merchandising covers all possible commodities. We have a televisually created politics of disillusion and disaffection. The end result is a series of implosions: conflict between labour and capital; between politics and entertainment; and between high culture and low culture. All such divisions collapse in on themselves to form a political void. The end result of this is often the 'sudden crystallisation of latent violence' (Baudrillard, 1993: 76), which appears as irrational episodes. Spectators turn themselves into actors; they invent their own spectacle for the gaze of the media. Baudrillard discusses examples such as the rioting at Heysel Stadium and the Real Madrid-Naples European Cup Final, and the violence in Thatcher's conflict with the miners.

For Baudrillard, in the Gulf War, we moved from the 'will to power' and the 'will to knowledge' to the 'will to spectacle': 'Just as everything psychical becomes the object of interminable speculation, so everything which is turned into information becomes the object of endless speculation, the site of total uncertainty'. (1993: 41). In other words, CNN provided all the pictures from the front line, but these pictures were edited into a form that the Pentagon not only approved of but also had designed in advance. The footage was presented in news programmes and in newspapers. Experts discussed the footage and other experts challenged their interpretation. However, the events were editorialised to such a degree that the pictures were depicting something that did not exist. So we have discussion on top of discussion, of events which did not take place: endless simulation, 'while the implosion of the apparatus of information along with the accompanying (Baudrillard, 1993: 42).

Christopher Norris (1992) has argued that Baudrillard's views are a reflection of the intellectual cowardice of postmodernists. Baudrillard and others simply refuse to stand up against the threat of the military power of the USA. Norris argues that Baudrillard merely attempts to 'deconstruct' the war as a simulated event and ignores the fact that the aerial bombardment of Iraq killed many thousands of people. His postmodernism does not allow him to take a moral stance against such horrific actions.

I do not think this is a fair or accurate reading of Baudrillard's position on the Gulf war. A key element of Baudrillard's argument is that untold numbers of Iraqi people were killed by aerial bombardment, but that this story was hidden by a smokescreen of images and propaganda that made the Gulf War look like a Hollywood blockbuster rather than what is was: a massacre.

It is important to note that in 'Baudrillard and the war that never happened', Norris does not condemn all postmodernist thinking or theorising. He clearly has a lot of respect for the work of Derrida. His critique is directed at Baudrillard alone: 'His absurdities shouldn't be treated as a standing indictment of the whole enterprise' (Norris, 1992: 16). Moreover, most of Norris's attack is of a personal nature and is not directed at Baudrillard's arguments. As Norris explains, 'It can scarcely be denied that Baudrillard's theses have a certain diagnostic value.' (Norris, 1992: 26). However, Baudrillard is described as having: 'a flair for publicity or the knack of avoiding peer-review.' (Norris, 1992: 22). In addition, at crucial points, Norris does not develop his own arguments. For example, he explains that one can accept Baudrillard's argument about the Gulf War: only 'if one accepts the postmodernist textualist premise: that reality *just* is whatever we make of it according to this or that predominant language game, discourse, or mode of signifying practice. Once reject that premise – as most people would unless drilled into accepting it by prolonged exposure to the fads and fashions of cultural theory – and the whole line of argument simply collapses' (Norris, 1992: 16). There are two problems with this; firstly, Norris does not explain why we should reject 'that premise'. Secondly, rather than presenting coherent arguments, Norris relies upon 'populism' – everybody would reject that premise, wouldn't they? – a tactic which Norris roundly condemns in Baudrillard's work.

The Persian Gulf distraction

Will Kaufman (1998) has looked at the presentation of the Gulf War in the work of the late US comedian Bill Hicks. What is most surprising is the similarity between the positions of Baudrillard and Hicks.

Many US stand-up comedians were seen as part of the cultural elite that were undermining the moral certainties of the Reagan years. Hicks, in particular, was demonised by the New Right's 'prohibitive spirit'. According to Kaufman (1998), Noam Chomsky was an intellectual mentor to Hicks, who once described himself as a 'Chomsky with dick jokes'. Hicks regarded humour as a form of intellectual self-defence against manipulation and control. Comedy is 'the last bastion of free speech' in the USA, claimed Hicks, and censorship one of the prime indicators of an anti-intellectual climate. The Gulf War had been presented through a pro-paganda model that contained a significant anti-intellectual element. As Hicks remarked at the July 1991 Montreal Comedy Festival, 'First of all, this needs to be said: there never was a war. ... A war is when *two* armies are fighting' (quoted in Kaufman, 1998: 67). The media generated a 'popular consensus' that was very much a top-down construction with demonisation of any available enemy:

- Quaddafi of Libya becomes a 'mad dog'
- Noriega of Panama becomes a drug-pusher
- Iraqi conscripts become savages carrying out the rape of Kuwait
- Saddam becomes the new Hitler

A central element of this popular consensus was the common perception that the Gulf War was a 'clean, precise and humanitarian operation'. Kaufman's argument is that Hicks went so far as to suggest that the media directed Bush into a number of shameful military actions against weaker powers: Grenada, Libya, Nicaragua and Panama.

Deleuze and Guattari: the war machine

One of the most challenging postmodern accounts of war is found in the work of Gilles Deleuze and Felix Guattari. For Deleuze and Guattari, the war machine is exterior to the state and is one of the key factors preventing the process of state formation from taking place. However, before we can fully comprehend what Deleuze and Guattari have to say about war and war machine, we need to be clear on how they theorise.

For Deleuze and Guattari, modernist thought takes the form of a hierarchy in which some ways of thinking are seen to be superior to others as in the notion of the 'tree of knowledge'. In contrast, they draw upon the Nietzschean concept of 'the will to power'; people whose ways of thinking are accepted as superior are simply making use of their ability to dominate others. Deleuze and Guattari criticise those discourses and institutions that repress desire and propagate fascist subjectivities. The discourses and institutions of modernity impose a definition of normality from the perspective of the powerful. In contrast, Deleuze and Guattari suggest that ways of thinking should take the form of a rhizome. These are ways of thinking that are not horizontal but spread like a strawberry plant, sending out both roots and shoots upon runners. In addition, Deleuze and Guattari attempt to decode libidinal flows brought about by the institutions within capitalism. They do this by attempting a 'schizoanalytic' destruction of the ego and the superego, and putting forward the notion of a dynamic unconscious. They refer to this as a process of becoming. This 'becoming' leads to the emergence of new types of decentred subjects, the 'schizo' and the 'nomad', who are free from fixed and unified identities, modernist/Freudian subjectivities and their bodies.

For Deleuze and Guattari, the war machine is an assemblage created by 'nomads', who are people that have come off the line of organisation, the state's preferred way that individuals should lead their lives. Nomadic people use the war machine to deterritorialise, or dissolve forms of organisation, that prevent us from fulfilling our desires by becoming whatever we wish. It is important to note that the purpose of the war machine becomes war only when it is appropriated by the state. The state has a need to draw upon its available resources to impose a form of organisation upon nomads; that is, to impose a form of territorialisation upon them. From the point of view of the state, the danger that can be unleashed by the war machine needs to be controlled by discipline. It is for this reason that discipline has such a high priority within the military.

What is postmodern war?

The term 'postmodern war' has been used by Chris Hables Gray (1997), Hables who argues that 'Postmodern war depends on international tension and the resulting arms race keeps weapons development at a maximum and actual military combat between major powers at a minimum' (Gray, 1997: 23). But why does Hables Gray use the term 'postmodern war'? Firstly, he argues that the logic and culture of war have changed significantly; notably, the political-ideological management of world and domestic relations has a much higher priority than in previous years. Secondly, the changes have a great deal in common with developments in other cultural areas.

The changing nature of war can be seen in the so-called drug wars. A significant turning point came with the US invasion of Panama to conduct a military 'arrest' of General Noriega. The division between the military and law enforcement has been broken. Moreover, the discourse of war has changed; the main moral justification for war is now peace. In addition, the 'emotional seduction of postmodern war is being disguised as rationality, especially to its most fervent admirers' (Hables Gray, 1997: 249). Postmodern war generates emotional needs and meets them. The postmodern war becomes a solution to every problem, including the problem of war itself.

Hables Gray: the characteristics of postmodern war

- The main moral justification for war is now peace.
- The main practical justification for repression is the fight for freedom.
- Security comes from putting the very future of the planet in grave risk.
- People are too fragile for the new levels of lethality; machines are too stupid for the complexity of battle. War is becoming cyborgian.
- There is a continual tension between bodies and machines; the human soldiers are much more valuable politically.
- The machines set the pace of battle, but the humans experience it.
- Advanced weapon systems are neither machines nor humans, but both: cyborgs.
- The battlefield is really a battle space. It is now three-dimensional and ranges beyond the atmosphere. It is on thousands of electronic wavelengths. It is on the 'home front' as the battle front.
- The battle space is also very constrained, politically acceptable targets.
- Battle now is beyond human scale – it is as fast as laser beams, extends for many thousands of miles and for 24 hours per day.
- Politics is militarized and needs representation.
- Genocide is technologically possible but morally not possible for most people.
- Industrialised countries want colonialism without responsibility and empire without causalities.
- Some people in the nonindustrial regions want Western technology without Western culture; others want neither.
- Soldiers are no longer uniform – the concept of male warriors is collapsing.
- Civilians and nature are more threatened in battle.
- New styles of war are invented.
- Information war makes the most advanced practitioners the most vulnerable.
- War proliferates into the general culture.
  (Hables Gray, 1997: 196–70)

Anthony Giddens on war

As we have seen, wars are serious in the modern world, not only because people are killed, but because the industrial base of a nation – including its workforce – is regarded as a legitimate target. Giddens has no general theory of the causes of war. However, wars are caused by the activities of human agents, which can have both foreseeable and unforeseen consequences. Wars are not caused by factors outside the control of the human agent, such as patriarchy, militarism or imperialism.

As we saw in Area 4, Giddens holds that all nation-states have a tendency to polyarchy, and, as such, the military becomes assimilated within polyarchic systems of domination. Moreover, within reflexive or high modernity, military service becomes entwined with citizenship rights. Not only does the military do as the civil authority tells it, but it needs to have at least the support, if not the mobilisation, of the masses. We find that within polyarchy, the leaders' control of resources, both authoratative and allocative, can give rise to action that is transformative of both the external world and social relations in the most violent fashion. In contrast to Deleuze and Guattari, Giddens argues that the military and war-related activities have played a key role in the processes of state for-mation. As Giddens explains, 'A combination of war and diplomacy shaped the emergence of the European state system, with some states surviving and expanding and most being absorbed or dissolved' (1985: 233).

In Giddens's view, modern warfare has changed from 'limited' to 'total war', from 'the traditional alternative of skirmish and battle' to the creation of fronts. Moreover, modern warfare involves the reallocation of time and space on the basis of leaders' strategic analyses; the plotting of military movements through time and space in order to achieve recognised and agreed goals:

> The territoriality of nation states reflects a genuine internal administrative unity and it is hardly surprising that boundary disputes, or incursions of one state across territory claimed by another, are serious matters. Unlike in the case of traditional states, a threat to a segment of the territory of a modern state is a potential challenge to its administra-tive and cultural integrity, no matter how barren or 'useless' that segment of territory may be. (Giddens, 1985: 291)

Why is Giddens's theory of the causes of war to be found in 'human agency'? Through the processes of structuration, individuals create the structures in which they live. For Giddens, forces such as 'militarism' (glory in war preparation) are human creations, and have a life of their own independent of our discursive con-sciousness and practical consciousness. In this respect, Giddens differs from traditional social theories of war, such as that of Quincy Wright. Wright has analysed several historical states of war: animal, primitive, historic/civilised, and modern. War becomes probable whenever there is á change in the balance between the following four factors:

- Technology
- Social structure
- Law
- Network of opinions and attitudes

In Wright's theory human agency is of minimal significance.

One of the central problems with general theories, such as that of Wright, is that the character of war has changed significantly between modern and traditional societies, most notably with the development of nuclear weapons. As Giddens explains, 'The fighting of wars often had a ritual and "prepared" character, not just because traditions infused wars like other segments of social life, but because armies needed – and were often allowed – time to assemble on a pre-arranged terrain' (1985: 224).

Giddens's understanding of the nature of warfare has to be placed within his understanding of modernity, and most especially his discussion of the 'internal pacification' of states by surveillance. For Giddens, there has been an industrialisation of warfare in the modern world, which as suggested above, has brought about a change from 'limited' to 'total war'. Giddens identifies the following six factors that have helped to bring about the industrialisation of warfare:

- Weapons technology, in the application of industrial techniques of production to weaponry
- New modes of transportation and communication
- Professionalising the military and abandoning the use of mercenaries
- The reorganisation of the officer corps
- The discarding of spectacular aspects of warfare, notably brightly coloured uniforms
- Integration of military campaigns on land, sea and air

However, it would be wrong to suggest that Giddens looks to industrial capitalism as the ultimate cause of war. As he explains, 'Industrial capitalism provided the means for the industrialisation of war, but the activities and involvements of nation-states are at the origin of the phenomenon' (1985: 226).

In a later publication, Giddens reinforced his view that industrialised warfare is not by its nature essentially capitalistic:

No doubt capitalism, both as a real institutional force and as an ideology, has on occasion provided the motive power for war. Yet – as the advent of the Soviet Union and other socialists states made clear – the propensity to wage war is not simply an outcome of capitalist organisation. The accumulation of weaponry has its own internal logic.... Armies become self-serving bureaucratic organisations, interested in expansion of their resources, while technological transformations constantly increase the destructive potential of weaponry. (Giddens, 1992: 57)

Two key phrases stand out in this passage: 'own internal logic' and 'self-serving bureaucratic organisations'. What Giddens is suggesting here is that the military has become an agency involved in an ecological competition for resources; and the force, or internal logic, behind this competition is beyond the manipulation of human agency. What staff have to do within the organisation is to 'ride the juggernaut' of the self-serving bureaucratic organisation, and find a place within its own internal logic. This is very much against the letter and the spirit of Giddens's theory of 'structuration', in which human agency creates structures.

With the end of the Cold War and the emergence of the new world order, the world has become a more fragmented and dangerous place. There are new and less predictable threats to our security, new forms of risk. Although many people expected to see a peace dividend when the Soviet Union ceased to be a threat to Western security, the armed forces have had to expand their role: peace-keeping, providing humanitarian relief and even law enforcement – in the case of the US invasion of Panama.

Area Summary

In this area we have contrasted the notion of 'modern' war with 'post-modern' war. We have argued that the sociological research on the nature of warfare has suggested that the nature of war did change over the course of the twentieth century, most notably since the creation of the new world order. This change was most pronounced with the Gulf conflict. This was a change not simply in terms of the technology used, but also in terms of the war aims and the targets of the war.

We started by looking at the contribution of Clausewitz on war and went on to look at the nature and the possible causes of war in the works of Chomsky, Giddens, Wallerstein, Deleuze, Guattari, Baudrillard, Gunder-Frank. The area raised a number of questions. Are economic factors the most important in our understanding of the nature and causes of war? What is the nature of 'limited' war in the post-Vietnam era? Of what significance are psychological factors? Of what significance is the media? Did the Gulf War take place?

References

Ahmad, E. (1996) 'Portent of a New Century' in P. Bennis and M. Moushabeck (eds) *Beyond the Storm*. New York: Olive Branch Press.

Aruri, N. (1991) 'Human rights and the Gulf crisis: the verbal strategy of George Bush', in P. Bennis and M. Moushabeck (eds), *Beyond the Storm*. New York: Olive Branch Press.

Baudrillard, J. (1995) *The Gulf War Did Not Take Place*. Sydney: Power Publications.

Baudrillard, J. (1993) *The Transparency of Evil': Essays on Extreme Phenomena*. London: Verso.

Bennis, P. (1991) 'False consensus: George Bush's United Nations', in P. Bennis and M. Moushabeck (eds), *Beyond the Storm*. New York: Olive Branch Press.

Boulding, E. (1998) 'United Nations peacebuilding in Namibia' *Conflict Research Consortium*.

Brock-Utne, B. (1985) *Feminist Perspectives on Peace and Peace Education*. London: Pergamon.

Brodie, B. (1973) *War and Politics*. Basingstoke: Macmillan.

Brzezinski, Z. (1991) 'The Gulf war', in *International Herald-Tribune*. April 22, 1991, pp. 5–6.

Chomsky, N. 'After the Cold War: US Middle East policy', in P. Bennis and M. Moushabeck (eds), *Beyond the Storm*. New York: Olive Branch Press.

Cohn, C. (1987) 'Sex and death in the rational world of defense intellectuals' *Signs*. No. 12 pp. 687–718.

Deleuze, F. and Guattari, F. (1988) *A Thousand Plateaus*. London: Athlone Press.

Eisler, R. (1987) *The Chalice and the Blade: Our History, Our Future*. San Francisco: Harper.

Fox-Keller, E. (1985) *Reflections on Gender and Science*. New Haven: Yale University Press.

Freud, S. (1938) *The Basic Writings of Sigmund Freud*. New York: Random House

Freedman, Lawrence and Karsh, Efrain (1993) *The Gulf Conflict 1990–91: Diplomacy and War in the New World Order*. New Jersey: Princeton University Press.

Giddens, A. (1985) *The Nation State and Violence*. Cambridge: Polity.

Giddens, A. (1992) *Modernity and Self Identity*. Cambridge: Polity.

Glover, E. (1947) *War, Sadism and Pacifism: Further Essays on Group Psychology and War*. London: Routledge.

Graubard, Stephen, R. (1993) 'Mr Bush's war' in S.R. Graubard (1993) *Exit from Communism*. New Jersey: Transaction.

Greenhouse, C. (1987) *Praying for Justice: Faith, Order and Community in an American Town*. Ithaca. New York: Cornell University Press.

Gunder-Frank, A. (1991). 'Third World War: a political economy of the Gulf war and the new world order', *Economic and Political Weekly*, September.

Hables Gray, C. (1997) *Postmodern War*. London: Routledge.

Harding, S. (1986) *The Science Question in Feminism*. Ithaca. New York: Cornell University Press.

Holt, Robert (1987) *Ormulum*. New York: AMS Press.

Kaufman, W. (1998) *Comedian as Confidence Man*. Albany, NY: University of Albany Press.

Malcolm, N. (1998) *Kosovo: A Short History*. Basingstoke: Macmillan.

Millis, Walter (1935) *Road to War: America 1914–1917*. London: Faber and Faber.

Money-Kyrle, R.E. (1951) *Psychoanalysis and politics: A Contribution to the Psychology of Politics*. London: Duckworth.

Murphy, A.B. (1991) 'Territorial ideology and international conflict: the legacy of prior political formations', in N. Kliot and S. Waterman (eds), *The Political Geography of Conflict and Peace*. London: Belhaven Press.

Norris, C. (1992) *Uncritical Theory: Postmodernism, Intellectuals, and the Gulf War*. Amherst, MA: University of Massachusetts Press.

Ramsbotham, O. (1991) 'The conflict in comparative perspective', in P. Bennis and M. Moushabeck (eds), *Beyond the Storm*. New York: Olive Branch Press.

Rascovsky, A. (1995) *Filicide: The Murder, Humiliation, Mutilation, Denigration and Abandonment of Children by Parents*. New York: Jason Aronson.

Reardon, B. (1995) *Educating for Human Dignity: Learning about Rights and Responsibilities*. Philadelphia: University of Pennsylvania Press.

Roach, C. (1991) 'Feminist peace researchers, culture and communications', *Media Development (Journal of the World Association for Christian Communication)*, 2.

Roxborough, I. (1994) 'Clausewitz and the sociology of war', *British Journal of Sociology*, 45(4): 619–637

Smith, E.S. (1993) 'George Bush's war' in S.R. Graubard (1993) *Exit from Communism*. New Jersey: Transaction.

Snow, D.M. and Drew, D.M. (1994) *From Lexington to Desert Storm: War and Politics in the American Experience*. New York: M.E. Sharpe.

Thorne, B. Kramara, C. and Henley, N. (1983) *Language, Gender and Society*. Boston: Heinle and Heinle.

Wallerstein, I. (1991) 'The Gulf war', in *Economic and Political Weekly*, April.

Wright, Q. (1990) *A Study of War*. Chicago: University of Chicago Press.

9

Voting Behaviour

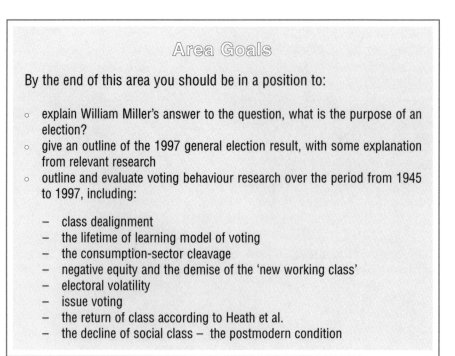

Area Goals

By the end of this area you should be in a position to:

○ explain William Miller's answer to the question, what is the purpose of an election?
○ give an outline of the 1997 general election result, with some explanation from relevant research
○ outline and evaluate voting behaviour research over the period from 1945 to 1997, including:

- class dealignment
- the lifetime of learning model of voting
- the consumption-sector cleavage
- negative equity and the demise of the 'new working class'
- electoral volatility
- issue voting
- the return of class according to Heath et al.
- the decline of social class - the postmodern condition

What is the purpose of an election? William Miller (1990) asked a sample of people from his larger study of the 1987 general election campaign if they agreed with the following list of purposes a lot, some, or not at all. The six purposes were as follows:

Table 9.1 *What is the purpose of an election?*

Elections are a way to:	A lot	Some	Not much
Choose among particular policies	60	27	12
Hold governments accountable for their past actions	48	28	23
Advance the interests of a social class	28	30	40
Gain particular things for oneself and family	34	35	23
Comment on the state of the country	60	27	12
Keep politicians honest	28	25	45

All numbers are percentages.
Source: Miller et al. 1990: 269

The early part of this area looks at the 1997 general election. Below are some of the important statistics from that election. Very often, it is possible to evaluate sociological theories of voting, as outlined in this area, by looking at the relevant facts. The information given below can be used to formulate your own evaluation of different theories.

Election Facts 1997

The final overall results were:

Labour	419 seats (on a 44.4% share of the vote)
Conservative	165 seats (on a 31.4% share of the vote)
Liberal Democrat	46 seats (on a 17.2% share of the vote)
SNP	6 seats
Plaid Cymru	4 seats
Others	19 seats

Turnout: 71.3%
Labour majority: 179
Swing: 10% Conservative to Labour
There were 117 female MPs in the House of Commons – approximately twice as many as in the previous Parliament.
There were 5 women in the Cabinet:
• Margaret Beckett (President of the Board of Trade) • Harriet Harman (Social Security)
• Mo Mowland (Northern Ireland) • Clare Short (International Development) • Ann Taylor (Leader of the Commons)
Non-Cabinet appointments:
• Helen Liddell (Minister of State for the Treasury)
A total of 494 out of 659 constituencies were fought on new boundaries at the 1997 general election.

The following constituencies had majorities of under 1,000:

Rank	Member (Party, Constituency)	Majority
1	M.J. Oaten (L Dem, Hampshire, Winchester)	2
2	A.M. Sanders (L Dem, Torbay)	12
3	E. Davey (L Dem, Kingston-upon-Thames, Kingston and Surbiton)	56

4	I.C. Bruce (C, Dorset, South Dorset)	77
5	D. Heath (L Dem, Somerset, Somerton and Frome)	130
6	Sir W.D. Madel (C, Bedfordshire, South West Bedfordshire)	132
7	P.D. Stinchcombe (Lab, Northamptonshire, Wellingborough)	187
8	P.A. Sawford (Lab, Northamptonshire, Kettering)	189
9	P.L. Atkinson (C, Northumberland, Hexham)	222
10	M.L.D. Fabricant (C, Staffordshire, Lichfield)	238
11	B. White (Lab, Buckinghamshire, North East Milton Keynes)	240
12	P.C.M. Nicholls (C, Devon, Teignbridge)	281
13	D. Ruffley (C, Suffolk, Bury St. Edmunds)	368
14	A. King (Lab, Warwickshire, Rugby and Kenilworth)	495
15	Hon. D.P. Heathcoat-Amory (C, Somerset, Wells)	528
16	Mrs. C.A. Spelman (C, West Midlands, Meriden)	582
17	Sir R.B.F.S. Body (C, Lincolnshire, Boston and Skegness)	647
18	Mrs. E. Gordon (Lab, Havering, Romford)	649
19	C.J. Fraser (C, Dorset, Mid Dorset and Poole North)	681
20	Sir J.M. Shersby (C, Hillingdon, Uxbridge)	724
21	T. Clark (Lab, Northampton, South)	744
22	D.W.G. Chidgey (L Dem, Eastleigh)	754
23	J.D. Cran (C, Humberside, Beverley and Holderness)	811
24	Sir A.D. Steen (C, Devon, Totnes)	877

(David Boothroyd's web site)

Understanding voting behaviour

For many psephologists, (people who study voting behaviour), the period from 1945 to 1970 was characterised by the following features:

- Two-party dominance
- Uniformity – people voting in a similar fashion all over Britain
- Class alignment – people voting on the basis of social class, with working-class people voting Labour and middle-class people Conservative

However, many researchers argue that the period since 1970 has been characterised by the following features:

- Increasing electoral volatility – people voting differently at different elections
- Above all, class dealignment and the rise of 'issue voting' – people no longer voting on the basis of social class, but on the basis of party policies on the key issues of the day

Most of the research into voting behaviour is concerned with examining the condition of the link between an individual's social class and voting intention. Traditionally, working-class people were supposed to have a Labour identification and to vote Labour in much greater numbers than other groups in the population. In contrast, middle-class people were said to have an identification with the Conservatives that led to their higher rates of Conservative voting. People who did not vote for their 'natural' class party were, according to the research at the time, said to be 'deviant voters'. However, much of the research in the area now suggests that this class alignment has been steadily breaking down since the 1970s; so much so, that by 1983, social class could be used to predict 'correctly' the votes of less than half of the British electorate. Voters were said to be moving away from their 'natural' class party. Since the early 1980s, the common view among psephologists is that people vote on the basis of issues rather than class alignment or identification.

However, before we look at the research into voting behaviour in the post-war period, we need to put into context what happened at the 1997 general election. During the 1980s, many, if not all, researchers in the area seemed to assume that the Conservatives would always win general elections. Mark Kirby (1995) outlined the arguments for the Conservatives' continued electoral dominance as follows:

- The Conservatives won four successive general election victories in 1979, 1983, 1987 and 1992, irrespective of the economic circumstances that the country was in
- Traditional class identification was said to be breaking down; the link between class and voting no longer existed
- Electorally, the working class was divided, with skilled manual workers voting Conservative in greater numbers
- New divisions, such as home ownership, had replaced social class within the electorate, and these new factors were to the benefit to the Conservatives electorally

The 1997 general election

In 1997, Labour won a landslide victory, and Tony Blair became the first Labour prime minister since 1979. In addition, Paddy Ashdown's Liberal Democrats gained more than 25 seats. In contrast, the Conservatives lost all their MPs in Scotland and Wales. In terms of representation in Parliament, the Conservatives for the first time became a wholly English party. Many Conservative Cabinet ministers lost their seats, including Michael Portillo, who was seen by many as the obvious successor to John Major.

The campaign was dominated by 'sleaze'. Martin Bell, a BBC war reporter at the start of the campaign, stood as an 'anti-sleaze' independent candidate. With

Table 9.2 *Vote by group*

	Con %		Lab %		LibDem %	
	1997	Change since 1992	1997	Change since 1992	1997	Change since 1992
Men	31	−11	45	+8	17	0
Women	32	−12	45	+11	17	−2
Ages (years)						
18–29	22	−19	56	+18	18	+1
30–44	26	−15	49	+15	17	−5
45–64	33	−14	43	+9	18	+1
65+	44	−3	34	−1	17	+1
AB voters (managerial, professional)	42	−14	31	+11	21	0
C1 (white collar)	26	−15	47	+15	19	−4
C2 (skilled workers)	25	−13	54	+13	14	−4
DE (semi-skilled, unskilled, state pensioners	21	−16	61	+15	13	−2
Own home outright	41	−14	35	+10	16	−2
Mortgage-payers	31	−16	44	+15	18	−2
Council tenants	13	−8	66	+1	15	+4

Sample: 2356 voters polled on Thursday 1 May, having just voted.
Source: http://www.bbc.co.uk/politics97/analysis/kelltab1.shtml

the support of both Labour and the Liberal Democrats, who stood down their candidates, Bell easily won Tatton, one of the safest Conservative seats in the country, defeating the former minister Neil Hamilton.

According to Peter Kellner (1997), 'At the heart of the 1997 election result is a conundrum. The defending government was presiding over steady growth, low inflation, falling unemployment, a buoyant housing market, cheap mortgages and falling income tax rates – yet it lost power; and not only was it ejected from office, it secured a lower share of the vote than any governing party this century. How come?' (www.bbc.co.uk/politics97/analysis).

Kellner's analysis of the BBC's exit poll, conducted by NOP on 2356 individuals as they left the polling stations around the UK on election day in 1997 (Table 9.2) is interesting. This study is important for sociologists because NOP not only asked about people's voting intentions, but also asked those sampled to supply, anonymously, personal information about themselves, such as their age, social class, gender, and housing. This information let NOP compare the representatives of their sample and also put together a detailed description of how different groups voted. In addition, as the same information was collected at the 1992 election exit poll, it was possible to make some valid statements about how the allegiances of different groups in the electorate changed between 1992 and 1997.

Table 9.3 *The classification of occupations into status grades*

Market research designation	Our designation	Grade	Examples[1]
A	I	Higher managerial or professional	Doctor, dentists, university teachers, senior government officials, architects, surveyors, engineers with professional qualifications, clergmen, barristers, solicitors, scientists with professional qualifications, company directors, senior managers with more than 25 subordinates, self-employed builders with 10 or more employees, farmers with over 500 acres.
B	II	Lower managerial or administrative	Farmers with 100 to 500 acres, shop proprietors with 4–9 employees, senior managers with 10–25 subordinates, other managers with over 25 subordinates, qualified nurses and pharmacists, company secretaries without professional qualifications.
C1	III	Skilled or supervisory non-manual	Farmers with 30–90 acres, telegraph operators and radio operators, typists or secretaries with at least one subordinate, civil service executive officers, local authority officers without professional qualification, commercial travellers, manufacturers' agents, salesman with at least one subordinate, shop proprietors with 3 or less employees, managers with less than 25 subordinates, draghtsmen, bank clerks.
C1	IV	Lower non-manual	Shop salesman and assistants, policeman, caretakers, loding-house keepers, street vendors, factory guards, waiters, telephone operators, non-supervisory clerks, inspectors (transport).
C2	V	Skilled manual	Coal miners (faceworkers and fireman), glass and ceramics makers, telephone installers and linesmen, furnace and foundry operatives, workers in electrical trades, fitters, instrument makers, wood workers, textile and clothing workers, food, drink, and tobacco workers, paper and printing workers, skilled construction workers, painters and decorators, firemen and guards, drivers of road goods vehicles.
D	VI	Semi-skilled and unskilled manual	Agricultural workers, gardeners and groundsmen, postal workers, quarrymen, miners (other than faceworkers and firemen), unskilled factory and process workers, laundary workers, dockworkers, warehousemen, porters, roundsmen, domestic workers, cleaners, messengers.
E[2]	VII	Residual, on pension or other state benefit	Persons not elsewhere classified (all were retired and supplied no evidence about their own or their spouses' previous occupations).

Notes

1 The examples are taken from Michael Kahan, David Butler and Donald Stokes, 'On the Analytical Division of Social Class', *British Journal of Sociology*, XVII (1966), 122–32, pp. 131–2. Butler and Stokes divided the middle class and working class between grades III and IV in the first edition of *Political Change in Britain* but between IV and V in the second edition. We have adopted the latter course.

2 Category VII is not included in our tables on occupational grades.

Source: Sarlvik, B. and Crewe, I. (1983) 'Decade of Dealignment – The Conservative Victory of 1979 and the Electoral Trends of the 1970s' Cambridge, Cambridge University Press.

According to Kellner, the NOP survey suggests the following conclusions:

○ Memories of the recession in the early 1990s were more important in shaping attitudes about the Conservatives and affecting how people voted than feelings about the following recovery. As Kellner explains, 'the Conservative slogan, "Britain is booming", may have been counterproductive, for it induced some voters to reflect, "Maybe it is, but I am not." Of those voters who said the economy was stronger, but their family's standard of living had deteriorated, more than eight out of ten voted Labour or Liberal Democrat.'

○ Labour succeeded in neutralising many of the negative perceptions that people had had of the party at the 1992 general election. Blair's leadership struck a chord with the electorate that Kinnock's had not.

○ The Conservative Party was perceived as divided, while, in contrast, Labour was seen as united. As Kellner explains, 'A majority of more than two-to-one thought the Conservatives good for one class, rather than good for all classes; but a similar majority thought Labour good for all classes, not just one. Worse even than that for the Tories, as many as 84% saw the Tories as divided – whereas 66% saw Labour as united.'

○ Blair was seen as a much stronger and more competent leader than Major; he outscored Major by 14 points, although Major was perceived as trustworthier. A Tory advertisement depicting Blair as a puppet of the German Chancellor Helmut Kohl did not strike the intended chord with the electorate.

○ In terms of policy, the majority thought Labour policies would make the situation better; in contrast, a considerable number of people in the sample thought that Conservative policies would make the situation 'a lot worse'. As Kellner suggests, 'Labour was seen as the party of hope.'

○ The swing in favour of the Labour Party among women was greater than among men.

Was there a 'gender gap' in the 1997 general election?

According to Kellner,

> For the first time since 1945, the votes of women alone were sufficient to give Labour an overall majority. In 1964, 1966 and October 1974 – the other post-war elections at which Labour secured an overall majority – men voted Labour in sufficient numbers to ensure an overall majority; had only women voted, Labour would either have lost the election or, at best, been able to form a minority government.
>
> (http://www.bbc.co.uk/politics97/analysis/kelltab1.shtml)

The data suggest that there has been a traditionall 'gender gap' in voting behaviour. According to Kellner, 'Young voters swung to Labour to a remarkable extent.' However, the swing to Labour was perceptibly lower in each subsequent age group: among 30–44-year-olds, 45–64-year-olds and those over 65, the swing to Labour was greatest among mortgage payers or council tenants.

Nicholas Jones (1997) gives us an informed journalistic account of the 1997 campaign. He suggests a number of reasons that the Conservatives lost. First, and most importantly, 'The feeling that it was time for a change was deep-seated in the electorate' (Jones, 1997: 271). Moreover, the Tories made a number of grave tactical mistakes. Major decided to have a long election campaign, thinking that the longer the period of electioneering, the more opportunities there would be to undermine Labour's policies. However, in Jones's view, there was poor morale within the Conservative Party as well as a lack of self-discipline among Conservative MPs – notably, outbursts from the Euro-sceptics and issues of misconduct and financial impropriety, which became known as 'sleaze'. These issues prevented any real effective attack upon Labour. In addition, the long campaign 'heightened [the] exposure of ministers who were seen to be out of touch with public opinion' (Jones, 1997: 113).

In particular, Jones argues that Blair came across as bold and imaginative with overwhelming support from his party, notably in the rewriting of Clause 4 of the Labour Party constitution and the abandonment of other outmoded commitments. In contrast, Major had to contend with a high level of indiscipline among his MPs, and he came across as indecisive on key issues such as Europe. As the Press Association reported, during the campaign, Robin Cook, then shadow foreign secretary, claimed that a 'clear majority' of Conservative candidates opposed Major's 'wait and see' policy on a single European currency. In response, Major had to appeal to his own party not to bind his hands by rejecting his 'negotiate and decide' policy on the single currency. In addition, Major felt he had to offer new concessions to the Euro-sceptics in the form of a free vote in Parliament on the single currency. Major also had to defend the right of Conservative MPs to declare their objection to the single currency, although he did later admit that he found the objections to the single currency frustrating.

It is not surprising, then, that Jones argues that Major was unable either to influence or control the news agenda during the campaign. Labour had very effective 'spin doctors': 'Blair's spin doctors had spent years perfecting their routines for generating unwelcome publicity for Major and his ministers' (Jones, 1997: 114). In particular, Blair's team adopted the strategy of 'rapid rebuttal' first used by the Clinton administration in the USA. Rapid rebuttal was an attempt to counter the Conservatives' negative campaigning.

In October 1995, the Labour Party purchased the impressive software program Excalibur for £300,000. This system allowed very large numbers of documents – official statistics, press releases, ministerial statements, etc. – to be loaded onto a large database. Excalibur allowed searches of key words to enable Labour to rebut Conservative attacks 'quickly and with confidence' (Jones, 1997: 20).

Jones also places a great deal of emphasis on news management in Labour's election victory, particularly the decision of the *Sun* newspaper to support Labour in the campaign. However, research by NOP suggests that the media did not have a great deal of influence.

'Sleaze' and 'Smears'

The General Election campaign exploded into life as Labour leader Tony Blair and the Prime Minister traded insults over 'sleaze' and 'smears' in their final acrimonious clash of the Parliament.

Ten Tory MPs were left with a question mark hanging over their probity after publication of an interim report on the 'cash-for-questions' investigation.

But the Prime Minister made it clear that he had no intention of altering the General Election time-table to enable the full report to be published.

Mr Blair said John Major's handling of the affair left 'a stain on the character of your government'. Mr Major said Mr Blair and his frontbench were guilty of having 'smeared and smeared and smeared again'.

Mr Blair and Liberal Democrat leader Paddy Ashdown were involved in 'a political stunt' designed to eclipse good employment figures, the Prime Minister insisted.

In perhaps the fiercest exchanges since the Labour leader first took up his place at the dispatch-box opposite John Major two-and-a-half years ago, all pretence of a keenly fought, gentlemanly election-battle was ditched as the row became bitterly personal. It means that the row over 'cash-for-questions', which was first raised in the campaign at Question-Time on Tuesday, now looms as one of the largest issues on the agenda.

After the steadily building pressure for publication of the report prompted Parliamentary Commissioner for Standards Sir Gordon Downey and the Commons Standards and Privileges Committee to agree to publish an interim report, a simple two-page volume was issued.

Sir Gordon exonerated 15 of the 25 MPs whose cases he had investigated – a group which included Defence Secretary Michael Portillo, former Cabinet Minister David Mellor and all four Opposition MPs under scrutiny.

But it left a question-mark hanging over 10 Tory MPs. Six of them have been identified: former Trade Minister Neil Hamilton; former Northern Ireland Minister Tim Smith; former whip Michael Brown; aide to Scottish Office Minister Lord James Douglas-Hamilton, Nirj Deva; and backbenchers Sir Andrew Bowden and Sir Michael Grylls.

Though Sir Michael is standing down at the next election, the other five go into the next election unable to lift formally doubts about their probity because Mr Major ruled out any extension of the Parliamentary session to enable the full report to be published next week.

(Murphy and Cordon, 'Blair and Major in bitter clash over sleaze', PA News)

Many people regarded Major's decision not to allow publication of the full report on 'cash for question' a mistake, reflecting his poor leadership.

Television and radio

I would suggest that Labour's relentless and imaginative efforts to guide and shape political coverage on television and radio and in the newspapers were partly responsible for turning their already near-certain victory into a record-breaking triumph. (Jones, 1997: 271)

Media coverage did not change voting decisions – survey findings

More than four out of five Britons interviewed in an NOP survey published today [8 May 1997] say that their own voting decision in last week's General Election was not influenced by any of the election media coverage. This was highest amongst people over 55 (89 per cent).

The survey – undertaken by the NOP Research Group Ltd, one of the UK's leading market research organisations – also found that 59 per cent of under-35s believe there is scope for change in the British approach to election campaigns, compared with only 46 per cent of over-55s. In addition, over half (55 per cent) of under-35s think that an American-style TV debate between the main leaders would have made the campaign more interesting, compared with only 30 per cent of over-55s.

Other key findings:

○ Over three-quarters say they feel that, overall, media coverage of the election campaign was 'fair and balanced'. Some 69 per cent of these were under 35, compared with 80 per cent of the over-55s.
○ Two in five (21 per cent) of the under-35s say they think that media coverage of the campaign was not fair and balanced, compared with just over one in ten (12 per cent) of the over-55s.
○ 54 per cent believe there is 'scope for change' in the British approach to General Election campaigns compared with only two out of five who feel it 'works as it is'.
○ Almost half (48 per cent) of people in the South agree with the idea that an American-style, televised debate between the main party leaders would have made the campaign more interesting, compared with only 35 per cent in the North.

Tony Lees, NOP's consumer research director, commented: ' Despite the extensive and prolonged media coverage of the events and issues leading up to the recent General Election, most Britons do not feel that this coverage influenced their decision on whether and how to vote. Nonetheless, the findings also indicate that future election campaigns may need to adapt if they are to appeal to the more discerning demands of the younger members of the electorate.'

Electoral volatility

How does political allegiance change between elections? In an effort to investigate this and related issues, the British Election Panel Survey, undertaken by the ESRC (Economic and Social Research Council) Centre for Research into Elections, interviewed a group of 3500 people periodically from the 1992 election to the 1997 election. Although many people dropped out of the panel, just under 2000 people were part of the panel in 1997. The survey aimed to clarify the following issues:

○ Why voters change their allegiances and votes
○ How perceptions of the state of the economy shape individuals' attitudes to government
○ The impact of political leaders on party support
○ The influence of the mass media
○ How changes in social attitudes affect voting behaviour

The survey suggested the following conclusions:

- Labour is thought to have moved towards the centre ... while voters themselves have moved to the left;
- Before 1994 Labour won most of its support from the Conservatives ... but since then it has come mostly from the Liberal Democrats;
- Tony Blair appeals to the middle class ... but no more than he does to the working class;
- Voters have become more sceptical about Europe ... but more voters think Labour are closest to their own views;
- The critical tone of the traditionally Tory press since 1992 has not helped the Conservatives ... but it has not done them much harm either;
- Elections are supposed to be about the economy ... but now it seems to be image that matters.

(http://www.bbc.co.uk/election97/polls/jcbeps1.htm. This web site gives a great deal of information about the 1997 general election. If you wish to find out more about the British Election Panel Survey (BEPS), the following web site is worth looking at: http://www.strath.ac.uk/Other/CREST/polaleg.html.)

In 1997, the electorate unquestionably accepted that the Labour position had changed, and were less likely to regard Labour as in favour of nationalisation, increasing taxes, higher spending and reducing inequality. Labour is now seen as no longer supporting increased taxation or state ownership. In addition, in 1997, voters assumed that the Conservative Party had moved further to the right on these issues. However, the survey showed the electorate had moved to the left. Voters in 1997 were more enthusiastic about nationalisation, higher taxes and spending, and government undertakings to decrease inequality than they were in 1992.

In terms of the economy, the survey suggests that, according to most observers in the 1980s, the Conservatives kept winning general elections because they were able to demonstrate that the economy was in a healthy state. However, during the period of the research, support for the Conservatives fell in opinion polls while the economy was doing well. In addition, those voters who continued to be faithful to the Conservatives were not especially inclined to have an optimistic view of Britain's future economic performance. In addition, voters assumed that the Conservatives were 'no longer "capable of forming a strong government" and those who no longer think that the party is "good for all classes" have been most likely to switch from the Conservatives.'

Evidently voters are interested not just in how much money there is in their own pockets. What matters to them even more, it seems, is that the government should appear to have some control over events and be felt to be looking after all sections of society.

The survey also looked at the flow of the vote between the main parties.

British election panel study

Before 1994 Labour won most of its support from the Conservatives. ...

Although elections are often thought of as battles between Labour and the Conservatives, individual voters rarely switch directly between these two parties. Instead, rises and falls in the overall level of Conservative and Labour support are normally the consequence of individual voters switching between one of those parties and either the Liberal Democrats or abstention.

But it has been widely argued that since the last election, Conservatives have found it easier to switch all the way across to Labour, encouraged perhaps by the repackaging of Labour as 'New Labour'.

Between 1992 and 1994, prior to Tony Blair's advent as leader, Labour did win slightly more new voters from the Conservatives than from Labour. Of those saying they would vote Labour in 1994, 12% were Conservative voters in 1992 while 10% were Liberal Democrats.

Even so, this was as much because relatively few Liberal Democrat voters switched to Labour than because Conservatives now found it easier to switch to Labour. It was still the case that more Conservatives switched to the Liberal Democrats between 1992 and 1994 than did so to Labour. One in five of those who voted Conservative in 1992 supported the Liberal Democrats in 1994 compared with only one in eight who switched to Labour.

Five times as many people switched from the Liberal Democrats to Labour between 1994 and 1996 than switched from the Conservatives. Only 4% of those who supported the Conservatives in 1994 have subsequently switched to Labour, compared with no less than a quarter of Liberal Democrat supporters. Former Conservative supporters are then still relatively reluctant to switch all the way to Labour. The repackaging of Labour as 'New Labour' under Tony Blair has in fact been most successful at winning over Liberal Democrats.

(http://www.bbc.co.uk/election97/polls/jcbeps3.htm)

Sociological research on voting behaviour

Let us move away from cut and thrust of the issues which dominated the 1997 election campaign and look at the sociological research published over recent years. Most researchers in the area of voting behaviour argued after the 1992 election that Labour's decline was permanent.

Ivor Crewe silenced?

Taking into account the arguments above about the 1997 general election, read the quotation below from Ivor Crewe (1992):

Labour's performance [in the 1992 general election] whether measured by its share of the vote (34.4 per cent) or its distance behind the Conservatives (7.4 percentage points) was its third worst since 1945 – an improvement only on the immediately preceding elections of 1983 and 1987. For the sixth consecutive election Labour failed to reach 40 per cent of the vote. The 1992 election confirmed its status as a long-term opposition party. (Crewe, 1992: 2–3, quoted in Kirby, 1995)

Richard Rose (1992) argued that the Labour defeat at the 1992 general election was 'shattering', because most of the short-term factors were in Labour's favour.

- Labour was united
- The SDP-Liberal Alliance was damaged by the quarrelsome merger between the two parties
- Unemployment was high
- The economy was still in a lengthy recession
- The Conservatives ran a poor campaign
- The Conservatives had had two leadership battles which had exposed splits and divisions within the party

Research into voting behaviour is primarily concerned with debates about two related concepts: partisan dealignment and class dealignment. Partisan alignment is about how people identify with a political party. Class alignment is concerned with the relationship between a person's social class position and party choice. Most research suggests that since the 1970s there has been a significant decline in both class alignment and partisan alignment. In other words, people no longer vote on the basis of their social class (they have become class dealigned), and they no longer strongly identify with a political party (they have become partisan dealigned). Since the end of the 1970s, people are said to vote on the basis of issues rather than on the basis of class or blind partisanship.

David Denver (1989) suggests that people have become less partisan because of an increase in political awareness since the 1950s. We spend more time at school, college and university than people in the 1950s, and we look for evidence rather than emotional attachment in our analysis of political arguments. In addition, most people in Britain have access to a television. Politicians are questioned aggressively on television; they are made fun of by satirical programmes; and, in addition, we are given a huge amount of information which allows us to cast doubt upon what politicians would have us believe. There is also the implication that television has made both its presenters and audience sceptical of entrenched ideological positions, in favour of the balanced and neutral position of the news programmes. Denver also suggests that in most of the post-war period the performance of the political parties has not been good. This poor performance by the parties has made us believe that no party has all the answers.

Class dealignment is related to the following factors:

- Embourgeoisement – the argument that the working class is becoming merged with the middle class

- Changes in the occupational structure – notably the significant de
  manufacturing sector and the expansion in the white-collar sector
- New or cross-class locations – the principle that people come to id
  homeowners if they own their own home irrespective of their class
- The fragmented nature of working-class interests, because of the en
  of a 'new' working class in the more affluent South of England

This is the accepted view that emerges from looking at electoral studie
1980s and 1990s. Let us look at some specific research into some of these

The lifetime of learning model of voting

An informed contribution to the study of voting behaviour was published in
by Rose and McAllister under the title *Voters Begin to Choose: From Cl
Class to Open Elections in Britain*. In this book, they construct what they c
'cumulative through a lifetime of learning' model of voting. They argue tha
choice that a voter makes on election day is not made in a timeless vacuur
number of factors affect how people vote, and these factors change over
course of their lives. The first stage is pre-adult socialisation or family loyalti
then come the following factors:

- Adult socialisation experiences
- Political principles – which include socialism, welfare, traditional morality an
  racialism
- Party performance in Parliament
- The election campaign

Socialisation is an ongoing process of personal development in which a
person learns the culture, values and ways of behaviour in a society. Parents are
a key factor in this learning process, and part of what we learn from our parents
is political ideas and prejudices. Many of these parental prejudices stay with us
and influence our adult voting intentions. As Table 9.3 from Rose and McAllister
(1990: 52) suggests, 19.75 per cent of the influence upon our adult voting intention is based upon such family loyalties.

Rose and McAllister clearly state the difference between political principles
and issues or the current performance of political parties: 'Because political
principles are durable, they can properly be considered prior influences upon
the choice of the vote at a particular election. By contrast, many questions about
topical issues reflect judgements made after a person decides which party to
support' (1986: 118). In addition, a little later in the book, they explain that 'the
influence of principles has been increasing [and] transitory events and issues
appear of little direct importance on election day' (130–1).

In their later book *the Loyalties of Voters: A Lifetime Learning Model* (1990),
Rose and McAllister further outline their 'cumulative through a lifetime of learning'

Table 9.4   *Influences in a lifetime of political learning*

	Variance explained 1987	
	%	Cumulative
Family loyalties	19.7	–
Socio-economic interests	9.3	29.0
Political values	27.9	56.9
Social and political context	1.7	58.6
Current performance of parties and leaders	10.5	69.1
Party identification	3.4	72.5

Source: Rose and McAllister, 1990: 52

model of voting (Figure 9.1). They still argue that the choice that a voter makes on election day is not made in a timeless vacuum.

Rose and McAllister argue that people are *forced* to choose which party to vote for, because parties they may have previously voted for no longer exist or have changed radically. Individuals who voted Labour in 1979 had to decide whether they had more in common with SDP-Liberal Alliance in 1983. Similarly, people who voted Conservative had to decide whether they had more in common with Labour in 1997. However, 'Even though parties change, the concerns of ordinary people can remain stable, for they reflect a lifetime of experience' (Rose and McAllister, 1990: 7).

Against the class-based models of voting they argue that 'intraclass differences' – in other words, differences between people within a social class – have expanded due to the education system. This means that people in the same social class have little in common with each other.

Against the issue-voting models, Rose and McAllister argue as follows:

> If parties act in ways that are inconsistent with the stable values, interests and loyalties of ordinary people, then voters are forced to think afresh about how to cast their ballot. An individual can remain constant to a lifetime of learning by making a reasoned choice in favour of the party supported before or by voting for another party that is now closest to him or herself. (1990: 17)

As we suggested above in the discussion of their earlier study, values are defined as normative and durable, are relevant to public policy and are different from issues which are concerned with current events, such as 'a particular strike, sterling crisis or a scandal' (Rose and McAllister, 1990: 92). In other words, values persist, but issues are transitory. Rose and McAllister explain that the most recent evidence available to them gives no support to an issue-based model, that people voted on the basis of the parties' stances on the key issues of the day:

> The instrumentalist theory of voting assumes that people who think the government has handled issues badly will vote to turn it out of office, in order to see if the opposition can do better. If everyone had voted according to their rating of the government's handling of issues, then the Conservatives would have lost the 1987 election, for only 35 per cent of voters on average gave the Conservatives a positive rating. (Rose and McAllister, 1990: 131)

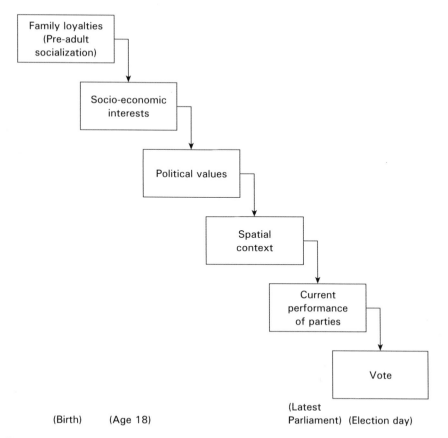

Figure 9.1 *Lifetime learning model of voting (Rose and McAllister 1990: 226)*

Rose and McAllister go on to explain that, according to the 1987 British election survey, the government's handling of issues accounted for only 2.5 per cent of the variance in the vote.

In the 1990 study by Rose and McAllister, values are grouped together into nine coherent clusters, which are outlined in Table 9.5, together with the percentage of the electorate allied to that cluster in 1987 and some typically associated with it. Parties have to attempt to put together a winning combination by appealing to as many values clusters as they possibly can. The data for the 1987 general election is also given in Table 9.6.

The lifetime of learning model can also be used to examine the influence of ethnicity, gender and age on voting intention. Ethnicity may also be related to voting intention. Afro-Caribbean and Asian voters are much more likely to be Labour supporters. This may be partly explained by the social class background of many ethnic minority members. However, a number of Asians have experienced upward mobility in the 1990s, and 23% of Indian men are self-employed, a factor which is only partly reflected in the shift in voting intention from Labour to the

Table 9.5 *Values of voters: a cluster analysis*

Electorate %	
7	*Victorian right*
	Cut social benefits, control unions, anti-permissive, pro-authority
17	*Social market*
	Favour privatisation, business, and social benefits
11	*Conserve environment*
	Put environment before jobs, housing
8	*Strong defence*
	Pro-nuclear weapons, international commitments
8	*Anti-nuclear centrists*
	Average except for opposition to nuclear weapons
11	*England alone*
	Against international commitments, pro-nuclear defence
18	*Muck-and-brass welfare*
	Put jobs, houses before environment; pro-welfare programmes, unions
15	*Soft left*
	Anti-nuclear weapons, pro-unions, pro-welfare, against privatisation
5	*Hard left*
	Anti-nuclear weapons, international commitments, pro-welfare, pro-unions, anti-authority, pro-permissive society.

Source: Rose and McAllister, 1990: 185

Table 9.6 *Voting by value clusters*

Total %		Con	Alliance (% within rows)	Lab
7	Victorian right	92	6	2
17	Social market	86	12	1
11	Conserve environment	69	25	5
8	Strong defence	63	29	8
8	Anti-nuclear centrists	39	35	23
11	England alone	31	29	39
18	Mark-and-brass welfare	15	34	51
15	Soft left	5	28	64
5	Hard left	1	13	84

Source: Rose and McAllister, 1990: 185

Conservatives in 1992. The limited amount of research on voting intention by issues suggests that ethnic minorities have similar attitudes to other people in the population on a wide range of issues.

Investigations into voting intentions of senior citizens suggest that support for the Conservative Party increases as individuals get older, while support for the Labour Party decreases. A number of factors may be at work here. Firstly as Goldthorpe et al. (1987) have shown, when people first enter the labour market they are much more likely to have a poorly paid job and therefore to make more use of the benefits system. In addition, as most people have children early in their adult life, younger adults make more use of welfare state services such as family credit, child benefit and the education service. As people move into middle age, their class position may change, and their income increase, as does the amount of tax they pay, and they make fewer demands upon the welfare state. This combination of factors might cause a change in older people's view of the world. In other words, people may experience changes in what Rose and McAllister call their socio-economic interests or their social and political context.

In the 1950s and 1960s, it was commonly assumed that men voted Labour in greater numbers than women because men were much more likely to work full time outside the home and to be involved in the trade-union movement. With the significant increase in women entering the labour market from the 1970s onwards, there has been an increase in women voting Labour. However, according to research cited by Bea Campbell in *Iron Ladies* (1987), this may be due to the fact that Labour policies on welfare and defence appeal more to female voters.

An informed summary of the possible influence of pre-adult socialisation, family loyalties, adult socialisation experiences, and political principles is provided by Johnston et al. in *A Nation Dividing* (1988):

> People are socialised into particular sets of political attitudes that reflect their occupational class origins and local contexts within which they learn the political meanings of their class positions. This produces the general pattern of voting by occupational class that is known as the class cleavage. That cleavage is far from complete, because of a variety of other influences, but it remains the single most important influence on the development of political attitudes and the identification of voters with particular political parties that follows. (Johnston et al. 1988: 269).

Against this view, it could be suggested that people make their party choice by intentional choice rather than by being driven by forces outside their control such as processes of socialisation.

The consumption-sector cleavage

Patrick Dunleavy attempts to classify people according to their overall involvement in public/private consumption across several sectors: housing, transport, health and education. These consumption experiences play a key role in voters' political alignment. I shall concentrate on housing as an example of what Dunleavy is discussing. It is important to stress that the consumption sectors are not a simple reflection of social class, although home or car ownership depends upon income, with professional households almost three times more likely to own a house and twice as likely to own a car, than unskilled manual workers. Housing and car ownership are not simple correlates of class because even as far back as 1979, at least half of skilled manual workers were homeowners, and 49.6% of homeowners were manual workers. Moreover, 57% of manual workers had access to a car, and 53% of car owners were manual workers.

In the initial versions of this analysis, which were greatly influenced by the work of the neo-Marxist Manuel Castells, Dunleavy argued that powerful ideological

Table 9.7 *Housing and voting*

Social class	Tenure	Labour	Conservative	Alliance (Lib Dem)	Con lead over Lab	n
Manual workers	Council rent	54	23	23	–31	166
	Other	46	33	21	–13	24
	Homeowner	36	33	31	–3	150
Non-manual	Council rent	33	49	18	+16	33
workers	Other	21	43	36	+22	14
	Homeowner	14	49	37	+35	152

Data from 1983 general election.
Source: Dunleavy and Husbands, 1985: 138

hegemonic structures were created and maintained by the dominant classes. Hegemony moulded the perceptions of individuals within the different social locations. Therefore, within the dominant ideological structures, voters were instrumentally aligned with 'the party most clearly identified with the interests of their consumption location' (Dunleavy, 1980: 78). Although the Labour Party was never solely committed to council housing as a form of housing tenure, it is not seen to be committed to the private sector in the same fashion as the Conservatives, who clearly are ideologically committed to the free market. Dunleavy's data showing the link between housing and voting is presented in Table 9.7.

What is significant about Dunleavy's research is that the explanation moves beyond the social psychological-individual-based explanation upon which most of the early research, for example, that of Goldthorpe and Lockwood (1969), was based.

Negative equity and the demise of the 'new working class'

With the election of the Conservative government of Mrs Thatcher in 1979, the relationship between housing and voting became much more controversial, as the Conservatives attempted to use housing policy to enhance their own chances of re-election. In effect, they attempted to provide the conditions under which what Ivor Crewe (1992) refers to as the 'new' working class can emerge. This 'new' working class is a class based upon consumption, notably consumption of housing. However, mortgages hurt, and mortgages with negative equity really hurt, reducing consumption and adversely affecting job mobility. This was a situation compounded by the financial market liberalisation during the Thatcher years, which has had the consequence of building up debt, a debt that made consumers much more vulnerable to upward movements in interest rates. Moreover, if social class is defined in terms of consumption patterns, negative equity will produce a process of 'proletarianisation', as consumption is reduced in order to meet expanding debt demands. The reader may ask: Who are the 'new' working class?

According to Ivor Crewe (1992), in the elections of 1983 and 1987, Labour remained largely working class, but the working class was no longer largely

Labour. What he means by this statement is that the alignment between Labour and its working-class support was limited to a so-called traditional working class that live in the North of England or Scotland, are union members, work in the public sector and are council tenants. By contrast, the 'new' working class is made up of people who have been exposed to some aspect of middle-class life, such as share ownership, live in the South of England, work in the private sector in a non-union environment and are owner-occupiers. Support for Labour among this 'new' working class was said to have declined significantly during the 1980s.

According to Thatcherite theory, the market should provide housing, either by owner occupation or via the private rented sector. Local authorities and central government should merely facilitate individual participation in the market. From 1979 until 1997, government housing policy had the following four clear objectives:

- To encourage owner occupation
- To reduce local authority provision
- To encourage the growth of the private sector
- To target resources to those with greatest need

The Housing Act 1980 gave tenants the right to buy their houses and also made changes to the subsidy and rent systems in an effort to make owner occupation more attractive and council tenancy less attractive. The Housing and Planning Act 1986 allowed local authorities to transfer housing stock to other landlords, without the need for a ballot. The Housing Act 1988 further extended this provision by giving tenants the right to initiate the transfer process, by holding a ballot. If tenants do not vote in such a ballot, they are assumed to have voted yes. The 1988 act also contains provision for the establishment of Housing Action Trusts, whereby council estates can be taken out of local authority control for a period of up to seven years, improved, and then passed on to a landlord that may or may not be the local authority. The Housing and Local Government Act 1989 attempted to close up any loopholes in the existing legislation. The housing subsidy and housing revenue accounts of local authorities had changes made to them, so that any surpluses on account are used to pay the housing benefit of other council tenants. There was greater central control of rents, Housing Action Areas were abolished, means tests were introduced for home improvement grants, and Neighbourhood Renewal Areas were introduced. Areas of greatest need are targeted for additional resources; these areas must meet fixed criteria, be supported by a survey, and be approved by the minister. What effect did these changes have upon the way people voted in the 1980s and early 1990s?

Political scientists have for some years accepted that housing has a close relationship with political alignment, independent of the effect of social class. Even such a staunch supporter of class alignment as Peter Pulzer was forced to admit, in his *Political Representation and Elections in Britain* (1967), that

There is no evidence that high incomes, or the possession of consumer durables, predisposes working class people towards the right. The one exception is homeownership, which, at all levels of income, makes people with manual jobs feel more middle class, and more inclined to vote Conservative than those who rent their homes. (Pulzer 1967: 112)

Why did working-class homeowners continue to support the Conservatives, rather than any other party, until 1997? In their analysis of MORI's 1992 general election survey, Colin Rallings and Michael Thrasher (1997) were surprised to find that so many home owners continued to support the Conservatives, given that a house was no longer an inflation-proof investment. Rallings and Thrasher clearly believe that working-class owner-occupiers had interests that should have determined voting to a much greater degree than they did. The MORI analysis supports what has become the orthodox view of the relationship between housing and voting, which needed to be re-examined, particularly in the light of 'negative equity', the situation in which individual mortgage payers owe more to the building society than they could sell their house for. Table 9.8 shows the changes in voting intention as related to housing tenure.

In a speech to the Royal Economic Society's 1997 annual conference, Andrew Henley (1997) reported that negative equity peaked at 6% of owner-occupiers in 1993. There are significant changes in the level of negative equity that Henley outlines. His figures are as follows: 1991, 2.6% of owner-occupiers had negative equity; 1992, 4.7% of owner-occupiers had negative equity; 1993, 6.0% of owner-occupiers had negative equity; 1994, 4.6% of owner-occupiers had negative equity (http://www.res.org.uk/media/annconf97/henley.htm).

In *The British General Election of 1983* and *The British General Election of 1987*, Butler and Kavanagh (1984, 1987) have also attempted to show that changes in housing tenure undermined Labour's position, claiming that, whereas council tenants voted 49% for Labour and 29% for the Conservatives, the figures were the reverse for the working-class people who were buying or who already owned their own homes (26% to 47%) (Butler and Kavanagh, 1984: 296–7) In Ivor Crewe's view, these people are the 'new' working class.

An alternative view is put forward by Heath, et al. (1985) in the British Election Surveys (BES) of 1983 and 1987. During the 1960s, there were major changes in housing tenure. Owner occupation doubled between 1951 and 1971, although this was largely because of the contraction of the private-rented sector. The Conservative government's legislation since the 1980 act led to a 5 per cent reduction in the size of the local authority housing stock between 1980 and 1986. As Heath et al. point out, 'this has merely undone the expansion of the previous twenty years. The net increase in council housing over the period ... [1964–87] ... is therefore effectively zero' (1991: 206).

Heath et al. clearly recognise the 'association' between housing and voting. In the 1987 BES, they refer to Capderville and Dupoirier's concept of le patrimoine, the idea that a stake in the nation's wealth may be a major factor in determining

Table 9.8 *Home ownership and voting*

% of 1992 voters 31	Homeowners	1983 vote			1987 vote			1992 vote		
		Con	Lab	L/D	Con	Lab	L/D	Con	Lab	L/D
	Working class	46	25	27	43	32	23	41	39	17

Source: *Sunday Times*, 12 April 1992: 14

	Homeowners	1997 vote		
		Con	Lab	L/D
		35	41	17

Sunday Times, 4 May 1997: 23

Table 9.9 *Parliamentary constituencies with highest negative equity and percentage change in share of vote 1987–92*

Proportion of homebuyers (1988–91) who now had negative equity in 1992 and average amount held			Percentage change in vote 1987–92		
			Con	Lab	LibDem
Luton South	72	6700	−1.4	+6.8	−6.7
Newham South	69	5600	+4.3	+3.1	−7.2
Southend East	66	6600	+0.8	+9.6	−12.0
Leyton	65	5800	−6.2	+11.5	−8.5
Newham North East	61	5200	+0.5	+5.7	−8.0
Newham North West	61	5700	−0.2	+6.4	−6.2
Basildon	60	6500	+1.4	+3.9	−5.3
Erith and Crayford	59	5100	+1.3	+12.0	−13.3
Walthamstow	58	5600	−1.4	+10.7	−10.8
Croydon North West	57	4600	−3.5	+10.3	−10.8
Brighton Pavilion	57	4000	−4.2	+8.6	−6.8
Peckham	57	4300	−2.2	+7.2	−4.0
Woolwich	55	4800	−4.6	+7.2	−1.6
Lewisham Deptford	55	4800	−3.8	+11.6	−6.0
Brent South	55	5600	−1.9	+5.6	−5.5
Southend West	55	6600	+0.3	−4.7	−7.2
Southwark	54	7600	−2.5	−8.9	+9.4
Luton North	54	6000	−0.2	+6.1	−7.2
Dagenham	53	5800	−2.2	+7.8	−5.6
Hove	53	4800	−9.9	+6.2	−2.4

Net figures: Conservative −1.8%; Labour +7.2%; Liberal Democrats −5.8%. In addition, in 1992, Labour gained three of the above seats: Walthamstow, Croydon North-West and Woolwich.

how people vote, but they are not convinced of a causal link between housing and voting.

In the 1983 BES, Heath et al. explain that purchasers of council houses were more likely to have been Conservative voters in 1979, but the statistical significance was not great. Among the council tenants in 1979, 23 percent had voted Conservative and 68 percent voted Labour. However, of the former council tenants who had bought their house between 1979 and 1983, 40 percent voted Conservative and 52 percent voted Labour. It must be stressed, however, that purchasers were no more likely than other tenants to abandon Labour. Purchasers defected from Labour, but so did many tenants. Three-quarters of the former Labour supporters who bought their council houses continued to vote Labour in 1983. This was almost the same figure as former Labour supporters who remained tenants; the exact figures were 76 per cent to 79 per cent. Moreover, as only 2 per cent of the 1983 sample planned to buy their council houses in future years, Heath et al. observe that any future gain for the Conservatives was likely to be limited. On the basis of the 1983 survey, Heath et al. reject Dunleavy's assertion that housing is a sectoral cleavage, but argue that housing 'acts as a separate source for the maintenance of the class cleavage' (Heath et al. 1985: 54).

In the 1987 BES, Heath et al. again show that purchasers were more likely to vote Conservative. In 1979, Conservative voting was 15 percentage points higher among future purchasers; in 1983, Conservative voting was 20 percentage points higher, when some of this group had completed their purchases; however, in 1987, it was only 14 percentage points higher, when the whole group had completed their purchases. Again, there was little evidence that the sale of council houses produces many new recruits for the Conservatives. Although the Labour vote fell by 8 per cent more than it fell among tenants, only 6 per cent of the electorate were purchasers, and 8 per cent of 6 per cent is only 0.5 per cent of the electorate.

In this area of voting behaviour, as in a number of other areas, Heath et al. present themselves as revisionists; they challenge the orthodox view that changes in housing tenure cause changes in voting behaviour. They are the only researchers to have attempted a longitudinal study into the effects of housing on the electorate in the 1979, 1983 and 1987 general elections.

Class and voting

Class has been seen as the most important factor influencing voting, and examination questions on voting behaviour usually focus on issues concerning class. The research suggests that for many psephologists, the period from 1945 to 1970 was one of two-party dominance, uniformity and class alignment. However, the period since 1970 has been one of increasing electoral volatility and above all class dealignment. The link between an individual's social class and voting intention, which traditionally involved working class people voting Labour and middle class people voting Conservative, has been steadily breaking down. So much so, that by 1983 social class could 'accurately be used to forecast the votes of under half of the British electorate. Voters were said to be shifting political allegiance away from their 'natural' class party.

For Ivor Crewe (1992), changes in the social structure, particularly the growth of working-class home ownership, have produced a diminution of class consciousness. More people are finding themselves under cross-class partisan pressure because they have mixed class characteristics; these are the 'new'

Table 9.10 *Summary*

Author	Explanation
Crewe. (1992)	Home ownership a key factor in the emergence of the 'new' working class, and in the process of class dealignment. Method of defining class – the social grade schema, similar to market research categories, based upon consumption patterns. Effect of negative equity: shrinking of the 'new' working class, possibly greater class alignment, certainly greater proletarianisation, because of decline in income.
Rose and McAllister (1990)	Social class declined in significance in determining voting behaviour, replaced by housing tenure. Method of defining class – the social grade schema, similar to market research categories, based upon consumption patterns. Effect of negative equity: greater class alignment, certainly greater proletarianisation, because of decline in income.
Johnson et al. (1988)	Owner-occupiers more likely to vote Conservative irrespective of social class. Method of defining class – the social grade schema, similar to market research categories, based upon consumption patterns. Effect of negative equity: greater class alignment, certainly greater proletarianisation, because of decline in income.
Dunleavy and Husbands (1985)	Individuals vote on the basis of a consumption sector, rather than social class. Method of defining class – the social grade schema, similar to market research categories, based upon consumption patterns. Effect of negative equity: decline in significance of the consumption sector, greater class alignment.

working class, and this group is likely to expand in future years. Again according to Crewe, since 1970, voters' party choices have become more closely associated with their positions on a range of issues.

Mark Franklin (1985) has provided the clearest statement on issue voting and class dealignment. In his study, Franklin argues that there has been a significant decline in class alignment since 1964. Moreover, as class dealignment has become more common among the electorate, issue voting has become of much greater significance. However, unlike many researchers in this area, Franklin is very clear on what he understands by class voting and he explains, why he believes that 'Butler and Stokes were able to write about the 1964 General Election mainly from the perspective of social class, while Sarvik and Crewe were able to write about the 1979 General Election mainly from the perspective of issues' (Franklin, 1985: 4).

Franklin builds a model of class voting derived from Butler and Stokes, which identifies the following indicators of working-class identity: parental party as Labour, working-class occupation, living in a rented home, parents in the working class, union membership, and leaving school at the minimum school-leaving age. Franklin traces the declining significance of each of these indices since 1964. The number of people living in the rented sector has declined, the number of trade unionists has declined, the number of working-class occupations has declined; the school-leaving age has increased and the number of people staying on at school after the minimum school-leaving age has significantly increased.

However, some criticism can be made of the social grade schema, which is the concept of class used by Crewe. The social grade schema originated in the annual report of the Registrar General (1911), and it consisted of five hierarchical grades. Under the influence of Research Services Limited in the 1950s, this was modified into a sixfold categorisation (A, B, C1, C2, D and E) of occupations. Unskilled manual workers are in group E and professionals in group A.

No research has been carried out to show whether or not this conception of class reflects the structure of classes in society. Critics could call them 'arbitrary market research categories' rather than a class system. Outside the area of voting behaviour, the social grade schema is not used by any reputable social scientist, perhaps because this way of defining 'class' takes the family as its unit of analysis, not the individual. This is a polite way of saying that the social grade schema ignores women, and assumes that all people in the household have the same social class position as the oldest male. Not only is this sexist, but it ignores the fact that, according to Marshall's Essex Mobility Study (1988), up to fifty per cent of people live in cross-class marriages. In other words, half of married people have a partner with an occupation in a different social class.

People who use the social grade schema have left themselves open to the criticism that the class dealignment thesis is a product of attempts to determine the relationship between voting and class with faulty measurement devices.

In addition, we might also want to cast doubt upon some of the assumptions behind the concept of 'issue voting'. It is assumed that the issue voter is a rational voter who attempts to get maximum personal benefit for minimum outlay. In other words, the rational voter is a 'rational utility maximiser'. According to Crewe, voters assign more weight to their own affluence than they do to impersonal issues or difficulties. This is clearly based upon the assumption by Anthony Downes (1957) that rational individuals have the following characteristics:

- They can always make a decision when confronted with a range of alternatives
- They can rank alternatives in order of preference
- These preferences are logically consistent
- The choice is always from the highest preference available
- They always make the same decision when confronted with the same alternatives

One problem in this type of analysis is the question of why people vote for parties when it is not in their financial interest to do so. Many working-class people voted Conservative in the 1980s when that party had a policy of raising money from VAT rather than income tax. Similarly, why do middle-class people vote for Labour, why do people vote for the Green Party?

The major problem with this analysis is rational abstention. In other words, the rational voter knows that the effect of one vote is very small, and the cost of going to vote will always outweigh the benefit of voting. It is always rational for the rational voter not to vote, and to let others bear the cost of voting.

In the 1980s, Heath et al. (1985 and 1991) conducted the British Election Surveys, and attempted to show that social class was still the most important factor in determining how people vote. Building upon the research of John Goldthorpe, they redefined social class, claiming that the working class made up about 34 per cent of the population. In addition, they made a distinction between absolute class voting and relative class voting. Absolute class voting is the total number of working-class people voting Labour, and this has declined at each election from 1966 to 1983, with slight increases in 1987 and 1992, and a significant increase in 1997. Relative class voting is the strength of Labour support within the working class. Absolute class voting has declined, but relative class voting has shown 'trendless fluctuation'; this is because the number of people within the working class is getting smaller at each election, but the remaining working-class people continue to vote Labour. Heath et al. claim that this means that no significant class dealignment has taken place.

In addition, Heath and his team cast doubt upon the notion of electoral volatility. In 1984, Crewe had argued:

> As partisan and class ardour cooled, however, considerations other than habitual party and class loyalties began to influence the voting decisions of more and more electors. In particular, campaign-specific factors – the outgoing government's record, the major issues of the day, the party leaders' personal qualities, specific and perhaps quite trivial incidents – took on a greater significance. Judging from the opinion polls, the three-to-four week campaign has had a stronger impact in recent years. Moreover, even the votes of those adhering to their usual party in the campaign are prone to waver more. Between 1964 and 1979 the proportion of voters who left their final voting decision until the campaign jumped from 17 per cent to 28 per cent. In addition, the proportion claiming to have thought seriously of voting differently in the course of the campaign rose from 24 per cent to 31 per cent. The committed electorate has begun to make way for the hesitant electorate. (Crewe, 1984: 203–4)

According to Heath et al. what Crewe is suggesting here is a theory about the changing psychology of the vote. This, together with the declining solidarity of class and class cultures, has created very high levels of electoral volatility. However, most of the volatility has been into or out of non-voting. Heath et al. argue that most of this non-voting is 'forced non-voting', caused by ill health, death or other factors outside the control of the individual voter. Heath et al. found that 81 per cent of the people who voted in both the 1983 and the 1987 elections voted for the same party on both occasions, leaving only 19 per cent who voted for different parties at each election.

The level of volatility, then, was much lower than Crewe had suggested. But what had caused the volatility that did exist? Heath et al. point to the following *political* changes:

- The increase in the number of Liberal-SDP and nationalist parties standing was one such change. Clearly, the more opportunity people have to vote for different parties, the more volatility one would expect to find
- Policies were changing within the two major parties; major changes in policy on issues such as nuclear weapons or in leadership may enhance volatility

However, by way of critique of Crewe, Heath et al. point out that between 1964 and 1970 there was no significant increase in volatility, and between 1974 and 1987 there was no significant increase in volatility. The big increase in electoral volatility took place while Crewe was responsible from the British Election Survey, between 1970 and 1979. During this time, there were a number of significant changes in the wording of various questions asked of the sample. For example, in 1964, people were asked: 'How long ago did you decide to vote that way?' This rather open-ended question was changed in 1974 to the more closed question: 'How long ago did you decide that you would <u>definitely</u> vote the way you did – a long time ago, some time this year, or during the campaign?' (cited in Heath et al. 1991 p. 14). The word definitely was underlined in the survey question. Again, in 1964, the following question was asked: 'Did you think of voting for any other party?' This was changed in 1974 to 'Was there any time during the election campaign when you <u>seriously</u> [original underlining] thought you might vote for another party?' (cited in Heath et al. 1991 p. 15).

Heath et al. conclude: 'There is a serious danger that the change is artifactual.' (Heath et al. 1991 p. 15). In other words, it is likely that the increase in volatility that Crewe found was a consequence of the change in the questions asked.

All of the theories of voting behaviour assume that forces outside their control, such as class or rationality, drive people. We might want to argue that people's behaviour is not determined, and that voting is a question of choice.

1997 British election survey

Tony Blair appeals to the middle class ... but no more than he does to the working class.

Historically, the Labour party has widely been regarded as a working class party. It was founded by the trade unions in 1900 in order to increase the number of working people in parliament. But it is often argued that one of the Labour party's successes since 1992 has been to widen its appeal amongst the middle class.

Labour's support undoubtedly rose amongst the middle class during the last parliament. But equally it rose amongst all groups in society. The key question is whether Labour support rose more in the middle class than the working class.

At first glance it looks as though it did. Between 1992 and the spring of 1995, when the Conservatives were at the height of their unpopularity, there was a 21 point swing from the Conservatives to Labour amongst those in salaried professional and managerial occupations. In contrast there was only an 11-point swing amongst those in the working class.

But these swing figures are potentially misleading. Conservative support was more than 20 points lower in the working class than amongst those in salaried occupations in 1992. This means it was almost impossible for there to be a 21-point swing against the Conservatives in the working class, it would mean there were hardly any Conservatives left in the working class at all!

Statistical analysis of the panel suggests that once this is allowed for, those in salaried occupations were not significantly more likely to have defected from the Conservatives after 1992 than those in the working class. All kinds of Conservatives switched at more or less the same rate.

(http://www.bbc.co.uk/election97/polls/jcbeps3.htm)

In their comparative analysis of the political and ideological importance of social class in Britain and the USA, Joseph Gerteis and Mike Savage (1998) make use of the Comparative Project on Class Structure and Class Consciousness. First, they examined the relationship between class and political identification in Britain and the USA, taking into account a range of socio-economic factors. Second, they investigated whether differences in political identification are related to the weaker significance of class in the USA, or whether the US political system reduces the impact of class on political mobilisation.

Gerteis and Savage (1998) measured an individual's class position by using Goldthorpe's class schema, but they also took into account sex, race and age. They show that class divisions are much more significant in Britain in terms of people's political choices. In the USA in contrast, social class is less significant in shaping political choice, but is still a significant factor in industrial relations. Gerteis and Savage (1998) found that people who earned money from investments were much more likely to be right-wing in both Britain and the USA. In Britain, employment divisions translate into political identification; in the USA, this is not the case. One possible explanation suggested by Bellah et al. (1996) for the limited significance of social class in the USA is the strength of US individualism. A possible consequence of this, claims Gerteis and Savage (1998), is the tendency of Americans from very different socio-economic backgrounds to define themselves as middle class. Devine (1997) points out that only 27% of Americans define themselves as working class. However, this may be due to the wording on questionnaires.

The 2001 general election

On June 7th 2001, Prime Minister Tony Blair entered the history books by winning Labour a second term. Over the four-week campaign period there were very few highlights, except for an incident involving a punch up between Deputy Prime Minister John Prescott and an egg-throwing protestor. The turnout for the election was 58%, the lowest for eighty years. Most of the post election discussion was centred on the possible reasons for the apathy. The Electoral Commission, in their initial report on the election argued that only politicians could break voter apathy.

Current state of the parties in the House of Commons

Party	Seats	Vote %
Labour	412	40.69
Conservative	166	31.70
Liberal Democrat	52	18.21
Ulster Unionist	6	0.82
Scottish Nationalist Party	5	1.76
DUP	5	0.69
Plaid Cymru	4	0.74
Sinn Fein	4	0.66
SDLP	3	0.64
Richard Taylor independent	1	0.10
Michael Martin, Speaker	1	0.06
UK Independence Party	-	1.48
Green	-	0.63

On 8 June 2001, the Conservative Party leader, William Hague, resigned as leader of the Party mainly because the Conservatives had made little headway since 1997 Initially, five candidates stood for the Conservative leadership; Ancram, Michael, Clarke, Ken, Davis, David, Duncan-Smith, Iain, Portillo, Michael

Ken Clarke and Iain Duncan-Smith were selected by Conservative MPs to appear on the short list from which party members would choose the leader. Iain Duncan-Smith won with 61 percent of the vote. However, there were some complaints about the new leadership election arrangements and it is unlikely that they will be used again.

The decline of social class – the postmodern condition

The Industrial Revolution brought with it what many sociologists consider to be clear and coherent classes. These classes were said to affect all aspects of life chances, to be a key factor in the formation of a person's identity and to determine people's thought, culture and ideas. However, class analysis has a tendency to point to the consequences of class and assume that this is sufficient justification for the existence of class. For postmodernists, it is not. Class analysis involves the invention of a set of analytical categories that are imposed on the world. To say that education failure or ill health is a consequence of class, or that there are class differences in child-rearing practices, is to make some questionable assumptions. It is to say that, like the pinball in a pinball machine, what people do and why they do it, is not of their own making or of their own choosing. In other words, it is to say that agency is exercised through the individual by some outside force, namely, the class structure. Class analysis is built upon the defective presumption that people are driven by forces outside their control. But it is people who fail in the education system; it is people who suffer from ill health; and it is parents who bring up children, not classes. Every social action has an intention behind it; and every social action has a number of alternatives. You as an individual person make choices, and all choices have consequences. Some of the consequences may be foreseen; some may be unforeseen.

Let us start by looking at the bourgeoisie. According to Peter Gay in his *Pleasure Wars: The Bourgeois Experience, Victoria to Freud* (1998), the definition of the Victorian bourgeoisie depended as much on self-perceptions as it did on economic facts. Even in the nineteenth century, the term 'bourgeois' was both elusive and used inconsistently. Gay attempts to contrast the character of the bourgeoisie in the four cities of Manchester, Munich, Paris and Vienna. The bourgeoisie in these four cities differed in their attitudes, aspirations, taste, patronage and power. If we look at the bourgeois class culture in relation to literature, music and the visual arts, we can find no equivalent of the Halle Orchestra or the Whitworth Gallery in Munich, Paris or Vienna. Not only were there distinctions in terms of class cultures, but, more importantly, the bourgeoisie differed in its composition across Europe. In France, there was a distinct *petite bourgeoisie*; in Germany, a *Großbürgertum*, *Mittelstand* and *Kleinbürgertum*. In England, there was no *haute bourgeoisie*, an urban bourgeoisie passing on inherited wealth and prosperity across several generations, as found in many European societies, except for the Chamberlains and the Kenricks in Birmingham.

Classes are always made up of countless individuals with differing tastes and temperaments. As there was no class culture among the bourgeoisie across Europe, so there was no working-class culture. The working classes did not spend all their time in the pub and music hall and breeding pigeons. Instead of the Marxist concept that ideas, in this case, in the form of a distinct class culture, are formed within the superstructure and determined by the forces and relations of production which make up the economic base, ideas are independent of any economic determining factor. There never was a class culture because there never was a class. There were only ever individual human agents drawing upon their own distinct skills, abilities and resources to make a life for themselves; constructing and drawing upon different tastes, styles and fashions, to fit in with their own ideas, attitudes and beliefs about life and how to lead it.

Sociology was invented to make sense of this modern industrial society of the nineteenth century. The 'social' that sociology attempted to describe and explain was believed to be both class based and class determined. The question was, which form of class analysis provided the most informed conclusion? On the one hand, there was the economic analysis of Marx, in which class was a product of the labour theory of value. On the other hand there was the more market-oriented class analysis of Weber, in which class was a product of 'market situation' and 'work situation'. In the twentieth century, class analysis continued to provide not just the explanatory framework for sociology, but its conceptual backbone. Even today, many researchers write books and papers about the salience of class, including John Goldthorpe, Fiona Devine, Mike Savage, Gordon Marshall, Rosemary Crompton and John Scott, to name but a few. However, for the post-modernist, the notion of class is redundant as a conceptual device that enables us to make sense of the contemporary world.

As we argued in Area 3, the bonds of social class decline in significance for people within the postmodern condition. In other words, social class relations do not determine how people organise their lives. Most sociological theories of social class assume that there is some form of common values, or sharing of ideas and ways of living within a social class. Marxists, for example, assume that working-class people are victims of false consciousness; by this, we understand that working-class people have ideas placed in their heads by the ruling class. This set of implanted ideas, which we term 'ideology', does not support the eco-nomic interests of working-class people. The notion that people have their ideas determined is undermined in the postmodern condition, in which individuals have to create their own thoughts and their own bonds of community. In contrast to most sociologists and Marxists in particular, postmodernists believe that class is dead and that we live in a post-class society.

We have seen the emergence of a 'new' middle class, or 'service' class, which is made up of 'professionals', often social and cultural specialists, who are cul-turally, but not necessarily financially, privileged. In addition, to this emergence of this 'new' middle class, the working class has 'fragmented'.

Malcolm Waters (1997), whom we discussed in Area 3, is relevant again here. As you may recall, Waters argued that the stratification system is moving from a class-based economic system to a culturalist or status-conventional phase. This social transformation is part of the movement from modernity to postmodernity. According to Waters, the status-conventional form of stratification is based upon the following four concepts:

○ Culturalism – lifestyle choices, aesthetic preferences and value commitments
○ Fragmentation – shifting and unstable associations
○ Autonomisation – in contrast to the concept of the 'rational voter', the disap-pearance of ordered nature of such preferences .
○ Resignification – the constant change of subject interest, choice and emotion, regenerating people's feelings and fears of distress, abuse and desire

What is significant about these changes that Waters outlines is that 'occupation' is now only significant as a 'badge' of status that indicates a person's ability to enjoy the finer things of life. Occupation is no more important than our 'consump-tion status', our ability to demonstrate to others that we can fully appreciate the finer things.

Postmodern stratification – the '*globals*' and the '*locals*'

In *Globalization: The Human Consequences* (1998), Bauman shows that the postmodern world is a stratified one. However, it is consumption, not production, that provides the foundation for stratification. In addition, stratification is a 'caste-bound experience' (Bauman, 1998: 101), and postmodern cities are described as '*apartheid à rebours*'. Bauman's discussion of stratification is built upon an earlier essay on the nature of identity in the postmodern world.

Within modernity, life had a secure and logical feel. In contrast, postmodernity is the form of society we are left with when the process of modernisation is complete, human behaviour has little or no direct dealing with nature and we live in a fashioned or manufactured environment. In the postmodern condition, the world has an abandoned, and unprotected feel for the individual human agent.

According to Bauman (1996), identity was a modern innovation. In the modern world, the problem of identity was a problem of how to construct and maintain our identity in an effort to secure our place in the world and avoid uncertainty. The creation of modern identity is seen as a pilgrimage. Without our pilgrimage to a secure identity, we may become lost in the desert. In the first instance, on our journey to a fixed identity, we need a place to walk to. This is our life project, which ideally should be established early in life and be used to make sense of the various uncertainties, fragments and divisions of experience which make up the post-traditional world. In other words, by creating a fixed and secure identity, we attempt to make the world more ordered and more predictable for ourselves.

In contrast, in the postmodern world, the problem of identity is one of avoiding a fixed identity and keeping our options open by avoiding long-term commitments, consistency and devotion. In place of a life project established as early as possible that we loyally keep to, postmodern people choose to have a series of short projects which are not fixed. The world seems to be a continuous present. The world is no longer agreeable to pilgrims. In place of that of the pilgrim, there are a number of other lifestyles that emerge: those of the stroller, the vagabond, the tourist and the player. These lifestyles are not new to the postmodern world, but whereas in previous times marginal people in marginal situations practised these lifestyles, they are now common to the majority of people in many situations.

As we saw in Area 3, the pilgrim has been replaced by the following four successors that represent postmodern life strategies:

- The stroller or *flâneur*
- The vagabond
- The tourist
- The player

In the postmodern world, we are all cast into the role of consumers; however, not all of us have the resources to be effective consumers. Some of us are 'tourists' and our choices are 'global', whereas some of us are 'vagabonds' and are cast in the role of 'flawed consumers' whereby we are forced to live as 'locals': in 'the world of the globally mobile, the space has lost its constraining quality and is easily traversed in both its "real" and "virtual" renditions … [in] the world of the "locally tied", of those barred from moving and thus bound to bear passively whatever change may be visited on the locality they are tied to, the real space is fast closing up' (Bauman, 1998: 88).

In other words, the globals enjoy their travel. Such global travel is a key element in postmodern freedom. Whereas the locals travel very little, are often illegally arrested and deported, wherever they go they are unwelcome. This local experience is postmodern slavery.

Sociological theories of class, then, are derived from either Marx or Weber, both of whom assumed that classes have causal power over life chances and are the only significant component in the construction of individual identity.

For the postmodernist, in the traditional sociological analyses of class, the fundamental problems are 'passed off' as 'the boundary problem'. The boundaries between classes are arbitrary, moralistic and totally lacking in any real foundation. There is no class culture, no class solidarity; class has no role in the formation of identity. The concepts that we find at the foundation of class analysis are unable to generate coherent classes. What we have, in effect, are individual human agents, with skills and abilities competing within a labour market for resources to construct a life for themselves. 'Occupation' is only significant as a 'badge' of status in the status bazaar of the labour market. Class is a set of conceptual instruments that have no reality outside the minds of the people who use them.

Area Summary

The literature on class and voting behaviour can be summarised as follows. Traditionally, it was assumed that people voted on the basis of social class. Middle-class people who voted Labour and working-class people who voted Conservative were said to be 'deviant' voters. In the 1970s, working-class people were said to have lost the taste for class-based politics, and this was reflected most clearly in the work of Ivor Crewe. By 1985, Heath and his colleagues were suggesting that class was still a significant factor in determining how people vote. In contrast, postmodernists would take issue with the idea that people's behaviour is determined, and with the notion of class.

continued

One of the most interesting things about doing research on voting behaviour is that in many respects all you need is an outline of election results to do informative and stimulating research. An outline of the British election results from 1945 to 1997 can be found at the following web site: http://www.gn.apc.org/ers/page2.htm.

References

Bauman, Z. (1996) 'From pilgrim, to tourist – or a short history of identity', in S. Hall and P. Du Gay (eds.), *Questions of Cultural Identity*. London: Sage. pp. 18–36.

Bauman, Z. (1998) *Globalization: The Human Consequences*. Cambridge: Polity.

Bellah, R., Sullivan, W.M., Swidler, A. and Tipton, S. (1996) *Habits of the Heart: Individualism and Commitment in American Life*. Berkeley: University of California.

Best, S. (1997) 'Power and Politics', in Nik Jorgensen (eds), *Sociology: An Interactive approach*. London: Collins Educational.

Best, S., Griffiths, J. and Hope, T. (2000) *'Active Sociology'*. Harlow: Longman.

Butler, D.E. and Stokes, D. (1969) *Political Change in Britain*. London: Macmillan.

Butler, D. and Kavanagh, D. (1984) *The British General Election of 1983*. London: Macmillan.

Butler, D. and Kavanagh, D. (1987) *The British General Election of 1987*. London: Macmillan.

Capdevielle, J. and Dupirier, E. (1981) 'L'effet patrimoine' in J. Capdevielle *France de Gauche vote a Droite*. Paris: Presses de la FNSP, pp. 169–230.

Campbell, B. (1987) *Iron Ladies*. London: Virago.

Crewe, I. (1984) *British Parliamentary Constituencies: A Statistical Compendium*. London: Faber and Faber.

Crewe, I. (1992) 'Why did Labour lose (yet again)?', *Politics Review*, (September).

Denver, D. (1989) *Elections and Voting Behaviour in Britain*. London: Phillip Allen.

Devine, F. (1997) *Social Class in Britain and America*. Edinburgh: Edinburgh University Press.

Dunleavy, P. (1980) 'The political implications of sectoral cleavages and the growth of state employment' Part I: 'The analysis of production cleavages', *Political Studies*, 28: 364–83: Part II: 'Cleavage structures and political alignment' *Political Studies*, 28: 527–49.

Dunleavy, P. and Husbands, C.T. (1985) *British Democracy at the Crossroads*. London: Allen and Unwin.

Downes, A. (1957) *An Economic Theory of Democracy*. New York: Harper and Row.

Franklin, M. (1985) *The Decline of Class Voting*. Oxford: Clarendon Press.

Gay, P. (1998) *Pleasure Wars: The Bourgeois Experience, Victoria to Freud*. London: Harper Collins.

Gerteis, J. and Savage, M. (1998) 'The salience of class in Britain and America: a comparative analysis', *British Journal of Sociology*, 49(2).

Goldthorpe, J.H., et al. (1987) *Social Mobility and Class Structure in Modern Britain*. Oxford: Clarendon Press.

Goldthorpe, J.H. and Lockwood, D., Jowell, R., Evans, G., and Witherspoon, Field, J.(1969) *The Affluent Worker*. Cambridge: Cambridge University Press.

Heath, A., Jowell, R. and Curtice, J. (1985) *How Britain Votes*. Oxford: Pergamon.

Heath, A., Jowell, R. and Curtice, J., et al. (1991) *Understanding Political Change*. Oxford: Pergamon.

Jones, N. (1997) Campaign. London: Indigo.

Johnstone, R.J., et al. (1988) *A Nation Dividing?* Harlow: Longman.

Kellner, P. (1997) 'The 1997 general election', http://www.bbc.co.uk/politicvs97/analysis.

Kirby, M. (1995) *Investigating Political Sociology*. London: Collins Educational.

Marshall, G., et al. (1988) *Social Class in Modern Britain*. London: Hutchinson.

Miller, W. (1990) *How Votes Change: The 1987 British Election Campaign in Perspective*. Oxford: Clarendon Press.

Pulzer, P.G. (1967) *Political Representation and Elections in Britain*. London: Allen and Unwin.

Rallings, C. and Thrasher (1997) 'Housing and voting' *Sunday Times*, 4 May, pp. 23.

Rose, R. (1992) *Politics in England: Change and Persistence*. Basingstoke: Macmillan.

Rose, R. and McAllister, I. (1986) *Voters Begin to Choose: From Closed Class to Open Elections in Britain*. London: Sage.

Rose, R. and McAllister, I. (1990) *The Loyalties of Voters: A Lifetime Learning Model*. London: Sage.

Waters, M. (1997) 'Inequality after class', in D. Owen (ed.), *Sociology after Postmodernism*. London: Sage.

Index

Abercombie, N. 84, 104, 120
Adie, Kate 216
Adorno, Theodore 30
Ahmad, Eqbal 210
AIDS 44, 192
Aid 175–177
Albrow, Martin 14
allegory 43
Alter, P. 168–169
American Civil War 218
Amnesty International 220
Angelou, Maya 12
Appadurai, Arjun 185
Arab Organisation for Human Rights 220
Aruri, Naseer 220
Ashdown, Paddy 239, 244
Ashley, David 33–34, 48, 200–201
assignments 2–3
ATSS foreword, 11
authority 6, 10, 12–39, 68

Ba'ath Party 215, 221
Bagguley, Paul 147, 150, 158
balkanisation 24–25
Barnes, Barry 120, 130
Bartelson, Jens 198
Baudrillard, Jean 4, 43, 52–53, 84–86, 209,
    219, 226–228
Bauman, Zygmunt 1, 5, 18–19, 22, 41, 44–46,
    48–50, 52–55, 57–58, 60, 63–68, 87, 133,
    266–267
Beck, Ulrich 152–153, 161
Bell, Martin 239
Bellah, Robert 263
Beng-Huat Chua 101

Benn, Tony 117
Bennis, Phyllis 221
Bentham, Jeremy 21
Bessel, Richard 10–11
Best, Shaun 5, 38, 65, 77, 95, 190–191
Best, Steven 64, 73, 77
Bienefeld, Manfred 188, 193
Blair Project, The 3
Blair, Tony 69, 71, 100, 117, 120, 122, 124,
    239, 242–247
Blumer, H. 145
Boulding, Elise 216
Brezhnev doctrine 214
British Election Survey 245–247, 256,
    257–258
Brock-Utne, Birdgit 216
Brodie, Bernard 212–213
Bruce, Steve 28
Bush, George 219–223
Butler, David and Kavanagh, Dennis 256
Butler, Davis and Stokes, Donald 259
Brzezinski, Zbigniew 221

Callinicos, Alec 78, 92–94
Camp 43
Campbell, Bea 253
Capderville, J. and Dupoirier, E. 256–257
Capgras' syndrome 44
capitalism 7, 41, 120
Capra, Fritj 153
Carter, Angela 21–22
Castells, Manuel 253
Childrens Act (UK), The 9
Chirac, Jacques 177
Chomsky, Noam 209, 221

citizenship 106
CJD 43
class alignment 238–239, 248
class dealignment 236, 238, 248–249
Clausewitz, C. 209–210
Clinton, Bill 71, 100
Coates, David 84, 104, 120
Cockerham, William 170
coercion 10
Cohn, Carol 217
Cold War 215, 233
colonialism 169, 187
Communist Party of Great Britain 110
Communitarianism 3, 120–128
Connor, Steven 43
Conservative Party 105, 113, 134–141, 255
    National Union of 137
    Reform of 139–141
consumption-sector cleavage 236, 253–256
Contact Group 215
Cook, Robin 243
Cooley, Charles 100
Cooperative Party 116
Cox, Robert 187
Crewe, Ivor 247–248, 254–255, 258–259,
    260–262
Crook, S. 33, 38, 197–198
Crowley, D. 174–175
cultural globalisation 185

Dahl, Robert 107–109, 160
Dahrendorf, Ralph 131–132
Day, G. and Robbins, D. 150
de Cuellar, Perez 225
De Gaulle, General 114
Delanty, Gerard 152
Deleuze, Gilles 209
Deleuze and Guattari foreword,
    47, 228–229, 231
demographic change 196
Demos 127
Denver, David 248
Devine, Fiona 263
devolution in the UK 142
Diani, Mario 155–156
disorganised capitalism 42, 146, 148–149, 202
Dobson, Andrew 153–154
Downes, Anthony 260
Dunleavy, Patrick 253–254, 285
Durkheim, Emile 128, 151
Duverger, Maurice 105, 112, 114

eclecticism 43
education 192
Education Reform Act 1988 (UK) 64
Einstein, Albert 216
Eisler, Riane 216

electoral volatility 236, 238, 261–262
end of history 68, 185, 190
Engels, Friedrich 79
Enlightenment 20–21, 24, 128, 153
environment 194–195
Environmental Movement 153–155
epistemological insecurity 3–4
epistemological uncertainty 43
ethnic cleansing 215
Etzioni, Amitai 105, 121, 124, 127–128, 130
European Union 168, 215
Eyerman, R. and Jamison, A. 146

Fabian Socialism 119
Fanon, Frantz 193
Featherstone, Mike 42, 62
Feher, Ferenc 68–69
Feminism 40, 42, 56,
filicide 216
Finkelstein, Joanne 9, 38
Finer, S.E. 134–135
flaneur 49
Ford, Henry 199
Fordism 200
Fosler, Scott 196
Foster-Carter, Aidan 193
Foucault, Michel 6, 20–22, 35, 48–49,
    73, 156
Fox-Keller, Evelyn 217
Frankel, Boris 152, 160
Franklin, Mark 259
Freedman, Lawrence 218–219
Freud, Sigmund 30, 38, 180, 216
Fukuyama, Francis 166, 185, 190–191
functionalism 40, 42

Gaia hypothesis 153
Garfinkel, Harold 180
Gay, Peter 264
Gay Times 157
Geller, Ernest 64
General Agreement on Tariffs and Trade
    (GATT) 175
George, Vic and Wilding, Paul 136
Gerteis, Joseph and Savage, Mike 263
Gershung, Jonathan 130
Giddens, Anthony 4, 6–9, 38, 41, 53, 78, 105,
    109, 122–124, 126, 129, 145, 161–163,
    166–170, 209
    agency and structure 178–185
    critique of Marxism 97, 189
    nationalism 88–89
    reflexive modernisation 4, 184
    war 230–233
Gilbert, A. and Guyler, J. 193
globalisation 166–208
Glover, Edward 216

Goffman, Erving 14, 38, 129
  total institutions 14–15
  frame 149
Goldsmith, Sir James 60–62
Goldthorpe, John, H. 252, 261
Gramsci, Antonio 36, 38, 83–84, 120, 186
Gradard, Stephen, G. 219
Greenhouse, Carol 217
Gulf War 198, 209, 216, 219–220
Gunder-Frank, Andre 209, 216, 222–225

Habermas, Jurgen 6, 22–24, 25–27, 38, 69,
    73, 132–133, 145, 158–159
Hables-Gray, Chris 229–230
Hague, William 137–141
Hall, John, A. 87–88
Hall, S. and Du Gay 101
Hall, S. and Jacques, M. 146
Hamilton, Neil 240
Hannerz, Ulf 168
Hardie, Keir 115
Harding, Sandra 217
Harvey, David 166, 198
Haseler, Stephen 135
Hayter, Tersea 176
Heath, Anthony 263, 256–258
Hebdige, Dick 87
Held, David 30, 38, 163, 166–168, 177
Heller, Agnes 68–69
Henley, Andrew 256
Hicks, Bill 228
Hoggart, Richard 72
Hoogvelt, Ankie 198
Horsman and Marshall 172
Houghton, Peter 131
Hintze, Otto 36, 38
Hirst, Paul 109–111
Holocaust 18–19, 46, 54
Holt, Robert 217
Horton, Michael 48
Hussein, Sadam 215–216, 219–220, 224

identity 48–52, 71, 101, 147–148, 168–169
IMF 176, 187
limited war 218–219
industrialism 7, 41
interfarda 225
Iran-Iraq War 220–221
Iraq 220, 222
irony 43
Irving, David 10, 38
issue voting 236, 238

Jameson, Fredric 72, 78, 89–92
japanisation 171
Jefferson, Thomas 129
Jenkins, Roy 131

Johnston, RJ 253
Jones, Nicolas 243
Jordan, Tim 156

KLA 215
Karmal, Babrak 214
Kaufman, Will 228
Kavanagh, Dennis 134–135
Kellner, Peter 240, 242
Keynes, John Maynard 199
Khmer Rouge 213
King, Roger 35, 38
Kinnock, Neil 117, 242
Kirby, Mark 147, 169, 239
Kirchheimer, Otto 105, 112, 114–115
kitsch 43
Kohl, Helmut 242
Korean War 219
Koro syndrome 44
Kosovo 214–215
Kurds 220
Kuwait 22, 219, 225–226

Labour Party 72, 105, 112–113, 115–131,
    160, 252
Laclau, Ernest and Mouffe, Chantal
    72, 89
Lang, K. and Lang, G. 146
Lash, Scott and Urry, John 148, 200, 202
Laski, Harold 212
Lees, Tony 245
Le Grand, Julian 135–136
Lenin, V. 187, 169, 212
Liberal Democracy 131, 133–4
Liberal Democrats 105
Liberal Party 131
Lifetime of learning model 249–253
Lindblom, Charles 108–109, 111
Locke, John 211
Lukes, Steven 7, 38
Lyotard, Jean-Francois 33, 38, 41, 55–56,
    61–62, 75, 91, 159

McAllister-Groves, Julian 149–150
McCarthy and Zald 155
McDonaldisation 201
MacEwan, Arthur 186
MacIntyre, Alasdair 130
Macmurray, John 105, 124–125
McCullagh and O'Dowd 28, 38
Major, John 112, 137, 239, 243
McKenzie, Robert 105, 112–114
Malcolm, Nole 214–215
Mann, Michael 35, 38, 186, 191
Mannheim, Karl 78, 94–95
Marris, Peter 47
Marshall, Gordon 260

Marshall, T.H. 106–107
Marx, Karl 76–80, 151
Marx, K. and Engels 148
Marxism 40–42, 59–60, 79, 119, 154
    contrast with elite theory 99
    conception of power 78–104, 105–106
    critique of pluralism 109
    globalisation 186
    ideology 82–83, 110, 119
    labour theory of value 80–81, 92
    mode of production 79
    strength of 81
    weakness of 81
Mason, Angela 157
Mayo, Elton 203
Mburugu, Edward 196
Mead, G.H. 129
meaning 47
Mestrovic, Stjepan, G. 24, 38
Michels, Robert 15, 38, 79, 105, 112–113
Miliband, Ralph 83, 109, 119, 159
military 7, 41, 99
Mill, J.S. 211
Miller, William 236–237
Millis, Walter 212
Mills, Charles Wright 78, 99–101
Milosevic, Slobodan 212, 215
Mintzberg, Henry 17, 38
Modernisation 170
Modernism 50
Modernity 40–41, 45–46, 50, 54, 68, 90, 92,
    123, 183
Money-Kyrle, Roger, E. 216
Mosca, Gaetano 78, 98–99
Muligan, David 127
Murphy, Alexander 211
Murry, Robin 186, 199

Naess, Arne 153
Najib, Mohammed 214
national identity 8
nationalism 88–89, 168–169
National Republican Union 114
Nazis 10–11, 18–19, 46
neo-colonialism 170, 187
neo-medieval 52
new cultural intermediaries' 42
New Deal 126–127
New Right ideology 111–112
new social movements 3, 15–16, 51–2, 69,
    82, 145–165, 172
new world order 209, 219, 221–222
Nordlinger, Eric 36, 38, 186
Norris, Christopher 86, 97, 227–228
North Atlantic Treaty Organisation
    (NATO) 168
Northern Ireland 27–29

Norton, Philip 134
Notestein, Frank 196

Oberai, AS 195
OECD 187
Offe, Claus 148
old social movements 52, 69, 145, 147,
    159–160
oligarchy 79
    iron law of 97–98, 112–113
Ono, Shin'Ya 109
ontological plurality 3, 43
OPEC 131, 190
organisations 16–17
Orwell, George 191
Outrage 156–158
Owen, David 131

Panama, US invasion of 233
Panitch, Leo 187
Pareto, Vilfredo 78, 98
Paisley, Ian Rev. 28–29
parody 43
Parsons, Talcott 54, 170–171
    on power 106
People's Action Party (Singapore) 101
People's Democratic Party of
    Afghanistan 213
    Babrak 213
    Khalq 213
Piore, M. and Sabel, C. 200
Pizzorno, A. 115, 144
pluralism 3, 9, 105, 107–110
Poggi, G. 35, 38
political parties 111
Pollock, Gary 200
polyarchy 105, 107–110, 160, 231
Portillo, Michael 239
post-fordism 15, 199–200
postmodernists 3, 59–60
postmodernism 40–44
    Best and Kellner critique of 73
    class 263–267
    disetatisation 197
    Giddens critique of 74–75
    Marxist critique of 72
    New Right critique of 73
    War 229
postmodernity 53–55, 68, 110
postmodernization 112
Post-communism 87–88
Poulantzas, Nicos 83, 119
Powell, Colin
Powell, Enoch 136
power 8, 41, 45
Prishtina 215
Pulzer, Peter 255–256

Queer Culture 156–158

Rabinow, Paul 20, 38
Rallings, Colin and Thrasher, Michael 256
Ramsbotham, Oliver 219–220
Randinelli DA and Kasanda JP 193
Rascorsky, Arnoldo 216
Raskovic, J. 5, 25, 38
Reardon, Betty 216
Reich, Robert 188
Renaissance 44
rhizome 47, 229
Ritzer, George 167, 201–202
Roach, Colleen 216
Robertson, Roland 166–167, 178–180
Robins, Kevin 101
Rodgers, Bill 131
Rodney, Walter 170
Rorty, Richard 64, 78, 95–96, 128
Rose, Richard 248
Rose, Richard and McAllister, Ian
    249–252
Rostow, W.W. 170–171
Roth, Guenther 19
Rousseau, J.J. 211
Roxborough, Ian 209–210

Sandel, Michael 130
Sarvik, B. and Crewe, I. 259
schlock 43
Schutz, Alfred 181
Schwarz and Schwarz 153–154
Scottish Parliament 142
Sennett, Richard 6, 14, 29–32, 38, 70–71,
    127–128, 199
Shiites 214
simulacrum 43, 90
Sklair, Leslie 167–168
Skocpol, Theda 36, 38, 186
sleaze 239, 243–244
Smelser, Neil 149
Smith, A.D. 194
Smith, John 117
Snow, Donald, M. and Drew, Dennis, M. 218
social 45
social action 8, 32
social class, decline of 56–57
Social Democratic Party 131
Social Democracy 119, 131–133
Socialism 41, 56–60
Spice Girls 45
Star Trek 190–191
state 6, 8, 20, 41, 54, 78, 120, 186
    disetatisation 197
    postmodern conception of 32–34
state-centred theorists 6, 35–37, 186
Stones, Rob 42

Sunni Muslims 214
surveillance 7
Sztompka, Piotr 145–146

Tatchell, Peter 157
Taylor, Charles 130
Taylor, Frederick 15, 199
Thatcher, Margaret 111, 113, 134
Thatcherism 84, 134–137, 187
Third Way 3, 126
Thorne, Kramarae, and Henley 216
Tilly, Charles 155
Tito, Marshall 211
total war 218
Touraine, Alain 151–156
Trumbore, Samuel A Rev. 122
Turner, Bryan 106
Turner R and Killian, L.M. 146, 155

United Nations 168, 173–175, 219
unsicherheit foreword, 1
urbanisation 195–196

Vietnam War 210, 219

Wagar, Warren 191
Wagner, P. 50, 77
War 209–235
War of American Independence 218
Waters, Malcolm 58, 180, 190, 265
Wallerstein, Immanuel 166, 188–190, 209, 225
Weber, Cynthia 198
Weber, Marianne 10, 38
Weber, Max 3, 6, 10, 12–35, 54, 100, 102,
    151, 159, 189
    bureaucracy 13–14
    rationalisation 17, 132–133, 197
    amtsehre 17
    staatsraison 18
Webster, Andrew 170
Welsh Assembly 142
Westphalia 211
Wheale, Nigel 42
Williams, Shirley 131
Willis, Paul 84, 105
will to power 47, 227, 229
Wolpert, S. 193
World Bank 176
World Trade Organisation 168, 187
Wright, Quincy 231–232

X Files 3

Yom Kippur War 131

Zald MN and Berger MA 146, 155